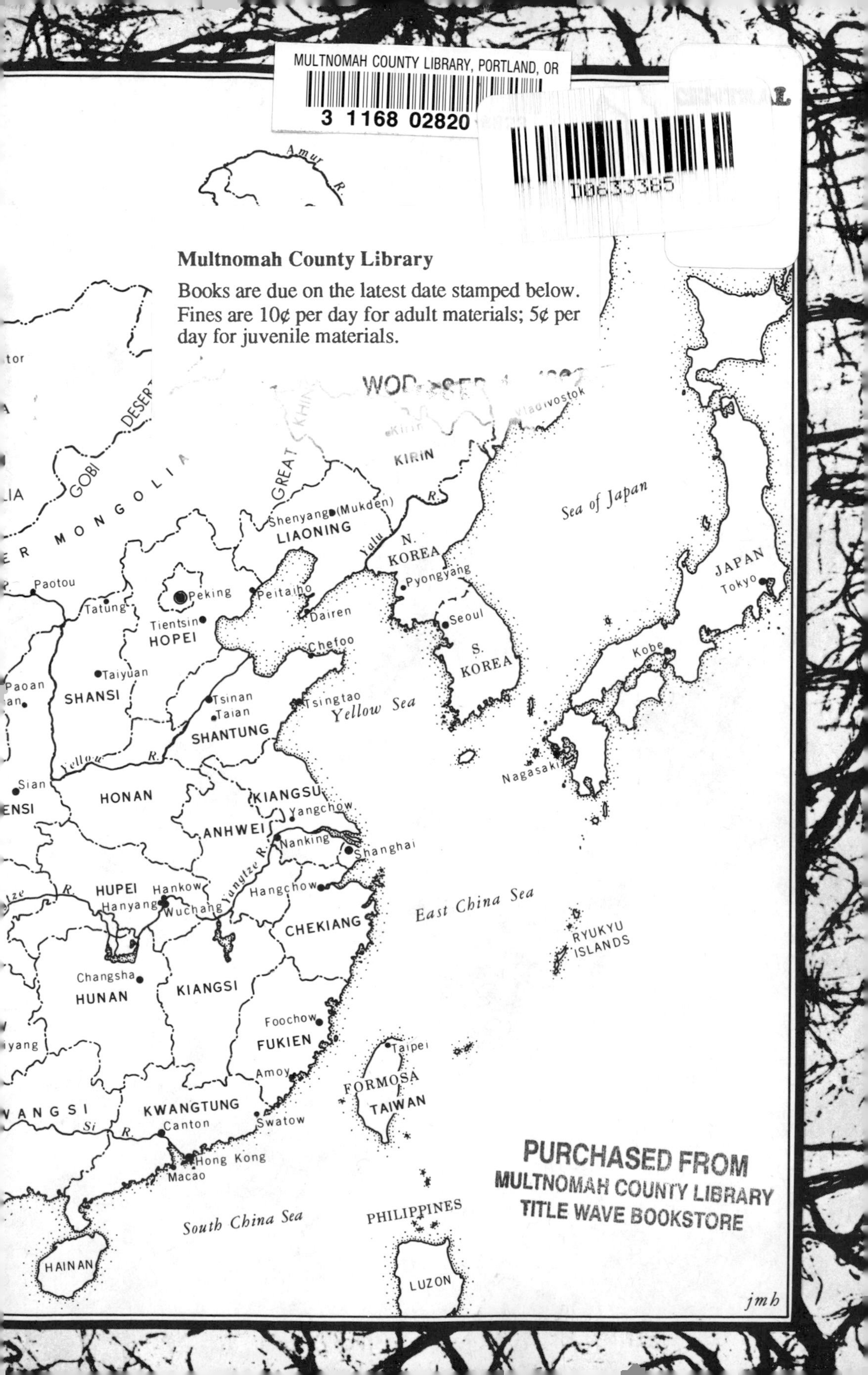
Amur R.
GOBI DESERT
MONGOLIA
GREAT KHINGAN
KIRIN
Vladivostok
Shenyang (Mukden)
LIAONING
Yalu R.
N. KOREA
Pyongyang
Seoul
S. KOREA
Sea of Japan
JAPAN
Tokyo
Kobe
Nagasaki
Paotou
Tatung
Peking
Peitaiho
Dairen
Tientsin
HOPEI
Chefoo
Taiyuan
SHANSI
Paoan
Tsinan
Taian
SHANTUNG
Tsingtao
Yellow Sea
Yellow R.
Sian
HONAN
KIANGSU
Yangchow
ANHWEI
Nanking
Shanghai
Yangtze R.
HUPEI
Hankow
Hanyang
Wuchang
Hangchow
CHEKIANG
East China Sea
RYUKYU ISLANDS
Changsha
HUNAN
KIANGSI
Foochow
FUKIEN
Taipei
FORMOSA
TAIWAN
Amoy
KWANGTUNG
Si R.
Canton
Swatow
Hong Kong
Macao
South China Sea
PHILIPPINES
HAINAN
LUZON
jmh

EDGAR SNOW

EDGAR SNOW

A Biography

John Maxwell Hamilton

INDIANA UNIVERSITY PRESS
Bloomington and Indianapolis

Photo credits: All photographs courtesy of the Edgar Snow Collection, University of Missouri-Kansas City Archives, and used with permission of Lois Wheeler Snow.

Manufactured in the United States of America

Library of Congress Cataloging-in-Publication Data

Hamilton, John Maxwell.
Edgar Snow, a biography.

Bibliography: p.
Includes index.
1. Snow, Edgar, 1905–1972. 2. Foreign correspondents—United States—Biography.
3. Foreign correspondents—China—Biography.
4. Sinologists—United States—Biography.
5. China—History—1937–1945. 6. China—History—Civil war—1945–1949. 7. China—History—1949–1976. I. Title.
PN4874.S5715H3 1988 070'.72'4 [B] 87–46366
ISBN 0-253-31909-9

1 2 3 4 5 92 91 90 89 88

To Gina

I am said to be a revolutionist in my sympathies, by birth, by breeding and by principle. I am always on the side of the revolutionists, because there never was a revolution unless there were some oppressive and intolerable conditions against which to revolute.

—Mark Twain, 1906

Revolutions are not caused by revolutionaries or their propaganda. Revolutions are caused by intolerable conditions under bad, incompetent and corrupt governments. In China the Communists also won because they convinced more people that they had something worth fighting for and dying for than Chiang Kai-shek was ever able to convince.

—Edgar Snow, 1955

CONTENTS

Acknowledgments

I began research for this book shortly after Edgar Snow died in 1972. In the years since, I have worked on the project off and on, between assignments overseas as a journalist and in government service. Along the way scores of people who knew Edgar Snow helped, consenting to interviews, providing papers, and often just giving good advice. An extraordinary number of those people were object lessons in courage, social consciousness, and decency. I am indebted to them in ways that transcend this book.

The names of those who were interviewed or provided papers are woven in the notes at the back of the book. I want to single out some here, beginning with Lois Wheeler Snow. Although she did not authorize this book, Mrs. Snow faithfully answered my questions and facilitated access to her husband's papers. I admire the strength of her convictions and her sense of responsibility toward her husband and toward improving U.S.-China relations. The late Mary Heathcote, a woman who also lived her convictions, encouraged me from the beginning—and listened to me talk when she knew far more. Helen Foster Snow, Edgar Snow's first wife and herself intimately involved in 1930s China, provided useful background, including two long interviews and many letters. John S. Service, an exemplary figure in the history of the period, read the complete manuscript and made invaluable comments. I am also grateful to J. Howard Snow, Mildred Snow Mackey, Dorothy Salisbury Davis and Harry Davis, Sylvia and Bill Powell, Robert Barnett, Louise and Randolph Sailor, Trudie Schafer, and former Foreign Minister Huang Hua, who gave me an entire evening of his time. At their request, I have not included in the notes the names of other Chinese whom I interviewed on trips to their country. I respect their wishes and thank them here collectively.

Friends and colleagues helped along the way. John H. Sullivan, a friend of unfailing good humor, contributed research ideas from his own extensive knowledge of Asia and commented on the entire manuscript. Charles Alexander reviewed the manuscript and was always there with good advice; George Krimsky, Paul C. Nagel, and Donald Shanor made helpful comments on portions of the book. Leo Ribuffo and Howard Gillette, as well as Lawrence Martin at a much earlier stage, provided scholarly guidance. Donald Gillin, Susan Eckert, Michael Edgerton, Roy Fisher, A. Tom Grunfeld, Repps Hudson, Louise Montgomery, and Paula Sullivan contributed pieces to the puzzle. The late Michael H. B. Adler made all the difference by encouraging me at a critical point.

Staff at a number of libraries gave important help, but none more than those at the Edgar Snow Collection at the University of Missouri-Kansas City. Though not otherwise a center for Chinese historical research, the Snow collection holds materials of use to scholars interested in China generally as well as in Snow. No one at the collection was more important than Marilyn Burlingame, who always answered my questions quickly and carefully. Kenneth Cramer at Baker Library, Dartmouth College, helped greatly with the Grenville Clark Collection. Brian Sullivan, Miriam Disman, and Thomas Duffy proved diligent, effective researchers.

Portions of the volume appeared originally in the *Pacific Historical Review* and the *Missouri Historical Review*. I made good use of their editorial suggestions and acknowledge here their permission to use portions of the articles in this book.

Peter Shepherd, a thoughtful, patient man who truly deserves the title *literary* agent, always cared about me and the book more than the money. John Gallman at Indiana University Press has, in the months we worked on this volume, shown himself a friend and intellectual colleague.

Regina N. Hamilton, who had other things to do, made constructive comments on the entire manuscript and was unswerving in her support. Maxwell J. Hamilton proved, throughout, that some men are born inherently good.

A Word on the Chinese Language . . .

and how it is used in this book. This book argues that America has failed to understand China, but it does not argue that the task of understanding is easy. The difficulties presented by the Chinese language are a case in point. As if romanization of Chinese weren't enough of a challenge, two different systems of transliteration have been used widely in this century—Wade-Giles and Pinyin. In addition, many place names, for example "Peking," were influenced by early French direction of the Chinese postal system. For the purposes of this book, I have used the Wade-Giles system prevalent during Edgar Snow's time. Mindful that readers are becoming familiar with the newer Pinyin system, the Pinyin equivalents for frequently used names and places in this book are listed below.

Wade-Giles	*Pinyin*
Amoy	Xiamen
Anhwei	Anhui
Canton	Guangzhou
Chang Hsueh-liang	Zhang Xueliang
Chang Kuo-t'ao	Zhang Guotao
Ch'en Yi	Chen Yi
Chiang Ch'ing	Jiang Qing
Chiang Kai-shek	Jiang Jieshi
Chingkangshan	Jinggangshan
Ching Dynasty	Qing Dynasty
Chou En-lai	Zhou Enlai
Chungking	Chongqing
Chu Teh	Zhu De
Darien (Port Arthur)	Luda or Dalian

Hangchow	Hangzhou
Ho Lung	He Long
Honan	Henan
Hopei	Hebei
Hupei	Hubei
Kansu	Gansu
Kiangsi	Jiangxi
Kuomintang	Guomindang
Kwangsi	Guangxi
Kwangtung	Guangdong
Lin Piao	Lin Biao
Liu Shao-ch'i	Liu Shaoqi
Lu Hsun	Lu Xun
Mao Tse-tung	Mao Zedong
Nanking	Nanjing
Paoan	Zhidan (renamed)
Peitaiho	Beidaihe
Peking	Beijing
P'eng Te-huai	Peng Dehuai
Po Ku	Bo Gu
Shansi	Shanxi
Shantung	Shandong
Shensi	Shaanxi
Sian	Xian
Soong Ch'ing-ling	Song Qingling
Sun Yat-sen	Sun Zhongshan
Szechwan	Sichuan
Teng Hsiao-p'ing	Deng Xiaoping
Teng Ying-ch'ao	Deng Yingchao
Tientsin	Tianjin
Ting Ling	Ding Ling
Tsinan	Jinan
Tsinghua	Qinghua
Tsingtao	Qingdao
Yenan	Yan'an

Prologue

On October 1, 1970, Edgar Snow stood next to Mao Tse-tung on the balcony of T'ien An Men Gate, the ancient structure that overlooks Peking's central square. Below, thousands upon thousands of Chinese trooped past in celebration of the twenty-first anniversary of the People's Republic of China.

Snow was near the end of an extraordinary odyssey. It began in Missouri, which imbued him with a romantic vision of independence both for himself and for others. The odyssey marked out a long list of journalistic accomplishments, including the most prescient reporting on China in this century. It was punctuated by ostracism in his own country during the dark days of anti-Communist hysteria. The odyssey created a man who called himself a citizen of the world and uncomfortably bore responsibility as the single most important link between China and the United States.

How did Snow come to stand that October day where no American had ever stood before? What did his odyssey say about American perceptions of China—and the world generally?

Those are the subjects of this biography.

EDGAR SNOW

Youth: An Introduction

It was just an off-the-cuff observation, but Charles White's judgment comes the closest to summing up Edgar Snow. White, a physician, grew up with Snow in Kansas City, Missouri. The two boys belonged to the same Westport High School fraternity and together struck out for California one summer after working in the Kansas wheat fields. White saw Snow only once after their school days and could recall reading one or two of Snow's eleven books. He casually followed the trajectory of Snow's journalism career: as stowaway to the Far East where Snow became an authority on the Chinese Communists in the 1930s; as a foreign correspondent for the prestigious *Saturday Evening Post* during the 1940s, covering the Soviet Union, Western Europe, and India; as the target of allegations in the bitter McCarthy years that he was "un-American." These charges White could not believe.

"Look," he told me after musing a moment, "Ed was not a Communist. He had been raised like the rest of us. He just saw more."[1]

Edgar Snow, born on a hot summer Wednesday, July 19, 1905, grew up in Kansas City at a time when the country self-confidently looked forward to becoming a world power, economically and morally. He died in his small Swiss farmhouse in 1972, near the end of the long war in Vietnam that left Americans wondering what had gone wrong.

Throughout those turbulent decades, Snow did see more. Many of his peers casually vacationed abroad as boys. Snow lived overseas. Independent, he traveled off the beaten track of government publicity handouts, away from reporters who flocked around routine stories. He matured among the nascent revolutionary movements that toppled Western colonialism and erected in its place scores of new states following their own dictates. Snow empathized with these national movements, he romanticized them. Yet he did not lose his American identity. While others learned to get along in the corporate world that emerged in the twentieth century, Snow clung stubbornly to American storybook ideals nurtured on the prairie—ideals that elevated the dignity of the individual, the "little man," and that honored self-determination and glorified its ultimate expression, revolution.

Snow saw twentieth-century history at close range. He was among the first American reporters to contemplate peasant rebellions in Vietnam and Burma. He covered World War II from its bloodiest vantage point, the western front in the Soviet Union; he slipped into Vienna at the end of the fighting to write the first reports of Austria under Soviet occupation; he watched the wartime United States-Soviet Union alliance unravel into global Cold War. He became the second American reporter to enter Riyadh and was on hand to cover Indian independence and Gandhi's assassination in 1948.

Snow saw the most in China. In 1936 he literally discovered the Chinese Communists, cut off for nearly ten years from Western observers. His report that they were not mere "Red Bandits," as Nationalists depicted them, but a coherent force with a loyal peasant following, was news not only abroad but in China itself. *Red Star over China,* accurately observed John King Fairbank of Snow's book-length report, became "an event in modern Chinese history." A primary source on the lives of Mao Tse-tung and other Communist leaders, on the Long March, on Communist guerrilla strategy, and on the course of the revolution, the book is viewed by historians as well as revolutionaries in other countries as "essential reading." Snow had unequaled access to Communist China after the fall of the Nationalists in 1949. In 1960 he was the first American reporter with prior experience in China to visit the People's Republic. He became the last reporter to visit before the outbreak of the Cultural Revolution and the first to return.[2]

Snow's own bent toward activism thrust him deeply into foreign affairs. He helped Peking students mobilize Chinese public opinion against the Nationalist government when it was about to cede North China to the Japanese in 1935. During the Sino-Japanese War he helped start a behind-the-lines industrialization campaign that created 1,850 cooperatives at its peak. He took sides in his writing and offered private advice to Franklin D. Roosevelt and other leaders. He tried to bridge the gulf that divided the Chinese Communists from the United States after 1949. He argued vigorously against involvement in Vietnam, a war he believed Americans could not win with honor.

Pressed up against rapidly changing events, Snow made the mistakes that journalists make. His involvement in history gradually colored his interpretation of events. But Snow excelled. Literary critic Maxwell Geismar placed him among America's best contemporary writers.[3] Although his few attempts at fiction and poetry went nowhere, Snow took the genre of "personal history" reporting to its highest level, putting himself in the story to make it more interesting and honest but not letting his presence overshadow the facts. More important than how he wrote, however, was what he wrote. Contrary to popular impressions, Snow remained both a thorough reporter and a brilliant interpreter of the meaning of events. He not only managed to be where other reporters were not, he had a capacity for understanding what he saw and for seeing ahead. Many critics came to view him as naive. He could be romantic, especially about his own country. Nevertheless, he was a hardheaded realist.

Snow's significance, however, goes well beyond his accomplishments to the inherent drama in his life, the tension between what he saw and American reaction to his reports. During the first half of his career, Snow enjoyed enormous popularity and acclaim. During the second, he could not find outlets for his work. Yet, a fundamental consistency underlay the roller coaster of emotions about Snow. Throughout his career, Americans viewed his work, as they did China, through the prism of their hopes and aspirations. During the 1930s, Americans deeply worried about being drawn into the world war taking shape. They eagerly embraced Snow's reports of Chinese Communist determination to mount an indigenous resistance to the Japanese in a united front with the Nationalists. In their eagerness to find anti-fascist allies, Americans ignored Snow's conclusion that the Chinese Communists were what they said they were, Communists. Instead they used his book to "prove" that the Reds were mere agrarian reformers, not Marxist revolutionaries. It did little good for Snow to protest this incomplete interpretation. During the post-World War II witch hunt for those who "lost China," Americans blamed him for misleading them about the true nature of Mao Tse-tung and his followers. Seeing a Red tide that "will smash across the Pacific Islands and cover the United States—all according to Soviet plan," Americans ignored Snow's reports on the Chinese Communists' economic and social advances after their take-over in 1949 and ignored news he bore of Communists' willingness to improve relations with the United States.[4] In the end, the tragedy was not that Snow misled Americans. It was that they did not listen to him.

The tensions that surrounded Snow produced wildly distorted, conflicting views of him, not least of all on the Left. Leo Huberman, editor of the self-styled "independent socialist" *Monthly Review*, called Snow a "Marxist when he thought about it."[5] While he may have liked Snow, Mao considered him bourgeois. And the American Communist Party, which provided virtually the only strong criticism of *Red Star* when it first appeared, labeled Snow a Trotskyite. On the Right stood Richard Nixon. Along with those who called Snow a careerist and a Communist tool, Nixon promoted the virulent Red baiting in Congress that eventually compelled Snow to leave the United States. Then, in 1972, just before making his historic opening to China, Nixon sent a letter to Snow, mortally ill with cancer in Switzerland, praising his "distinguished career."

For all this, Snow was not a man who courted controversy.[6] He was not flawed by tragic personality traits that tortured his soul or earned him enmity. Even his harshest critics, who accused him of purveying Communist propaganda, admitted they liked him. As one of his editors at the *Saturday Evening Post* put it, "Ed was the one correspondent I would bring home to meet my mother." Snow was not vain or pompous. When he left Missouri for New York as a young man, he did not don a top hat and carry a cane, as was *de rigueur* among gentlemen like Walter Lippmann, or resort to such sophistications as using his middle name. (Snow's was Parks. He thought Edgar bad enough.)

Snow craved adventure. He took risks, often on impulse. But he was not erratic or wild, even as a young man. Before leaving for Russia, young John Reed frolicked on New York's Fulton Street docks late at night, half drunk. Snow visited alone, quietly roaming the wharfs and dreaming of travel.

Snow was uncomfortable pontificating in front of audiences, and he was terrible at it. By constitution, he was not strident or self-righteous or brittle. When high-strung Peg Snow, his first wife, engaged someone in violent argument, he often ambled off. Contemporary journalists like Agnes Smedley or Anna Louise Strong, whom Snow liked, thrived on being in opposition. Not Snow. In his youth he went his own way quietly, as when he reluctantly lost faith in Catholicism while an altar boy. Knowing how much the Church meant to his mother, he continued to attend mass until he left home. He was the kind of boy who would dance with his older sister, Mildred, at the Jack-O'Lantern soda shop near their home. Although colleagues considered him as stubborn as a Missouri mule during the 1950s, when he refused to write on less controversial subjects and save his job at the *Saturday Evening Post*, Snow wanted American acceptance.

The truth about Edgar Snow was rooted, as Charles White knew, not only in what he saw on his extraordinary journeys but where he came from. Although nothing in Snow's youth suggested he was destined for greatness or controversy, the setting in which he was raised and his youthful personality profoundly prefaced his life. Ed Snow, wrote another friend, who knew him as a mature man, "was always from Kansas City, Missouri."[7]

Located on the jumping-off point to America's frontier, Missourians liked to think of their state as a microcosm of their robust country. During Snow's youth, Kansas City made the transition from a small town to an industrialized metropolis with breathtaking speed and confidence. Fatal traffic accidents were divided between runaway horse teams and careless automobile driving. The 1905 city directory, published several days after Snow's birth, reported that the Metropolitan Railway carried seventy-seven million passengers annually, more than a two-thirds increase in five years. Real estate transfers had leapt 250 percent over the 1900 level. The local Chamber of Commerce called Kansas City "the most American city," and townsmen held themselves up as an example to others on the prairie. The year Snow turned four, one hundred members of the local Commercial Club and fifty other businessmen hired a special train to take them fourteen hundred miles through eighty-three towns in Missouri, Kansas, and Nebraska. They hoped to meet 170,000 people and make them aware of the dynamic spirit of their city, with its slogan "Keep something going on."[8]

Oil refineries, automobile assembly plants, and factories making ready-to-wear garments and paint rose up on the prairie. By the time Ed Snow enrolled in high school the value of Missouri industrial production outstripped the value of farm production. The state ranked eleventh nationally in manufacturing.

The transition from agrarian to corporate America would transform the independent farmer from a dominant reality into an icon. But during Snow's boyhood, Kansas City had men and women who remembered when their parents first turned the prairie sod—and they were far enough removed from the experience to romanticize it. Kansas Citians clung to Missouri's "Show Me" agrarian conservatism. Those values, as one historian described them, held "that the hope of America lay in free citizens immune to coercion as a result of their widespread ownership of the land."

Kansas City's history and location in the state accentuated its feeling of independence. "It began and remained," as historian Paul Nagel perceptively noted, "as a speculative venture—the city was established by a private company." The city always had a sense of becoming. It never developed a stable sense of community. In addition, the city was not comfortable about its place in the state. A wide gulf divided it from

St. Louis, on the east side of the state and more oriented to the established Atlantic coast culture. Kansas City faced the West, the unknown. At one point it flirted with the idea of joining Kansas, just across the river. As a result Kansas Citians were mistrustful and supremely individualistic.

Kansas City projected these attitudes toward its politicians. The political machine that Jim Pendergast created and his brother Tom fine-tuned had a well-deserved reputation for its sway over local politics. Often overlooked, though, the Pendergasts could not ignore democratic sentiment. Tom gave citizens illegal liquor and lower telephone rates. When he held court, anyone wishing a favor had to wait his turn in line, no matter what his status in town. Even then Kansas Citians did not always let the Pendergasts have their way. Pendergast candidates lost elections, and eventually Tom went to prison.

The dual idea of material advancement and individualism was part of Snow's heritage, though his forebears came west by different routes and with different backgrounds.[9]

Snow's mother, Anna Catherine Edelman, was a first generation American. Her mother, Mary Fogarty, hailed from Menagh, Tipperary; her German father, John H. Edelman, was born in Silesia. The Edelmans moved west to Kansas City, via Columbus, where Anna was born in 1878. John Edelman, a grumpy old man when Edgar Snow knew him, owned a construction company. Mary Fogarty, remembered as a sweet lady, and other Irish relatives in town had harsh words about British imperialism, a sentiment that ran strong among Midwesterners.

Edgar Snow's paternal relatives, who dominated his immediate family circle, had roots deep in the American past. Edgar Snow's great-great-great-grandfather William Snow, a Virginian, fought in the Revolutionary War. Afterward, he settled the family in the Cumberland mountains of Kentucky. Edgar Snow noted with special pride as an adult that the Kentucky Snows did not keep slaves. As a young man he boasted, though apparently without much proof, that an ancestor came to America on the *Mayflower*'s second voyage. Later in life, when critics questioned his American standing, Snow played with the idea that his antecedents included Samuel Snow of Salem, Massachusetts, the United States' first merchant consul in Canton sometime after the Revolutionary War.

Horace Parks Snow, Edgar Snow's flinty grandfather, pushed west from Kentucky to farm. With the money H. P. made from the land, he set up a general store on Main Street, Winfield, Kansas. By the time of his death, he owned farms in three states. He equated every expenditure with the amount of interest he could earn in one year on a bank deposit. His grandchildren visited the family farm and cattle spread in Burden, Kansas, during the summers. H. P. regularly trumpeted to them that he never worked a day in his life for another man.

James Edgar Snow—Edgar Snow's father—was born in Kentucky in 1873, seven years before H. P. moved west to Kansas. J. E., as he was called, left the farm but not its values. He repaid H. P. for his short stint at Southwestern College, near Burden, and was proud of it. In search of work, he landed in Kansas City, Missouri, where he met Anna Edelman and married her in June 1899. After working a few years for a sheep commission company, a job that took him to Salt Lake City and Chicago, he settled in Kansas City. He used his savings to buy a small printing business downtown that carried his name. For a time he published a cattleman's paper. For J. E. and Anna's children—Mildred born in 1900, John Howard born in 1902, and young Eddie—Kansas City was home.

The idea of material success was one thing, achieving it quite another. Notwithstanding the widely shared reverence for commercial free enterprise, the pursuit of profits and the pursuit of independence did not always reside easily together. Some men were just too individualistic. J. E. Snow was such a character.

J. E. worked hard. His business motto was "Printing When Promised." Whenever the *Kansas City Star* needed a commercial printing job done in a hurry the purchasing agent called Snow. Ed and Howard were expected to work, either down at the printing business or elsewhere. Ed had odd jobs as a soda jerk and selling the *Saturday Evening Post*. In high school he toiled with other boys as a harvest hand in the wheat fields. The hard work shocking wheat by hand and hauling it by horse-drawn wagon wore out a pair of gloves a day. In the Snow house a boy learned that progress was possible, that things were supposed to get better—and that you had to work for it.

At the same time, J. E. was attracted to the printing business, or at least the trade as it had flourished in the previous century, for reasons that went far beyond pure commercial interest. The West had a tradition of journeymen printers whose transportable skill and everyday access to the written word gave them independence and a window on literature. "How strong must that student feel who can walk through a library with the consciousness that he knows the plans and purposes of all the leading books!" J. E. wrote in a 1893 essay at Southwestern College. "What a world of information is a library to its master!"[10] At home J. E. wandered about reciting long passages from Goethe in German. While young Ed worked in the print shop on Main Street, J. E. shouted out Hamlet's soliloquy in cadence with the presses.

Acquaintances nicknamed the small, often absent-minded J. E. "the dreamer." "He was something of an idealist . . . whose philosophy went deeper than the printing industry," Charles White recalled. "One of the phrases that he often used was that he was 'thinking about something or other in the back of his head.' He probably was." J. E. railed against the Pendergast machine and supported "independent citizens" reform organizations, even though it didn't help his business.

Ed would exhibit those same traits in later life, habitually letting coffee perk on the stove until the pot melted into the burners. Conscientious as he was about getting facts straight in his reporting, he never mastered travel schedules. He seemed determined to be late, even for interviews with Chinese premier Chou En-lai. And like his father, he did not let money get in the way of principle.

Not surprisingly, J. E. was far from prosperous. He resisted suggestions from Howard, who emphasized the entrepreneurial side of Kansas City, that he should expand the business. Ed remembered that his father preferred shooting pool with his printers to playing bridge with his customers.

The Snows formed a familiar family scene. They lived in more than one house in Kansas City. All were strictly middle class, like the square two-story home on Charlotte Street when Snow was in high school. It was in the "Kansas City shirtwaist" design—so called because the exterior of the first level was brick or stone and the second was wood and because the style was so common in the city. Anna, whose working life centered around the practically designed home, was a good cook. For pleasure she had her bridge games and sewing circles. J. E. smoked cigars only occasionally and brought hard liquor into the house just for use in toddies to cure colds. He enjoyed dressing up in his Shriner regalia. He took the children to play tennis at nearby courts and put up the croquet set in the backyard. J. E. called for discipline; Anna, to whom Edgar was deeply attached, pleaded mercy when one of her children transgressed.

J. E. was a Republican, and Anna a Democrat. But the big difference was religion. J. E. broke his family's strong Protestant tradition by marrying a Catholic, and a strict one at that. Although he at first agreed that his children should go through the normal progression from baptism to confirmation and beyond, J. E. quickly lost patience with the Church. He had become so intolerant by the time Eddie came along that he refused to let the boy enter parochial schools as Mildred and Howard had done. While Anna tried to coax J. E. to Mass, he devoted Sunday afternoons to inveighing against the inconsistencies of Catholicism and reading to his son from the forbidden books on the Catholic Index.

J. E.'s anti-Catholic counterpoint seized the household. The children remembered it ruefully. Perhaps because of this, Snow asserted in his autobiography that it was not his father's arguments that disillusioned him about the Church; it was the revelation that the communion wafers had ordinary origins. Whether Edgar Snow's adult aversion to confrontation came from J. E.'s negative example or the positive one set by Anna's forbearance, he gave little credit to his father for teaching him the habit of reading from forbidden books.

J. E. wasn't Ed's only window on the written word. Lucy Smoot, principal of Norman Grade School, was a tough taskmaster. Students, she wrote in 1922, "learned that doing dirty work and being a quitter were the most unspeakable crimes."[11] She insisted that no one reached the third grade if he couldn't really read. The tiny dynamo made such an impression that Snow corresponded with her for years after he left Kansas City. Katherine Theresa Edelman, an Irish woman married to Anna's brother, was a local literary figure; her poetry, eventually collected in *Shamrocks and Prairie Grass*, appeared regularly in the *Kansas City Star*. The crusading *Star* itself held special charms. Young red-headed Eddie often lugged his father's packages to the massive red brick building on Grand Avenue and talked to the journalists in the newsroom.

As a boy, Snow fit in. At Westport High School, he went out for sports, though with little apparent distinction, joined clubs, and belonged to Delta Omicron Omicron fraternity. Fraternal gatherings involved intramural sports, Panhellenic dances, and weekly meetings in which the boys were expected to criticize each other. Snow's most notable accomplishment came in the Boy Scouts, which he joined at the age of thirteen. Within a year he filled the right sleeve of his olive drab military style scout tunic with twenty-one merit badges and belonged to the city's first group of Eagle Scouts.[12]

Befitting the environment in which he grew up, young Ed Snow gravitated toward creative enterprises. In high school he started a fraternity newspaper, *The Delt*. Blending his literary interests with a Kansas City appreciation for business, he served as business manager. He composed fraternity songs. In 1923, after graduation from high school, he attended the Junior College of Kansas City, across the street from Westport High. During his one year there, he worked on the school paper. Jazz caught on in Kansas City during his youth. Snow and his chums, among them drummer Buddy Rogers, listened to Cab Calloway and Count Basie, who played in suburban coffee shops. Snow played the drums and the saxophone with modest proficiency and managed and performed in the Blue Bell Jazz Band.

Sitting in a classroom was another matter. Snow's mediocre grades in high school, as much as independent-mindedness, may have prompted him to choose a somewhat defensive aphorism to accompany his senior year photograph: "But respect yourself most of all." In his two semesters at junior college, he earned the equivalent of three B's, seven C's (four in English), and an F in botany. He did not complete mathematics-trigonometry.[13]

Kansas City suburbs offered boys swimming holes and stretches of woods in which to play. If the environment didn't have the romance of Mark Twain's Hannibal of a generation before, it did give a boy scope for dreaming Mark Twain dreams. Indeed, as his friends later joked, Snow was born reading Mark Twain. (Years after leaving Missouri for good, Snow wrote in the margin of Harold Laski's *The American Democracy*, "see Mark Twain on this.")[14] Like Huck Finn and Tom Sawyer, as well as characters he read about in *Robinson Crusoe, The Swiss Family Robinson,* and *Treasure Island,* Snow wanted adventurous travel. The cards he had printed to advertise his jazz orchestra noted "Out of Town Jobs a Specialty." He worked during high school as an office boy for the Missouri-Kansas-Texas or "Katy" Railway line, which gave him free rides to the Ozarks. His most outstanding childhood transgression involved a car, a Stevens driven by sister Mildred's boyfriend. One day when he was sixteen years old, Snow slipped into the front seat and drove off. Returning home, he spotted his waiting parents. He became nervous, pushed on the gas pedal by accident, and smashed into a tree. He had to sell his musical equipment to pay for the damage. Snow was never a good driver.

Huckleberry Finn inspired Snow and another boy to plot a raft trip down the Missouri River. Those plans did not materialize, but in the summer of 1922 he traveled west with Charles White and another boy, Bob Long.[15] The journey began with little promise of adventure—or so Snow indicated to his parents. Ostensibly the three headed for the wheat fields near Salina, Kansas. But once the boys made some money as harvest hands, they set out for California in Long's black Model T touring car, on whose side they boyishly wrote "The Unconscious Three." They followed the Santa Fe Trail most of the way, tracing a route to Colorado Springs, then down to New Mexico. They cooked their own breakfast and dinner and bought lunch at restaurants and slept under the open sky on pleasant nights.

By the time the boys arrived in Los Angeles, their money was gone. The beat-up car, limping along on a scored cylinder, brought

$95. Long's mother and brother came out to get him. Snow and White set out to ride the rails back to Kansas City.

The plan had two drawbacks. The national railroad shopmen's strike, begun in early July, had brought out a large contingent of detectives to protect the trains from sabotage. In addition, White and Snow knew nothing about hopping trains. Their first effort to hitch a ride bore the familiar signs of Snow's life-long penchant for missing connections and bumping into trees. The boys jumped on a train they thought was heading east and spent the night hanging off a boxcar ladder. The next morning they were in Sacramento. With funds in even shorter supply, they looked for work, ending up about twenty miles away in Roseville, a central point for fruit packing. For five days they waited on dining tables in a heavily guarded compound set up for Mexican strike breakers.

Back on their way they became more adept at hitching rides. They learned to pick the express trains and to find comfortable, if precarious, places to stow themselves. At one stop, Snow awoke from a sweaty sleep to find himself resting under the wheel of an idle boxcar. Railroad employees threw them off a train at a water station in the Nevada desert. At the last minute the boys managed to sneak onto the cowcatcher. While riding the Atchison, Topeka & Santa Fe, they were caught again in Lamar, Colorado, not far from the Kansas border. This time they spent the night in jail. In Kansas "harvest bandits" robbed Snow of fifty cents and took summer wages from migrant workers on board.

The railroad strikes had little social or political significance for the boys. Their parents may have agreed with criticism in the press that the workers' demands for higher wages held up food shipments and cost consumers dearly.[16] What interested Snow was the rough adventure, the ordinary people he met, and, as he often reminisced late in life, thoughts of the exotic world that lay beyond the Pacific Ocean, which he had seen for the first time.

A boyhood fling at travel, even if it took one overseas for a time, fit neatly into the spirit of the insouciant 1920s. Apolitical and brimming with footloose adventure, Richard Halliburton, whose romantic travelogues Snow read, captured the spirit of the age. American youth faced little to fear in satisfying their wanderlust. Unlike colonial powers, the United States had earned few enemies overseas. With the economic boom, money presented no real obstacle for many either. One of Halliburton's early travel companions was from Kansas City, which had its share of wanderers. Bob Long went overseas for nine months with a group of Kansas City college boys, visiting China among other places.[17]

After two semesters at junior college Snow gave up school for a year. For a while he joined Howard, who dropped out of school to make his way in the business world of New York. Recollections are not clear about what Ed did there, though Howard recalled he found a job. Records at Columbia University show that Snow took two courses at night school during the 1925 spring semester. He earned an A in advertising writing and "no credit" in advertising psychology "by reason of irregular attendance."[18] In any event, Snow was back in Missouri in the fall of 1925. He enrolled at the University of Missouri, a popular school for Kansas City boys.

The University of Missouri resided in quiet, rural Columbia, in the center of the state. The setting belied the temptations the journalism school offered young people like Snow already seized by the desire to travel. Missouri's was the first journalism school in the world, started in 1908, and its founder, Dean Walter Williams, had an international reputation and outlook. He organized international journalism meetings before Snow was born and founded the Press Congress of the World. Through special connections Williams developed with American editors overseas, he sent a steady stream of bright young graduates to foreign jobs.

Williams was especially successful at placing graduates in Japan and China. More than fifty journalists educated at the University of Missouri worked in the Far East by the late 1920s. Missourians pioneered journalism education in China and brought promising young Chinese to Missouri for education. People talked about a "Missouri News Monopoly" in China. Those Missouri ties eventually went beyond journalism to business and government. In 1920, a Missouri Society with 120 members was organized in Shanghai. Williams, who became president of the university, was mentioned as a candidate for the post of minister to China in the early 1930s.[19]

This international perspective was hardly lost on Snow. On November 10, 1925, during his first semester on campus, the most recent journalism graduating class dedicated a gift to the school. They had chosen a meridian plate, which they placed in front of Neff Hall, the home of the journalism school. The plate ticked off the miles to foreign cities—Moscow, 5,273; Delhi, 7,730; Shanghai, 7,136; New York, 983. . . .

Snow enrolled in the journalism school's advertising sequence. He earned better grades than at junior college, although he received a D in Dean Williams's course on the history and principles of journalism.[20]

He joined a social fraternity, Beta Theta Pi, where he disliked the hazing, and the national advertising fraternity, Alpha Delta Sigma. He worked as a campus correspondent for the *Kansas City Star*. But following the meridian marker in front of Neff Hall interested him more than classes, which he regularly skipped. Combined with an inherited feeling that his father should not have to shoulder the financial burdens of a university education, Snow left after only a year to join Howard again.

The Roaring Twenties was Kansas City optimism on a colossal scale in 1926. New York, especially, glittered with possibilities. Snow took a job with Scovil Brothers & Company, an advertising firm that represented Wall Street financial institutions, then riding the crest of the boom. While brokers traded securities at a furious pace, ad executives proclaimed a long, glorious mission: "Consumption engineering does not end until we consume all that we can make," proclaimed Earnest Elmo Calkings, one of the city's most respected advertising men.[21]

The Snow brothers rented a small apartment at 56 West 55th Street, around the corner from the Ziegfeld Follies theater. Buddy Rogers lived with them for a time; so did a young man in charge of the aviation section at the *New York Times*. Howard, whose good looks landed him a job modeling Spur bow ties for a full-page ad in the *Saturday Evening Post*, filled the apartment with a parade of parties and bright, talented guests, including Bette Davis, then an unknown actress living with her mother.[22]

With his easygoing manner, Snow quickly made friends and cultivated mentors. None was more important than Charles Hanson Towne. "Mr. New York," Towne had enjoyed a sparkling literary career with *Cosmopolitan*, the *Smart Set*, *McClure's*, and *Harper's Bazaar*, where he was editor when Snow arrived. The round-faced and avuncular journalist took special pride in discovering young writers. As an editor on the *Smart Set*, he reminisced, "I used to pick up each manuscript and say to myself, 'It may be here. This may be it.' Every prejudice was in the writer's favor."[23]

Snow liked the heady sky's-the-limit feel to New York. He did not relish the day-to-day grind of an advertising firm. The men did not seem particularly talented and the narrow field restricted his personal freedom, he thought. Snow didn't receive a salary raise because he was habitually late, even when meeting with his boss. Only his ability to make friends saved him. Kelly Graham, a notoriously tough businessman who became president of the First National Bank at the age of thirty-six, liked Snow and gave Scovil his much-sought-after advertising account. When Graham invited him to a dinner with Senator Edward I. Edwards, Snow saw a chance to land an account with a security firm in which the legislator had an interest. Snow become so absorbed in the conversation, however, he forgot to raise the subject.[24]

In what would be characteristic fits of homesickness, Snow talked about returning to "dear old K.C.," but he always delayed homecoming. "I am determined to raise my head above the crowd and amount to something in a larger way than at present seems possible in Kansas City," Snow wrote to his father half apologetically and not at all certain which direction to take. He considered law school. He won the World Wide Letter Contest sponsored by the *Savings Bank Journal* and over the next months thought about a career as an independent author, perhaps writing fiction or movie scripts. He toyed with the idea of acting, and applied for a job as assistant to an executive at Samuel Goldwyn Motion Picture Company. The job didn't materialize, but the movie mogul said, with keen foresight, that Snow had "dramatic instinct!"[25]

When Snow turned a modest stock investment into eight hundred dollars in late 1927, his dramatic instinct told him he had an answer to his future, a year of adventurous foreign travel. Banker Kelly Graham encouraged the idea, as it was something he would like to have done as a young man. Snow persuaded Alvin Joslin, a Kansas City pal and fraternity brother, to go along. Through Charlie Towne, Snow met Theodore Roosevelt's son, Kermit, president of the Roosevelt Steamship line. Roosevelt offered Snow and Joslin jobs as deckhands aboard the *Radnor*. The pay was twenty-five dollars a month. The itinerary included Panama, Hawaii, the Philippines, China, and, depending on the cargo taken aboard in the Far East, India.

Snow hastily laid his plans. From Walter Williams he obtained names of Missouri graduates overseas. Towne and Roosevelt armed him with a blanket letter to American "counsels [*sic*]," as Snow put it. For twenty-five dollars he bought a secondhand Number 4A Kodak camera and approached several editors about filing stories during his travels. Towne agreed to act as his agent and deposit earnings in Graham's bank.

In a letter that his parents would not receive until he pulled out of port, Snow explained his decision.

> I have been somewhat depressed by the monotony of existence and the thought that I labored, a cog in a gargantuan machine, while youth, life, was slipping by. Brooding over my stereotype style of living had to have a culmination. I determined it should be a happy one. And to me, fond ones, happiness at the moment meant but one thing. And that was travel!! Adventure! Experience! I wanted to overcome difficulties—physical hardships—and enjoy the tokens of triumph! I wished to know peril and danger! I wanted to fill my youth with something

> more than the pious, pitiful platitudes which I felt surrounded me. And the consistent drabness of the days through which I have been wearily dragging myself, aggravated my nerves and put me to dreaming of fabled, far-off places. Names of cities kept insisting themselves upon my consciousness and intruding upon my efforts at concentrated thought. "Calcutta!" and then "Palestine!" "Shanghai!" said the small voice; "Iliolu!"; "Baghdad!"; "Mecca!"; and "far Damascus!" How could I labor over the lifeless little duties spread before me when this song of cities was beating in my brain![26]

Despite the Halliburtonesque terms in which he explained his adventure, Snow sensed the perilousness of his decision. He asked his parents not to say much about his trip to friends and relatives. "Should my plans—as there is always an imminent possibility—be defeated, I and all of you might be open to some ridicule." Even a reassuring thought, that he had been promised a job at another ad agency when he returned, seemed flat in view of the course his peers were taking. Bob Long, soon to appear in *Who's Who in Kansas City*, gave up aspirations of a diplomatic career to enter his father's lucrative insurance business.[27] Charles White was on his way to a good medical practice, and Buddy Rogers was already a star. While Snow laid plans to leave New York City, Howard took an advertising job with the *American Banker's Association Journal*. Howard decided to acquire wealth first, then use his mature years in search of knowledge.

Snow saw it the other way around. Although he grew up like other boys in Kansas City, he chose not to stay home and mature amid the changes transforming the country into a world power. Armed with a vision of Mark Twain's agrarian America, he was bound to see more.

Adventure Bound

1

About the time Edgar Snow was born, a warm sympathy for the Chinese, beleaguered by foreign interlopers, took hold in the United States. But when Americans like President Theodore Roosevelt described China as of "the keenest national concern," it was just talk. The Open Door Notes of 1899 and 1900, demanding that the Great Powers make room for American interests and ideals in China, were a bluff, a colossal exercise in national self-delusion. Although senators might proclaim that "we must have the [China] market or we shall have revolution," capitalists found other markets for their prodigious industrial production, many of them right in burgeoning American cities. In 1910 less than 1 percent of total U.S. exports went to China. Secretary of State John Hay, architect of the notes, concluded that public opinion simply would not support concerted government action to protect China from foreign encroachment.[1]

Little had changed by the time Snow embarked on his travels. Less than 2 percent of total United States trade involved China in the peak year of 1928. Americans still talked in grand terms as evidenced by the Kellogg-Briand Pact, signed August 27, 1928, outlawing war. Pervasive economic nationalism pushed United States tariffs to their highest point in history. Symptomatically, American press coverage of China went into a three-year decline starting in 1928. Snow had every reason to expect he would find the country as had Halliburton, who lounged in Peking for "twenty, happy, full, care-free, December days." Instead, while Americans watched themselves slip into the Great Depression, his wanderlust brought him face to face with poverty and oppression. His idealism would not let him look away.

Life on the *Radnor* was everything Snow hoped it would be. Tanned and temporarily moustached, he stood watch and took a turn at the ship's wheel, a privilege "'deck boys' are seldom accorded," he told Charlie Towne in an exclamation mark filled letter. "I even induced the mate to let me steer part of the way through the Canal, just for the thrill of it." In Panama City he visited the saloons that stretched for blocks and experienced the importuning of young prostitutes in the "infamous Coconut Grove."[2]

As the *Radnor* steamed toward Hawaii, Snow felt he was getting to know the sailors, veterans like "Singapore" Sam Morgan, with whom he stood the eight to twelve watch. He envied their taut physiques and their "carefree, blithesome spirits and the utter content in the unglorified lives they live," he told his brother Howard. But his visions of seeing the Far East with these men faded when the ship's boiler blew. The planned six-hour layover in Hawaii dragged on for weeks. Snow's voyage with the *Radnor* was over.

Snow and Joslin took rooms at the Army & Navy YMCA. Uncertain what the next step might be but eager to get adventure where he could, Snow lolled on Waikiki and tested himself surfing in the turquoise sea. He and Joslin looked for Sans Souci, Robert Louis Stevenson's home; partook in a luau ("as we of Missouri would say, 'a stemwinder' "); leisurely drove around the island; and ogled at Ola. Ola was a hula dancer whom they persuaded to perform for them. "A trifle too robust and a day or two beyond maidenhood," she undulated until exhausted to the tune of "Sweet Lei Lehue," scratched out on an old phonograph. Snow and Joslin sold pineapple juice at a stand on the YMCA grounds to earn money. In addition to producing articles that he hoped Towne would place in the United States, Snow wrote three poems that appeared in the *Honolulu Advertiser*. After a nauseating ninety-seven mile trip in steerage to Kauai, he spent three "idyllic" days tramping around the island. He wrote an article on the trip for *Paradise of the Pacific* magazine.

Joslin, Snow commented, had "two consuming fires," beer and home. Before long he decided to "retreat" to Kansas City (where he entered the advertising business—handling transportation accounts!). Snow wanted to go on. After more than two months in the islands, however, he could not afford to buy a berth on a vessel, and work as a deckhand was scarce. A chance to work his way to Japan aboard the *Yomachichi* disappeared when the job was given to another at the last minute.

Snow was on his way back from watching the *Yomachichi* glide out of port when he saw a throng of Japanese heading past him toward the docks. They were seeing off the *Shinyo Maru* bearing the Japanese ambassador and his daughter, who was returning to wed Prince Chichibu. The *Shinyo Maru* was scheduled to depart that afternoon, and Snow remembered that one of the passengers was an acquaintance, Dan Crabb, a Princeton man bound for Port Said and "an adventure into 'darkest Africa!' " Snow decided to bid Crabb farewell. When it turned out Crabb had a huge first-class cabin, big enough for two, the two boys impetuously agreed on a stowaway scheme. Or so Snow would later recount in a romanticized story for the *Kansas City Journal Post* and in excited letters home.[3]

Thinking he would be discovered in an hour or two, Snow gave a hasty, unceremonial good-bye to Joslin. That Snow actually pulled off the scheme—an accomplishment that became something of a legend in the Orient—was due apparently to his casual manner. He would mingle one day in second-class spaces, the next with first-class company, which included seven Americans. Emboldened, he and Crabb struck up a bridge game with the princess-to-be and her mother. During another bridge game an elderly American school teacher abruptly asked Snow, "Just what class passenger are you? You seem to be on the first-class decks and yet I never see you in the dining room saloon."

"Why, I'm—I'm in a class by myself, rather," Snow replied, recounting later that she was "a lady and not too inquisitive and having an admirable sense of humor, she laughed with me and we returned to the bridge game, where, to direct the conversation definitively into safer channels, I trumped my partner's ace."

Snow slept on Crabb's sofa and rose before the cabin boy came to make up the room. He ate Crabb's breakfast, the sole meal served in the rooms, and tried to fill up on sandwiches during cocktail hour. The Japanese cabin boy caught Snow pulling on his trousers one morning. "I told him I was in second class and that Dan and I were good friends," Snow wrote Towne, "and, if he kept 'mum' about me sleeping in Dan's cabin, the reward would be munificent indeed. I gave him ¥11 (about $5)."

On June 22, nine days and eight breakfasts after leaving Hawaii, the *Shinyo Maru* put into Yokohama early in the morning with one nervous passenger, now fourteen pounds lighter, pacing the deck. Snow did not have the landing pass required to go ashore. As he looked at the hundreds of Japanese shouting "banzai" in welcome to the future empress of Japan, he had visions of landing in jail.

His salvation this time was an English newspaperman who came out to the *Shinyo Maru* in a pilot boat with a horde of other reporters to cover the royal arrival. When Crabb and Snow took him aside and told their story, he was amazed.

"Why, do you know it's the first time it's ever been done?" he said. "Many have tried, but they've all failed. Now we have got to get you ashore to make a perfect score."

The plan was simple. In the company of the Englishman and several other Western reporters, Snow marched off the docked ship, nonchalantly nodding his head at the customs officials, displaying a sheaf of notes and some pictures, and, in Japanese, saying, "Reporters, *Japan Advertiser.*"

In Tokyo the journalists celebrated Snow's successful passage, made at Japanese expense, in the American Club. That night Snow joined O. D. Russell, the managing editor of the *Japan Advertiser,* and his wife for dinner, a long-awaited relief from bacon and eggs.

Russell offered Snow a job on the *Japan Advertiser,* long a conduit bringing Missourians to the Far East. Snow turned it down. A letter from Charlie Towne encouraged him to stick with his original plan, to travel at his own speed writing free-lance articles entitled "Adventure Bound." The affable editor said he was publishing a piece on Snow's Hawaii stay in *Harper's Bazaar.* Snow, paid five hundred dollars for his work, replied he was "treading with winged sandals on clouds of pink bliss!" The news was "the sort of thing that happens only in Alger books."

In Japan, Snow wrote a piece about his escapade on the *Shinyo Maru.* Russell, who wanted to publish it, promised to wait until Snow and Crabb were well out of the country. Other journalists promised not to break the news either. The boys made a trip to the mountain city of Nikko, then checked into a comfortable inn. When a Japanese police inspector stopped by, asking how they arrived in the country, they hurriedly packed their things.

From Yokahama, they went down the coast to Fuji, Nagoya, Kyoto, and Kobe. There they bought third-class passage aboard the *Empress of Asia,* which steamed through the inland sea of Japan, awash with green inlets and oddly rigged sailing vessels. In Nagasaki, Snow bought a silk kimono for his father and sailed on to China.

Snow arrived in Shanghai on Friday, July 6. He had never seen so many people. Half naked coolies, their heavy burdens suspended from bobbing bamboo poles, trotted past fierce Indian policemen. Englishmen in shining Austins competed for the roadways with man-powered rickshaws. Chinese signs, banners, and flags hung everywhere, except along the foreign-controlled Bund where somber gray European-style stone buildings looked over the Whangpoo River.

Snow found a room at the Navy YMCA on Szechwan Road. Later he pushed his way through the crowds to Avenue Edward VII, a street that wandered like an endless "S" between the International Settlement and the French Concession. He turned in at No. 4, the Great Northern Telegraphy Building, and climbed to the sixth floor offices of the *China Weekly Review*. In addition to the usual clutter of a newspaper, books were piled everywhere, on desks, tables, and chairs, and crammed into glass-enclosed sectional bookcases stacked shakily to the ceiling. This was one of the best private libraries in China. The owner of the library and the editor of the *Review* was J. B. Powell, to whom Snow presented a letter of introduction from Missouri Dean Walter Williams. Though he had no inkling of it, Snow's career as a China Hand was about to begin.

Powell, born and raised in Missouri, was a breath of home. So was the *Review*.

The *Review* had been founded by Thomas Franklin Fairfax Millard, another Missourian, regarded as "dean of American newspapermen of the Orient." After completing his studies at the University of Missouri, Millard began his career in journalism at the *St. Louis Republic*, where a characteristic fit of stubbornness cost him his job. He refused one day to cover a fire. He went on to the New York *Herald* and assignments as a foreign correspondent covering the Boer War, the Spanish-American War in the Philippines, and the Russo-Japanese War, as well as hostilities in Central America and, in 1900, the Boxer Rebellion in China, the country that held his interest.[4]

Millard hated European imperialism. During the Boer War, his dispatches criticizing British colonialists and glorifying their enemy so irritated Lord Kitchener that he had Millard deported. Millard was not opposed to enlarging American commerce in China, so long as that commerce helped the Chinese. He stridently criticized the Chamber of Commerce, bankers, and other Americans who resisted change in order to preserve United States business interests and imperial life styles in the foreign concessions. He called on the United States government, whose views he tried to shape, to adopt a policy of "felicitous aggressiveness," meaning it should become the prime force helping China even if the effort required economic warfare against other powers.[5]

Millard recognized that China was on the brink of an upheaval. His most ambitious effort to project his views onto that rapidly changing scene came in 1911, when he started the *China Press* in Shanghai. Millard intended to make the enterprise "substantially Chinese in backing and sympathy," among other things breaking with the colonial convention of ignoring "native" news. And he soon had plenty of Chinese news to report. On October 10 that year the *Press* broke the story of the anti-Manchu rebellion, which led to final dissolution of the Ching dynasty. Carl Crow, a Missourian working on the paper, thereafter had an exclusive weekly interview with the new chief of state, Dr. Sun Yat-sen.

Powerful members of the foreign community, especially the rival British-owned *North China Daily News*, objected to Millard's views, especially when he refused to side with the British in the Great War shaping up in Europe. Losing revenue and generally disgusted, Millard sold the paper in 1915. Two years later the determined editor tried again, starting a weekly, *Millard's Review of the Far East*. Upon Dean Williams's recommendation he brought John B. Powell to Shanghai to help with the editing chores. When Powell arrived and asked what the paper would print, Millard answered characteristically, "Anything we damn please."[6]

Powell and Millard cut different figures. Millard, cocky and often rude, always dressed fashionably and lived comfortably. He was immaculate, even when covering a battle. Powell, born to a northwest Missouri farm family, graduated from the University of Missouri journalism school and later taught there. Unlike Millard, he had no international experience before he came to China. All his journalism work was with Midwest newspapers. Also unlike Millard, he projected a simple friendlinesss, dressed casually, and sometimes smoked a corncob pipe. In 1922, when Millard decided to become an adviser to the Chinese government, he sold Powell his interest in the weekly. Characteristically, Powell did not put his name on the masthead. He changed the name simply to *China Weekly Review*.

The differences were cosmetic. Powell, a populist who disliked bankers and pressure from anyone, was also anti-imperialist and pro-Chinese. It was years before he would ride a rickshaw; when he finally got used to the idea of one human being pulling another, he always overpaid the driver. Like Millard, he believed the United States should play a special role in protecting and helping China. "In practical American terms," Powell wrote, "the Open Door in China means a first rate anti-trust law for China." Also like Millard, he published anything he damn pleased, supporting little-known Chinese leader Chiang Kai-shek over the vehement objections of fellow Westerners.

Rather than producing a strong central government, the 1911 revolution had disintegrated into a collection of competing warlords. Challenging the nominal central government in Peking, erstwhile leader

Dr. Sun reorganized his Kuomintang party and established a rump government in Canton, which in the 1920s developed ties with the Communists. Sun died in 1925. Chiang, one of his lieutenants, moved to take control of the newly proclaimed Nationalist government. In 1927 he began to enlarge his zone of control. Powell, like Millard, had no love for communism, but he did not agree that Chiang's campaign northward amounted to a "Red tide on the Yangtze." He believed that Chiang would split with his "Red" allies and bring sweeping reforms to improve conditions for the Chinese and end unequal treaties. Powell cheerfully reported that the Coolidge administration would not help Shanghai's foreign residents, who set up a "free city" to protect themselves from the Nationalists. He called on Westerners to give up extraterritorial rights voluntarily. The Shanghai American Chamber of Commerce charged Powell with "lending aid to disruptive" elements and called for his resignation from the organization. Powell headed off a vote on his ouster and declared he had "no intention whatever of changing my views."

Powell was right about Chiang. Chiang entered Shanghai, and with the help of the opium trafficking Chinese underworld engineered a bloody "white terror" that left, by some contemporary estimates, five thousand dead and the Communist Party in disarray. He then continued northward.[7] On July 3, 1928, just three days before Snow arrived in Shanghai, Chiang reached Peking. Real national unity was still a dream, yet the prospect of stability was sufficient to convince Powell to make plans for a special "New China" edition. Needing help with the project, Powell asked Snow if he wanted a job. Snow, who owed money to Dan Crabb and saw China as a good stopping place, agreed to interrupt his wanderings, temporarily. He wrote home that he had succeeded "in getting one of the prize jobs of the year!"

If Snow knew nothing of China, he instinctively shared the friendly, balding editor's distaste for the extraterritorial privileges foreigners enjoyed on Chinese soil. "Strange, isn't it," he wrote home only three days after landing in Shanghai, "that this, the most progressive, the wealthiest port in China should be controlled by foreigners! Yet the British and the Americans say it is all right; doubtless it is—for them."[8]

Snow ordered a linen suit to combat Shanghai's steamy humidity and, together with Chinese assistants, set to work assembling copy and coaxing advertising out of clients who previously abandoned the *Review* because of Powell's politics. To those who met Snow that summer, he seemed friendly, shy, and serious. He read avidly from Powell's library and listened intently to the editor's stories about China and its future.

The 198-page supplement appeared on October 10, the anniversary of the 1911 revolution. The *Review* described the issue as a "commemoration of the efforts which have been executed over a considerable number of years to bring about the development and modernization of the Republic of China as an independent member of the family of nations." The long list of contributors included many of the leaders of the young government. Articles extolled the reconstruction of China's railways and telegraphic system, China's "human wealth," the growth of rural cooperatives, and improvements in public health. In terms not unlike those used by the *Kansas City Star* to describe local prospects, the *Review* predicted that in fifty years China would have "palatial buildings in every city . . . on the same lines as skyscrapers of America, with numerous elevators. Rickshaws will be abolished, and only motor cars will be in use."

Snow's single signed contribution drew explicitly from his Missouri experience. "A few decades ago paved roads were still uncommon in many rural sections of the United States," he wrote, describing American self-help programs. Now, he continued, "there is a spirit, or at least the hopeful semblance of a spirit, of 'Lift China out of the Mud!' "

Before the supplement appeared, Powell offered Snow a job as the *Review*'s assistant advertising manager. The salary was about $180 a month. While the job carried administrative chores, it offered opportunities for reporting. Caught up in events, Snow agreed to stay a while longer.

In mid-October Powell sent Snow to Nanking, the Nationalists' capital.[9] Foreigners had not established themselves in that city as they had in treaty ports. Unlike in Shanghai, pidgin English was not much use in communicating with Chinese. Snow could not explain to the staff at his hotel that his room had bedbugs. When he finally showed them the welts on his body, they put a mosquito net over his bed.

In Nanking Snow got a contract for twelve months of advertising from the National Registration Bureau, shook hands with Chiang Kai-shek, and interviewed ministers T. V. Soong, C. T. Wang, and Sun Fo, the son of Dr. Sun Yat-sen. The trip reinforced Snow's conviction that "China is changing with a swiftness unparalleled in the history of any country of the world."

A trip north to Shantung in December gave Snow a chance to see the heavy hand of imperialism, Japanese style. Since its major victory over the Chinese in 1894, the Japanese had sought to enlarge their influence in the country. They had been especially active in Shantung. When the Nationalists approached the province in 1928, Japan sent in five thousand troops to protect Japanese nationals. Skirmishes erupted.

Japan used the occasion to exert more control. In the next months it curtailed rail traffic and commerce. To draw public attention to the problem, which the Japanese denied, Sun Fo invited Snow and Al Batson, a reporter with the British *North China Daily News*, to see for themselves.

Just after Christmas, the reporters boarded a special train car arranged for the trip. Because the government was concerned about wear and tear on its equipment, the locomotive lumbered along at only fifteen miles an hour. At each station, Snow saw rice, beans, millet, flour, kaioliang, and other cargo languishing on loading platforms, sometimes piled so high they obscured the station.

On Sunday morning, December 30, they arrived in Taian. It took twenty-two hours before the Japanese let the party proceed to Tsinan, Shantung's capital, and then the journey was fitful. Under duress from the Japanese, station managers along the way would only let the train through after bitter protests. Three miles south of Tsinan, Japanese officials held the train up, saying it did not have permission to enter the city. After a three-hour wait, the reporters decided to travel the last stretch on foot.

Altogether, Snow estimated that the Japanese had detained 51 locomotives, 492 goods wagons, 33 passenger cars, and 9 service cars, costing the Nationalists forty thousand dollars a day in lost revenue. The Japanese, he also concluded, were stalling on repair of the Yellow River Bridge, blown up by dissident Chinese forces retreating before Chiang's armies. "There is no doubt whatever, in my opinion, that the Japanese have prevented the movement of rolling stock at Tsinanfu, that they have interfered with the administration of the railway, and that they show every indication of continuing to hinder the progress of the rehabilitation of the line."

Overall, Snow regarded the ten-day trip as an extremely lucky adventure. Al Batson told Snow marvelous stories about his earlier career as a Canadian army officer, seaman, cross country walker, actor, and advisor to the Nicaraguan freedom fighter Augustino Sandino—the latter job ending when the Marines landed and tossed him out of the country. On the way back to Shanghai, Snow climbed the six thousand-odd steps up sacred Tai Shan mountain in Taian, cold excitement even Batson thought foolhardy. Best of all was an erroneous report that the Japanese had arrested the party. For several days, "White Cloud," Snow's Chinese name, was on the front pages of papers in Tientsin, Peking, Canton, Hongkong, Wuhan, and Tsingtao.

When the news of his good fortune reached home, Snow's mother implored him to return immediately. "I hope you will not be sent on any more investigations, that if you are you will refuse to go. . . . You have already had too many adventures."

Undeterred, Snow took another travel assignment from Powell, this time to prepare a Baedeker of sights tied together by the Chinese rail system. Together with S. Y. Livingston Hu, a Harvard-educated technical expert with the Ministry of Railways, he spent four months viewing China from swaying coaches, at various stops wandering through the streets and outlying countryside. In April he traveled south of Shanghai to Hangchow and Ningpo, and northwest to Nanking. Later he rode the Tsinpu route, running from Nanking north to Tientsin. In May and June he headed further north to Manchuria and on into Korea, which was under odious Japanese suzerainty. Snow returned to Peking to make a July swing west to Suiyan.

Powell's ulterior motive in running the four-part series was to show that, under the Nationalists, China's "romantic railways" offered safe, pleasant, interesting travel.[10] Snow's copy, banged out on a balky Corona, described clean, comfortable trains, "serving excellent foreign food," efficiently run Chinese hotels, young girls with peach blossoms behind their ears, scenes comparable to the Grand Canyon or the Royal Gorge (which he had seen on his boyhood trip west with Charlie White and Bob Long), and modern electric light plants side-by-side ancient temples. In his article on traveling over the Peking-Mukden railway, he ridiculed the white-tiled, Japanese-built Yamata Hotel in Mukden, "a magnificent inverted bathroom," and in a separate article drew attention to Japanese imperial designs: "Deep within the heart of every Japanese in Manchuria is a conviction that until the Rising Sun floats unrivaled across South Manchuria, Japan cannot rest." But Snow stressed the new spirit he thought he saw in the Nationalists. "It does not take a prophet to observe that it is here, in historic Nanking, that the great things of China are going to have their center in the future."

As much as Snow looked for romantic sights, images of Chinese poverty and hardship built up one on the other wherever he traveled.[11] On his railway inspection trip with Batson, he walked behind the Tsinan Club, "that neat modern little building the foreigners have constructed for themselves." He found Chinese families living in semicave dwellings, "shivering with the cold, weary and emaciated looking." The frigid climb up Tai Shan brought him face-to-face with beggars living in "trembling straw lean-tos, scarcely larger than dog kennels, from which the wretches crawled into the biting wind." But the most searing experience came at the end of his four-month railway journey.

Over the objection of his traveling companion, Hu, Snow insisted on taking the Peking-Suiyuan line well into famine-ravaged districts on the drought-dry southern edge of the Gobi desert. Along the way they met Rewi Alley, a brawny, rawboned New Zealander who worked as a factory inspector in Shanghai. Alley was using his vacation to help with relief efforts. Snow considered Alley better company than Hu, whom he thought effete and supercilious like all Harvard men. Not put off by scares over typhus and the omnipresent dust that settled in eyes and ears, Snow got off the train at Kweihwa with Alley. The next day they rode about sixty miles to Saratsi together. Snow come back without a touch of *sans souci*.

With O. J. Todd, an engineer from Michigan working with the International Famine Relief Commission, Snow walked past scenes on Saratsi's fetid streets that haunted him the rest of his life. They stepped over half-alive bodies. Children, their faces bloated by disease, stared vacantly ahead. A withered young woman dug into the ground for the roots of a scrawny tree. "We came to a picture that was surely the most heartwrenching I have ever seen," he reported in a story for the *Review*.

> A little boy, scarcely six years old, sat beside an old man, either dead or in the last moment of earthly life. The child was thickly coated with dust and filth—and nothing else. . . . I walked over to the spot, knelt down beside the child and put my hand on the old fellow's pulse. There was no response. His heart, too, apparently had ceased beating. Gently pulling the bewildered infant away from the body, we took him with us, and I saw to it that at least one empty stomach was well fed that day.[12]

While Snow was in Peking finishing his travel series, Powell wired him to return to Shanghai at once. Powell served as the China correspondent for the *Chicago Tribune*, and the *Tribune* wanted him to cover Marshal Chang Hsueh-liang's efforts to take over the Soviet-controlled Chinese Eastern Railway in the north. By the time Snow reached Shanghai, Powell had gone, leaving instructions to take over editorship of the weekly as well as his local *Tribune* duties, jobs that stretched out for several months when Powell extended his trip into Russia.

In his second year in China and at the helm of the *Review*, Snow had matured. Now in his mid-twenties, he had seasoned physically. The lines framing his broad smile deepened. The brows over his brown eyes thickened. Brown hues replaced the red in his curly hair, which, when he attended to it, was parted high on his head, slicked back. Standing a little under five feet nine inches, Snow did not tower over Americans or Chinese; but flesh and muscle clung tightly to his frame, giving the impression of compact energy.

Putting that energy to good use, he had seen more of the country than many who lived in the foreign concessions for years. He counted among his friends many of the journalists and other Westerners who dropped by the newspaper office to talk about politics or borrow books. With one of them, John Allison, a young Nebraskan who worked as local advertising manager for General Motors, he moved out of the YMCA into a small apartment on Seymour Road.

Snow was also something of a professional success. During his first months as the *Review*'s assistant advertising manager, the number of ads had doubled to twenty pages a week. In addition to conferring responsibility for running the *Review* on Snow, Powell had given him the title of assistant editor. Filing for the *Chicago Tribune* added to his prestige. Snow expressed his self-confidence in an article for the *Review* lamenting the "American college boy 'vagabond' . . . drifting insouciantly through the East."[13]

Snow's literary output was expanding beyond the *Review*, though in no certain direction. He sold free-lance articles to the *Kansas City Journal Post* and the *New York Herald Tribune* magazines, *Travel* magazine, and *Advertising and Selling Age*. He tried fiction, writing a piece portraying a "fair-haired" young American customs officer in Shanghai, who is duped by his beautiful, dope smuggling, Russian sweetheart. "Never trust a Russian, Johnny," the girl warns the now wiser boy in a parting note at the end of the story. Snow admitted the story was "lousy" and probably only published by *Liberty* magazine because the editors wanted to claim it had an author in far-off China.[14]

Gradually Snow began to form his own opinions about China. He still shared Powell's belief that the best future lay in Nationalist hands.[15] He wrote his mother that he was proud of the signed photograph Sun Fo gave him after the railway series appeared. But, as Snow saw it, the Nationalists had a long way to go before they truly transformed China. He was deeply bothered that Chinese walked by the dying in Saratsi. Chiang seemed unable to make rapid change. His inability to check feuding warlords in the Northwest had "succeeded in so crippling the railway and impoverishing upper Shansi and Chihli that these avenues of relief were closed." In a letter home, Snow called Chiang a "dictator" of "mediocre abilities." The Generalissimo succeeded largely because of his "remarkable" wife, whom Snow found beautiful and articulate. China, Snow wrote home in early 1929, "needs a crusader, a towering pillar of strength, a practical idealist who can lead his people out of the stench and decay, the misery and suffering and national agonies, an individual who can emancipate her from the sins of corruption and greed and ignorance in which she now languishes."

Toward the end of 1929, Snow's correspondence home hinted at interest in the Communists. In the coming months he pieced together from secondhand sources one of the few articles written at the time on the little-known Chinese Communist movement, struggling for survival in the countryside. With keen insight, Snow noted that Chiang's failure to keep his promises was one of the Reds' more effective weapons. Snow was far from a Communist sympathizer, however. From Shanghai acquaintances, he learned details of Chiang's alliance with the notorious Green Gang and their bloody purge of the Communists in 1927. To Snow, Chiang's action seemed a step toward law and order.

For all his interest in strong leadership, Snow also wanted greater democracy. The two values existed side by side in his American experience. It bothered him that Chiang showed little sign of relinquishing one-party Kuomintang rule. In an article that appeared in the *New York Herald Tribune* Sunday magazine and the *Kansas City Journal Post,* Snow criticized undemocratic deification of Nationalist party founder Sun Yat-sen. "Apparent to all is the fact that this name is constantly being used and abused by politicians and militarists who have not the faintest sympathy with the high ethics or dogma of the idealist that was Sun Yat-sen." When Snow's father suggested it might be unwise to challenge government propaganda, Snow replied with an argument probably calculated to appeal to his father's anti-Catholic outlook:

"Do you see any great difference between the methods used here and those which Spain employed in enslaving the Americas three centuries ago? Spain used the incense and the idolatry of Catholicism to break the spirit of races she conquered; the National Government is interpreting Sun Yat-sen as a deity and making a cult of the beliefs of a man who despised worship in any form. Both of them are betrayers. Spain betrayed Christ; the Kuomintang may yet betray Sun Yat-sen."[16]

Snow's travels also put flesh on his instinctual dislike of special foreign rights. He was as outraged by Western indifference to the human suffering in Saratsi as he was depressed by Chinese indifference. He stepped in himself to help unfortunates, on one occasion demanding that an old Chinese woman stop beating a small girl who could no longer carry her heavy load. On another occasion, in Shanghai, a coolie whose clothes had caught fire fell "within shouting distance" of Snow, who was out for a night on the town. While Chinese stood around and watched, Snow rushed over and threw his camel coat on the man.[17]

In Powell's absence, Snow did not hesitate to throw the *Review* into pro-Chinese causes.

The building housing the *Review*'s offices had two elevators, one reserved for Westerners. When a Chinese visitor complained about the discrimination, Snow editorialized on the "arrogant, insulting piece of effrontery" of the building's British management. "The Great Northern Building," he wrote, "is managed by men still harboring the intolerant view of their predecessors who established the white man's domain many decades ago."[18]

This was just the kind of issue that sparked fierce debate among Shanghai's foreign community. The British-owned *North China Daily News*, which for years had traded insults with the *Review*, jumped at the chance to attack Snow's editorial. "That Ishmael among local journals has distinguished itself by the utter disregard for truth," wrote "A Lover of Truth" in the letters column of the *North China Daily News*. "I would . . . appeal to you once more (as I did in my letter of May 29 last)," wrote "John England" in another missive, "to take the initiative or whatever steps are necessary towards running the editor of the 'China Weekly Review' out of town."

Snow responded in the next edition of the *Review*:

> Regular readers of the *Review* know that this journal is not anti-foreign, nor is it avowedly anti-British. It is an American magazine, striving always for the spirit of fair-play and if it sometimes seems that the *Review*'s attitude is pro-Chinese at the expense of foreign interests, it is because the editors attempt to wield the scalpel for what is morally right; that which is justice. And we aim to attack bigotry in all its manifestations because it is opposed to that justice.

The British building owners changed the elevator policy. Several months later, when Powell had returned, they got even by refusing to renew the *Review*'s lease. Powell moved his offices down the street to No. 38 Avenue Edward VII, where he rented a five-room suite on the fourth floor of a nearly windowless building. It was a fond memory of Snow's that his boss "never uttered a word of admonition."

In letters home Snow swore that he was about to leave China. Once he finished his railway stories, he wrote Howard, who had just landed a six-thousand-dollar-a-year advertising job, "Nothing will persuade me to stay away from home any longer." But something always seemed to put off the event, and that something came down to one point, as he explained a year later, when he was still in China: "I hate the thought of going back to the old 9 to 5 routine. Any experience in discipline which I might have had has long ago been spiked by this personal management freedom of two years and more." Even as he advanced at the *Review* and traveled widely, he complained that the job encroached too much on his freedom.[19]

In early 1929 Tom Millard, who for years had shuttled between the Chinese government and journalism, was about to go to work for the Nationalists. That would leave his position as correspondent for the *New York Herald Tribune* open. Millard, who belonged to the same fraternity as Snow and liked the younger man, was able to appoint his successor and asked if Snow was interested. Becoming a correspondent for the prestigious *Herald Tribune* was a great opportunity for a reporter Snow's age. Nevertheless he turned it down. The job had a major drawback. It would commit Snow to stay in Shanghai.

A perfect opportunity came late in the year in the form of a cable to Powell from Drew Pearson and David Lawrence. Pearson and Lawrence had organized the Consolidated Press Association to funnel news to the New York *Sun*, the *Chicago Daily News*, and more than fifty other dailies. They needed a part-time roving correspondent in the Far East, an unmarried man free to look for out-of-the-way news. They didn't care if the young journalist wrote magazine articles on the side or also reported for non-U.S. newspapers. Powell recommended Snow, and on December 2 a cable confirmed that he had the job. To Snow's chagrin, Powell prevailed on him to stay with the *Review* for a few more weeks while he made another trip.

On March 22, 1930, the last day Snow's name appeared on the *Review*'s masthead, one major reason for returning home suddenly vanished. Snow's mother died unexpectedly of peritonitis. In subsequent correspondence, his father related that staff at the Catholic hospital treating her had been rude and careless, something staunchly Catholic Anna had admitted before she died. The news of her death left Snow crushed and feeling guilty that he had not been home. Years later he still shed remorseful tears.[20]

The Consolidated Press made relatively few demands. Concerned about cable charges, the editors discouraged correspondents from filing breaking news covered by the major wire services unless, as Snow put it, he had "a scoop on the assassination of Chiang Kai-shek or a virgin birth."[21] During the summer, Snow reported on Chiang's campaign to keep a coalition of warlords from taking control of Peking, prepared several advertising booklets for the Nationalist government's Ministry of Railroads, and wrote free-lance articles.

In one of those free-lance pieces, published in August by H. L. Mencken's *American Mercury*, Snow loosed a salvo at the foreign community and its offensive extraterritorial ways.[22] In "The Americans in Shanghai," Snow lambasted nearly every one of Mencken's whipping boys—joiners, Christianity, municipal corruption, the YMCA, general hypocrisy—and in enough detail to take the breath out of nearly every foreign resident, American or not.

According to Snow, virtually every foreigner came to China to make money. Even "the missionary goes to sell the Bible," he wrote, no longer constrained by his mother's religiosity. "Among them are some wealthy hierarchies, rivaling the exploiters who looted the Hawaiians while confounding them with the wonder of 'salvation from sin through the Son of God, our Savior Jesus Christ.' " He criticized the American chairman of the International Settlement, who propagandized "against the withdrawal of American marines and sailors, and against the abolition of extraterritoriality." Snow listed the addresses of brothels "maintained exclusively for foreign civilians." He called the local British administration "uniquely feudal . . . one of the narrowest oligarchies surviving in the world today."

American Randall Gould, editor of the *Shanghai Evening Post & Mercury*, "thought Ed a trifle unfeeling and callow, [but] I had to admit that basically he had our sinful avaricious cruel town pretty much to rights." Mostly, people were outraged. "Mr. Edgar Snow appears to be a master of fallacious and untruthful, but ear-tickling journalese," concluded a British official when news of the article reached the Foreign Office in London.

That Shanghai's foreign community had reason to run Snow out of town did not trouble him much. He wanted to leave anyway. He had played with various travel plans. His first thought was to visit Russia. When no visa was forthcoming, he asked his editors if he could travel overland to India. Seeing the chance to fill clients' papers with colorful stories, Consolidated Press notified Snow in late August that it was giving him three hundred dollars a month to make the trip.

Snow left Shanghai on September 25. According to plan, he headed south via Formosa, Foochow, Amoy, Swatow, Canton, Macao, and Hanoi. From Hanoi he took a two-day train ride across the Tonkin plains and up the Yunnan plateau, sixty-four hundred feet above sea level, reaching Kunming on December 7. Known as "the eaves of the foot of the world," Kunming was China's last outpost toward the west. There Snow laid plans to become one of the few Westerners to trek to Upper Burma, a notion he acquired in reading Marco Polo's travels.

The local U.S. Consul, Harry Stevens, unsuccessfully tried to dissuade Snow from making the journey through four hundred miles of bandit country. The day after he arrived, Snow lunched with Dr. Joseph F. Rock, a Viennese-born naturalist-explorer who had earned a worldwide reputation for his travels through Yunnan. Rock was experiencing a tortured bout of indecision, wavering over an offer from the National Geographic Society to make a plant-hunting expedition in the region.

Snow's plans seemed to crystallize his own thinking. Rock decided to organize a caravan and invited Snow to come along, insisting however that they delay their departure until January when the hills would be safer.[23]

While Snow impatiently waited, he stayed in Stevens's rambling, cold, Chinese house, going out during the day to explore. The city was filled with exotic sights, Tonkinese in brown and white pajamas, gaudily dressed Chinese, and shaggy Tibetans. Marring these scenes, though, were revolting human conditions that raised more questions about the Nationalists' effectiveness. En route to Kunming he had seen evidence that Nationalist officials were not improving society but plundering it. In Canton, the Kuomintang heartland, a local publisher subsidized by the Kuomintang confided that "every official here is getting rich off the tax racket." In Kunming, malnourished children sucked sugarcane pacifiers coated with opium; slavery ran to half a million people; absentee landlordism left less that one-third of the peasants with their own land to till. Snow was distressed to learn that children worked the semi-government-controlled Kochiu tin mines and that for years the chief mining engineer had been an American. "Forty percent [of the miners] die of arsenic poisoning after three or four years," he wrote Dick Walsh, editor of *Asia*. "In a few months their skin turns nearly green, the arsenic eating into their bodies very rapidly. The average wage paid is around $20 yearly."

The arrangements with Rock were not as good as they sounded. Rock rarely met a man he liked. The only exception seems to have been Dr. J. A. Watson, head of the Church Missionary Society hospital in Kunming. And Rock never traveled with Watson, as his biographer pointed out about her unsympathetic subject. Snow accepted the protection of Rock's Nashi tribesmen, admired his familiarity with every stone and plant in the province, and his willingness to treat native illnesses. But he disliked the naturalist's imperial trappings, which included a folding bathtub and regal table settings, and he had little appreciation of Rock's caution. At their first meeting, Snow proposed to use potassium cyanide to disinfect the plants he would eat on the trip. Snow, Rock wrote in his diary, would "kill himself in the bargain. *Sancta simplicitas*." The journalist, he concluded, was "an uncouth American youth, inexperienced and learned in ill names . . . he carries the general air of the provincial American ignorant of his own ignorance."

When Rock became feverish, he hired Szechwanese coolies to carry him, a royal annoyance to Snow. When Snow broke out in an unaccountable rash, Rock simply remarked, "I hope it is not contagious." In one village where they spent the night in a rundown temple, they found inscribed on the wall, "Joseph R. Rock. Will I ever come here again? No, never. Jan. 28, 1930." Snow struck out the "No, never" and wrote "yes, again, Feb. 7, 1931." Rock wrote in his diary, "Never again shall I ask anyone to go with me."

About two weeks after setting out from Kunming, the caravan reached Tali, where Snow and Rock separated as planned. With his own small caravan of ponies and mules, a cook and muleteer, Snow attached himself to a well-guarded merchant caravan descending toward Burma. Two weeks later he arrived at the gleaming Irrawaddy, bearded and favoring a swollen knee inflicted by the kick from one of his mules. He quickly came down with malaria.

A Burmese girl, Batalá, nursed him back to health while he rested in the British commissioner's house. He met her again in Rangoon, where fever struck once more. Snow described her in a New York *Sun* dispatch as a slender, fragile girl of 17, with "eyes provocative in their dark merriment"; her inky hair gleamed in the night.[24] Snow lounged along the bamboo-lined Irrawaddy for a month, listened to her sing folk songs, and followed her through local festivals, theaters, and temples. Rested, he moved on to India, where he spent four months traveling in the vast expanse between the arid Kyber Pass and verdant Ceylon.

Snow made the most of his adventures in his copy. Like Halliburton, he seemed to find a riveting experience wherever he ventured. A visit to the courtyards of the Delhi fort made him feel "magically transported into a place of illusion and romance." Some of his stories in the genre, like his recounting of the Shan village woman in Yunnan who tried to marry him to her daughter, came off quite well.

At the same time, the journey opened a window on upheavals soon to reshape the political landscape. In Formosa, where he narrowly escaped an aborigine uprising in the central mountains, he observed the nearly total transformation of native culture by the Japanese, who had taken over the island after defeating the Chinese in 1895. In Hanoi, he encountered the familiar sight of French hotel clerks berating Annamite bellhops and Western train conductors slapping the cheeks of native passengers too slow to produce their tickets. Snow filed brief, secondhand stories on the Communist-inspired rebellion taking place at the time. The harsh French retaliation bothered Snow, as did his experience that the Vietnamese moved "sullenly aside when you pass too close to them, and they cower. They have no spirit." Snow's sympathies were on the side of those who rebelled. He was the only American on hand to record the uprising of landless Burmese peasants under Saya San, who also evoked Snow's sympathies. Saya San's rebellion was "a movement from the soil." With its well-trained and equipped army, Snow correctly predicted in a dispatch, the British would eventually put down the uprising and kill Saya San. Afterward, the rebel would become a martyr, "one more grievance to stir hatred of the Burmese against rulers whose domination appears to grow more and more intolerable to the Middle East."[25]

India offered Snow a close look at strong political leaders challenging imperial rule. Maverick journalist Agnes Smedley, a frequent visitor to the *Review* offices in Shanghai, had given him a letter of introduction to Jawaharlal Nehru. Snow presented it in Bombay and was immediately impressed with the Indian's practical idealism. He was less enthusiastic about Gandhi, whom he met in the cool summer capital of Simla. He wrote his sister Mildred that Gandhi was "a considerable bore." The austere leader was negotiating the end of the 1930 disobedience campaign. Gandhi's exaltation of sexual abstinence, nonviolent techniques, and poverty clashed with Snow's belief in direct, practical action. Snow also worried that the Mahatma's boycott of British textiles developed a market for Japanese piece goods in India. "Curiously," he wrote in a news story, Gandhi "still appears to believe it is possible to replace machines with handlooms." When Snow revealed these misgivings to the Indian leader in an on-the-run interview, Gandhi advised him to "study some more."[26]

Snow covered the trial in Meerut of thirty-one conspirators charged with organizing a militant labor movement of textile workers. All but three of the accused were Communists. During the trial they "conducted a brilliant and interesting defense," each presenting "in great detail some special phase of Communism."

"When one reads back through the newspaper files since the trial began," Snow reported, "it is an education in the economics of Karl Marx, and their revolutionary application by Lenin, his associates, and their successors."

Sarojini Naidu, a woman activist and close follower of Gandhi, introduced Snow to her Communist sister, Suhasini, whom Snow thought the most beautiful woman he had ever met. Suhasini took him on forays into the mill districts where he saw the cruel conditions in which workers and their families toiled.

Sarojini and Suhasini were members of the Chattopadhyaya clan, "the most interesting family I have known anywhere," Snow reported. One radical member of the family had a common-law marriage to Agnes Smedley in Germany. Another sister was an authority on Indian art, and yet another, a spinster, ran the first Montessori school in the country. What he liked about the four women reflected what he disliked about India. Snow would always admire liberated women. And these ladies, as he wrote in an article celebrating them, set a badly needed example for other Indians. "Victimized by their own religion and archaic social structure, a system of government that has kept them in dark ignorance and illiteracy and a philosophy based on one of the most fundamentally corrupting of all superstitions—that the suffering one endures in this life is the result of sin in a previous existence—the millions of Hindu women in semislavery need to be awakened to the needless futility of their lives and to be shown how release is possible."

Although Snow had started to read Marxist literature on his own, he did not embrace Communist solutions any more than he did Gandhi's. Suhasini called him "Mr. Iceberg" because he did not succumb to her fervent political convictions. But exposure to Marxism gave Snow a new vocabulary explaining the oppressive nature of imperialism and its commercial exploitation. The poverty he saw in India and in his other wanderings also impressed on him the need and possibilities for urgent change. His thoughts particularly revolved around China and the steps needed to release national energies there.

Newsman William Shirer, who met Snow in Simla, sensed that China had captured the young Missourian's interest. India had its beauty, Snow told his father, but "I do not find the Indians I have met (with a few exceptions) are as attractive as the little men of Japan, China, or even Annam & Tokien [*sic*]."

Snow considered going on from India to Europe and the United States but changed his mind. Running out of money and fearing "that it would be necessary for me to get a job almost at once" in New York, Snow told his editors he wanted to return to China. When no response came, he assumed they agreed and took the sea route aboard the *Chichibu Maru*.

Snow was not beyond relishing the adventure as the ship worked its way toward East Asia. "I fell in love with the Balinese, as everyone does," he wrote to Towne. "There is some secret of life and laughter there that the rest of the world has lost or never knew."

Pacing back and forth on the deck of the ship, resting in Singapore harbor, Snow was vividly reminded of how far he had come since he was a stowaway on the *Shinyo Maru* three years before.

The Japanese skipper approached, sizing him up with apparent distaste.

"Are you Mr. Edgar Snow?" he asked.

"Yes, I am," Snow replied, about to move on.

"Ah, Mr. Snow—you have got ticket?"

"Oh yes, certainly."

"Please, Mr. Snow, may I see?"

Snow impatiently pulled out his papers. The captain looked them over at leisure. Handing them back, he said meditatively, "Mr. Snow—I was captain—of *Shinyo Maru*!"

It was the kind of story that China Hands loved to tell over whisky in their clubs. Snow, ready to enter their foremost ranks, left his stowaway days out of his memoirs.[27]

The Second Act

2

When Snow set out from New York in 1928, he sought carefree adventure, no more. "You will say I am omitting the 'sordid details'—giving a picture which is only half-true," he told Howard after a few days of traveling. "Yes, there is plenty of unpleasantness—but why bring that up? One easily forgets the pain when any pleasurable sensation quickly follows it."[1]

Returning to Shanghai from India in 1931, Snow had a different view. He still wanted his freedom. He still relished adventure. He planned to complete *South of the Clouds*, a travelogue describing his trek from Yunnan to Burma, rather than return home where the Depression and higher living costs would force him into "selling advertising, or some silly stunt like that, and with no time for what I really want to do," as he told Towne. But as much as he might resist the notion, the real attraction of China ran deeper. In the turbulent months ahead, Snow was drawn more and more into the country, tormented from the outside by imperialist aggression and from the inside by persistent political, social, and economic tyranny and confusion.

"What I hate of course is the filth of the country, the hopelessness of the people, the apparent poverty, distress, disease, inequality everywhere," he told Howard after coming back to China. "Yet it is irritation and this provides a stimulation much more real and perhaps deeper in humanity than one derives from living in the sameness that is America."

Snow's Shanghai homecoming in August 1931 was anything but happy. People had not forgotten his *American Mercury* article. The weather was oppressively sultry. He immediately came down with a 104-degree fever. The doctor thought it was malaria. Snow went to bed for three days. As soon as that passed Snow had an attack of prickly heat and a bout of homesickness. "I've given the East one year more," Snow told Towne. "Perhaps not that long, but certainly no longer."

The Nationalists had made little progress since Snow left on his South Asia trip.[2] They firmly controlled only two provinces, Kiangsu and Chekiang on the coast. Elsewhere the best Chiang could achieve was a loose federation with local warlords, whom he had to fight or buy off or both. In nearby Kiangsi, the Communists organized a soviet, prompting Chiang to throw precious resources into his third "bandit suppression" campaign in June 1931. Meanwhile, reforms remained a distant dream. At the local level, time-secure officials managed co-operative banks for their own benefit, borrowing low interest money themselves and lending it to peasants at traditionally high rates. Chiang's central government in Nanking seemed far less efficient than enterprising local bureaucrats.

On the street in Shanghai, Snow encountered a young Chinese acquaintance. When they first met, in 1928, the young man was about to become secretary to a Nationalist minister and enthused that "China is on the road at last." Now he was a bank clerk. The Nationalists had failed to pay his salary for three months. "I couldn't afford to stay in Nanking even if they had made me minister," he told Snow.

Snow had barely unpacked his bags when the Yangtze swelled to historic proportions leaving two million dead and twenty-five million homeless.[3] He made his way up the surging river in a small launch, plowing past submerged villages where Chinese clung to anything that remained above water. On a single day in Yangchow, he saw a dozen dragon junks glide into port, their decks loaded with four thousand coffins. Snow praised "brilliant" T. V. Soong, the Nationalist Minister of Finance, for effectively managing the National Flood Relief Commission. He had little good to say about the government as a whole, which initially spent more time bickering internally than organizing a relief effort. The indecision and wasted effort, he charged in an article on the flood, was typical of the "militaristic regime which for callous indifference, tyrannous oppression and ruinous incompetence has not been surpassed anywhere in this era."

A second test of the Nationalist regime came on September 18, the day Snow returned to Shanghai from his Yangtze River trip.[4] A small bomb exploded on the tracks of the South Manchurian Railway. Saying they were taking defensive measures, the Japanese moved on Chinese positions in Mukden and within twenty-four hours controlled nearly the entire Kwantung peninsula. The speed and efficiency of the operation suggested to Snow and other Western observers that the Japanese had contrived a pretext for taking control of Manchuria.

The Japanese pressed on into Manchuria. Although Chiang Kai-shek did not want to put up resistance, Chinese General Ma Chan-shan in Tsitsihar vowed to fight "to the last man." By the time Snow, Powell, and a handful of other reporters sent by their papers to cover the fast moving events reached Tsitsihar, the fighting was over. Ma and his ill-supported army were in flight for the Siberian border. The mangled, frozen corpses of Chinese soldiers, some half-eaten by wolves and wild dogs, littered the outskirts of the city.

In Mukden, Snow interviewed the newly appointed Chinese governor. The former Ching imperial official, somewhat bewildered by his new position, admitted that the Japanese put him in the job against his will, that he had not approved the new budget because it hadn't yet been translated into Chinese. Snow had a good story. He returned to Shanghai in December certain that Japan was only beginning its transparent tactics of using proxies to gain control of China.

"Such a phantasmagoria as existed in Manchuria under the name of government did not, perhaps, deserve to survive," he commented privately of the overthrown Chinese regime. "But the ethical problem still remains: has any nation the right to take over the land, property and government of another merely because that latter is hopelessly incompetent?"

While the Japanese consolidated their gains in the north, civilian Chinese in the south unexpectedly took matters into their own hands. They boycotted Japanese goods and refused to work for Japanese employers, shutting down sixty Shanghai factories. The Shanghai Chinese Bankers' Association made it impossible for Japanese to clear business transactions.

On January 18 blood was shed. Five Japanese monks wandered into Chapei, a Chinese-run area of Shanghai just north of the International Settlement. Although the precise causes remained in dispute, a riot followed, leaving one of the priests dead. The disturbance gave the Japanese another pretext for action. This time it issued an ultimatum, among other things demanding the arrest of Chinese accused of assailing the monks, the breakup of anti-Japanese organizations, and an end to the boycott.

The Nationalists agonized over their decision for more than a week. It was clear to anyone walking through the streets, which began to look like an armed camp, that the Japanese were prepared to take military action. Full compliance with the ultimatum would not spare the Chinese from attack, Snow accurately predicted. Four hours before the deadline on January 28, Chinese officials notified the Japanese that they would meet all demands. Admiral Shiozawa next demanded that all Chinese troops evacuate Chapei before midnight. The message was not delivered to the mayor until 11:30, by which time the Japanese troops were moving into assault positions.[5]

Having word of the impending action, Snow left shortly after eleven o'clock for the North Station Railway terminal in Chapei. He warned the unsuspecting station traffic manager that Japanese troops were en route. Snow suggested he disperse Chinese waiting for trains. Coming back, Snow encountered the advancing Japanese and saw the first Chinese soldier fall, shot by a Japanese bullet. Snow's dispatch, appearing as the banner story on page one of the *Chicago Daily News* and the New York *Sun*, was the first filed on the fighting. Editors changed his melodramatic lead—"The streets of Shanghai are red with blood tonight"—and cabled their congratulations for the scoop.

Snow worked that night without sleep. The next day he witnessed a mid-day Japanese air raid on civilian targets, the first such bombardment in the 1930s. That night, Snow reported from the blazing city, "scarlet shafts of light pierced the moonless and starless heavens, throwing a wavering eerie light over a scene of wild confusion and death."

Chinese General Tsai Ting-kai pledged not to "yield an inch of territory." To the surprise of the Japanese, his troops mounted a tenacious defense. For nearly five weeks, Snow stayed in the middle of the fighting. His succession of front-page stories took him back and forth across the lines. He was the first foreigner to arrive after the Japanese dropped six-hundred-pound bombs on Chenju. Wanting to verify whether Chinese had withdrawn from positions or still held them, he picked his way across battlefields pitted with twenty-five-foot-wide bomb craters while Japanese planes soared overhead. Coming back from an interview with General Tsai, he walked for three hours in the dark, getting arrested twice. Another time, when he hunkered down behind a grave marker on the Japanese side of the lines for an hour, a Chinese sniper put a hole in his hat. "I would describe the Chinese defense as heroic," Snow reported early on, making no secret of his sympathies.

Often there was little Snow could do to help the Chinese. During one reporting visit, the Japanese herded Chinese civilians out of their homes into a bamboo thicket, which they set on fire. Snow watched helplessly while the soldiers shot the bewildered peasants running out of the blaze. Snow was more successful when he spotted a young girl wandering amid flaming wreckage after a bombardment. Her father, a railway worker, had been killed. Snow took her back through the rear-line barricades. Later he found a home for her "with a Chinese whose goods I rescued from his mansion in Hongkew." The North Station Railway traffic manager won a promotion, a cash award, and a decoration for acting on Snow's advice and dispersing rolling stock and people before the initial Japanese attack on Chapei. He gave Snow a banquet.

At the end of the month, the Japanese finally claimed their victory. Snow went out to survey the destruction patrolled by vindictive Japanese soldiers. He stopped to help victims, among them a young girl, part of whose leg and hand were blown off. "I have seen enough," concluded Snow. "In my mind runs a panorama sharp with images of horror and carnage. . . . I think of the agony and loss and death among hundreds of simple and guiltless folk, massacred without cause and with little warning."

In early March the Japanese declared a new state in Manchuria, which they named Manchukuo. At its head they put Henry Pu Yi, the last Ching ruler. A year later, when the Lytton Commission of the League of Nations concluded that the Japanese had been the aggressors in Manchuria, Japan withdrew from the league and, showing its defiance, took control of Jehol province, whose southern border was less than fifty miles from Peking.

The valiant Chinese defense against much better outfitted and trained Japanese soldiers gave Snow some hope for the future. Since coming to China in 1928, he had searched fruitlessly for evidence that the Chinese people would take matters into their own hands. With the fighting in Shanghai he saw "something like patriotism, as the term is understood in the West." Merchants donated material, food, and clothing. Chinese Boy Scouts carried messages. The Chinese commander, General Tsai, carried himself in a way that appealed to Snow. He dressed simply and spoke directly and forcefully. China's problems, Snow believed more than ever, lay with its political leadership, not its people.

Chiang showed little regard for public opinion, as Eugene Chen explained to Snow shortly before the fighting began. Chen had just resigned as the Nationalist foreign minister. Known for his grand oratory with journalists, Chen told Snow how he opposed Chiang's decision to give in to Japanese demands because such a decision would destroy the people's movement and "any government which ordered that did not deserve to survive." According to Chen, Chiang replied: "The people be damned. We will lead them by the ears. They will do as we say."[6]

After the fighting was over, Snow's contacts with anti-Kuomintang critics grew. One of the most important was Mme. Sun Yat-sen. Snow first met her when she agreed to talk with him at the Chocolate Shop on Bubbling Well Road. Mme. Sun was known for her beauty, warmth, and aversion to publicity. As their conversations continued, Snow assembled rare interview material for a profile that appeared first in the New York *Sun* in October 1932. He did a longer piece the next year for the *New York Herald Tribune* Sunday magazine. Soong Ch'ing-ling (her maiden name) made good copy. She was a member of China's most powerful family. One of her sisters married Chiang Kai-shek; another married H. H. Kung, a perennial Nationalist minister. Finance Minister T. V. Soong was her brother. Mme. Sun had ignored family wishes when she married Dr. Sun, thirty years her senior. She showed as much independence after his death in criticizing Chiang's stewardship of the Kuomintang (KMT).

"Under the Kuomintang taxes have passed into the category of plunder," she told Snow. "Schools have decreased, illiteracy has actually increased, education has lapsed to a low not touched since the days of the Empire. Famine has spread over wide areas and national reconstruction has scarcely been commenced. . . .

"If Dr. Sun were alive today he would disown this Kuomintang and see it dissolved rather than have its name applied to the administration of feudal militarists. . . . After six years there is not even a simple bill of rights for the people. There is not yet any kind of constitution." Although Mme. Sun was not a Communist, she told Snow that the Chinese Communist Party was the only truly revolutionary force in China.[7]

Speaking in terms that Snow appreciated, Mme. Sun quickly won a devoted admirer. "I have never met anyone who inspires such instant trust and affection as Madame Sun," concluded Snow.

Snow became a frequent guest at Dr. Sun's old home on the Rue Molière in the French Concession, where a stream of foreign and Chinese activists congregated around China's Mrs. George Washington, as Snow called Mme. Sun. Among those who passed through Mme. Sun's doors were American journalists Agnes Smedley and Randall Gould, Chinese writers Lu Hsun and Lin Yutang, and Dr. Yang Ch'uan, who founded the Academia Sinica and served as secretary of Mme. Sun's China League for Civil Rights, patterned after the American Civil Liberties Union. An outspoken critic of the Kuomintang, Yang was impressed with Communist organizing in the countryside, something that increasingly interested Snow. It was widely believed that Yang's assassination in the French Concession in 1933 was the work of Chiang's henchmen. Snow considered the murder one more piece of evidence of Kuomintang tyranny.[8]

From a personal point of view, Snow had reason to consider himself fortunate. He was on hand to cover the Japanese aggression in the north and in Shanghai, both major international news events. In the process he proved himself an able war correspondent. In February 1932 the London *Daily Herald* recruited him as a stringer.[9] He was developing a wide range of Chinese contacts, which gave him an edge over other reporters.

Putting aside thoughts of his *South of the Clouds* travelogue, he started a book on the events he had witnessed since his return. Like his involvement with China, the process quickly consumed Snow's energies.

Howard found him an agent, Henriette Herz. In May, when Snow had roughed out only several chapters, Herz said she needed a completed manuscript by the first of August. Although he protested that he could not possibly finish a good book before the end of the year, he received a leave of absence from Consolidated Press and plunged ahead. While he wrote, Shanghai temperatures hovered around 100 degrees. The air was so humid that a saucer of water sat three days in the sun before evaporating. Adding to Snow's misery, the management decided to modernize his apartment building, creating an ear-splitting din for a month. Snow finished the first draft on July 19, his twenty-seventh birthday.

The book aimed to present—as Snow originally proposed to Herz—"stories of action, dramatizing the human element in the conflict." It also marked Snow's intellectual path.[10]

No longer under the spell of Powell's hopeful vision of the Nationalists, Snow was utterly disillusioned with Chiang and the party. Under the Generalissimo, "the unification of China was still chimerical." What organization Snow saw stemmed from Chiang's construction of "private fascist 'cells' within the Kuomintang." The prospect of far-reaching social, political, and economic reforms, "seemed more remote, under Kuomintang leadership, than in 1928."

If Snow saw the period as a "phase of militarism in China's evolution toward modern statehood," he was unclear what would or should come next. He believed that some Nationalist officials were sincerely interested in transferring control of the government from the military to the people. Some reforms had come. Improvements in railways and roads were one bright spot, and Snow continued to write travel literature for the government. The Communists were a giant question mark. Mme. Sun described her husband's political career as "a steady progression to the Left." Snow did not disguise his enthusiasm for what the Communists might be. He attributed much of the early success of the Kuomintang to its alliance with the Communists. He pictured the Communist activities in central China as "one of the most remarkable mass movements in history," with peasants, often armed with only pitchforks, forming ranks behind the Reds who were under steady Kuomintang army attack. But real information about the Communists was sketchy, and Snow was not at all sure that the movement could coalesce an entire nation: "So far its performances indicated that its triumph probably would mean the triumph of ochlocracy."

"It is depressing," he wrote to his sister, Mildred, in a dark moment, "no longer to be sure of anything."

As uncertain as Snow was about Chinese domestic solutions, he had developed a fixed view of China's external difficulties and of the activist role that the United States should play in helping China toward nationhood.[11]

Influenced by Oswald Spengler's book on the decline of Western prestige as well as by his own firsthand observations, Snow perceptively foresaw that Japan's rise marked the end of occidental mastery of Asia. The East was learning that the West was not invincible. That did not bother Snow. The rise of Japanese imperialism, stifling the rise of Asian nationalism and democracy, did. At the same time Snow thought that Secretary of State Henry Stimson's nonrecognition policy of the puppet state in Manchuria, which kept the United States half-heartedly in Asia without providing any deterrence, would not stop Japanese aggression. "The United States," he observed, "seems to be drifting toward war with Japan."

Snow projected a view of American idealism on this troubling scene that broke sharply with Millard's turn-of-the-century optimism about commerce serving as a spearhead for American ideals in China. Colonial activity in China, as well as Southeast Asia and India, convinced Snow that the rush for profits by the United States and other Western powers only brought bondage to vast numbers of workers and farmers, deprived Asians of their nationhood, and blinded them to the positive force of American democratic principles. "Can Easterners ever take these ideals seriously when the very basis of our civilization seems to belie them?"

Snow's solution for avoiding war and emancipating China was for America to redeem itself with an act of unrestrained idealism. The United States should supplement Stimson's nonrecognition policy with "evidences of good faith . . . to strengthen the Japanese moderates" and to provide moral leadership in Asia. Specifically, the United States should liquidate its "imperialist adventure in the Philippines (always a losing investment)"; that policy "should be used as a lever to get other powers to make similar undertakings in the Orient."

Snow acknowledged that his idealistic plan "for establishing harmonious relationships between the earth's families of men . . . will be rejected as 'visionary.' " In fact, few Americans paid any attention to *Far Eastern Front,* which did not appear until October 1933, after he made extensive revisions. The Century Company, which indicated an interest in the manuscript before Snow began writing in earnest, ultimately declined. Herz approached sixteen more publishers before Harrison Smith of Smith & Haas accepted the book, which Snow dedicated "To C. H. T. [Charles Hanson Towne] friend of youth." Americans bought only 675 copies, not enough to earn Snow any money beyond his $250 advance. French, English, and Chinese editions were later published. But in mid–1935 Snow calculated he still had not made more than $1,000.[12]

The book's melodramatic prose drew snickers from Snow's fellow correspondents.[13] Bullets "spat death," Chiang "sanguinarily crushed the labor movement," "Japanese bayonets daily thrust deeper and deeper into the heart of Manchuria," "bullets spat venomously," and Japanese shells "arrived with messages of death and hate." Japanese-held Darien was the "hilt of [Japan's] lance thrust into the continent." And it was "the heraldic talisman of the latest race to attempt to erect a base of power for expansion in Manchuria." Of Snow's style, the reviewer for the *Saturday Review of Literature* observed that *Far Eastern Front* "reads like an alarm-clock rendering of *Time.*"

Despite the overwriting, *Far Eastern Front* showed signs of Snow's later genius as a popular writer. Like other contemporary journalists, particularly Vincent Sheean whose *Personal History* became a best seller in 1934, Snow put himself in the book, giving the reader the feeling of being on the scene rather than witnessing it from afar. If Snow rejoiced too much in his own in-the-thick-of-it reporting, he engaged reviewers with his passion. They responded with mostly generous comments: "It is easy to see that the author . . . has thrown his sympathies with China—as did most of the world," said a typical reviewer. "However, the book is interesting from beginning to end."

Although Snow's vision of American foreign policy ran counter to the expansionist ideas that shaped United States policy in an earlier era, it did not sound alarms with most of his countrymen. In the 1930s the average American had come to many of the same general conclusions as Snow had, if for different reasons. The Depression brought a crisis of confidence to the country. Not only had the glitter of foreign markets in China proved illusive, but the American economic system itself also seemed flawed. While Snow's doubts about capitalism mounted as he observed colonial conditions, Americans watched their overheated economy rapidly turn to ashes. Not only domestic liberals agreed on the need for some kind of collective economic planning. The U. S. Chamber of Commerce acknowledged in a 1931 report that Americans "are living in a period in which national economy must be reorganized as the controlling factor," though of course they saw big business as having responsibility for engineering the change.[14] That same year *Baltimore Sun* editorial writer Gerald Johnson noted that "substantial Americans—and by that is meant the great mass of families whose incomes range between $2,500 and $25,000 a year—are not cherishing any serious doubts about capitalism, [but] they have developed a new and decidedly critical attitude toward certain details of the capitalist system as it has been developed in this country."

Consumed by their own troubles, Americans had no objection to relinquishing the Philippines. Congress was considering long-standing Filipino pleas for independence. The central question was not whether to pull out of the islands, but how quickly. "I want Asia for the Asiatics and America for the Americans," summed up Senator Huey Long in the final days of debate, reflecting the views of constituents who wished to stanch the flow of duty free Philippine sugar, copra, and oil into depressed U. S. markets. The real motive behind the drive to free the Filipinos, noted one reporter, was not "so much the desire of the Philippines to be independent of the United States as it is the desire of the United States to become independent of the Philippines."

Likewise, as most reviews of *Far Eastern Front* expressly stated, Snow's broad sympathy for the Chinese did not trouble Americans. They shared it. After several years of scant newspaper coverage of China, Japanese aggression put the Chinese on the front page. Hearst and other publishers urged their reporters to get graphic stories of the fighting. News of the victimized Chinese brought on a "rush of sentimentality over China's plight," as one reporter put it. Of course, stepping in to help the Chinese was another matter altogether, but Snow's proposal could easily be seen, as he acknowledged, as a mere extension of the Stimson Doctrine to do nothing. And the Stimson Doctrine was one of the most popular foreign policy initiatives of the Hoover administration.

These similarities masked the reality that Snow and Americans had parted company. Americans acquired skepticism of unallayed capitalism in breadlines. Snow acquired it the way many Chinese revolutionaries did, in treaty ports run by Westerners. His skepticism would be permanent. Moreover, United States withdrawal from the Far East was for him an act of involvement. For most Americans it was simply a way of distancing themselves from Asian problems.

An editorial in the *Kansas City Star* forthrightly described the prevalent American attitude: "Evidently Japan is taking advantage of the preoccupation of the Western powers with their own affairs to get a strangle hold on China. . . . The only thing the rest of the world can do is to make a record of protest—and trust that Japan may be able to enforce a measure of order on the Chinese chaos."[15]

Such inaction only proved to Snow the limitations of capitalism. Western nations found it easier to support Japanese imperialism than to follow through on pledges to protect Chinese sovereignty. "I think reactionary tactics will be dominant in the foreign policies of all nations of the imperialist class (which includes the United States, of course) for at least a decade to come," Snow wrote to his father in words that showed his increasing familiarity with Marxism. But a process of change was underway, Snow added, in America as well as Asia. "We are entering a period of consolidation of the forces of capitalism and imperialism against our rapidly increasing masses who are the victims of the system." The result might not be exactly the same everywhere but capitalism wouldn't survive.

Snow's palliatives were naive, though they were no less realistic than Stimson's. But Snow's observations also had practical applications missed by Americans preoccupied with their own troubles. Snow was one of a handful of American writers who recognized that the world was headed toward war with Japan. Five years later journalist John Gunther would remark with some understatement that *Far Eastern Front* was "not so widely known as it should be."[16]

By the time *Far Eastern Front* appeared, Snow's life had changed in two ways. He was married, and he was living in Peking.

Helen Foster arrived in Shanghai aboard the *U.S.S. Lincoln* about the time Snow returned from India in 1931. Even in that exotic port city, Peg, as she was called, stood out. Lithe, blue-eyed, and twenty-three, she was strikingly attractive. Tremendous energy lay behind an inquiring mind and a bruising personality. "I was brought up exactly right," she reminisced later in life. "There was nothing wrong with it because it worked. I loved school. I loved every class. I took for granted that I should study; and I was the teacher's pet and the most popular girl in the school. This is a combination that isn't easy to find."[17]

When she arrived, Snow was leading a comfortable bachelor life.[18] He had a two room flat on Bubbling Well Road. Shanghai's social whirl was always lively. He had his precious freedom. And yet he was not altogether happy. "I grow heartsick at times and weary with a malaise that troubles me vastly and the cause of which I do not quite understand," he told his sister. Although he attributed part of this to China's struggles, part lay in loneliness, which contrasted with his siblings' lives. Mildred was married. News that his brother had decided to marry, too, depressed him "for a great many days," he admitted—though he soon was sending warm, welcome-to-the-family letters to the bride.

Strong female personalities attracted Snow, and Peg's worked like a magnet. Peg offered the prospect of affectionate intimacy that was missing from his life. Her steady outflow of ideas about current affairs, political theory, and changing the world resonated with his increasingly active involvement with China.

Their first meeting was on the day Peg arrived. Through her father, a Utah attorney, she had lined up a job as a clerk at the American consulate, but her real ambition was to become a writer. She had read Snow's dispatches before coming to China and set out to interview him immediately after landing. Westerners, still smarting from his *American Mercury* article, warned her away from Snow. In their first meeting, Peg made a point of saying that she was not eager to give up her freedom for marriage. But when Snow had an attack of sinusitis within several weeks of their meeting, he wrote home that she was the one bright spot in the illness. By the summer of 1932, Snow was relating excursions they took together outside the city. When Peg wanted a writer's name, he thought of "Nym Wales," a combination of the Greek for "name" and her Welsh ancestry, which stuck. In December, when most of the work on *Far Eastern Front* seemed out of the way, Snow took Peg for a walk along the cold Shanghai waterfront and proposed they get married right away. They could move to Peking and be free together pursuing their writing interests.[19]

The marriage took place quickly and with little fanfare. At Peg's insistence Snow bought Harris tweeds to replace an ill-fitting lavender pinstriped suit he had bought in India. They told only a few friends, including Mme. Sun, who gave them an electric percolator and a Cantonese dinner party. Peg insisted that the ceremony take place at noon, Christmas day, in Tokyo. With less than a week's notice, John Allison, Snow's old Shanghai roommate and now with the Foreign Service in Japan, made the arrangements—dealing with the complicated Japanese registration procedures and finding someone to officiate despite the holiday. Even Peg could not keep her husband-to-be from missing the train from Kobe to Tokyo. They arrived at the embassy with two minutes to spare.

The honeymoon took the couple to Formosa, Bali, Singapore, and China's coastal ports. In February they arrived in Peking and settled into a small house in the center of the city. "I do not know exactly when or how it happened, or in what gown she first smote my orbs, but it was another occasion in life when destiny rode high and splendid over many petty obstacles," Snow told Towne. "It is done, and we are marvelously happy."

Peking presented an ideal setting for Snow's energies, though the place seemed to be more for idle contemplation than anything else.[20] At the time there was a joke, passed around and around at Peking cocktail parties, of a former Western member of the community who moved to Shanghai, thereby raising the standards of both cities. Behind this comparison lay the reality that Shanghai was hell-bent on the pursuit of profits while Peking, with its antique shops and serene old imperial grounds, reached for sublime enrichments.

The one thousand or so Westerners scattered around Peking were mostly in the unprofitable professions of education, art, diplomacy, and journalism. At the endless round of parties, where guests nibbled on dried lotus root hors d'oeuvres, one could hear German-born Karl August Wittfogel spin out his Marxist theories, chat with Swedish explorer Sven Hedin, who in 1933 was mapping out an expedition on the Silk Road, meet budding China scholar John Fairbank and Owen Lattimore of the Institute of Pacific Relations, discuss literature with J. P. Marquand who was writing his Mr. Moto books, or converse with John Service, one of the many young Foreign Service officers who came to Peking for Chinese language training. U.S. diplomat O. Edmund Clubb put on regular Saturday luncheon discussions, which Snow attended. L. C. Arlington, perhaps the most venerable local sinologue, frequently came by to talk with Snow on Sunday afternoons. Teilhard de Chardin, a tall, spare, French Jesuit paleontologist who earned the enmity of the Church for daring to apply evolutionary concepts to Catholic theology, visited to discuss philosophy and fascism. For relaxation, the Snows rode horseback, swam at the American legation where a Shanghai friend, Marine Corps officer Evans Carlson, now served, or picnicked at a temple rented by a friend in the tawny Western Hills outside the city.

The Snows lived in three different homes during their nearly five years in Peking, two in the city and one outside near Yenching University, overlooking the summer palace. Rent and food could run only thirty-five dollars a month. Servants, good cooks, gardeners, and a private rickshaw coolie cost little more.

Snow continued to lay plans to go home in a month or two. Although he complained that his work was too demanding, the relatively slow pace of newsgathering combined with the ease of living gave Snow plenty of freedom to write longer articles on subjects that interested him. The real threat to that liberty came when the Depression forced cutbacks by Consolidated Press. In April 1933 the news service reduced his salary; at the end of the year it had to terminate the relationship with him altogether. Over the next months Snow wrote letters from time to time to see if the *New York Herald Tribune*, the *Chicago Daily News*, or another American newspaper could use him as a correspondent. Although nothing came of those inquiries, somehow good fortune seemed always to intervene both to keep food on the table and preserve his independence.

The most notable episode of good luck involved the Associated Press, which offered Snow its Peking bureau. Snow did not want the job because it would tie him down, but he needed the money. Deciding to leave the decision to fate, he bet part of his savings in two races at the Paomachang track. Miraculously, he won nearly $1,000 and turned down the job. He had another boost when the conservative *Saturday Evening Post* bought an article adapted from *Far Eastern Front*, for which they paid $750. The magazine also suggested that he contribute other articles. Snow figured he could live off his new wealth plus income from a weekly column for the New York *Sun* and occasional dispatches for the London *Daily Herald*.[21]

China gave Snow not only a journalist's education in the real world of politics and economics but also the time to indulge his peripatetic reading habits. In Peking he wandered widely among thinkers like Emerson and Freud. He subscribed to the British New Left Book Club, and he was particularly fond of George Bernard Shaw. He and Peg had read Shaw's *The Intelligent Woman's Guide to Capitalism and Socialism* to each other and during their honeymoon went out to see the author when his ship docked in Hongkong harbor. Snow was amused when Shaw told a Hongkong University audience that "If you are a Red today at 20, you may be a man fit to live in the world by the time you are 40." The remark made the British furious.[22] The other side of Snow's growing interest in Leftist thinkers was fear and revulsion, common in the 1930s, with fascism. Fascism had immediate importance for Snow and others in Peking, who feared that Chiang might actually join the Axis powers rather than resist Japan. Chiang seemed adept at using Fascist police tactics against his own people. When John Leighton Stuart, head of Yenching University, asked Snow in late 1934 to deliver a talk to the faculty on fascism, he undertook serious study of the subject.[23]

Snow's talk drew on writers ranging from Adolf Hitler to the British Marxist John Strachey, who equated capitalism with fascism—a point of view Snow found appealing. Fascism, as Snow defined it, included key elements of capitalism, and it stood for everything he did not: imperialism, racism, intolerance of individual freedom, "state-controlled capitalism, or perhaps more properly expressed as capitalism-controlled state." Theoretical communism, in contrast, intrigued Snow. Its ultimate objective had a ring of democracy about it. Communists conceived "of proletarian dictatorship as being part of a dynamic process, a necessary evil preliminary to the establishment of a classless society, and hence transitory, while the Fascists, with the theory of Absolute State, believe they have achieved the ultimate political form."

Snow's talk was dull. Although friends like flashy *Chicago Tribune* correspondent Floyd Gibbons gave him pointers on how to put ideas over to a live audience, Snow was an incurably slow talker and ill at ease on a rostrum. The fascism speech was all the worse because his heavily theoretical talk was written in a dry academic style drawing almost exclusively from European examples, of which he had no first-hand experience. Snow's strength lay in writing about what he saw and heard for himself.

Snow's interest in contemporary Chinese literature was one area where he effectively combined intellectual pursuits with active concern about Chinese affairs. A growing body of native writing broke sharply with the past. Rather than the traditional art-for-art's-sake approach written in a classical style only the elite understood, these authors wrote in vernacular and sharply criticized political and social conditions. Snow compared one of the most important writers, Lu Hsun, to Russia's Gorki and Mark Twain for attacking such "evils in Chinese society as squeeze, bribery, usury, child slavery, selfishness, superstition, 'confucianism,' militaristic exploitation of workers and peasants, muzzling of the press, destruction of the people's organizations, nonresistance to Japan and other phenomena observed in modern China."[24]

"Chinese fiction and philosophy," Snow believed, "are more valuable than all the thousands of pages poured through the lens of twisted foreign perspective."

Few Chinese works had been translated into English. Snow began to think about undertaking a book of short story translations about the time he was married. Encouraged in a Shanghai meeting with Lu Hsun, Lin Yutang, and other writers on the way back from his honeymoon, he undertook the job in Peking.

Snow had learned only a smattering of Chinese during his first years in the country. To prepare for the translation task he began to study seriously under a long-gowned Chinese instructor from the Foreign Service officers' language school. Snow soon could write a few hundred characters and carry on a conversation, though with a Missouri accent, as his friends laughingly noted. He did the short story translations with bilingual Chinese assistants, initially a Shanghai writer and later students, who wrote out the story in English as best they could. Snow discussed each sentence, searching for the best literate rendering of the Chinese. "I assure anyone interested," Snow commented, "that I would much prefer to write three books of my own rather than have to repeat the operations that have gone into the making of this one."

Snow's collection offered the English-speaking world a unique opportunity to read Chinese writers, but the manuscript experienced rejection after rejection until British publisher George G. Harrap & Co. agreed to bring it out in 1936. The next year Dick Walsh, editor of *Asia* magazine, published *Living China* in America through his house, John Day. The book earned excellent reviews, enhanced Snow's reputation with the small group of Americans interested in China, and made little money.[25]

Dedicated to Sun Yat-sen's wife, Soong Ch'ing-ling, "whose incorruptible integrity, courage, loyalty, and beauty of spirit are burning symbols of the best in living China," *Living China* also marked Snow as a Nationalist antagonist. The Chinese authors whose work he translated were enemies of the regime. The Nationalists banned books by many of them. The Blue Shirts jailed writers Ting Ling and Sun Hsichen, and in 1932 the Kuomintang executed six Left-wing authors, including Jou Shih, whose story of the tribulations of a slave mother Snow had translated. Nationalist repression only pushed the writers further to the Left. When U.S. Ambassador Nelson Trusler Johnson, remarkable for his ability to speak Chinese, praised *Living China*, Snow replied that he had learned much in his translation efforts, "probably too much, along certain lines, for the powers that be to look upon me benignly again. You cannot enter into a thing like this very deeply without coming to share some of the feeling that produces it—and to begin to have feelings about the country and its people may prove a good road to ruin for a 'foreign correspondent.' "[26]

Snow had good reason to worry. When he was on the *China Weekly Review*, a White Russian told the chief of the political department of the Shanghai International settlement, Pat Givens, that Snow's real name was something like "Lavinsky," and that he was an agent of the Third International and traveling under a false passport. A copy of the dossier that Givens prepared fell into the hands of Marine Corps officer and friend Evans Carlson, who passed it on to Snow. Before being literally kicked out of the *Review* offices by Powell, the Russian said he had fabricated the story as a joke on the strongly anti-Communist Givens.[27]

The bogus report followed Snow to India in 1931. At least that was the best explanation why a Hindu secret service agent made a point of sitting with Snow on a train ride between Delhi and Calcutta and asking questions. Afterward the Indian professed to believe that Snow was not, as originally suspected, a narcotics smuggler and Comintern agent who entered the country illegally. Nevertheless, the charge surfaced again in Bombay. According to a young British army officer who befriended Snow, the local chief of police contemplated deporting Snow, or worse. Snow immediately rushed off to see the American consul, who promised to rectify matters.

Snow's files in Shanghai continued to grow when he returned to China. Authorities noted with careless insinuation that marked the Red Scare period in the 1950s in the United States that he was friendly with the radical American journalist Agnes Smedley and that he received literature from suspected Communist agents. Rumors about his sympathies circulated again in Peking during 1933. This time Snow went to Ambassador Johnson, whom he viewed as a kind of protector. Snow told the ambassador that he was friendly with "Mme. Sun and one or two others of the younger Chinese group in Shanghai who have been prominently engaged in the propagation of liberal ideas" and that with several other newspapermen he had joined her civil liberties organization. But, Snow insisted, he was not a subversive radical and asked Johnson what he should do.[28]

In almost thirty years of service in the Far East, Johnson had developed complex codes of behavior. The United States, he thought, should help China, among other things by relinquishing extraterritorial rights. Americans should not, however, sacrifice their own freedom of action—a principle he attributed to the Oklahoma frontier where he spent four boyhood years—by becoming actively engaged in domestic Chinese causes. Snow was crossing the line. Not particularly sympathetic, Johnson gave advice that drew from another philosophical view, summed up by the Taoist motto on a scroll in his office: "Through not doing, all things are done." Johnson suggested that Snow simply ignore the personal attacks. "A dossier such as Mr. Gibens [*sic*] apparently had built up regarding him," Johnson noted in a memorandum of conversation, "was as hard to change as the morgue of a newspaper." Snow should leave "his actions and his writing to prove the falsity or truth of it."[29]

That presented Snow with a problem. He realized that being labeled as a Communist could destroy his credibility with mass American publications, like the *Saturday Evening Post,* for which he had begun to contribute regularly. He cared passionately about appearing in those establishment organs. Twisting absentmindedly at his curly hair and smoking Camel cigarettes, he would work for hours writing and rewriting, trying to make his articles about China intelligible and interesting to American audiences easily confused by the mass of Chinese names.[30] Yet the whole point of reporting was to do just that, report. His concerns about his reputation notwithstanding, Snow was not willing to curb himself in reporting Nationalist transgressions. The certain result was that the stories he produced were positive proof to many of his subversive character.

Two articles in *Current History* demonstrated Snow's prevailing attitude. In the first, a profile of Chiang published shortly after his conversation with Johnson, Snow said the Nationalist leader was "not a great statesman, nor really a great general, and in some ways he is a mediocrity. . . . His traditional conservatism, strengthened by his acquisition of wealth and power, seems to have narrowed his social and political outlook." The second piece examined the troubling pattern of Nationalist censorship. The Nationalists went to often absurd lengths to constrain Chinese publications. On one occasion a censor squelched a Chinese government explanation of Sino-Japanese fighting in the north. Foreign correspondents were not immune. When Chinese censors got their hands on copy, they often mangled it without bothering to tell correspondents of the changes they made. When the Nationalists took exception to *New York Times* correspondent Hallett Abend's reporting in the early 1930s, they forbade government officials from meeting with him and refused to let him use government-operated telegraphs to file stories. Although Abend could use foreign-controlled communications facilities in the treaty ports, filing from inland cities like Peking was a problem. Personally troubled by censorship and concerned about attacks against Leftist writers he supported, Snow's article laid out a long list of abuses: book burning, paying spies to lurk around schools, banning old tales that might have "symbolic meaning," and condoning the activities of the Blue Shirts, "a secret fascist organization created to combat communism and to promote Chiang Kai-shek's policies."[31]

When Howard, who had just gone to work for the conservative National Association of Manufacturers, wrote about rumors floating around at home that his brother was becoming "leftist" or "Communistic," Snow's hot reply showed both concern for his reputation and his unwillingness to back down.

> Don't tell me these things anonymously. You must know very well that it will do me no good in my work to have such stuff circulating. There is hardly an editor in America who would print a thing by me if it were thought I was a Communist. And for your satisfaction, I am not. I belong to no political organization; I don't attempt to interpret facts as I find them from any ready-made economic or political doctrine whatever, whether Marxist or Leninist or Mussolinian or Rooseveltian. The worst handicaps I have are that I have a lingering belief in such things as the rights of men to equal opportunity, a belief in the fundamental soundness of such concepts as freedom of speech, freedom of press, freedom of assembly, and a somehow undying faith in the notion that the highest degree of individual freedom (in the largest social sense) is not necessarily incompatible with democratic political forms. I will get over this when I see Huey Long seriously on the way to the White House. Meanwhile I believe it will be possible (though I'm by no means convinced that it is probable) that we Americans will be able to maintain a certain consistency with the original ideals of the founders of the great republic, and they were very advanced men in their time, and work out a decent civilized system of life and economics which will fairly soon put the control of the means of production in the hands of the people, and for the widest social benefit. If this is treason, tell the Liberty League, or whatever it is called, to prepare the noose.[32]

In personal conversations, Snow came across as sincere and pleasant, rarely argumentative. He was slow to talk about himself. He didn't pry into others' affairs. These traits, plus his disregard for time, led Peg to describe him as somewhat sinicized. But rather than keep Snow out of trouble, his personality helped him come in closer contact with dissident Chinese, including the politically active students he met while teaching part-time at Yenching University.[33]

Yenching, five miles outside Peking's walls, was the largest Christian-run university in the country. Because of high tuition and the loss of face for students who could not afford costly socializing, it attracted the sons and daughters of wealthy Chinese. Inside its walls a student could live a dreamy existence, studying beside the lake or playing tennis. Nevertheless, widely popular professor Randolph Sailor calculated that at least one-third of the students were highly politicized. Although Peg complained that many of her husband's students lacked social consciousness, the journalism school particularly attracted politically concerned students because its relatively easy courses left time for extra-curricular activity.

Snow taught the first course on feature writing at the journalism school, which had both Chinese and American professors educated at Missouri and benefited from substantial University of Missouri financial support. In his first class, Snow impressed his students by telling them he "came to China not to teach, but to study, and that in his view, there was much to learn from China." Students soon congregated at his house to help with translation work, borrow suitcases full of books on the Kuomintang's list of forbidden reading, and talk about politics.

The issue that consumed politically active students, as well as Snow, was Japanese aggression and the Generalissimo's willingness to give ground rather than stand and fight. After 1932, Japan made massive investments in Manchukuo. On trips into the region Snow found the Japanese "as prosperous as any army of weevils in a flour mill." Under the Japanese Army dictatorship, as Snow described the government, the Chinese faded more and more into the background. Following a trip in 1935, Snow speculated in a *Saturday Evening Post* article that it was "not only conceivable but probable that Manchuria may be made to finance the polishing off of the conquest of China." That year the Japanese forced the Nationalists to declare the area just south of the Great Wall a neutral zone. Their next move was to demand that the zone become an autonomous region with Peking the capital.[34]

Late in 1935 Chang Chao-lin, a journalism student from Manchuria and a Yenching student leader, visited Snow to ask about rumors that Sung Che-yuan, the Chinese general responsible for the northern region, was on the verge of capitulating. Snow said a source had just confirmed the reports. Chang went over to the large living room window and stared out on to the patio to hide his tears. Snow was touched. When Chang revealed that he and other students hoped to put pressure on Chiang to resist, Snow and his wife encouraged the students and agreed to help.[35]

Although the students did not tell them everything of their activities, they shrewdly viewed the Snows as valuable, willing allies. The Snows' home was one of several Western residences where they could meet and talk safely. As a Western reporter, Snow could also publicize student demands through his dispatches, and he provided a good vehicle for private communications inside the country. When the students wanted to solicit Soong Ch'ing-ling's views on the proper course of action, the Snows typed their letter in English and forwarded it. Later the students gathered in the Snows' home to read her answer: Don't worry about Nationalist injunctions against political activity, she counseled, "you should show your mettle and swing into action!"

The Japanese had given China until December 10 to establish the new autonomous region. If the students could pressure Chinese leaders into refusing to capitulate, Snow and his wife thought, the Japanese might back down. "I stressed . . . the immediate necessity for a positive demonstration of student opinion," Snow told a friend of his advice to the students. "Events of the last ten days have moved so rapidly that any kind of action, if [it] is to have any effect on mass opinion, must be taken without further delay. I suggested a mass demonstration, to be organized not later than the 10th." Seeing that something dramatic was needed, the students came to the same decision. On December 8, Wang Ju-mei, Yenching's delegate to the Peking student union and one of the young people who met regularly in the Snows' living room, informed Yenching colleagues that plans were made. The students would take to the streets the next morning bearing a nine-point manifesto calling on the Nationalists to use all their resources to fight Japanese imperialism and to restore civil liberties so that patriotic Chinese could speak out.

That night the Snows helped translate student broadsides into English. The next morning they were on hand when, at 7 A.M., eight hundred students from Yenching and Tsinghua Universities marched through the freezing cold toward the city, shouting slogans and carrying long banners. As these students streamed through the streets, others climbed over school walls to join their ranks; shopkeepers and coolies applauded and rushed out to snatch copies of the leaflets. At one juncture Snow saw a column of marchers meet a Nationalist army officer. The officer dismounted his bicycle and cried as he embraced the students who gathered around him, themselves weeping. Elsewhere Chinese police, reinforced by Japanese gendarmes, beat the demonstrators with leather belts and tore their standards to shreds. The students, Snow noted, unflinchingly pressed on and at eleven o'clock presented their demands to General Ho Ying-chin, Chiang's representative in Peking. Afterward they started to look for other columns of demonstrators locked out of the city. When the students, now numbering two thousand, approached the legation quarter, the fire department turned hoses on them, an effective tactic in the cold weather. Before their retreat, the students managed to turn the water on police and cut the hose.

"Demonstration viewed gravely here," Snow wrote in cablese to the London *Daily Herald*, "likely to be cause japoprotestupset expected northern settlement stop sinohistory often altered parstudent movement . . . stop student program definitely revolutionary."

Buoyed by their success, the students went out on strike the next day and staged a second demonstration, this time almost eight thousand strong, on December 16. Attempting to control the protest, officials told one column of marchers to enter the city at Hsunchihmen gate. When the students arrived they found it drum tight. Foreign correspondents watched to see what would happen next. Recalled UP correspondent Mac Fisher, a friend of Snow:

> There were special police armed with Mausers, wearing black leather coats and helmets. And there were ordinary garrison troops with fixed bayonets, and the fire department with hoses all laid out. It was a standoff. All of a sudden from the head of the column of students a small girl dashed out and ran right up at the bayonets and the Mausers of the police. We had seen the police beat students like anything and everyone gasped. She ducked under the police and flopped down on the flagstone street and rolled under the gate.[36]

The police stopped the girl before she could open the gate and began to beat her. Snow and Victor Keen, the *New York Herald Tribune* correspondent, rushed over hoping their presence would shame the police into stopping. Her act was one of many that gave a heroic quality to the demonstrations and provoked a nationwide outpouring against appeasement of the Japanese. By the end of the year, sixty-five demonstrations occurred in thirty-two cities, including the capital, Nanking. "The Peiping students have lit a flame that is sweeping the country,"Agnes Smedley wrote to Peg from Shanghai.[37]

Foreign correspondents filed stories on the demonstrations and personally sided with the students. Powell, in town to give a speech on journalism at Yenching, covered the December 16 march and agreed it was a "patriotic demonstration against alien aggression." He blamed the Japanese, not the Nationalists, for the harsh repression. American newspaper editor William Allen White of Emporia, Kansas, also in Peking, spoke approvingly of the student demands over dinner at the Snows'.

Snow followed the demonstrations closely, recording the historic event with his movie camera. Afterward students continued to meet at his home. He and his wife helped many of them. They sheltered the heroic girl who stormed the gate, Lu Ts'ui, a student at Tsinghua University, and spirited her out of the city to Shanghai. Police arrested and beat Wang Ju-mei in early 1936. After his release Wang hid at the Snows', sleeping on the old day bed in their living room. The

Nanking government revoked Snow's press privileges for several months, although he was able to make a special arrangement with the local telegraph office to cable his dispatches.

The December 9th Movement, as it came to be called, achieved its immediate objective. When the protests first erupted, old General Sung told Doihara he would not resist public opinion. In the next weeks he continuously avoided Japanese importunings. As Snow had suspected, the Japanese were not prepared to use force and recalled Doihara. Most observers realized, however, that it was only a matter of time before the Japanese renewed their efforts. "We are seeing the last half of the second act," William Allen White commented to Snow, "and the play's a tragedy."[38]

The movement also proved an important turning point in another drama.

The Communist Party later portrayed itself as having inspired the December 9th Movement. The claim was inflated. As explained by Wang Ju-mei, who became a senior Communist official in the People's Republic of China after 1949, he and other students who planned the demonstration were not Communists at the time. They did have limited Communist contacts, though, and heard reports that the Red leadership, isolated in the countryside, supported all-out opposition to Japan. In the early part of 1936 Wang and others who were determined to maintain their resistance joined the party. Just as Nationalist intransigence and repression drove many Chinese writers into opposition, the events in December mobilized student activists against the regime.

In the coming months Snow, who had played a supporting role with both writers and students, doubled his efforts to see for himself the political force that attracted these patriotic Chinese.[39]

Red Star over China

3

The best way to define a man's authentic character, William James observed, is "to seek out the particular mental or moral attitude in which, when it came upon him, he felt himself most deeply and intensely active and alive. At such moments there is a voice inside which speaks and says, 'This is the real me!' "[1] For Edgar Snow that exhilaration could only occur when he encountered men and women acting out a drama that brought his Missourian sensitivities about popular action and democracy into full play. Snow had looked for such a moment in China for years. It finally came in 1936 when he discovered the Chinese Communists.

Snow began to think seriously about a journey to Red territory about the time he completed *Far Eastern Front.* "It seems that the only books on China that can succeed here are novels," publisher Harrison Smith wrote to Snow in 1933 about the book's dismal sales, "but I do believe that soon some writer, and I don't see why it shouldn't be you, will write a book that is not fiction, but of such compelling interest that this strange taboo will be broken!"[2] Shortly after, Smith & Haas publishers gave Snow a $750 advance for a book, due at the end of 1934, on "Red China or another topic."

Allowing for "another topic" was prudent. Reaching the Chinese Communists was as problematic as writing a popular book on China. The Communists had suffered setback after setback in the bloody wake of Chiang's Shanghai purge in 1927. On orders from Moscow, they tried desperately to maintain an alliance with the Left-wing Kuomintang government in Hankow. "For a few months in 1927," wrote Vincent Sheean, among the last Western reporters to see Chinese Communist Party (CCP) leaders close up, "Hankow concentrated, symbolized and upheld the hope for a revolution of the world."[3] But with the defection of a key warlord ally, who like so many worked out a deal with Chiang Kai-shek, and with mounting disillusionment on the part of their Kuomintang allies, the Communists were soon under attack in Hankow, too. Marxist orthodoxy, promoted by Stalin's Comintern advisors in China, insisted that true social revolution could germinate only in urban centers. Acting on this premise, the Communists directed their forces toward Changsha, Nanchang, Swatow, and Canton. In each place they suffered stunning defeats. By the end of 1927, CCP membership had dropped from more than fifty thousand to less than twenty-five thousand. Communist forces retreated to enclaves in the countryside, where they remained under Nationalist attack.

More than a dozen soviets in all sprang up, including one in Hupei-Anhwei-Honan under Chang Kuo-t'ao and another, farther north, in Shensi. Teng Hsiao-p'ing's first major party assignment was organizing guerrilla operations in the far southern province of Kwangsi. The largest and most successful soviet began in the rugged Chingkangshan mountains astride the border between Hunan and Kiangsi provinces. Mao Tse-tung arrived there with a tattered unit, only one thousand strong, in October 1927. Within thirteen months Generals Chu Teh and P'eng Teh-huai joined him with their soldiers. Emboldened, the enlarged force came down from the mountains and in 1931 proclaimed the Chinese Soviet Republic.

"News" about the Communists presented a confused, often bizarre picture. While the Communists clung to their alliance with the Left-wing Kuomintang in Hankow, the *North China Daily News* reported "naked body" processions: "Those who are familiar with the modesty of Chinese women, during the past centuries, require no further or more conclusive proof of the pernicious influence of Russian Communism."[4] After the coalition fell apart in July 1927, no Western journalist visited the fragmented Chinese soviets, which no doubt had difficulty communicating among themselves. Reporters had no choice but to rely on secondhand information. A typical 1930 United Press dispatch based on information from missionaries described both Communist brutality and land redistribution schemes, the latter making them "popular with the poorer people, who have nothing to lose." Mao was intermittently reported as deathly ill or outcast by his comrades. Moscow, which supposedly directed the CCP, knew as little as everyone else. In March 1930, *Inprecorr*, the official Comintern organ, ran Mao's obituary, saying he died of tuberculosis.

The Nationalists quickly quelled Red slogan-shouting that erupted from time to time in Shanghai streets. Small groups of party members met under strictly clandestine circumstances, and then with no assurance they were safe. Western police arrested thirty-six at a meeting in the International Settlement in 1931 and turned them over to the Nationalists, who did not report the execution of twenty-three of them. The KMT banned the circulation of opposition publications and used their propaganda machine to grind out a steady flow of news depicting the Communists as "Red bandits" and baby killers, devoid of ideological passion. Among the few Westerners who cared one way or the other, this protrayal often fell on receptive ears. Many found it hard to believe that communism could take root in China. As one observer put it, "The psychology and tradition of the Chinese render them less susceptible to Marxist doctrines than any people in the world." Columbia University China specialist Nathaniel Peffer and *New York Times* correspondent Hallet Abend wrote of "so called" Communists.

Although he portrayed them as successes, Chiang's military campaigns against the Communists raised questions about the validity of his anti-Red propaganda. Four times between 1930 and 1933, the Generalissimo drove his armies into Kiangsi to destroy the Communists. Four times he failed. The Reds held out, even though they suffered half a million casualties, according to KMT reports tabulated by journalist Agnes Smedley. If KMT body counts were accurate, the number of Communist dead equaled the size of the radical Taiping rebel army that stormed Nanking in 1853. If the figures were exaggerated—if this was a small outlaw force—how did it withstand the Nationalist armies? And if the CCP weren't promoting real revolution, why did Chiang proclaim that without exterminating the Red bandits, "we cannot preserve the old morals and ancient wisdom handed down from our ancestors"?

Snow took the Communists seriously and was willing to consider the possibility that they stood for real revolution. "Communism is no longer—if it has ever been—merely the hallucination of alarmists in China," he concluded in the *Current History* article he pieced together before leaving for India in 1930. Back in China, Snow developed extraordinary contacts among those very few people asking hard questions about communism.[5]

Agnes Smedley had the best access to Red sources of any Western reporter. She attended secret Shanghai meetings to hear reports on CCP activity, and at one point a Red Army commander secretly convalesced at her home. Before he was murdered, Mme. Sun's colleague Dr. Yang Ch'uan assembled information on the Communists and their loyal following from documents captured during Chiang's extermination campaigns. Snow read his report. Through Peg, Snow would have known about inquiries into communism made in 1931 by Jay C. Huston, an

American foreign service officer in Shanghai. Consul-General Edwin Cunningham took litle interest in Huston's two reports, written on off-duty hours. Ill and feeling isolated, Huston befriended Peg Snow soon after she went to work at the consulate and showed the reports to her. In 1932, the year Huston died, Edmund Clubb evaluated Communist activity in the countryside. A vice-consul in Hankow, Clubb drew on Snow's *Current History* article. Snow and Clubb became friends in Peking. In late 1934 Snow was also in contact with Norman Hanwell, who in the course of his research in the countryside pieced together information on the Communists. Meanwhile, Snow amassed his own library of clips and other materials on the Communists. Snow tried everything he could to understand the Reds.

Clubb and Huston made the usual quota of mistakes. (Clubb, who chose words with all the care a master chess player gives his moves, reported that Red leader Chou En-lai was dead.) They presciently concluded, however, that Communist successes derived in large part from shortcomings of the Nationalists, whose armies existed "for the sole objective of plundering the people." Snow came to the same conclusion in his *Current History* article. It was uncertain what the Reds would do with power but clear why they acquired followers: "the Kuomintang's inability to keep its promises."[6]

Snow did not change his mind later. "Remember that real revolution in China, just as anywhere else in the world, is tried only when every other means of resolving intolerable situations has been exhausted," Snow told his brother in 1935. " . . . You would not, if you came here, see much resemblance between the Red Army and an American election, and in appearance there is none. But when you had been here as long as I have you would begin to see that this revolution is merely an expression of a historic need of the masses, too long suppressed, too long denied, and now become volcanic and catastrophic in its manifestations. It is the people's thumbs down on the rulers of the realm."

About the time of his marriage in 1932, Snow told his agent Henriette Herz that he tried to get "a 'passport' [in Shanghai] from local Reds, for a visit to Soviet China. I nearly succeeded, but at the last moment the CP's through whom I worked became suspicious of me, and disappeared." A visit seemed possible again when Snow signed the Smith & Haas contract in 1934. Chiang's fifth Communist extermination campaign had come to a standstill. But within a few weeks fighting resumed, and Chiang wrapped a tight blockade around the Kiangsi soviet. In April the Nationalists decisively beat the Communists at Kuangchang. Some four thousand Communists lay dead on the battle-field, and panic swept through the ranks of the survivors. Desertion, Red leaders admitted, became "an enemy even more fearful than Chiang Kai-shek." Snow notified New York that plans for a book on Red China were "fast dwindling." He had an interesting talk with the Generalissimo, and if the Nationalists' "claims are fact, it appears that the Communist base in Kiangsi has been virtually wiped out."[7]

While Snow turned to "another topic," his *South of the Clouds* travelogue, the Communists undertook one of history's greatest treks, a desperate six thousand-mile "Long March" to escape the Nationalists' grasp. For a year the Red column, savaged by skirmishes, harsh weather, forbidding terrain, illness, and lack of food, wound its way through China. As usual, reports on their activities presented a muddled picture. American foreign service officers filed a flurry of dispatches describing the march as it moved west, then north. The dominant impression was of a force that had spent itself, though there were dissenting views. Clubb thought the Communists would emerge a more powerful force than ever. Arthur Ringwalt, the American vice-consul in Yunnan, described the Communists, who came near his post, as under superior leadership, with strong morale and an ability to attract followers. Meanwhile, newspapers carried horrifying accounts of Red brutality. The most notorious was the murder in southern Anhwei of two young American missionaries.

"We actually know nothing about the Communist movement," Nathaniel Peffer wrote in 1935. "What you believe about Communist China still depends on whom you prefer to believe—whose sympathies you share or whom you respect enough to accept his intelligent estimate as carrying weight."[8]

By the time Mao's forces straggled into Shensi province in October 1935, the Reds were far less than 10 percent of their former strength, still vulnerable to future Nationalist assaults, and not entirely in step. Chang Kuo-t'ao, in charge of the Fourth Front Army, resisted Mao's leadership. Chang's disagreements with Mao dated back to the early 1920's. In recent years he had operated relatively independently in a separate soviet. When his column joined with the First Front Army and Mao in Szechwan, Chang argued against Mao's plan to continue north. Though Chang lost, a political compromise was struck. The armies reorganized. Chang and Chu Teh took a west column having the majority of the Fourth Front Army; Mao, with the main part of the First Front Army, took the east flank. It was a fragile agreement. Several weeks into the march, a flooded river separated the two forces. Chang turned south taking Chu with him, according to many accounts, as a prisoner.

But the marchers who arrived in Shensi under Mao had reason to rejoice. It was a major propaganda victory to have arrived at all, and in this new soviet the Communists were better positioned than before. In the south, the Communists had been fragmented. Here they had the beginnings of a unified base. Because Shensi was one of China's poorest provinces, it promised a rich harvest of recruits; because it was close to Japanese-controlled territory, it offered a rallying point for patriotic Chinese. As early as 1932 Mao and Chu Teh had declared war against the Japanese, though with no real prospect of engaging the enemy. In the Northwest they could. Within a few weeks the Communists crossed the Yellow River, ostensibly to fight their way north to the front and engage the Japanese. The real reason was to scout base areas, recruit additional forces, and collect food and revenue, but the Communists scored a propaganda victory just the same. Chiang's plan to smash the Communists once and for all was a tragic blunder. Rather than snuffing them out, he drove them to the high ground.

Snow realized that the Communists put the Nationalists in an awkward position. "For the Communists there is nothing to be lost by a war with Japan, and there is a socialist world to be won," Snow wrote. "For the warlords, on the contrary, there is everything to be lost, and nothing to be won but honorable mention in history."

Snow saw unmistakable signs of the Communists' growing appeal in Peking. In the wake of the December 9th student demonstrations, which occurred just after the Communists arrived in Shensi, Wang Jumei and other student leaders secretly joined the Communist Party. Colonel Joseph Stilwell, the United States military attaché in Peking and one of those who did not believe it "in the nature of the Chinese to be Communists," saw a spirit in the Red Army he did not find in Chiang Kai-shek, a "goddamned fool" who was not fighting the Japanese. "I don't know what [the Communists are] preaching," he told Snow, "but it looks to me like they've got the kind of leaders who win. I mean officers who don't say, 'Go on, boys!' but 'Come on, boys!' If that's the case and they had enough of them, they could keep the Japs busy here till kingdom come."

The headquarters of the Bandit Suppression force in Sian, about six hundred miles southwest of Peking, was also a center of growing doubts about Chiang's leadership. Young Marshal Chang Hsueh-liang, who commanded the force, had staunchly supported the Generalissimo for years, beating back separatist plots and loyally following orders to retreat before the Japanese as they moved into his native Manchuria. But his Tungpei, or Manchurian, troops were less and less enthusiastic about pursuing the civil war. Skirmishes with the Communists brought defeat, for one thing. For another it was not clear the Communists were really enemies. They released captured officers who returned with stories about Red zeal to fight the Japanese. Many Tungpei troops crossed the lines to join Communist ranks. Following the December 9th demonstrations, the Young Marshal made it known that all anti-Japanese students, no matter what their political beliefs, could come safely to the city. Many students made the journey, among them two Yenching journalism students close to the Snows, Chang Chao-lin and Chen Han-p'o, who took positions on a local newspaper writing anti-Japanese propaganda.

Hoping to capitalize on Chang's growing doubt, a Communist emissary visited the Young Marshal in early 1936. The emissary was a Red Cross official and sometime Christian known among his Communist contacts as Pastor Wang. Wang told Chang that the Communists wanted to join forces against the Japanese. After long discussions with CCP leaders, Chang agreed to an unofficial cease fire and to allow some Reds to work in Sian disguised as Tungpei soldiers. The understanding was so secret Chiang Kai-shek's ubiquitous underground did not know exactly what was afoot.

Snow had hints of Chang's changing attitude. A December 9th student activist who visited Chang at his Sian headquarters saw Snow in early March 1936. The student said that Chang, while professing his allegiance to Chiang Kai-shek, added ambiguously that "Unfortunately, I cannot tell you everything that is happening here in Sian nor in Nanking. However, I think that you will be satisfied with my eventual policy. . . . I deeply sympathize with your movement." The student told Snow that a large segment of the officer corps in Sian was sympathetic to the Communists.

While the Communists were on the Long March, Snow despaired of reaching them, although he was unable to put the trip out of his mind. He could not seem to finish his long overdue travelogue. He applied for a Guggenheim grant to study the agrarian crisis in China. The underlying issue, he wrote in the grant proposal, "is whether, in a country the size of China, and overwhelmingly agricultural . . . a true communist or proletarian regime is possible." He did not get the grant. It went instead, he later joked, for a "study in Chinese racial and psychological characteristics as revealed by Chinese facial expressions." The Guggenheim fellow wandered through the Peking streets taking photographs of Chinese after his interpreter told them some emotionally evocative story.[9]

Peking residents with good contacts among the Communist underground did not advertise them. Doing so could be lethal. Likewise, there wasn't much point in asking people about their political affiliations. A person could guess, though, and Snow was alert for contacts that might be able to help him get into the Communist camp. One of those was Sergei Polevoy, a Russian who came to China just before the October 1917 Revolution. Sympathetic with the revolution in his own country, Polevoy developed friendships with a long list of Chinese Communists and may, for a time, have assisted the Comintern. When Snow met him, Polevoy taught Russian language and literature at Peking National University. After several general conversations, Snow asked if Polevoy would help him get in touch with the Communists. Polevoy, who swore Snow to secrecy, said he would do what he could. At least that is how Polevoy's son remembered the previously untold story years later.[10]

Another likely intermediary came in the form of a tall, pale Chinese boy wearing an unkempt gown. Yu Ch'i-wei had been an active member of the Communist Party underground as a student at Tsingtao University. (Among those he brought into the party was a pretty young actress who became his lover; she later married Mao Tse-tung and took the name Chiang Ch'ing.) Jailed for several months after a crackdown of Tsingtao students, Yu moved to Peking National University to work in the radical student movement. After the December 9th demonstrations began, he visited the Snows' home with student leaders. The Snows saw behind his student pose. David, as he called himself, assumed a grandfatherly attitude toward the others, who listened intently to him during their political discussions in the living room; he talked like a Marxist; he lived cautiously, keeping much to himself and never sleeping more than a few nights in any one house. When David needed help leaving Peking, the Snows gave him a suit and put him on a train for Tientsin. Before leaving, David said he would tell a contact, a mysterious Mr. K. V., that Snow wanted to visit Red China. In encouraging letters written at the end of March 1936, David reported he had pleaded Snow's case and expected an answer in a few days. "I think they have no reason to refuse your requirement. I hope it shall be realized. Please write to me before your travelling!" After Yu's optimistic letter, no positive response followed from Tientsin. Nor could Snow reach Yu, living the life of a fugitive.

Snow tried another tack in May. He went to Shanghai where he saw Soong Ch'ing-ling, Lu Hsun, and Agnes Smedley. Although Smedley seemed irritated with him—perhaps because she wished to get to Red areas first—Snow hoped his overture would produce results.[11]

Late in the month, when Snow was back in Peking, his luck changed. Hsu Ping, a local university professor whom Snow knew, came with a letter written in invisible ink. He instructed Snow to go to Sian where he would get safe passage to the addressee, Mao Tse-tung.

Snow apparently did not know Hsu was a Communist and had only a vague idea whence the letter came, though he always thought Soong Ch'ing-ling played a role in making the arrangements. Because of the extreme secrecy required, details remained unclear for years. Nearly twenty years passed before Snow learned that the letter was authorized by Liu Shao-ch'i—David Yu's "Mr. K. V."—who was head of the Communists' North China bureau secretly based in Tientsin. In 1937, after Snow's trip, David Yu told Peg that he was the number two man in the North China bureau. That supports the view held by at least some veteran Chinese Communist leaders in the 1980s that David played a role in engineering Snow's trip. Snow, however, never mentioned David's help or listed him as a member of the North China bureau. Sergei Polevoy told his son that he played a role in securing the invitation for Snow and that he considered the assistance one of his greatest accomplishments.

The questions surrounding Snow's invitation heightened the sense of intrigue and adventure he felt in preparing for his long awaited trip to "Red China." But the most important questions about the letter went far beyond the mere technical aspects of how it reached Snow to the reasons *he* was invited at all.[12]

An explanation lay in the nascent united front unofficially negotiated with the Young Marshal. From their new vantage point in the Northwest, the Chinese Communists mounted an aggressive campaign to reach beyond their borders. They sent invisible ink letters to Chinese students as well as to Snow, who was not the only foreigner invited to the Northwest. The Communists also welcomed American physician George Hatem. Discontent with his limited medical practice in Shanghai, Hatem decided he could better use his skills in the Red districts. Through Agnes Smedley he met helpful Soong Ch'ing-ling. From the Communist point of view, a journalist could play a special role by broadcasting that the Communists existed as a viable anti-Japanese force worthy of popular support. The truce in the Sian made it possible for Snow to pass through Nationalist lines; his reports could widen the breach further.

Another factor involved the Communist leadership itself. The intransigence of Chang Kuo-t'ao, who resisted Mao's authority, marked only one episode in the party's recent turbulent history. For years Red leaders were spread over China and in Moscow, and not altogether in harmony. The confusing reports about Mao's disagreements with other party leaders in the early 1930s had truth to them. Mao was a rebel among revolutionaries. His promotion of guerrilla tactics and his belief that the peasants, not the urban proletariat, possessed the greatest revolutionary potential, deviated sharply from the party line. Before the First Front Army broke out of Kiangsi in October 1934, the party's Central Committee expelled Mao for the third time. When the Long March column reached Tsunyi, Kweichow, the following January, he was elected chairman of the Revolutionary Military Council and chairman of the Politburo, the latter a new post. But the conclave had not included Wang Ming, titular head of the Politburo and located in Moscow, and Mao's support at the meeting came less from Politburo members present than from the generals brought in to make an enlarged conference. In 1936, with Chang Kuo-t'ao marching off on his own and Wang Ming still in Moscow, Mao was strong enough to court the press and weak enough to want to build up his image as a leader.

But why Snow? The answer to that lay in his nationality, his contacts, and his independence. A Chinese reporter, even if one could be found, had to file his reports without the extraterritorial protection afforded foreigners, while British, French, and German reporters were tarred by their countries' success in creating such odious foreign privileges in the first place. A Russian journalist would be suspect to the outside world and no doubt unacceptable to Mao and others who had disagreed with Moscow. That left Americans, and among those Snow stood out. The proliferation of people with Red affiliations who helped him—or at least thought they did—was remarkable. The only American journalist who had better contacts with the Chinese Left was Agnes Smedley, but her contacts were too good. She was an out-and-out partisan, with limited outlets for her work. Snow's articles, on the other hand, appeared in the *Saturday Evening Post*, the *New York Herald Tribune*, and *Foreign Affairs*, anything but radical publications. The Communists might not be able to control what Snow wrote, in the way they might if someone less independent came, but they had reason to believe that he would be fair and that people would read his reports.

Snow hurriedly prepared for the trip, taking so many inoculations so quickly he made himself ill. He gave Peg instructions to gather research materials and asked Mac Fisher to file occasional stories to the London *Daily Herald* while he was "in the interior." Snow was that vague to Peking friends. "I am leaving tomorrow for Red China, to interview Mao Tse-tung, and to travel, photograph, and write what I please," Snow notified his publisher in a "Strictly Confidential" letter. "If I get through, it will be a world scoop!" Characteristically, he nearly missed the train to Sian.[13]

As instructed, Snow checked into the Guest House in Sian. One morning soon afterward Pastor Wang, the Red emissary, took him to a hillock outside town where Snow literally found himself in the embrace of Teng Fa, chief of the Red Army's Security Police. Snow thought he had never seen a Chinese like him. Teng, staying in the Young Marshal's home, wore a Tungpei uniform. Beneath the stiff disguise, Snow perceived "no sedentary bureaucrat, but an out-of-doors man of action." Teng's intense eyes sparkled; he had a pantherish grace, a grip of iron. Good humor and excitement bubbled over as he hugged Snow repeatedly. "What a Red Chinese! What a Red bandit!" Snow exclaimed later.

George Hatem, the American physician invited by the Communists, was also at the Guest House waiting for travel arrangements to be completed. He and Snow passed the time talking, playing rummy, and listening to Wang's yarns. They told the curious hotel manager they were leaving on a scientific expedition as soon as the rest of their party arrived. At the suggestion of his contacts, Snow arranged for a translator to come with him, a young Chinese friend in Peking. The boy, however, changed his mind by the time he reached Sian and left for Szechwan with the money Snow advanced him. Snow notified Peg of the problem. In one of those fateful decisions, she approached Yenching student leader Wang Ju-mei, who agreed to go. Before leaving for Sian, Wang stopped by to see Harry Price, acting dean of the Public Affairs College at Yenching. Price considered Wang one of his better students and reminded him that he would miss final examinations and graduation, just a couple of weeks away. "Ed Snow has arranged for me to meet Chou En-lai," the future foreign minister of the People's Republic of China replied. "I can't refuse."

Snow and Hatem left Sian at dawn in early July aboard one of the Nationalists' six-ton Dodge trucks. (Wang Ju-mei came later.) They reached Yenan, one hundred miles away, the following day. At seven o'clock the next morning a solitary guide threaded them through the Nationalists' lines straight into the soviet. After two days picking their way through the sparsely populated fudge-colored hills, the two Americans reached the village of Paikiaping. There Snow came face-to-face with his first Communist leader, Chou En-lai. Snow spent two days interviewing Chou. On July 10, atop a swaybacked horse, Snow set out with a contingent bound for Paoan, three days away.

Roving bands of Nationalist soldiers not under the Young Marshal's command made routine forays into the soviet. At one point Snow had a near brush with a patrol. It was not the danger, however, that caused his adrenalin to flow so much as it was the Communists themselves. Everything, even their crude propaganda, was news. Snow poured out question after question, writing down the answers in his notebook. As he traveled the last leg to Paoan, an image of the Communists, walking alongside his mount and singing songs, took shape. "The Red Army has taught me to read and write," said Old Dog, a seventeen-year-old who made the Long March. "Here I have learned to operate a radio, and how to aim a rifle straight. The Red Army helps the poor."[14]

Snow descended into the green valley cradling Paoan amid the sound of blowing bugles. Crowds shouted, "Welcome to the American journalist to investigate Soviet China." A reception committee showed Snow to his quarters, one of four one-room huts near the equally primitive "Foreign Office."

"It was the first time I have been greeted by the entire cabinet of a government, the first time a whole city has been turned out to welcome me," Snow wrote in his diary. "Had I been called upon to make any kind of speech I would have been unable to do so. I was overcome at the warmth of the greeting, the incredible experience of receiving it far in the interior of the little city fortified by many-ribbed ranges of mountains, and the strange thrill of solemn military music in the stillness and vastness of those mountains."

That evening Mao Tse-tung walked down to shake Snow's hand. Tall and gaunt, the upper reaches of his face framed by two shocks of black hair, Mao had a rough-hewn simplicity and magnetism. Within a week, he invited Snow to his house, a cave carved out of the loess hillside. These were Mao's first interviews with a foreign journalist, and they stretched over many evenings. Hunched over a squat table, on which Mme. Mao served hot-pepper bread and sour plum compote, the men talked through an interpreter into the small hours of the night.

Chou En-lai had mapped out an itinerary for Snow. But it was Mao, the young journalist acknowledged, who set his course in the soviet.[15] There was no doubt of the importance Mao attached to the interviews. Snow submitted questions in writing. Mao spoke from notes and reviewed translations of the interviews twice, making revisions and amplifications. His principal messages became a leitmotif running through Snow's visit: that the "fundamental issue before the Chinese people today is the struggle against Japanese imperialism," and that this must be "realized simultaneously with the liberation of the oppressed peasantry"; that "the Communist Party of China was, is, and will ever be, faithful to Marxist-Leninism"; that "we are certainly not fighting for an emancipated China in order to turn the country over to Moscow!"

The talks were not entirely formal. Between the careful give-and-take, the two men joked and conversed casually. After twelve nights of dwelling on CCP policy, Snow convinced Mao to break with typical Communist reluctance to talk about personal matters and to recount his life. Mao had never done so before. The details were so obscure that Mao's wife hovered nearby to listen.

Mao was born to a prosperous peasant family in Hunan. As a boy he cut off his traditional Chinese pigtail in defiance of the Manchu rulers and joined one of the rebel forces that completed the Ch'ing overthrow. An adolescent during the warlord period when China remained weak, he became increasingly radical. He reached manhood in the Chinese Communist Party, whose founding he attended in 1921. In relating this progression, Mao was at times self-serving and misleading. He described something of intraparty feuding, including the feud with Chang Kuo-t'ao, who was now en route to Paoan with Chu Teh after a series of military blunders. But Mao skirted responsibility for his mistakes and exuded confidence. He deftly dismissed Wang Ming with the casual remark that his reports from Moscow were out of touch with the Chinese soviet's reality. Mao's deceptive comments notwithstanding, his story was an important one, illustrating the forces that conspired to produce Communists in China. He never related his personal history in anything approaching such detail again.

Other Red Chinese leaders confirmed in words and actions the impression that Mao spoke for the party and that the CCP was committed to revolution, a revolution that was Marxist inspired but Chinese led. The lone Comintern advisor in Paoan gave additional weight to that message. Li Teh, as he was called, was an experienced Comintern agent whose real name was Otto Braun. Snow first met Li in Peking during 1933, when he showed up with a letter of introduction from Agnes Smedley. Li was chiefly concerned with establishing his identity as a German newspaperman—and with drinking all their brandy, Peg thought. Unable to get beyond noncommittal political conversation with the Snows, he did not visit again. In Paoan, Li did not reveal his real name to Snow. He did relate how he secretly entered the Kiangsi soviet in 1933 and became the only Westerner to make the Long March. Despite his singular status, Li had little influence. The leadership, which criticized past Comintern advice, seemed to confer with him out of courtesy rather than any genuine interest in his views. "The Chinese after all understand their revolution better than any foreigner could," Li told Snow.[16]

Evidence that these Chinese were committed Communists was as obvious as the red stars and the hammer and sickle emblems plastered on uniforms and the walls of Lenin Clubs. Nearly every biography Snow recorded drew a picture of intimate involvement with the party, often not only in China but also in the Soviet Union. The director of an army public health bureau was a "convinced Marxist," Snow wrote in his diary after one typical conversation. Lo Fu, secretary-general of the Politburo, stressed that "the Red Army is not an army of the peasantry, although the troops are largely drawn from the peasantry. It is an army of the Communist party, first of all." Rank and file Chinese repeated Marxist slogans. Soldiers and "little Red devils" unabashedly stood before Snow reciting their Communist catechisms: "The Red Army is a revolutionary army"; "The Red Army is the army of the poor men!"[17]

Statements by peasants and soldiers were vastly more important to Snow than anything the leadership might say.[18] And what the peasants said suggested that the Communists succeeded where the Nationalists failed. Many poor farmers in the soviet criticized the Communist regime and voiced complaints, Snow noted in a telling observation, "but most of them talked about the Soviets as *womenti chengfu*—'our government'—and this struck me as something new in rural China."

Poor peasants in Nationalist-controlled parts of Shensi spent 65 percent of their income on taxes, according to reports at the time. Many sold their farms for a few bits of food. In contrast, the Communists ensured that everyone who wanted land and livestock got them; they reduced taxes, effectively abolished usury, and eliminated the power of privileged groups. In Shanghai children were routinely sold into factory jobs, as Snow had seen firsthand. After working twelve or thirteen hours they would sleep on dirty quilts beneath their machines. Factory wages for an entire family came to about a dollar a day. In Wukichen, a soviet industrial city so primitive it lacked electricity, conditions were Spartan but workers had clubs, food, and pay—and "they knew nobody was making money out of them," Snow thought. Chu Tso-chih, a well-known engineer, gave up a high paying job in Shanghai to join the Communists. His one serious criticism in Wukichen, he told Snow, was that the "people spend entirely too much time singing!"

Red propaganda reached into every corner of soviet life, an irritation to Snow. But literacy campaigns, while fledgling, had at least begun. Peasants were informed and vocal, and allowed to voice criticism. "Almost any farmer you meet can talk some very elemental politics with you," Snow told people later. Ting Ling, a writer whose stories Snow had translated and whom the Nationalists arrested in 1933, was a heroine in Paoan. Communist actors performed her dramatic skits in the people's theater. Anti-Communist propaganda could not compete. At the Red Army Academy, students used the backs of enemy leaflets for taking notes. To Snow's surprise, the Communists did not restrict his movement.

He saw no opium poppies, beggars, wife beating, prostitution, polygamy, or foot-binding. "I have seen comely young girls sit down beside bellows and pump the ancient instrument cheerfully for an hour or more to cook the soldiers' dinner, talking and joking with them meanwhile," Snow recorded in his diary. "During my stay here I have never seen a child struck nor an old man abused."

Altogether it was better than anything Snow observed in places where the Nationalists ruled. "I arrived here safely several weeks ago and began work at once on my botanical collection," Snow cryptically wrote to his wife. Life was austere, full of monotonous food and "bugs, which I am also collecting for the Smithsonian Institute: fleas, ants, spiders, bedbugs, lice, mosquitoes, flies, etc. . . . But being here is an experience worth all that & much more. It is exhilarating in many ways but most of all because of contact with heroic young scientists. . . . They go at the difficult labor of discovering a new scientific world like school boys to a football match!"

By the time Peg read the note, Snow was traveling with the soviet army over the rough, arid terrain of Kansu and Ningsia, the western part of the soviet. The trip offered the rough adventure Snow relished. He rode a sturdy black pony, carried an automatic for protection, and wore a battered army cap with a red star blazing over the bill. His cheeks bristled with red whiskers. Snow's host was P'eng Teh-huai, Commander of the First Front Army. P'eng wore no rank insignia, lived like his men, took obvious pleasure in strenuous physical activity, and avoided what Snow considered the objectionable qualities in some Chinese of evasion. Snow liked him.

Traveling with P'eng, Snow observed the Red leadership's efforts to instill united front sentiments in troops. It wasn't always easy. P'eng's troops observed Red dicta, such as paying peasants for needed supplies, but they had yet to fully learn the rules for wooing soldiers loyal to the Nationalists. P'eng "raised hell" over the wounding of a captured officer. At a meeting with his lieutenants, P'eng said they would have to explain better the aims of the anti-Japanese united front to their men.[19]

P'eng's efforts were only one piece of evidence that the Communists were determined to resist the Japanese. Military courses at the Red Academy in Paoan almost exclusively emphasized anti-Japanese warfare. Propaganda throughout the soviet seemed intent on the same thing. A performance by the People's Anti-Japanese Dramatic Society included the "United Front Dance," a routine depicting "the mobilization of China to resist Japan."

The Communists had talked about a united front before the Long March began, but precisely with whom they would form a united front and under what terms was vague and constantly changing.[20] In initial conversations with Snow, Mao and others spoke of "unification of the entire Chinese people." Yet Snow had reason to wonder if the Communists would go as far as to accept an alliance with Chiang Kai-shek. Chou called the Generalissimo a "bungling amateur" as a tactician who had several years earlier "reached the zenith of his power." While Snow visited the military front, the leadership resolved some of this ambiguity. In an "Open Letter Addressed to the Kuomintang," the Communists made their most conciliatory appeal yet. If the Nationalists agreed to join in fighting the Japanese, and if they would grant popular rights and intensify economic development, the Communists would accept the laws of a new National Defense Democratic Government, back away from land reform, and consider changing the names of their organizations. The Communists would not insist on representation in the cabinet of the new government, Mao told Snow when he returned to Paoan from the field, or organize mass movements opposed to the new government.[21]

Snow realized that this would make big news, provided he could get back to tell it. He had worried about leaving the soviet even before he arrived. With each Communist biography he took down, with each tale of the Long March, with each scrap of evidence that these were not merely Red bandits, he became more anxious about getting his news to the outside world. Mao's latest statement on the united front came on the heels of news that Peg had tried to reach Paoan and failed. In Sian, Nationalists were replacing the Young Marshal's Tungpei troops in preparation for another annihilation campaign against the Communists. These new troops tightened the blockade. Snow would have liked to meet Chang Kuo-t'ao and Chu Teh, who had not yet arrived, but decided to return home immediately.[22]

The four-month stay in the soviet deeply affected Snow. The simple rural setting, contrasting sharply with the reclining luxury of Peking and the steaming materialism of Shanghai, provided a perfect setting for Snow's agrarian sympathies to be realized. In contrast to their Nationalist rivals, the Communists "turned back to the deep soil-base of their country." After eight years of searching, Snow found a political movement that, while not a carbon copy of the populism that existed on the Midwestern plains where he was reared, attracted and harnessed people's energies for the common good.[23]

The Communists depended on voluntary action. They achieved that by creating an array of people's organizations that gave everyone jobs and put social pressure on those who reluctantly joined in. Though coercive, there was none of the brute force Snow saw in the Nationalist areas. The Communists did not need to use combat troops for police activities within the soviet. Citizens of the soviet projected pride, dignity, and a sense of purpose beyond their own narrow families to improve material conditions and oust the Japanese. For the first time Snow saw "joint enterprise of the political workers and the people" in which "the resources of energy, intelligence, patriotism and economy latent in the masses can be utilized to the fullest."

The Communist Party reached toward the common people and did so with a common touch. The old effete elitism Snow detested in China was gone. Peasants and intellectuals gathered together at the Red theater. The leadership sought no special privileges or personal material gain. Mao went out with "Saturday brigades" to work in the fields. Instead of banker's black, the intellectual finance minister, Lin Paich'u, one of the few officials over fifty years of age, wore a faded gray uniform and a ragged cap. A piece of string hooked his glasses to one ear.

Mao cut a remarkably American figure in some respects. Intellectually, he regarded himself as a Marxist, but as one historian put it, "populist ideas and impulses profoundly influenced the manner in which he adopted and employed Marxism." Mao's political orientation was toward the peasants, whose setting and life style he romanticized. Deeply nationalistic, he believed in the ability of the Chinese people to shape their destiny, rather than believing that historical forces, like some configuration of stars, must first be properly positioned. He distrusted intellectuals and bureaucrats.

Snow's first impression of Mao was "Lincolnesque." Snow's other impressions reflected equally American images. Though educated, Mao spoke to his followers in their own terms and seemed to possess a native shrewdness. Iron-willed, he worked for hours on end and during the Long March walked nearly as far as his men; his reputation for a charmed life, an American image of heroes, seemed well-deserved. Providence always seemed to intervene, Snow noted, saving Mao from capture or death. Despite his preeminence, there was no deification of Mao, nor did he seem to desire such status. Once while talking with Snow, Mao rolled down the waistband of his trousers to hunt for lice; on a hot day, while Snow was interviewing Lin Piao, Mao nonchalantly pulled off his trousers. An individualist, Mao shunned the close-cropped haircuts commonly worn in the soviet for his own long, awkward locks and smoked cigarettes inveterately, though the Communists considered the vice a sign of personal corruption. Like a good citizen soldier he rendered the most feeble salute Snow had ever seen. During a picture session, Snow had to loan his Red Army cap to Mao, who did not have one. Snow had a great deal in common with Mao. Each read avidly, dressed casually, disdained organized religion at an early age, and kept to his own schedule. Each put practical over theoretical questions.

Snow realized that the Chinese Communists were not Missouri democrats. The CCP was authoritarian and wanted control of the entire country. Any concessions the Reds made to the Nationalists, he noted, they "examined, debated, decided, and integrated in terms of Marxism—and the proletarian Revolution, which the Communists did not abandon as their ultimate purpose." All the same there was a democratic side to the Communists who attracted so many followers. First, the Communist idea was to redress ancient inequities in the Chinese system and eliminate foreign imperialists. Both meant to liberate the Chinese. Second, Communists' practicality and the primitive conditions in which they existed prevented establishment of an authentic Marxist regime. Instead, the CCP had to design policies to meet people's needs. "Chinese Communism as I found it in the Northwest," Snow concluded, "might more accurately be called rural equalitarianism than anything Marx would have found agreeable as a model child of his own."

The Communists' program, Snow believed, forced a crude democratic dynamic on all of China. As successful as the Communists had been, their victory was not assured. It depended on Chiang Kai-shek. He, too, could compete by responding to popular needs. The possibility of a united front, which provided a framework in which both sides could vie for power, seemed a particularly positive development brought on by the Communist threat. As Snow was to say, "The achievement of 'democracy' now in prospect would have been impossible without the ten-year presence of Communist Opposition."

This competition of two would-be totalitarian political movements was not neat democracy, as Snow knew it and liked it. But it was a big step forward from the unresponsive one-party rule of the Nationalists. Snow accepted it as a practical solution in a context that was vastly different from his origins. In making the compromise, Snow reconciled his values to the Chinese situation. Freedom of the press, for instance, remained one of his favorite subjects in China. He thought a reordering of the "feudal" system in China plus expulsion of imperialist forces could eventually produce such liberties. The hopefulness of the soviet, in contrast to the despair he witnessed in Nationalist territory, confirmed in his mind the possibilities of socialism furthering this process. He had learned to be a Missourian in an alien land.

Most of the time, Snow said later, he "felt as completely at ease as if I were with some of my countrymen."[24] That ease showed up in leisure activities. He, Dr. Hatem, and several Chinese challenged a team from the Wukichen arsenal in basketball. In Paoan he played hotly contested games of tennis with Li Teh and several Red Academy commissars on a rocky court near his lodgings. He taught a one-armed Commissar named Tsai Shu-fan to play rummy, a game that soon swept the city, and he introduced poker into evening sport. In his letter to her, Snow asked Peg to send the Communists *Man's Fate*, Malraux's book depicting the 1927 Communist purge in Shanghai, and two volumes by Agnes Smedley, as well as magazines, tea, chocolate, coffee, and a map-making device described in a circular. When Lin Piao invited Snow to speak on "British and American Policies towards China" at the Red Academy, Snow accepted. He was deeply moved by the commitment of the people, many of whom would probably be killed before he saw them again. "They are immensely brave," he remarked to Hatem during one convocation, when impassioned speeches were made on liberating the oppressed in China and the world.

Among the mementos Snow packed for the trip home were his Red Army cap, two copper coins minted in the Kiangsi soviet and presented by a soldier who had been on the Long March, and a black jade snuff bottle.[25] Hsu Hai-tung, another plain-talking general, gave Snow the bottle during their farewell on the Kansu plain. "Please take this as a souvenir from the Fifteenth Army and myself," he told Snow. "My men want you to have it so that you will not forget us. It once belonged to a Mongolian prince and is famous among peasants all over here. Take it and you will return home safely."

On October 12, three days after Chu Teh's troops linked up with military units in the soviet, Snow left Paoan. Hatem and Wang Ju-mei stayed. Mao was still asleep when Snow walked out of town, but a number of other political leaders bid him farewell. When Snow passed an open-air Red Academy class, students came over to wish him well. "Peaceful good road, Comrade Snow, ten thousand to you." As Snow rode off, he felt as though he were leaving home, not going to it.

Ten days later Snow, grinning through a prickly beard, appeared unannounced at the side door of his Peking home. Inside he pulled a Red Army cap out of one of his bundles, donned the battered trophy of his travels, and capered around Peg. While his dog Gobi pawed him, Snow asked the cook for a long awaited meal of eggs, milk, and coffee.[26]

Snow's return trip had been a near tragedy. The morning after he crossed from Communist territory into Nationalist, sympathetic troops smuggled him into Sian in a Kuomintang Army truck loaded with gun sacks. Snow used one sack to conceal his notes and film, and the photos given him by the Communists. Upon his arrival in Sian he was horrified to find that the sack had been mistakenly thrown off at an earlier stop. He spent a sleepless night while the drivers and a Tungpei officer retrieved it.

Now secure in Peking, he wanted to keep his four-month visit in Red China secret for a few more days. That would give him time to begin writing a serialized newspaper account and have his photographs developed before the Nationalist censors knew what he was doing. Unexpected news of his own death, however, scotched those plans.

Two days after his return, the Associated Press wire carried a report that "Snow fell into the hands of 'red bandits' and was shot when he was caught writing about them in his notebook." When Snow's father read the story in Kansas City, he immediately asked the *Kansas City Star* to send an inquiry to China over the AP wire. Snow's editors in Britain and New York cabled similar queries. That morning fellow Missourian Jimmy White, who manned the AP's Peking bureau, was on the telephone to Peg. Had she heard from her husband?

"Oh, I heard from him today," she said. "He's fine."

When White related the news reports, Snow got on the line himself. A few hours later he gave a press conference at the American embassy, which also called about his welfare. Snow enjoyed borrowing Mark Twain's remark that news of his death was premature. At the Peking news conference, he said someone else might have been killed in inner China. He was molested at no time during his travels. The Reds treated him well.

The Nationalists branded Snow's reports a hoax. "The Japanese-financed White Russian Fascist press of Tientsin," Snow ruefully observed, alleged that he was "in the joint pay of Wall Street and Stalin." For the most part, though, Snow's accounts of the Chinese Communists were taken seriously. Powell's *China Weekly Review* published his interviews with Mao, which Chinese read eagerly. Yenching students invited Snow to talk and show his photos. Reporters interviewed him. His account electrified an audience at the Peking Hotel. Randall Gould published a speech by Snow in the *Shanghai Evening Post & Mercury*. C. E. Gauss, the Consul General in Shanghai, thought Snow sympathetic to the Communists but believed he provided "the most comprehensive, authoritative and up-to-date account of the Chinese Soviet movement to come to the attention of this Consulate General. It is accordingly believed that it merits the close attention of the Embassy." Members of an informal discussion group to which Snow belonged gathered at John Service's home to hear about the trip. "Suddenly," thought Service, "there was a new factor, of uncertain but potentially vital significance, in the China equation."[27]

In the coming weeks the London *Daily Herald* gave front page play to Snow's serialized report, ran related editorials and large displays of his pictures, and promoted him to chief Far Eastern correspondent. The *New York Times* and the New York *Sun* quarreled over exclusive American rights to the series he gave to the North American Newspaper Alliance. Not knowing the details of the argument, Snow concluded that the newspapers were not running the stories because they wished to suppress them, and he took them back. To his surprise, *Life*, a new magazine published by Henry Luce, a supporter of the Generalissimo, paid one thousand dollars for Snow's photographs, splashing forty-one of them across eleven pages in two successive issues. Long articles by Snow appeared in half of *Asia*'s 1937 issues; the *New Republic* published a four-part series on Soviet China; *Amerasia*, eager for a piece by Snow, printed excerpts from his interviews with Mao; the *Saturday Evening Post* published an article.

"A piece of news that is one month early is as worthless as a piece of news one month late," journalist Vincent Sheean commented on lack of enthusiasm for his reports from China in 1927. Sheean had had advance information on the impending breakup of the KMT-CCP alliance, but his editors at the North American Newspaper Alliance simply were not interested. Snow experienced no such problem. From the time he filed his first news stories until he finished his book-length report, China was big news. Japanese aggression would reunite the Nationalists and the Communists, a union that had overwhelming appeal to Americans.

Initially after returning to Peking, Snow held out little hope that Chiang would give up the war against the Communists "unless under the emotional stimulus of a national anti-Japanese mass movement the greater part of his officers and army begins to break away from his command." Events quickly moved in that direction. On December 12, students in Peking staged a demonstration demanding that Chiang, in Sian to launch the new offensive against the Communists, turn his forces instead on the Japanese. After a hectic day of covering the protests, the Snows went to Ran and Louise Sailor's home for dinner. Jim Bertram, also invited, showed up with stunning news. Revolting troops in Sian had killed the Generalissimo.[28]

News of Chiang's death, like news of Snow's, was premature. The Young Marshal and other Tungpei "rebels" had kidnapped Chiang, not killed him. Chiang's detention, however, was no less astounding. Chiang's kidnappers hoped their act would serve to end the civil war, though that too remained obscure. The Nationalists, who heavily censored Snow's dispatches, forbade publication of the rebels' demands. At the same time they promoted erroneous reports that the Communists had occupied Sian, that the rebels nailed the chief of police to the city gates, that women were being "communized." When Nationalist representatives, including Mme. Chiang herself, traveled to Sian to plead for Chiang's freedom, no official mention was made that the Communists had joined in the negotiations. The Soviet Union's news service, *Tass*, complicated matters further by publishing reports that the rebels were pro-Japanese and intent on destroying the united front. These Russian reports perplexed and angered Snow. Sage comments from Moscow, he observed, "can add nothing but further confusion in the mind of a public already as deeply confused as it is possible for a strictly controlled and censored press to make it."

A Tungpei leader, Miao Feng-shen, asked Snow to accompany him to Sian. One of the brains behind the kidnapping, Miao thought Snow's presence would give him a cover. Snow declined but arranged for Mac Fisher and James Bertram, whom he deputized as a special correspondent for the London *Daily Herald*, to go instead. Neither of the two reporters knew Miao's true identity until he revealed it en route. Becoming nervous, Bertram and Fisher decided to destroy a secret letter Snow had asked them to deliver in Sian. After a comic effort to flush the envelope down a primitive toilet, the trio burned the contents and split up. Only Bertram and Miao reached Sian, arriving several hours after Chiang's release on Christmas day. Agnes Smedley was broadcasting news nightly from a Sian radio station, and Bertram agreed to help. As soon as his voice was heard over the air, Nanking said he was a Russian Bolshevik, a charge picked up on the Reuters wire.

Ambassador Johnson was singularly diffident to all of this. When Snow sent him copies of his published interviews with Mao, Johnson replied that "Mr. Mao Tse-tung talks very much like a lot of other Chinese leaders I have met. But then, after all, his case is not as bad as some of the others, for he had less access to information about conditions in the world than do others that I have met and talked with." Johnson considered the Sian Incident, as Chiang's kidnapping was called, just an attempt by Chang Hsueh-liang and his colleagues to compel "Chiang Kai-shek to give complete recognition to their talents. Just a kidnapping. As you know, I have always felt that the confusion and complications which we ascribe to the Chinese mind are very much the product of our much more complicated brain."

Snow could not agree. He had received a puzzling card from Hatem written shortly after the kidnapping. Hatem described jubilation in Paoan as well as speeches by Mao and other leaders calling for a mass trial of Chiang. Yet, although Chou was involved in negotiations over Chiang's release, no trial followed, and Chiang went back to Nanking. Snow did not learn for almost a year that Stalin had directed the CCP leadership to release Chiang or he would discredit them as bandits! Still later Snow concluded that it was the last occasion when Stalin managed to command a "critical decision in Chinese party policy."

Chiang took elaborate steps to obscure the bargain he struck for his freedom: agreement to call off the anti-Communist campaign and to enter into anti-Japanese alliance with the Communists. Young Marshal Chang helped him save face by returning as Chiang's prisoner (a status he continued to hold in Taiwan after the Communist takeover in 1949). While publicly affirming that his old policies remained in force, Chiang slowly and quietly negotiated with the Communists—so slowly that as spring gave way to summer, Snow worried that CCP-KMT rapprochement would disintegrate into another annihilation campaign. Then, on July 7, another Sino-Japanese incident erupted, this time at the Marco Polo Bridge, about ten miles outside Peking. Although the precise causes remained obscure, as usual, the consequences were not. Desultory fighting turned into pitched battle. On July 27, three squadrons of Japanese bombers and heavy artillery pounded the garrison at the South Barracks, Peking's last defense point. Two-thirds of the three thousand Chinese troops perished. The next day Snow ventured onto the blood-stained road with a Reuters correspondent. He saw wounded soldiers stumble along the thoroughfare. Chinese bodies lay in heaps. The Japanese, who estimated their losses at fifty, made their official entry into Peking a week later.[29]

Under the force of these circumstances, a united front rapidly coalesced. Not only did Chiang accept a partnership with the Communists. He also released nonaligned political prisoners who had decried his previous "Win the Civil War first" policies and lifted the ban on resistance songs and slogans. Dissident leaders, including warlords from Yunnan and Szechwan, rallied to the Nationalist banner.

The Japanese, meanwhile, rolled on. In late September, thirty thousand troops following the rising sun raped, looted, and murdered in Paoting, site of a Nationalist military headquarters along the Peking-Hankow railway. Spoiling for a fight that would draw international publicity and perhaps foreign military assistance, Chiang positioned his troops to provoke a confrontation in Shanghai. The ensuing battle lasted three months and received more press coverage than any fighting since the Allies broke through German defenses in 1919. A *Life* photograph of a terrified Chinese baby sitting amid the burned-out wreckage of a Shanghai rail depot became a searing image for Americans, who read daily eyewitness reports of Japanese aerial bombing of civilians in a score of cities along the China coast.

During one week in December, the Japanese sank the U.S. gunboat *Panay* in the Yangtze River, killing three Americans, and overran the Chinese capital of Nanking. An estimated three hundred thousand Chinese were killed, thousands of women were assaulted and raped. "Huge sections of the city," the *Kansas City Star* reported, "were nothing more than smoking heaps of masonry at points where Nippon's modern siege guns had battered huge holes and breaches in the massive piles of stone." The Japanese, Snow reported one *Panay* crew member as saying, "could not possibly" have mistaken the vessel for anything but a United States ship. The U.S. flag was flying and two were painted on her decks.

There could hardly have been a better scenario for the book Snow was writing. Everyone, it seemed, was interested in China. Executive branch cabinet heads now paid day-to-day attention to the country, rather than leaving diplomacy to foreign service officers. For the general public the heroic Chinese peasant, personified in the 1937 movie version of Pearl Buck's *The Good Earth*, became, increasingly, an object of sympathy. Polls showed 2 percent of the public pro-Japanese, 74 percent pro-Chinese. *Time* selected the Generalissimo and Mme. Chiang as "Man and Wife of the Year" for 1937. As Harold Isaacs would put it later, the Age of Benevolence in American views of the Chinese had ended, the Age of Admiration had begun.[30]

Coupled with sympathy for the Chinese was fear of Japan. The old enemy, economic depression, was giving way to the specter of a new one, world war spawned by fascism. In 1936 Hitler marched into the demilitarized Rhineland, Abyssinia fell to the Italians, German bombers leveled Guernica for Franco's Nationalists. Hitler and Mussolini established the "Rome-Berlin Axis," and days afterward Japan and Germany joined in the Anti-Comintern Pact. Then in 1937 came Japanese aggression in China. As the sinking of the *Panay* showed, the United States could be dragged into the fighting, something Americans did not want. A Gallup poll showed that sentiment in favor of total American withdrawal from the Far East jumped from 54 to 70 percent of the public after the *Panay* incident. Sympathy for the Chinese notwithstanding, polls also showed that a substantial majority of Americans wanted their country to stop selling war materials to Japan *and* China. In a thoroughly isolationist mood, Americans welcomed news of a KMT-CCP united front. A strengthened China might be able to fight its own battles against the Japanese.

At the same time that fascism seemed more and more menacing, the Communists looked more and more like allies. The fascist coalition also alarmed the Soviet Union, which began appealing to Western powers for cooperative action. In the Unites States, American Communists cultivated a popular front image befitting allies. On July 4, 1935, the *Daily Worker* carried pictures of Lenin and George Washington side-by-side with reprints of the Declaration of Independence. The Communist Party no longer pressed Roosevelt to move the New Deal Leftward. An organizational bulletin warned party members on WPA projects not to sound like "crazy Reds." One of those who resisted the drift toward respectability observed that the approach seemed designed not to "offend ancient contributors to *The Saturday Evening Post*."

Snow finished his book to the sound of gunfire outside Peking in late July 1937. The hefty volume, more than four hundred pages long, was in the fullest sense a report—of what he saw in the soviet and what he was told—as well as an interpretive analysis of what the Communists stood for and their impact on the fluid scene in China. He dedicated the book "To Nym," his wife. He initially entitled the book *Red Star in China*. When his agent Henriette Herz—possibly inadvertently, possibly diplomatically—referred to the title as *Red Star over China*, he realized he had the perfect name.[31]

Snow had been deeply anxious about the timing. He worried that swiftly moving events would outdate *Red Star* before it appeared; while he labored to add new chapters about the united front, he fretted that a competitor would come out with a related book before his. Random House, which bought Smith & Haas publishers and with it the contract for Snow's book, shared that sense of urgency and caution. Although delighted with the manuscript, Random House wanted Snow to write a quick postscript describing Japanese coastal attacks. Unable to contact Snow, by this time at the front, and as anxious as he not to be scooped, it finally decided to bring out the book on January 15, 1938. Learning that a book by Bertram on the Sian Incident was scheduled for January 3, Random House hastily moved up *Red Star*'s debut to the same day.

Neither Random House nor Snow need have worried. *Red Star* received the kind of acclaim authors dream about. A sampling of more than one hundred reviews in general circulation publications reveals not a single one that offered an overall negative assessment. They were larded with praise publishers conjure for dust jackets: "a dazzling journalistic feat" (Portland, Maine, *Evening Express*); "absolutely indispensable" (Bruce Catton in the *Knoxville Sentinel*); "the outstanding book of the year" (*Florida Times-Union*); "prophetic" (county librarian writing in the *Daily Republican*, Fairfield, California); "magnificent" (*Wisconsin State Journal*). The most influential newspapers and magazines were equally enthusiastic. The *Saturday Review of Literature* put Snow's picture on its cover. As Malcolm Cowley, book editor of the *New Republic* and an eminent writer himself, put it, "To Edgar Snow goes credit for what is perhaps the greatest single feat performed by a journalist in our century."[32]

In Great Britain, where it was published by Victor Gollanz in October 1937, *Red Star* became a Left Book Club selection and went through three printings in its first month. Sales quickly reached one hundred thousand copies. One month after publication in the United States, Henriette Herz cabled Snow that twelve thousand copies had been sold. Random House Publisher said orders arrived at the rate of six hundred copies a day. Editions soon appeared in half a dozen other languages. "This for a book about Communists in China!" exclaimed Cerf, who was not sure where total sales might end.

Sales figures did not fully measure *Red Star*'s fame. President Roosevelt's Secretary of the Interior Harold Ickes stayed up all night reading *Red Star*, he told a Chinese friend of Snow, and brought the book to FDR's attention. Snow's reporting inspired young people: One woman gave up her nearly completed Ph.D. studies to report on China. Theodore White took the advice of his Harvard mentor, John Fairbank, and set out for China to "do what Snow had done." The same year that *Red Star* appeared, Milt Caniff started his "Terry and the Pirates" comic strip at the suggestion of Joseph Patterson, publisher of the New York *Sun*. Desperate for background information about China, where the cartoon was set, Caniff followed Snow's pictures and text, by his own admission, "slavishly." For many intellectuals *Red Star* was the single best book of China reportage they ever encountered. Many, like Philippine journalist Alejandro Roces, could recall moving passages from the book fifty years later. With Pearl Buck's *The Good Earth*, it became regarded as one of the two most memorable books of an age when China was front page news.

The one exception to *Red Star*'s enthusiastic reception came, ironically, from American Communists.[33] The Worker's Book Shop banned *Red Star* from its shelves, and *New Masses* refused to take advertisements for the volume. The American Communist Party took its cues from Moscow, and Moscow had reason not to welcome *Red Star*. Snow wrote that the Chinese Communists were Marxist revolutionaries and that *"the Soviet movement and the Chinese Red Army began spontaneously, under purely Chinese leadership,"* a point Snow himself underlined. In so doing, he challenged Moscow's status as the center of worldwide Marxist revolution and, thus, the legitimacy of the soviet state. Snow also touched a raw nerve in the Kremlin when he wrote that "the Comintern may be held responsible for serious reverses suffered by the Chinese Communists." Over the objections of his rival, Leon Trotsky, Stalin had insisted on the KMT-CCP alliance that ended in so many Chinese Communist deaths in 1927. Now Stalin was urging the CCP to forge a new united front, a step to strengthen Russia's eastern flank against possible Japanese attack.

American Communists contrived typically comic contortions to salvage Moscow's reputation. A reviewer in the *Communist* labeled Snow "an irresponsible retailer of gossip and slander" who led readers into the "quicksands of Trotskyism" for attributing CCP setbacks to Comintern errors. An obscure German Communist whom Snow met in Shanghai and knew by the name of Heinz Shippe criticized *Red Star* in two letters to *Pacific Affairs*. Writing under the pen name of Asiaticus, Shippe said Snow was wrong to suggest "that the Reds *would* 'try out Communism' if they could gain control of the great cities" or that "the Chinese Communists used land redistribution merely as a maneuver to gain the power that would enable them to press forward to thoroughgoing Socialist changes, including collectivization." The Chinese Communists were not and could not be social revolutionaries. China had not reached a stage of development where socialist revolution could exist as it had in Russia. The CCP could only hope to pave the way for a socialist revolution by joining the Nationalists in throwing out the imperialists and eradicating "powerful feudal remnants in rural China." Others, led by Moscow, would carry out the socialist revolution later.

The Asiaticus critique in *Pacific Affairs*, which earlier ran a favorable review of *Red Star*, irritated Snow enough that he wrote two replies. Communist criticism, however, had virtually no impact on Snow's reputation. Had Snow known what the future held, he might have wished that Americans had paid attention to his Communist detractors. In another era Americans would charge that Snow misled Americans by portraying the Chinese Communists as mere agrarian reformers *with no Marxist objectives.*

The "agrarian reform" myth became, as Snow's critics would charge, a major impediment to the development of sound policies toward the Far East. The illusion prevented Americans from understanding the significance of the Communists. But "the birthplace of the eventful idea" was not in *Red Star*, as some would also charge.[34] It was in an American public little interested in thinking globally, utterly unwilling to apply its ideals abroad. Americans in 1938 were hungry for anti-Fascist allies, allies who would mount their own resistance to Japan, Germany, and Italy and leave the United States at peace. The Chinese Communists, in league with the Nationalists, offered such an anti-Fascist force. Americans embraced the Communists and, as if to make the love affair more palatable, wished away the complex factors that presaged a Communist revolution in China. The Chinese Communists, in the popular mind, could not be allies, it seemed, if they were not democrats.

Snow favored the Chinese Communists, he romanticized them, and he did so with great force. By the mid-1930s he had matured into a powerful writer. In *Red Star* he brought the reader into a vivid drama, flinging him into the arms of Teng Fa, letting him feel the uncertainty and fear of traversing the Nationalists' blockade, sitting him down in the primitive cave where Mao told his life story. Snow's description of the taking of Tatu Bridge during the Long March, where Red volunteers swung hand-over-hand on chains into the teeth of Nationalist machine gun fire, could make a reader leave tears on the page. Eager to communicate with Americans, Snow used American images to describe the CCP. The overall effect could be heady. Taken alone this offered Americans a comforting picture.

But this was only part of *Red Star*. Throughout the book Snow made clear that, however much he admired the Chinese Communists and however American he saw them, they remained revolutionaries. On the same pages that Snow wrote of "rural equalitarianism" in the soviet, he also wrote that the Chinese Communists were laying the foundations for "a true Socialist society."[35] That was why the American Communist Party criticized him; that was why he saw a *red* star over China.

Reviews showed how myopic Americans were, how one-dimensional their reading of *Red Star*. Heywood Broun, recently turned Catholic and violently anti-Communist, used his position on the Book of the Month Club to blackball *Red Star* as a club selection—or so Snow heard. But that, if true, was a major exception. As unbelievable as it would seem in little more than a decade, reviewers rarely raised the issue of communism. Some short reviews did not even use the words "communism," "Marxism," or "Red," except to quote the title of the book. The emphasis was on the anti-Japanese activities of the Communists, their short-term reforms, and Snow's adventures in getting the story. "The 'Red bandits,' " a *New York Times* reviewer concluded, "bear a close resemblance to the people we used to called patriots." Said the *Milwaukee Journal*: "One cannot help finding a degree of similarity in the faith of these young Chinese Communists and that of primitive Christians." A few reviewers noted that Snow sympathized with the Communists (about as many said flatly that he was an objective reporter) or that he may have been "unduly hard in his assessment of Chiang Kai-shek." Even then their ultimate comment was one of endorsement, as exemplified by Roger S. Greene in the *Worcester Telegram*. Greene worked for years in China, among other things representing the Rockefeller Foundation, and supported Chiang Kai-shek. Although he found "an emotional quality [in Snow's book] which at times arouses suspicion that his capacity for critical appraisal has been somewhat impaired, there is enough confirmation from other sources to convince me at least that his conclusion is essentially sound."[36]

"How Red are the Reds?" journalist John Gunther asked several years later. Citing Snow's interviews with Mao, he answered, "Not very, by our standards." The Communists wanted to nationalize production but that lay in "the remote future. . . . What the Chinese Reds stand for is agrarian reform."

A great divide separated Snow from the Americans he hoped to reach. Although as enthusiastic about an anti-Japanese united front as any American, he perceived the KMT-CCP alliance differently. Americans saw the CCP joining the KMT; Snow saw the KMT joining the CCP. Moreover, he had an entirely different view of domestic reform in China. First, he cared deeply, as Americans did not, that change take place; second, with his belief that unfettered capitalism had undermined democracy in China's treaty ports, he saw socialist revolution as positive. With economic growth on the upswing in the United States, however, American confidence in the capitalist economic system was at its highest point in more than half a century. Some polls showed that Americans, in fact, preferred Fascist to Communist systems of government. It was Fascist aggression that bothered them.[37]

One night sitting in front of a fire with Harry Price, Snow talked glowingly about his trip to Paoan. "Ed, now this is just too idyllic," Price said at last. "It seems impossible."

"Well," Snow replied, "I'm just telling you what I saw."[38]

For all the misunderstanding, *Red Star over China* was a monumental book. Although it had its flaws, those imperfections did not, on balance, gainsay the overall achievement. While much of that achievement rested on Snow's solid factual reporting, much lay in the romantic idealism and partisanship that Price detected. The initiative that Snow displayed in reaching the Communist Northwest came from his craving for adventure and his unwillingness to be strapped down by a job in Peking or Shanghai or by popular convention. His warm sympathy for people allowed him to penetrate in a way that conventional, cynical reporting did not. Chinese really talked to Snow in the soviet. With his intuitive understanding of the motives and aspirations that drove people to struggle against foreign oppression, Snow understood the attraction of communism for Chinese, the key to the CCP's future success. Not preoccupied with Marxist purity himself, Snow recognized that the Chinese Communists were molding Marxism to their own peculiar conditions.

"There are errors of fact in [*Red Star*], and doubtless errors of judgment and analysis," Snow wrote in response to Asiaticus in June 1938, the month the book appeared, "and some of these concern the Soviet Union."[39] Mao and his supporters had tried to use Snow as a vehicle for presenting their views and themselves to the world. As Snow seemed to suspect, he accepted too completely their criticism of the Comintern. Snow did not fully understand the dimensions of the power struggle within the CCP. He too quickly dismissed Mao's rival Wang Ming, mentioning him only once, and then to refer obliquely to Mao's disparaging remarks about him.

Snow had to rely on secondary material, which often could not be trusted. Errors crept into his biographical sketches of Ho Lung and Chu Teh, who were not in the soviet at the time. Yet, Snow effectively used a standard journalism technique to minimize the problem. He devoted a large part of *Red Star* simply to relating, with attribution, what the Communists told him. (Mao's biography, about sixty pages long, was told in the first person.) This did not ensure accuracy, but it saved Snow from presenting unverified material as if it were fact. The reader was warned that he was getting a subjective view. After years of hearing the Nationalist side, the world had a chance to hear the Communist point of view in China.

More significant than the errors Snow made was the fact that he made so few despite the enormous handicaps under which he worked. That he did not make more was a testament to his judgment and cautious journalist instincts and his independence.[40] Snow refused to write his reports in Paoan or let Mao check them over. He was a relentless questioner, meticulous in taking notes, working far into the night to sort out and ponder his material. Snow was also an acute observer and possessed a good eye for telling detail. His observation that Lo Fu, general secretary of the Politburo, had not seen a copy of the Comintern's *Inprecorr* for nearly three years said a great deal more than any policy statements about the day-to-day influence of the Soviet Union in Paoan. Snow discriminated about information and omitted material on the Kiangsi soviet precisely because he had no way of evaluating it. He was leery of Chou En-lai's statistics on the Red Army, writing in his notes that "Red Army commanders, like most Chinese commanders, overstate their numbers." In his writing, Snow expressed skepticism of some CCP claims, speculating that the Communists, despite denials, exploited the peasants during Chiang's fifth extermination campaign. He observed that the Communists used the Long March to the Northwest, which put them in a position to fight the Japanese, as "the biggest armed propaganda tour in history."

"Wherever my personal sympathies may lie," Snow told Ambassador Johnson of his report, "I continue to be from Missouri," the "Show Me" state.

Snow took great pride in the care with which he reported. When a reviewer in the New York *Sun* wondered if Snow accurately calculated the average number of miles the Communists traveled in a day during the Long March, Snow shot back a letter explaining how he arrived at the figure. It was vintage Snow.[41]

Red Star will probably be the greatest book of reporting by an American foreign correspondent in this century. It remains an enduring historical record, a primary source on the early Chinese Communist movement, the lives of Mao, Chou, and other leaders, and the Long March. It stands well ahead of reports by those who came to the soviet after Snow not only because of its accuracy but because of its clear vision of coming events in China: that the Chinese Communists aimed to achieve "a true and complete Socialist State of the Marx-Leninist conception," that they would not surrender their movement to Moscow, and that a social revolution could succeed in China.[42]

"The movement for social revolution in China may suffer defeats, may temporarily retreat, may for a time seem to languish, may make wide changes in tactics to fit immediate necessities and aims, may even for a period be submerged, be forced undergound, but it will not only continue to mature; in one mutation or another it will eventually win, simply because (as this book proves, if it proves anything) the basic conditions which have given it birth carry within themselves the dynamic necessity for its triumph."[43]

"Ed Snow's book," Arch Steele commented years later, "opened a window on the unknown and changed the thinking of millions."[44] Steele was only partly correct. Snow did introduce the Chinese Communists to the world. But he did not change the thinking of millions about the course of events in China. Americans glorified the Chinese Communists without fully understanding the significance of what Snow saw.

As Harrison Smith predicted, Snow broke the "strange taboo" against non-fiction books about China. In the process he became a hybrid, one foot firmly in Missouri and one in Northwest China. But Americans saw Snow at the time as strictly American, a Horatio Alger character. Only thirty-two years old when *Red Star* appeared, Snow was in the next edition of *Who's Who in America*. Widely quoted, emulated, he was a hometown hero.

"Most people lose the romanticism of their younger days and settle down in office or plant," the *Kansas City Star* reported. "Edgar Snow, whose recently published book, 'Red Star Over China,' has attracted favorable reviews throughout the country, has experienced the adventure he once dreamed of when a student at Westport high school and now finds himself a recognized authority on a confusing and complex country."[45]

Scorched Earth

4

Red Star over China's extraordinary popularity surprised Snow. In January 1938, the month it appeared in bookstores, he was covering the Japanese attacks along China's coast. Hearing nothing from Random House, which did not have his address, Snow worried that the publishers had lost interest and delayed publication. He wrote his agent that he didn't expect the book to sell well when it did come out.[1]

Snow's worry was easily explained as the fretting every writer experiences after delivering his manuscript, especially when he is half a world away from those who midwife his labors. Yet, Snow's angst reflected something else, too, something more profound and peculiar to him. Snow deeply desired American acceptance, but not the kind that comes by temporizing one's views. He wanted Americans to see what he saw in China. And everything he knew of United States attitudes suggested the opposite. Americans didn't care deeply about the Far East, let alone embrace his vision of it or of what the U.S. role should be. It did not seem to him that *Red Star*'s popularity, when glimmerings of it reached him, was based on solid footing.

The only response Snow knew was to work harder at explaining himself. Another journalist could have ignored an off-beat letter that appeared in the *Kansas City Star*. Written by a former missionary in China, it reported "huge groves containing as many as forty innocent children murdered in cold blood by the Reds" and criticized *Red Star*'s contention that the Communists were in the anti-Japanese vanguard. Snow wrote a two-page, single-spaced letter to the *Star* editor rebutting the "libel against the Chinese people."[2]

About the same time Snow wrote to Earl Browder, secretary of the American Communist Party. One of the party's complaints, as Snow understood it, was that *Red Star* described the Comintern as a bureau of the Soviet government rather than as the head of the international revolutionary movement. Browder had reason to take the criticism personally. He had worked for the Comintern in China for a time. "You know I am not a Communist," Snow told Browder, whom he had not met personally. "[It] was not expected that I should return with the report of a Comintern delegate." Moreover, Snow added, he could have said far worse things about the Comintern based on the "abundant information" available. The main thing was that internecine squabbles among Communists distracted them from the chief task of fighting fascism. "Good heavens, what is the point of such an attitude, and what role has it in an era of the Popular Front?" Snow asked. "China and the Communist army need all the help and sympathy they can get from every quarter. . . . It is help for China that primarily interests me."[3]

Snow's response was like that of many patriotic Chinese. "The literature of former days," as Lu Hsun wrote, "is like watching a fire from across the water; in present-day literature, the author himself is being scorched by the fire and he is bound to feel it deeply, and when he begins to feel it deeply, he is bound to take part in the social struggle."

Snow's reports on the Chinese Communists were an integral part of that struggle, as the Nationalists were painfully aware. Before 1936, Chinese, like Westerners, knew precious little about the Reds. Many thought that Chu Teh and Mao Tse-tung were one person, Chu Mao. Snow's visit changed the equation in China. Not only did he introduce the Red leaders, he was the first independent reporter to broadcast their anti-Japanese policies. Those policies gave credibility to CCP claims on national leadership. The Communists understood this. They distributed a special pamphlet of Snow's interviews with Mao. Snow realized that his mere presence in the soviet was important to the CCP, giving credence to its claims of being a truly international movement.[4]

Snow defied Nationalist censors by giving copies of his first news dispatches to Chinese professors and writers belonging to the National Salvation Association. These appeared in a Chinese language volume, *Impressions of Northwest China*. After finishing *Red Star* in July 1937, Snow passed a copy of the manuscript to the same group on condition that they give any revenues from their translation, innocuously called *Travels in the West*, to the Chinese Red Cross. Pirated Chinese editions appeared soon after, though the Nationalists did what they could to keep the book out of circulation. (After the 1949 Communist takeover, a Chinese scholar wrote that at last he could read *Red Star over China*.)

Snow supplied maps to young Chinese friends from Yenching who wanted to visit Red China. He found Chinese "in the most unexpected places" with a copy of *Red Star* "tucked under their arms," asking how they could enter one of the Communist schools in the Northwest. During a visit to the Communist-controlled Northwest several years later, impish journalist Israel Epstein routinely asked Chinese, "How did you get here?" Came a typical answer: "I read Snow's book." *Red Star*, as John Fairbank later put it, was "an event in modern Chinese history."

The Nationalists had tried unsuccessfully to discredit Snow's reports on the Communists. They were equally unhappy with his dispatches on Chiang's kidnapping, which related the mutineers' desire for an anti-Japanese united front. The censors butchered Snow's copy, and a government spokesman, T. T. Li, notified him that further "propaganda" would result in unspecified "measures," a thinly veiled threat to withdraw his press privileges. Although Snow expended considerable effort to head off such retaliation, he did so unflinchingly. His reports, he wrote to Li, were accurate and could not harm the Nationalists or China. Rather they helped by promoting accommodation with the Communists. "Quite aside from my tasks as a journalist, I believe that such a settlement could create the basis for a strong, united and effective China, in the very fullest sense of the word." If anything, Snow told Li in a line reminiscent of the one he sent Browder, he had "a rich store of material for 'attacking purpose' " that he had not used.

As Snow implied, he was willing to censor himself for the sake of China. In conversations with Snow, Chou En-lai had criticized Chiang as an inept horseman who did his troops the greatest disservice by going to the front with them. Later as the united front began to take shape, Chou worried that the comments would antagonize the Generalissimo. He sent word through underground channels asking Snow not to include them in *Red Star*. The request angered Snow, who had already incorporated the comments, but he agreed to delete them. *Red Star* was remarkably free of criticism of Chiang, and in spots Snow praised him.

Months after *Red Star* appeared, Snow interviewed Mme. Chiang. She had launched into a half hour tirade against her husband's critics that was so violent Hollington Tong, a Missouri journalism school graduate and the Nationalist government spokesman, could not keep his hands from trembling. Snow thought it would make a good story but agreed not to write it. He did not want to lose her support for an industrial revitalization project he was promoting.[5]

Snow's advocacy of a strong united front was not unique. Anti-Japanese sentiment ran high among people as diverse as pro-Communist Agnes Smedley and pro-Nationalist J.B. Powell, who were close friends during the period. As Powell put it, he preferred "Chinese bandits to those Jap scoundrels." Although longtime foes on nearly everything else, Powell's *China Weekly Review* and the British-owned *North China Daily News* favored the KMT-CCP united front. Reporters commonly held back criticism lest it weaken the alliance.[6]

If Snow was in good company, he nevertheless felt uncomfortable. His position was more complicated. Because he had such extraordinary access to Communist sources, his writing took on more authority. He felt an enormous sense of responsibility. Thus at the same time that he worried about damaging the united front, he felt obliged to convey the nuances of Chinese Communist thinking and policy. While he might leave out points, such as Chiang's horsemanship, which he considered relatively unimportant, he could not skirt issues of real importance. When Snow's interviews of Mao first appeared in the *China Weekly Review*, George Hatem wrote Snow from the Northwest with a request from Mao. In a note at the end of the interviews, Snow had conjectured that the Communists would not abandon the class struggle during a united front with the Nationalists. In the Hatem message, Mao said this was true, but he thought it better not to emphasize the point at the moment. Mao's request notwithstanding, *Red Star*, which appeared later, made clear that class struggle remained an important component of the CCP's thinking.[7]

Snow faced a similar request in 1938 in Hankow. American Communist criticism of *Red Star*, plus evidence that the Chinese Communists may have misled him on some points, troubled Snow. He spent considerable time reevaluating his impressions. In Hankow, he asked Po Ku about *Red Star*'s critical description of the Comintern's role in China. "You were a little too strong in your criticism," Po Ku replied. "Everything you say is true, but the thing is: we don't wish to talk about these things now."[8]

Snow did not heed the advice. Shortly after the conversation he wrote a brief update to *Red Star* and used the opportunity to make a few revisions to original portions of the text. Among other things, he took the edge off Mao's criticism of Wang Ming. Instead of describing Wang's reports on the CCP, written from Russia, as "astounding," Snow said Wang "must have found it very difficult at times to get accurate information even on the location of the main forces of the Red Army for his reports to the Comintern." Snow toned down some criticism of Otto Braun and of the Comintern for CCP setbacks.[9]

To Snow's critics these changes later became proof that he knuckled under to Soviet pressure. There is no doubt Communist criticism was on his mind. In his letter to Browder, he said he "voluntarily" excised some of the offending passages in *Red Star*—"sentences which I thought might be offensive to the party." Yet, whatever he may have said to curb Browder's criticism, a close reading of the revisions shows that Snow refined his points, not obscured them. If anything, they were more troublesome to Communists in and outside China. Snow still described the Chinese Communists as authentic social revolutionaries. The Comintern was still "responsible for serious reverses suffered by the Chinese Communists in the anguish of their growth." Snow did not alter his statement that "*the Soviet movement and the Chinese Red army began spontaneously, under purely Chinese leadership.*" As much as he wanted to ameliorate intra-Communist differences, the revised edition said that "the Chinese Communist movement was now aided only by a Comintern which could no longer command the vast resources of the 'base of the world revolution,' but had to limp along as a kind of poor stepchild which might be officially disinherited whenever it did anything malaprop." As such, the revisions did not make the book any more acceptable to Communists in the Soviet Union or the United States than it was before. Snow had reason to think it displeased the Chinese Communists, on whose doorstep he more clearly laid blame for past failures.[10]

The prevailing united front spirit entangled Snow in the publication of a new magazine dedicated to advance China's cause. The idea to start the magazine came from J. Spencer Kennard. A Left-leaning Baptist missionary, Kennard had published *Christian Graphic* in Japan until the military govern nent suppressed it. With one thousand dollars from the Friends Service Committee, Kennard hoped to start again in China and asked the Snows if they would edit his "journal of applied Christian ethics."[11]

With his regular duties for the London *Daily Herald*, his rush to finish *Red Star*, and the demands for magazine articles, Snow was already busier than he wanted to be. Peg, always the crusader and hungry for a pulpit, was eager to undertake the job, however, and dragged her husband with her—after a fashion. She would get the enterprise under way; he would be *an* editor as long as that meant his only responsibility was to write occasional articles. Others had to help with editorial chores and additional money.

The Snows assembled an editorial board, representing a wide range of opinion, and hired as managing editor John Leaning. A young Englishman who wore turtleneck sweaters and sported a long cigarette holder, Leaning had been secretary for Labour MP Hugh Dalton before starting a casual world tour that brought him to China. His main qualifications were that he had some journalism experience, he was not otherwise occupied, and he was willing to work in exchange for room and board in the cheap quarters the magazine rented.

The editorial board found plenty to disagree over. Long arguments broke out in the very first meeting. Peg did not help things by flooding the room with ideas: Why not have the magazine read from right to left, Chinese style? Why not eschew capital letters on the cover, where articles and by-lines were listed? Acceptance of the latter idea led E. T. Shaw, a principal at one of the local schools, to resign. He did not come to China, he said, to teach bad punctuation to the Chinese. Others soon followed. For his part, Leaning didn't want to call the magazine a "journal of applied Christian ethics." He eventually barred Kennard from his quarters and refused to publish any of his articles. Their disagreement caused such acrimony that the night the first edition was laid out, Peg broke down in tears. Snow, more involved with the publication than originally agreed, was probably just as glad he was in the hospital for a kidney stone operation.

The one thing everyone eventually agreed on was the basic mission of the biweekly, to keep the idea of democracy alive in China. In concrete terms, that meant opposing fascism and supporting "freedom of expression," as *democracy* pledged in its first issue.[12]

Snow commented in one of the initial meetings that the magazine would "champion lost causes." And J. B. Powell, an enthusiastic supporter, thought the odds were against the magazine succeeding. He expected *democracy*'s troubles to emanate from Bolsheviks and Fascists, but the Nationalists proved to be the major obstacle, at first. Chinese law required periodicals like *democracy* to have a Chinese guarantor, and the police looked for excuses to turn down each Chinese backer the editors presented. J. Leighton Stuart, the pro-Nationalist President of Yenching, could not persuade the police that the money to start *democracy* did not come from "the land of the hammer and sickle," as one board member put it. When the editors finally found impeccable backers—some Chinese bankers—their troubles were not over.

The maiden issue appeared with a large blank spot where censors deleted a picture of Mao that was to accompany an article by Snow. The KMT Department of Publicity subsequently informed two Chinese members of *democracy*'s board that the magazine "gives decided prominence to materials favorable to the Communist Party and to the Popular Front. This is highly inappropriate. From now on it is important that the press law be strictly observed." Subsequent issues carried articles, such as one by Chou En-lai, presenting Communist points of view, but pro-Nationalist pieces appeared too. Stuart wrote "General Chiang Kai-shek—An Appreciation"; another piece criticized Communist theory on democratic freedom. Nevertheless, a Nanking bookstore wrote to the *democracy* in June that it was unable to accept more copies of the magazine. The government forbade it to sell the periodical. Meanwhile, the Western-controlled Shanghai Municipal Police Department included Snow's involvement with the magazine in the dossier they maintained on him.[13]

Democracy's editors took solace in the magazine's wide appeal among English-speaking Chinese. Sun Fo, president of the Legislative Yuan in Nanking, and the mayor of Peking, not a member of the KMT, praised it. English- and Chinese-language periodicals reprinted its articles. But any hope of survival ended with Japanese occupation of Peking in July. The sixth edition of *democracy* never left the Chinese printers, whose presses were destroyed. In late August, a notice went out announcing the death of the journal and directing subscribers to write for refunds.

When the Japanese attacked Peking in July, Snow joined other members of the foreign community in aiding the Chinese. The Japanese made house-to-house searches, imprisoning people with modern books. Students buried volumes in Snow's courtyard. Manchurians put a shortwave radio station in his house, which quickly filled with Chinese on the Japanese blacklist. He helped some leave the city disguised as beggars, coolies, and peddlers. Others simply climbed over the city wall, which abutted his garden. He helped a guerrilla unit fence jewels looted from an imperial temple on condition they release several Italian friars they held for ransom. Ransoming friars, Snow counseled, would generate bad international publicity for the guerrillas. Snow wrote "a devastating analysis of the mistakes the Chinese command" made and how the Communists would have reacted. He showed the story to Jim Bertram but, not wanting to create friction among China's forces, did not publish it.[14]

Snow expected the Japanese to raid him any day. Peg's absence compounded his anxiety. In late 1937 the Communists had moved their capital to Yenan, nearer Sian, and with the easing in KMT-CCP relations, other journalists began to make visits to Red headquarters. Peg, stymied in her attempt to reach Paoan when her husband was there, tried again in April, accompanied to Sian by the young Communist David Yu. The Nationalists did not appreciate Western reporters likening Yenan to a "Boy Scout summer camp," as United Press reporter Earl Leaf did—even if the reporter sympathized with the Nationalists.

(Leaf later became a publicity agent for the Nationalist government.) But although police in Sian did their best to prevent Peg from making the trip, she jumped out of her second-story window at the Sian Guest House one night and took a private car to the Red capital.[15]

In notes to her husband, Peg wrote that she was ill with dysentery. Snow worried about her general safety. He considered going to Yenan with a small party, Owen Lattimore, T. A. Bisson, and Philip Jaffe and his wife. Jaffe, who made a fortune in the greeting card business, was managing editor of a new magazine called *Amerasia*. Lattimore and Bisson served on the editorial board. Snow tried to help the group make contact with Red Army leaders in Sian. Although he decided against making the trip himself, he asked Jaffe and the others to take supplies to Peg. By the time the Jaffe group, joined by a Scandinavian driver, arrived in mid-June, Peg had overstayed her visit by almost a month. She wanted to leave with Jaffe, who spent three days in the soviet. His 1924 Chevrolet was already crowded, however. And the party feared the presence of a new American face in their midst might alert border guards, whose vigilance was increasing. Peg decided to return with the next Red army truck. Unfortunately, a truck was not to leave soon. Heavy rains, lasting through July and August, washed out roads.

Snow lamented to friends that he missed his wife, something that seemed remarkable to many. Peking raised gossip to an art form, and one standard item was "how [Snow] could get along with Peg because she talked so much," recalled Ida Pruitt, a member of the *democracy* board and a social worker at the Peking Medical College. Although Snow was nearly universally liked, Peg was so shrill and critical that many acquaintances didn't socialize with the couple. Some friends thought that Peg seemed in competition with her husband. Years later, she reflected on their different personalities: "Once [Ed] said to me, 'Why do you criticize me? I never criticize you.' I was dumbfounded to realize this was true." Despite these differences, they shared similar views on China and a common sense of enterprise. Helen Snow's books were to become an important source on the period. Their marriage, though without much obvious affection, provided a solid base in an uncertain world.[16]

As Peg's absence stretched out, punctuated by hit-and-miss correspondence filled with commands and reprimands, he eventually became petulant himself. "You [are] always leaving by the next bus. Endless people ask when you're coming back, as everyone knows where you are. I should also like to know if you do not intend to return for some weeks or months so that I won't be worrying."

Peg's answer finally came, as the rain ended, via radio message. Though garbled, Snow could make out the words, "All right. Best you come here." Snow decided to get Peg and go on to Shanghai, where the London *Daily Herald* wanted him to cover the fighting.[17]

Before leaving, Snow undertook another mission to help endangered Chinese friends. Five months earlier Teng Ying-ch'ao, Chou En-lai's wife, had come to a temple outside Peking to recuperate from tuberculosis. When the Japanese attacked, she hid in the city at the home of Hsu Ping, the professor who had delivered the invisible ink letter inviting Snow to visit the Chinese Communists. Teng as well as Hsu's wife wanted to escape from Peking. Snow agreed to help them reach the port city of Tientsin.

Recollections of the episode varied in later years. Ida Pruitt recalled that the escapees whom Snow helped included a Red general hiding in her home. Neither Snow nor Jim Bertram, who accompanied Snow, ever mentioned the general. Mme. Chou later protested Snow's description of her disguise as that of a servant. In any event, the broad outlines of the story are clear enough: The escape was both uncomfortable and dangerous.

In early September Snow, Bertram, and their Red companions went to the Peking train station. The train they boarded was one of the first in several weeks to leave and the entire city seemed intent on cramming itself on the cars, which reeked of stale air. Snow found a place on the last step of the last car; Bertram balanced himself on the railing and waved to Pruitt as the train lurched out of the station.

With frequent stops to let Japanese troop trains pass, the normal two-hour trip to Tientsin took fourteen. En route Snow ran into John Service on the train. Snow confided that he would be in serious trouble if the identities of his entourage were discovered. His concern mounted when he pulled into the heavily bombed city of Tientsin that evening. Hawk-eyed Japanese sentries patrolled a several hundred yard stretch that lay between the station platform and the British concession. Soldiers yanked a dozen young Chinese from the train, heading them off to military trucks. One sullen guard examined Mme. Chou's straw luggage, spilling the contents on the ground before allowing the party to cross the barbed wire barrier.

After seeing their Communist charges safely on their way, Snow and Bertram decided to take a steamer south from Tientsin. Before leaving, Snow advised Peg by radiogram to leave immediately for the port of Tsingtao while she still could. A series of miscues followed. Snow and Bertram did not find Peg in Tsingtao and took the train to Sian hoping she had come at least that far. They arrived to find that she had left a few hours earlier on the Green Express. Anxious to reunite Snow with his wife and get him out of town, the Sian police telephoned down the line. Four gendarmes pulled her off the train and put her on a train back to Sian. Snow, his wife, and Bertram stayed up far into the night drinking and talking.

Bertram decided to head into Red China, which he had not yet seen. Smedley, who came back from Yenan with Peg, decided to go back. After thinking about joining them, the Snows headed back to the coast. Along the way they saw the Green Express, which Peg had taken out of Sian, wrecked beside the track. Shortly after she got off, the Japanese had bombed the train, killing a number of passengers.

In Tsingtao the Snows had the city to themselves. The war had driven tourists away. The couple spent two weeks visiting the German forts, strolling in rented swimming suits alone along the white beach, and consuming ice cream. They decided that Peg, still ill, would rest, close down their house in Peking, and rejoin her husband in Shanghai when it was safe.

Snow left on October 9 and arrived in Shanghai as Chinese troops launched a major offensive. "Shrapnel sprayed all round me to-night on the Bund as two squadrons of Chinese planes flew overhead to answer a Japanese raid in which at least 60 tons of bombs had been dropped," read his first dispatch. "One bit struck a door beside which I was standing."[18]

The fighting in Shanghai had begun in early August, with Japanese terror bombs creating awful carnage. J. B. Powell actually saw blood run in the gutters. Though a latecomer among the reporters who flocked to the story, Snow expected to see plenty of action—and he did while the fierce fighting lasted. But he badly misjudged how long the Chinese could resist. He reported in early November that Japan had "lost the chance . . . of a speedy victory"; the fighting had entered a "phase of slow trench warfare and heavy bombardment. This is likely to drag on for some time." Four days later he wrote the battle's epitaph: "China's commanders rang the curtain down at 1 A.M. to-day on an 88-day struggle that has cost their army 125,000 casualties."

On the last day of fighting Snow perched himself on a flimsy balcony in the French Concession, just fifty feet from Chinese territory. With a group of cameramen he saw Japanese troops, maneuvering behind tanks and a wall of aerial and artillery fire, push back the Chinese lines. After lunch Snow, the cameramen, Malcolm MacDonald of the London *Times*, and Marine Major Evans Carlson, now a military attaché in Shanghai, caught up with the shifting front. This time their vantage point was the platform of a French power plant. When Japanese machine gun fire rattled against a tower they were just about to climb, the group took cover behind a concrete wall. They came out to find blood dripping down from the tower. Snow watched Chinese troops, whose retreat had been cut off, clamber over barbed wire into the French Concession. Carlson ascended the ladder to the tower. He returned with the body of Pembroke Stephens, a *Daily Telegraph* correspondent, shot through the head.

London *Daily Express* correspondent O. D. Gallagher, feeling he could not scoop a colleague on his own obituary, sent his dispatch to Stephens's paper. That night Snow and Carlson opened a bottle of Napoleon brandy sent over by Mme. Sun, who was cleaning out her cellar before evacuating the city. They drank a toast to Pembroke, the only correspondent killed in the fighting. Not long afterward Snow took out a five thousand dollar life insurance policy.

In December Japan's superior fire power overwhelmed Nanking. But China did not fall. The government and the people began to retreat into the vast hinterland, leaving the scorched earth behind. "Look at the map and note the smallness of Japan compared to China," Chiang told Snow shortly after the war began. "Can anyone doubt that we shall triumph?"[19]

A new spirit of Chinese unity, regarded as a near miracle among many Western observers, provided the greatest hope that Japan would choke on the grandiosity of its ambitions. "Today," Mme. Sun proclaimed in a message she gave to Snow before secretly leaving Shanghai, "the Chinese people [are] more united than ever before to cooperate in the cause of world peace, the betterment of the social and economic order and against Fascism and war."

Throughout China pictures of Mao Tse-tung and Chu Teh hung alongside those of Chiang and Sun Yat-sen. In the new capital, Hankow, about six hundred miles inland on the Yangtze, Chou En-lai served on the Presidium of the Extraordinary National Congress of the KMT and was Vice-Minister of the Political Department of the National Military Council. Of the two hundred members of the People's Political Council, thirty were members of the CCP and other small parties. Communists freely published their organs, with KMT financial help, some thought.

Military successes followed. In 1937 Communist units, renamed with united front titles, killed, wounded, or captured more than four thousand crack Japanese troops in Pinghsingkwan Pass along a southern loop of the Great Wall and knocked out twenty-one Japanese planes at an airfield far behind enemy lines. In Hopei and Shansi, Communist-trained self-defense armies wiped out thirty-six small enemy garrisons in the space of four months.

Chiang, Snow wrote in the *Saturday Evening Post*, was using Chinese Communist tactics. Aggressive at last, he burned Japanese mills and factories in Tsingtao, "marking a new chapter in the war between China and Japan," Snow reported. Using mobile tactics, his troops delivered a humiliating blow to the Japanese at Taierchwang in April. It took the Japanese two months to recover.

Evans Carlson was impressed by the intense "work together" patriotism he saw in the defense of Shanghai, a sentiment summed up in the phrase "gung ho." After reading a draft of *Red Star*, he wanted to see for himself how the Red Army fought so successfully. Snow arranged permission from Mao. In a united front mood, Carlson's superiors and Chiang Kai-shek agreed to let him go. Later, after United States entry into the war, Carlson introduced Red tactics—as well as the term gung ho—into a special Marine Corps raider battalion.[20]

"On that vast stage, here between the rivers and mountains and in the plains and valleys of China," Snow wrote in a fifty-page update of *Red Star* that appeared in 1938, "Japan may meet not simply a great army in uniform but a foe made up of a whole people, scores of millions of men, women, and children, who are being prepared to resist, for as many years as necessary, in a revolutionary crusade for their homes, their freedom and their future."[21]

Inspired by these events, Snow sounded remarkably like Ambassador Johnson, who called Chiang Kai-shek the "living symbol of unity." Having thrown aside all pretense of conciliating Japan, Chiang was at last a national leader. He still considered the Generalissimo unexceptional intellectually, militarily, and administratively. Yet, in this mediocrity, Snow saw virtue. Instinctively seeking the mean, Chiang moved with progressive forces at large in the country. "Radical changes will be made peacefully by Chiang, and by the army and the government that he symbolizes as 'Tsung Tsai,' " or General Planner, Snow predicted in an article for *Foreign Affairs* entitled "China's Fighting Generalissimo." "That in turn implies more political liberty, democratic training and enfranchisement for the people; the completion of long-deferred anti-feudal agrarian reforms; the integration of the peasantry's mass power in political, economic and military organization; and consequent deep social changes everywhere."[22]

For all his positive feelings, Snow had a daily reminder of the difficulties China faced.[23] The window in his little office atop a midtown Shanghai building looked out on a depressing scene. Shanghai, home for 70 percent of China's industrial capacity, lay in mile after mile of smoldering ashes. Some eight hundred thousand Shanghai workers were jobless. Over half a million slept in the streets where Snow often walked with New Zealander Rewi Alley, the Shanghai Municipal Factory Inspector whom he first met during the 1929 famine. Lucky Chinese found places in refugee camps, five hundred in a hut, each family on one of the shelves stacked three tiers high. Deaths in these camps averaged two hundred a day. Snow saw sixty corpses hauled out of one camp during a single visit. When food shortages became especially acute Snow and Alley dropped steamed bread to starving Chinese from the top of a building in the French Concession.

In the ashes and despair, Snow saw the end of the old Western-run treaty port system. "The severance of Shanghai," financier T. V. Soong told Snow before the fighting ended, "would necessitate the organizing of a new type of economic base in the interior and modeling trade of the country on a radically different pattern." The question that Alley and Snow pondered over drinks in the evening was just what kind of organization could produce desperately needed new sources of cloth, chemicals, soya sauce, alcohol, paper, tobacco, machines, iron, matches, scientific instruments, rubber shoes, glass, and flour. When Peg arrived, in time to see the Japanese victory parade, an idea began to take shape for helping develop such a new economic base in China.

At a dinner party given by John and Stella Alexander the conversation turned to the economic causes of wars. Alexander, a British diplomat, argued zealously that a world of cooperatives could provide the framework for international peace. Cooperatives, he said, "are a democratic base in any kind of society—capitalist, socialist, communist, or what have you. There's no argument against them, for anything can be built on such a base."[24]

After turning the idea over in her mind, Peg agreed that cooperatives might provide work for displaced Chinese and give a big boost to the war effort. She began to prod. Although her husband did not agree as quickly as she wanted him to, the idea appealed enormously to his populist instincts—and squared with his past experience. Five years before, Snow had enthusiastically reported on a mass education program in Hopei province that combined many elements of cooperative self-government. He saw successful cooperatives in the Communist Northwest in 1936. The benefits of behind-the-lines industrial organizations, he eventually agreed, could be enormous. They could provide badly needed work, products to help in the war effort, and a chance for Chinese workers to manage their own organizations. Alley, whom Peg met on her first Sunday back in Shanghai, liked the idea too. Soon a handful of others, among them Alexander, former Yenching journalism professor Hubert Liang, and Chinese banker Hsu Hsing-lo, began to talk seriously about the "establishment of rural, industrial and consumer cooperatives." At the first formal meeting in the Snows' apartment on Bubbling Well Road, they agreed that "no one would be better suited" to lead the movement than Alley.

Such a project did call for someone like Alley. A rugged man who could crack walnuts between his thumb and forefinger, he came to China after fighting in World War I. He fell in love with the Chinese and, though a bachelor, adopted two Chinese orphans. With nearly boundless determination he sought to make Chinese factories safe. He readily accepted the challenge of starting cooperatives and drew up a plan that envisioned three wide bands of industrial cooperatives arrayed behind friendly lines, with the most mobile factories closest to the front and mines and heavy industry in areas farthest from the fighting. Snow named the enterprises the Chinese Industrial Cooperatives, which was often shortened to "Indusco," Alley's cable address. The Indusco slogan, like Carlson's, was "gung ho."

J. B. Powell, Randall Gould, and H. J. Timperley, an Australian reporting for the *Manchester Guardian*, occasionally sat in planning meetings and offered to help build public support for the scheme. The principal responsibility for that fell on Snow, chairman of the Membership and Propaganda Subcommittee. It was an enormous task. Despite their enthusiasm, the founders found little real interest or support from potential funding organizations or from the Nationalist government, whose approval was indispensable. They sent an early version of their plan to Chiang Kai-shek's military affairs commission, where it languished. As one of his first jobs Snow wrote a booklet, "The People Strike Back! Or the Story of Chinese Industrial Cooperatives." He and Alley paid for the printing in English and Chinese. When the booklet appeared in June, Indusco had acquired only a small contribution from French trade unions and still needed the government's approval.

With the arrival of a new British ambassador, Sir Archibald Clark-Kerr, Snow found a key ally. The ambassador had a reputation for disdaining Americans but was keenly interested in *Red Star*. Snow was one of the people he wanted to meet first in Shanghai. Snow liked Clark-Kerr's interest in picking nongovernment brains, his committed antifascism, and his call-me-Archie informality. Not only did Sir Archibald learn about Indusco from the Snows and John Alexander on his own staff, but from two house guests, Christopher Isherwood and W. H. Auden, who were gathering material for a book and toured the city with Alley. "China," they concluded in their narrative, "requires 30,000 industrial cooperatives." When Snow asked for help winning support from the Hankow government, the ambassador took the case directly to Mme. Chiang, who extracted grudging agreement from her sister and her husband, H. H. Kung, who was to oversee Indusco. Formal government approval materialized on August 5, though it quickly became clear that real support was not near at hand.

By that time, Snow was in Hankow, living in a two-room flat in the Navy YMCA, the center for newspaper reporters. The city was not a happy place. Frequent air raids and blistering heat contributed to the sense of doom among "last ditchers," those who stayed. Snow discovered that some foreign businessmen hoped for a Japanese victory. They expected the Japanese to "open up the river, they understand business, and we can deal with them," one man told Snow at a business luncheon. "The best thing is that law and order will be restored again. They will put an end to this Red business once and for all." The Generalissimo seemed as unrealistic as businessmen. "Japan," he told Snow in an interview, "has already suffered a spiritual defeat. Without the necessary spiritual foundations, military operations cannot succeed. Because her spiritual concepts are incorrect, Japan cannot win." Chiang's attitude seemed to explain the Nationalists' halfhearted interest in Indusco.[25]

Snow's enthusiasm for Chiang's mediocrity vanished as quickly as it had risen. Rather than drift toward the center of dynamic forces in the country, as Snow originally hoped, Chiang floundered in the backwash. On the same day Snow sent Ambassador Johnson his recently published *Saturday Evening Post* article praising Chiang, he confessed, "I am somewhat less optimistic about the future after a brief spot survey here, but I believe the possibilities in general remain the same."[26]

Snow's letter prompted an exchange of correspondence with Johnson revealing the sharp differences between Snow and American foreign policy makers generally. Despite early Chinese victories, Johnson replied, China would never put up an active resistance but a passive one. Ideas for mobilizing resistance simply did not work in a country "organized as China has been for the last thousand or so years." Johnson was willing to go along with Chiang and "vent out disappointments upon the bacon in the morning and try to report the results, with as little rancor as possible." Snow, much more of an activist, was not. His Indusco plans, he rejoined, "cannot be carried out by a Government organized as the present one is, and as China has been for the last thousand years or so. But I do not rule out the possibility of change, and of swift change in a situation moving at such a pace as the present one."

The Communists still seemed to be masters of that change. Snow visited Chou En-lai and his wife in their comfortable Hankow home and spent part of two days talking with Po Ku on Chou's staff. Revealing frays in the united front, Po said that CCP activity was difficult in Kiangsi, Kweichow, and Shensi. "Conditions were also bad in Kwangsi, but at least Red leaders were not being arrested." Although the Nationalists held political power, the bouncy Red envoy said the Communists possessed national leadership "from a tactical point of view."[27]

This claim rested on the same foundation as before. While the Nationalists squandered Chinese patriotism, the Communists actively recruited soldiers and workers to go into the interior to resist the Japanese. Even foreign Communists in Hankow seemed more patriotic than the Kuomintang. One of these was Wataru Kaji, whom Snow met over chocolate nut sundaes at the YMCA. A Japanese Communist who translated Lu Hsun's works, Wataru wrote anti-Japanese propaganda despite attempts on his life in Hankow. Korean and Japanese Communists assured Snow "they could easily raise a division in China, if given proper facilities and cooperation by the Chinese government."

The defense of Wuhan, as Hankow and its two adjacent sister cities were collectively called, seemed to highlight the differences between the Communists and the Nationalists. It was commonly understood that the fall of Wuhan was just a matter of time. One of Alley's first jobs was to help move the city's industry upriver, out of reach of the Japanese. Yet, Wuhan hung on longer than anyone expected. United Press offered Mac Fisher two hundred dollars a month if he would stay in Wuhan to the end. The salary was extravagant by wire service standards, but UP editors expected Fisher wouldn't be in the city for more than three or four weeks. Fisher stayed some six months. The Communists took advantage of the situation. Noting how workers in Spain valiantly defended Madrid from Franco for two years, they urged the government to "defend Wuhan to the death." Threatened by the vision of armed workers, students, and other citizens potentially under the control of the Communists, the Nationalists rejected the scheme. In late August, they broke up the Wuhan Defense Committee and temporarily halted publication of a pro-defense Communist periodical.[28]

"If the city masses in Wuhan and Changsha were organized, trained and armed, and if the 20,000,000 people in the environs of these cities were similarly mobilized," Snow wrote to Powell, "there is no doubt in my mind that the Japanese could not take Wuhan—which, properly defended, is virtually impregnable."

Han Ying, whom Snow interviewed in Hankow, exemplified this fighting spirit. The rough, gap-toothed general was field commander of the New Fourth Army, made up largely of troops that served as the rear guard for the Communist columns that escaped from Kiangsi in

1934. Unable to catch up with their brothers, Han's troops had regrouped, survived additional Nationalist attacks, and eventually joined the united front. By mid-1938 Han was building local village defense forces in the demoralized countryside around Japanese-occupied cities in Anhwei and Kiangsi. The unpretentious Han showed interest in Indusco's cooperatives and complained that the Nationalists did not adequately support his army, which swelled with patriotic peasants. Han Ying "was one of the few bright spots of my trip . . . a real army man, not a politician," Snow wrote to Peg when he returned to Hongkong.[29]

With Japan having gained control of so much of China, British-run Hongkong had become a logical place for international fund-raising activities on behalf of the Chinese. Mme. Sun headquartered her China Defense League, for which Snow helped raise funds, in Hongkong. On this stay he collected money, shoes, and medical supplies for Han's force and arranged a behind-the-scenes loan for Indusco from T. V. Soong, head of the Bank of China and one of the people with Nationalist connections Snow still liked. The loan, meant to demonstrate strong outside support for the cooperatives, helped convince H. H. Kung to release promised government funds.

Snow abandoned the idea of returning to Kiangsi with Han to see his troops in action. For one thing, he needed a rest. He suffered from stomach pains and had been unable to eat or sleep. For another, he worried that Peg would be "utterly disgusted" with his constantly shifting plans. Although he had turned his London *Daily Herald* chores over to Powell to give himself more time, Snow was far behind on magazine writing and a planned book. In September, after Peg joined him, he checked out of the Repulse Bay Hotel bound for Manila.[30]

The balmy Philippines offered relaxation and easy socializing. The *Manila Bulletin* had strong Missouri ties. A *Bulletin* editor and his wife greeted the Snows at Manila harbor and whisked them to their hotel. That night Peg, pinned into a Filipino costume, and her husband, wearing a native pineapple gauze shirt, went to Malacañan Palace where President Manuel Quezon was entertaining. Ed Snow was often the center of attention at such functions and, as usual, quickly made friends. Learning that the Snows were without much money, William and Polly Babcock took them into their home. Will Babcock was a import-exporter who had come to the islands thirty years before to teach. His home, once residence for the commander of the American occupation force, offered an especially comfortable retreat. Servants skated over the floors daily on coconut hemispheres, polishing the nara wood to a high gloss. The windows, framed by shutters made of sea shells, looked out on a large quiet garden shaded by banyan trees. Not long afterward the Snows moved to Baguio, the Philippines' cool, summer capital, staying with the Babcocks when in Manila.[31]

Amid Baguio's pine forested mountains, Snow wrote a poem musing on local Igorots, only recently headhunters. "Igorot Mutation," not-too-good verse, showed his mind and his heart were never far from the "avalanche of horror" he saw engulfing the world:

> But if this wild man in a single infloration
> can share in all that we aspire to be,
> what traffic law can designate
> one-way mutation down the road of time,
> what mind prevent a counter-change
> excepting unremitting change itself?
>
> Once yield the child of culture back
> to tribal witchery—a Fuehrer or a Duce,
> a Son of Heaven or a Falingista Chief–
> and in that same swift, single generation
> they'll render him a homicide again,
> with barbarous heart, and call it "Aryan Soul."

Rather than abating, Snow's fears of Japanese aggression mounted in the Philippines. His heightened anxiety prompted him to reevaluate his early view that the United States should withdraw from Asia. In keeping with his increasing activism, he called for direct intervention.

Snow met General Douglas MacArthur at a Manila dinner party given by the American High Commissioner, Paul V. McNutt. Formerly U.S. Army Chief of Staff, MacArthur now served as a Philippines military advisor, a job he got when, in a five-minute interview with President Quezon, he said the islands were defensible. MacArthur told Snow he would train 400,000 soldiers by 1940 and by 1960 military reserves would exceed 1,200,000 men. At any time in the interim Philippine forces could hold off an invading enemy until American forces arrived.[32]

As Snow saw it, the invasion had already begun. The Japanese had their eye on the islands' oil, nickel, rubber, copra, hemp, tobacco, gold, rice, iron, and timber. By Snow's reckoning thirty thousand Japanese had arrived. Japanese propagandists bombarded the people with visions of brotherly love between oriental races, while nearly one hundred Japanese corporations laid siege to plantations in Davao, Mindanao, which was fast becoming a Japanese fiefdom. Interviews with Filipino businessmen, journalists, doctors, lawyers, professors, housewives, and miners revealed a deepening dread of Japanese encroachment. Many, like an Igorot doctor in Baguio learning to speak Japanese, were preparing for greater Japanese control. With Will Babcock acting as translator, Snow interviewed General Emilio Aguinaldo, leader of the guerrilla uprising against the Spanish and American forces forty years before. The "marvelous" old general expressed faith in Japan's good will but was critical of Japanese actions in China. He asked Snow not to publish his anti-Japanese remarks.

Total United States withdrawal from the islands, scheduled for 1946, only hastened the process by which Japan remade the Philippines as it had Formosa and Manchuria, Snow thought. The Philippines needed markets for their raw materials, especially sugar. After independence its exports could no longer enter the United States duty free and therefore could not compete with American domestic and Cuban sugar. The only alternative was for Filipinos to seek the fatal embrace of Japanese fascism. "Every day that brings nearer Uncle Samuel's farewell to the Philippines," Snow wrote, "hastens the approach of Master Samurai."

Despite MacArthur's cocky assurances, Snow thought Japanese military aggression would "provide some rude shocks for the American people." Japan could launch a surprise attack, possibly in China. Some American ships might survive, dashing successfully back to Manila. While they huddled there, the Japanese would attack America's only fortifications on the island, at Corregidor. Corregidor's antiquated armaments could not withstand the assault. "It is doubtful if our main forces could penetrate the ring of highly fortified Japanese islands—the Marianas, the Carolines, the Marshalls, and Palaus—to aid Manila sufficiently to save the Philippines from falling to Japan." The U.S. Congress, Snow argued, had erred gravely when it voted down an appropriation, recommended by a special naval board, to upgrade the harbor and air base in Guam, a strategically located advance base. "Such a war would be incalculably more costly, a few years hence, than the price of a showdown at present."

Snow believed that American imperialism abetted this cultural, economic, and military threat to the Philippines. By seeking its own special privileges in Asia, the United States gave legitimacy to imperialism by other powers and contributed to the prolonged weakness of countries like the Philippines. Even so, American imperialism was far better than anything Japan would provide. Americans, as he saw it, had at least "liquidated a good deal of feudalism" existing under wretched Spanish rule. They improved education levels, even for the headhunting Igorot tribespeople, so that over half the islanders could read and write; built roads, hospitals, and public utilities; and taught democratic self-governance. Having stayed so long, there was only one proper American course of action: "continued American union with the Philippines, military, economic and political. Not dissolubly so, but until such time as the Filipinos are capable of successfully manning their own inner defenses alone."

Snow similarly revised his views on U.S. involvement in China. In early 1936, before he had gone to Paoan, he counseled that the best way to help China was to disengage, relinquish hoary unequal treaty rights, and "recognize China on a basis of full equality," that is as a country capable of taking its place among the family of nations. Americans selling "Chiang Kai-shek millions of dollars worth of munitions, airplanes and other materials of war every month" should be told they did so "at their own risk." Said Snow: "We cannot determine China's self-determination. Nobody can do that but the Chinese." In mid-1938 he remained less concerned with aiding China than with simply ending sales to Japan of scrap iron, steel, and oil, which appalled him. "An isolated China," he wrote during the first flush of the united front, "can defeat an isolated Japan."[33]

Now in the Philippines, Snow changed his mind. Although Americans should still renounce unequal treaties, he said, Japanese aggression had progressed too far for that by itself to make a difference. For the sake of their self-defense and their honor, Americans needed to bolster China with economic aid. "Prestige and self-respect," Snow told the readers of the *Saturday Evening Post*, "prevent us from handing Chinese sovereignty to the Japanese."

Snow worked hard in the Philippines to help China. Within the first weeks of arriving, he raised funds for the Chinese Defense League and the New Fourth Army. He helped start a Philippine Association for Industrial Cooperatives, which found strong financial support among local Chinese. He and Peg recruited Indusco supporters in Baguio, including the tiny but redoubtable Natalie Crouter, whose fund-raising parties became prestigious social events.[34]

Despite these successes, the experience was frustrating. The Japanese envoy tried to stop Snow from speaking on Indusco at the Teatro Nacionale in Manila. The American High Commissioner, whose wife chaired the Philippine Association for Industrial Cooperatives, successfully intervened. Other attacks were more difficult to fend off. Efforts to keep Indusco nonpartisan made it a target from all sides. The Left complained that Indusco aided the Nationalists; the Nationalists regarded Indusco as Leftist, if not "Red." Accordingly, Snow was asked, on the one hand, to raise money and, on the other, was criticized for being too visible and for giving Indusco a Communist image—unfair charges because he drew almost no attention to his own role in the movement and because he promoted Nationalist involvement.

Snow had barely set foot in the Philippines when Alley swamped him with woeful and slightly recriminating letters. "Sorry you are fed up with the show," wrote Alley only a couple of weeks after Snow arrived. "Of course, we should have an International Section and no one can do it except you." A week later: "You can't leave stillborn babies around." Soong's Bank of China, Alley wrote several days after that, would not give the entire loan unless Snow vouched for him "by formal resolution. You see, whether you will it or not, you are in this thing."

From his quarters at the Baguio Country Club, Snow vented his own irritation. "I've written you over a dozen letters. I get replies to about one out of two telegrams. This is hopeless," he scolded Alley, who shared Snow's casual attitude toward punctuality. Snow agreed that establishment of an international committee was critical to developing needed support. All the same he thought he couldn't afford to do much more. "I have not made a cent since I've been here, and have been living on my savings, which are rapidly dwindling," Snow wrote to his agent in March.

Nevertheless he was back in Hongkong the next month helping start the international promotion committee, of which Mme. Sun became president. The job dragged on for three months, with only bits of time for writing.

Besides being tired, Snow was homesick, as usual. And he felt a growing sense of dread about the approach of general war. His own existence, he realized, was becoming perilous. A few months before, he had been bumped at the last minute from a flight to Hankow that the Japanese shot down. The Japanese had earlier banned *Far Eastern Front* in their country. They now attacked him on Chinese soil. In early 1939 a pro-Japanese secret society in China announced a "death roll." Among those marked for "telling too many lies" were Powell, Gould, Smedley, and Snow. Japanese busily collected sixteen hundred copies of *Red Star* in Shanghai and anyone, including an American, entering the country with the popular volume tucked in his bag was liable to have it confiscated by surly Japanese guards. After finishing his work in Hongkong, Snow planned to visit Indusco cooperatives in the interior and gather material for a long delayed book. Before flying to Chungking, he sent his "Last Will" to Peg in Baguio.[35]

Snow found little to cheer him in Chungking, China's capital since the fall of Hankow. Correspondents considered it "a uniquely unpleasant place."[36] Much of the year a miasmatic mist engulfed the old Szechwanese city deep in the interior. Everything seemed covered with slime. Pigs wallowed in the narrow muddy streets. Government officials, diplomats, and journalists lived in rat-infested, airless houses. When the torrid summer heat burned off the fog, it also accentuated the stench from open sewers and cleared the skies for Japanese bombers that pounded buildings into rubble. It all looked worse because of the corrupt and inefficient government.

Despite having written his will, Snow displayed characteristic faith that good fortune was on his side. He overcame the housing shortage when *New York Times* correspondent Tillman Durdin and his wife let him sleep on a plaited bamboo bottom bed in their two-room house. Most nights the threesome spent several hours huddled with two hundred Chinese in an underground shelter waiting out the Japanese raids. One night, after Mme. Chou En-lai and a New Fourth Army commander dined at the Durdins', Snow suggested that they forgo the tiresome routine and stay in the house. The law of probabilities, he argued, made it unlikely that a bomb would fall on this house out of the tens of thousands still standing. Durdin's wife finally prevailed on the two men to go to the stifling shelter. They emerged several hours later to find the house in ruins. "I take back the whole goddamned law of probabilities," Snow said, staring at the wreckage. Learning of the close call, members of the press corps came around. They stayed until dawn drinking two bottles of liquor that survived on the bottom shelf of a bookcase.

Snow found that the Nationalists had lost a great deal of their enthusiasm for the united front. Their traditional power base lay in the coastal cities under Japanese control. In contrast the Communists had years of experience fighting guerrilla warfare in the countryside. The Red domain and influence was spreading. The Communists continued to advocate a united front, but alliance or no alliance they refused to put their victorious forces in Kuomintang hands. As Mao told Bertram, the Eighth Route Army—the new name for the Red army—would act "independently and on our own initiative." The KMT passed laws "Restricting the Activities of the Other Party" and "Guarding against Communist Activities in Enemy Occupied Areas." In Chungking, a powerful general and KMT political leader told Snow he considered Communist-run organizations illegal. Sporadic clashes between KMT and CCP guerrilla units had broken out in both the north and south.

Indusco's future was equally precarious. It was a choice target for ill-paid government officials. Political cliques, who considered the cooperatives communistic, attacked Indusco. In Chungking Snow learned that government officials arrested and dismissed Indusco workers. Indusco's best hope was H. H. Kung, but he was part of the problem. "Kung is not only corrupt, and incompetent," Snow wrote in a "strictly confidential" letter. "He is without any will and is pushed around like a flabby sack of meal by any force with which he comes in contact."[37]

In mid-August—after narrowly avoiding other Japanese bombs and nearly losing his only spare pair of trousers in a freak fire—Snow left in Indusco Truck No. 3 to troop the Indusco line running north into Communist-held territory.[38] Despite the Nationalists' attitude toward it, Indusco had made extraordinary progress. Sixty-nine cooperatives existed in December 1938. Within six months 724 co-ops produced minerals, clothing, alcohol, tools, soap, electrical equipment, tents, and food needed in the war effort. Run locally, the co-ops benefited workers. Paoki, "Indusco City," had retail stores, schools, "and its own club house equipped with the only shower baths in town." In Chengtu Snow bicycled to see a cooperative machine shop with 150 workers. "Men sang at their work, anti-Japanese tunes learned in their co-op training," Snow reported in his typical upbeat fashion about the cooperatives, "and it was all good to see and hear in the open air, remembering the dark prisons of workers in Shanghai."

In Sian Snow found additional evidence of Nationalist antipathy to Indusco and the united front. Indusco workers, including one of Alley's adopted Chinese sons, were in concentration camps even though their units provided materiel to the Nationalists. KMT troops curtailed traffic to the Communist capital in Yenan. Only because he carried letters from T. V. Soong to local Nationalist commanders and served as a delegate of the International Committee for Indusco was Snow able to hitch a ride on one of the few Yenan-bound trucks—and then the trip was an uncertain one. At the end of the first day rains turned the roads into brown soup. Snow made the best of the layover, teaching poker to other passengers and recruiting a cook for Yenan's new "Foreign Guest" cave. The party rolled into Yenan a week behind schedule.

The stated reason for Snow's visit was to see Indusco operations, which had made a slow start. In early 1939 Alley set up an Indusco depot in Yenan and arranged loan funds for local producer societies. Additional funds did not get through from Chungking. The Communists, in any event, were suspicious of Indusco's bourgeois character. Snow had tried to allay those concerns, writing Mao that Indusco's principles fit with the Communists' own mixed economy. By the time Snow arrived, fifteen Indusco factories were in operation. When Snow pressed Indusco's case with Mao, the Red leader offered a strong statement of support for use by the International Committee. Three months after Snow left, an All-Union Cooperative Conference in Yenan voted to reorganize about 140 existing producer societies along Indusco lines.[39]

Yenan looked better than Chungking to almost every Western visitor, and not simply because of the weather. The Communist political program pursued the same positive reforms that commanded Snow's enthusiasm in 1936. "Thousands of new caves have been built," Snow wrote to Evans Carlson. "A whole mile of . . . shops make up a new shopping street. Indusco products are prominent among the goods displayed." Notwithstanding intense Japanese bombardment, agricultural production was up and sanitation was good. The Lu Hsun Academy of Fine Arts housed five hundred writers, artists, dramatists, and composers. Literacy was a priority. Yenching student leader Wang Ju-mei, who had taken the name Huang Hua, was secretary of a youth organization and head of an outlying school. Enthusiasm for the war effort was unabated. Oxford-educated George Hogg gave up his job as a United Press reporter and went to work for Indusco until he died in 1945 of malnutrition and lack of medical care. He summed up the Yenan spirit, as it was called: Chinese came to find "a place where comradeship and equality in a national cause were placed above everything else. It was as simple as that."

Mao was more in charge than ever. Chang Kuo-táo had rejoined his colleagues in disgrace. After the CCP Central Committee tried and sentenced him to study his mistakes, he defected to Nationalist controlled areas. When Mao's other rival, Wang Ming, returned from Moscow in 1937, the Central Committee rebuked him for wanting to retreat from Mao's line and return to an urban oriented strategy. He was later criticized for acting independently. Snow met Wang during his visit and thought him charmingly urbane, astonishingly young (he was only thirty-two at the time), and, as far as Snow could tell, without much influence.

During his ten-day stay in Yenan, Snow met informally with Mao over dinner and games of poker and bridge, which the Red leader had learned to play. Mao had a new wife, slender, attractive Chiang Ch'ing, who joined in. He was heavier, wore his hair shorter, and had acquired a "kind of benignity," Snow recorded in his diary. Mao dressed as shabbily as ever. His three-room cave was furnished with a rickety chair and a low sofa with bad springs. The Communist leader, Snow concluded, "was still the plain man of the people, the queer mixture of peasant and intellectual, the unusual combination of great political shrewdness and earthy common sense."[40]

Snow worried about the kind of welcome Mao would give him. During the three years since they first met, rumors circulated that Snow was a foreign agent. The origin of the rumors was murky. In China all sorts of half truth made the rounds. At one point Snow tied the spy allegations to Agnes Smedley. If he really thought she was to blame, though, it did not prevent them from becoming close friends over the next years. Meanwhile Philip Jaffe heard from Chinese sources in New York that Chou En-lai thought Snow was a spy. One thing Snow knew for certain was that Heinz Shippe, author of the Asiaticus critique in *Pacific Affairs*, told Mao that Snow made serious errors. Snow also learned indirectly that Mao defended him, though without endorsing his writing: "Snow came here to investigate our situation when nobody else would, and helped us by presenting the facts. You did not come. Even if he later did something which we detest, we will always remember that he did a great service for China."

Mao quickly allayed Snow's concerns in Yenan. He did not mention Shippe's criticism. When Snow asked about the accuracy of *Red Star*, Mao said the book correctly reported party policies and his views. At a mass meeting Mao introduced Snow as the author of a "truthful book about us."

With Huang Hua acting as interpreter, Snow pressed Mao for clarification of CCP policies during two days of formal interviews. To Snow's question whether the Communists had become mere reformists, not social revolutionaries, Mao responded unequivocally: "We are always social revolutionaries, we are never reformists. . . . For the present the revolution is national and democratic in character of its aims, but after a certain stage it will be transformed into social revolution." The united front notwithstanding, Mao confirmed that the CCP "has never sacrificed its independence for one day, one hour, or one-half a minute."

The previous month the Soviets had signed a nonaggression pact with Nazi Germany and within the next several weeks divided Poland between them. Mao provided a bizarre explanation justifying Stalin's action, a *volte-face* after five years of vilifying Hitler. Chamberlain with the help of Roosevelt, he said, was organizing a world front of "so-called democratic countries" whose ultimate objective was to defeat Germany and isolate the Soviet Union. Chamberlain was quite prepared to "sacrifice China in order to make an ally of Japan." The Soviet Union acted in self-defense without abandoning its fight against imperialism. "Hitler," Mao observed, "is in Stalin's pocket." As for Poland, its government, "acting under instructions of British finance capital," was so hostile to the Soviet Union it rejected aid from Moscow. "It revealed its incompetence when, after but two weeks, it buried itself under the iron heel of Hitler."

Snow replied that Stalin may have simply strengthened Hitler and made enemies of people who had supported the Soviet Union through the Popular Front. It might turn out that "there is a hole in Stalin's pocket," he observed. Later, when the British tried to appease Japan by closing the Burma Road, China's supply line to the west, Snow began to wonder if Mao was not right about Britain's intentions.

The Yenan press carried a transcript of the interview. The report reached Chungking before Snow did and caused a big stir. The Generalissimo had previously stated that Britain would continue to back China. Po Ku, in the CCP's Chungking office, told Snow that Mao needlessly alienated allies. Snow thought Po Ku "seemed more keenly aware of the 'contradictions' in the Kremlin's turncoat policy than Mao, whose views went unchallenged in Yenan."[41] Though Po Ku wondered if it was necessary for Snow to publish the interviews, they appeared several weeks later in the *China Weekly Review*. Not long afterward the Nationalists blockaded the Communist-controlled area. Snow was the last foreign journalist to visit Yenan for five years.[42]

The deterioration of the united front was a source of great despair for Snow. It prompted him to write reports that other journalists, centered in the Nationalist capital, held back. Agreeing with Chungking censors that negative reports about the united front aided the enemy, reporters maintained the fiction of Kuomintang-Communist cooperation after the erstwhile partners began to skirmish. For similar reasons reporters blinked at Nationalist inefficiency and corruption. Snow shared this loyalty to the Chinese but thought extreme self-censorship simply let the Nationalists pursue their ineffective war strategy. Fed up, he had barely rejoined his wife in Baguio when he broke the silence with a *New Republic* article on "China's Precarious Unity," which appeared in mid-1940. Although still restraining his criticism, Snow recorded anti-united front comments by Nationalist officials in Chungking and described Nationalists' attempts to isolate the Communists, concluding that the united front had not produced "either democracy or basic harmony."[43]

A few months later in *Asia* Snow reported "There has apparently been no fundamental reform in the government, which is still a dictatorship and will never voluntarily become anything else. Outside the guerrilla districts under the influence of the Communists, the land system remains about the same. Outside industrial cooperatives, it is impossible to point to any new right won by the working class."

Snow's criticism of the Nationalists made him a major exception among his colleagues. Not until 1944 did other journalists voice similar concerns.

Snow was the first and the last Western reporter to visit CCP headquarters in the 1930s, an accomplishment that underscored his status as the foremost authority on Chinese Communism. Despite this, he was aware that Western readers misunderstood his portrait of the Chinese Communists as well as of the war in Asia. When Snow sat down in Baguio to write his book, he tried to clear up the misunderstandings. The resulting volume was called *The Battle for Asia* in the United States and *Scorched Earth* in Great Britain.[44]

Snow presented the Communists as having some democratic characteristics. Mao shattered the Confucian mold that shaped Chiang. He was "leader only by common consent and all his decisions are the result of discussions and collective judgment." More definitively than before, Snow stated that the Communists were not able to practice anything like Marxism. The Chinese Communists were as correct to call themselves Marxist as followers of Christ were to call themselves Christians. Both were waiting for the advent of an age when they could truly practice what they preached. The Communists viewed the creation of a democratic republic as the next necessary stage en route to that utopia. "The Communists are today the last people to suggest that China is 'going Communist' in the near future."

Time would show that Snow used an unfortunate analogy, suggesting that the true coming of communism in China lay in some era beyond anyone's lifetime. In other respects, though, he was on the mark. Although the Communists shed the red stars from their military caps in the spirit of national unity, he observed, they pinned the emblems "just inside their left breast pockets." Those red stars were beacons for social revolution. "The Chinese Communist Party stands quite apart from all other offspring of the Comintern" in being largely self-sufficient, Snow added. Although Stalin directed aid to Chungking, leaving only speeches for the CCP, revolutionary words from Moscow defined the regnant philosophy in Yenan. Men like Ambassador Clark-Kerr erred in believing that the Communists were "nineteenth-century agrarian democrats," Snow wrote. "How all these people reconcile such interpretations with the Chinese C.P.'s loyal adherence to the Comintern I do not know. . . . My personal feeling in the matter is that liberals who build up hopes that the Communists of China are 'different' and 'only reformers' and have abandoned revolutionary methods to achieve their program, are doomed to ultimate disillusionment." Snow's analysis stood in overwhelming contrast with the many reporters who returned from Yenan with breathless descriptions of the "lovable" Communists.

As before, Snow believed the war offered an opportunity for real change in China by creating conditions that destroyed petty parochialism, ancestor worship, defeatism, illiteracy, and reliance on treaty ports. "Out of the valley of slaughter a greater nation than the one which entered it will emerge—and greater than the one which is seeking its extinction," Snow concluded in a *Saturday Evening Post* article extolling the patriotic spirit he saw in China.

While in Yenan he had expressed enthusiasm for this new self-reliance before an assemblage of two thousand Red soldiers. "Your leader Mao Tse-tung has said that every man and woman must learn to 'fight with his teeth, his hands and his feet,' so that China can win alone. And he is right. Depend on no one but yourselves."

As much as this exhortation squared with his Missouri view of self-reliance, he delivered it ruefully. China, he believed, could not recover its lost territory without "external military aid." Another credo, equally American, told him that the United States had an obligation to help China. The real question, Snow argued in his strongest case yet for direct American action, was not whether Americans should be involved but on what terms.[45]

Snow's argument was that the United States could not avoid being drawn into the conflict in Asia so long as it was involved in Europe. Neutrality, even out-and-out appeasement of Japan, was not feasible, for that would force Great Britain to fight on European *and* Asian fronts. "We could not forsake Britain in the East without appeasing her opponents in Europe." Yet, as much as Snow built his case on Americans' interest in Europe, *his* concern did not lie there at all. It lay in Asia. "There is nothing real in this [European] war . . . to invite sacrifice of American lives," Snow confided to Will Babcock as well as old friends like Charlie Towne. The choice for Americans was whether their involvement preserved European domination of Asia or promoted Asian independence.

To wage a strong war in Asia, Snow wrote in his book, the United States should renounce extraterritoriality and cancel all loans made to China before war. He speculated that Britain and other colonial powers "would probably take the strong hint" and do likewise. As a condition of involvement in war, the United States should insist on promises for a decolonization program afterward: liberation of India and Burma as well as all countries under Japanese control; a comprehensive education program leading to independence for more backward colonies; financial, technical, industrial, medical, and other aid plus a program of colonial industrialization based on state-coordinated cooperatives or collective economy; and assistance in developing a federation of decolonized democratic states.

Snow thought it reasonable to invite the Soviet Union to join such a pact as a way to keep open a "last line of cooperation" and to make a Russia-Japan pact less likely. "If the British Empire is a democracy, with six-sevenths of its total population denied democratic rights, perhaps we should be able to stretch a point in the case of Soviet democracy."

The United States must ensure that it supported democracy in countries it assisted during the war. "If democracy is to prevail, our loans must be made direct to democratic organizations inside those countries, such as Industrial Co-operatives in China, concerned with developing their own internal market and strengthening the economic basis of democracy, and not with exploitation of cheap labor and raw materials for purposes of collecting tribute at home and abroad."

For Snow the war was fundamentally a conflict of ideas, democracy versus Japanese *and* Western imperialism. That was why he thought that if a war did start, American planes should bomb Japan with "millions of leaflets containing the emancipation proclamation." Much of this sounded naive, and, at one level, it was. American ideals would have had no impact on Britain; as time would show, it was unrealistic to expect Americans to invest much effort to shape British policy on decolonization. "The evidence of history to date," Snow admitted, "indicates that capitalism is incapable of intelligent co-operation or planning or anticipating change in any joint international scheme combining progress with security." But his perception that the war was more than a war between Great Powers, which was the way most Americans saw it, was keen. Colonial nations, learning that their European masters were not invincible, saw in the rise of Japan the prospect for their own independence. The question was whether the Allies would appear as liberators or as oppressors. "The deepest meaning of this struggle is man's needs for social and economic progress," Snow wrote, "and in the end it will be won or lost everywhere in terms of the political strategy which best expresses those needs."

The only choice for America, he believed, was to provide a positive reinforcement of those aspirations not only to help Asians but to affirm its own fundamental beliefs. "Our decisive frontier is not in China and it is not in England," Snow declared. "It is on our own soil and in our own soul."

While Snow worked on his book in Baguio, his idealistic investment in Indusco paid impressive returns.[46] By mid-1940 Indusco had 1,850 cooperatives with thirty thousand members. According to one estimate, the cooperatives accounted for 1 percent of total Chinese industrial production. A *Time* magazine article on Indusco coincided with major fund-raising events in the United States. The article, which included a photo of Snow, described the cooperatives as the engine for democracy in China. Snow had a point when he pronounced Indusco a success, "no doubt about it." Altogether the Indusco movement made remarkable advances.

All the same Indusco had serious problems. Robert Barnett on the staff of the New York City-based Institute of Pacific Relations discussed some of them in an IPR report: insufficiently trained personnel, irregular bookkeeping, ignorance and suspicion of local populations, inadequate equipment and materials. Moreover, Barnett noted, some critics "felt that foreign participation rendered the movement artificial and weakened an activity which properly should be run by the Chinese." The latter hinted at a fatal flaw. The decentralized, self-governing concept that Snow favored for Indusco was at odds with the Nationalist government, and yet Indusco could only succeed if the Nationalists let it succeed. The International Promotion Committee, which Snow helped establish, could not permanently by-pass national leaders by providing funds directly to the cooperatives.

Snow did not agree with the headline over Barnett's article—"China's Industrial Cooperatives On Trial." As he saw it, the Nationalist government was on trial through the industrial cooperatives. In his writings Snow had put Indusco in the best possible light, playing down corrupt Kuomintang practices. But privately he was more candid. In a letter to Edward Carter, Barnett's chief at IPR, he acknowledged troubles and admitted that success was not certain.

As peaceful a spot as Baguio was, Snow found little rest there. His commitment to Indusco took weeks of his time. All the while he worried about finishing his book before it was outdated by the new round of Japanese aggression he saw coming. At the end of 1940 he was forty pounds underweight and suffering from a vitamin deficiency—though he did not know it at the time.[47]

When Snow finished the book he did what he had done so often before: made plans to return home and, as usual, went somewhere else first. He returned to Shanghai in early December and, with J. B. Powell, put Peg on a ship bound for California. Not wanting to let go of Asia so quickly, Snow accepted an assignment from the *New York Herald Tribune* to return by way of Siam, Burma, India, and Europe, which he had talked about visiting for some time. He hung on in Hongkong a few weeks as if hoping some miracle would hold him back one more time.

China seemed bent, instead, on disappointing him. In late December Snow reported fears "that civil war may be renewed on a large scale." The chief concern was a Nationalist demand that the Communists' increasingly strong New Fourth Army move north of the Yangtze River by the end of the month. According to later Communist claims, Chiang acceded to Chou En-lai's last minute request for a different retreat route, one that did not take Communist forces near Japanese garrisons. In any event, the new year found the New Fourth Army headquarters detachment and a rear guard south of the river. Nationalist troops attacked, leaving hundreds dead.

Nationalist officials released a skimpy announcement on January 17 that the New Fourth Army had revolted and was now disbanded. By underground leaflet and word of mouth a different story spread, one that described carnage and betrayal by the Nationalists. Thanks to his contacts, Snow got a detailed report from the Communist side and, though reluctant to provoke further hostility, broke the story when he was certain the facts were accurate. His *Herald Tribune* report of the nine-day battle, leaving four thousand casualties and two thousand prisoners, created a furor. The Nationalists had been unable to stop his story, which he filed from Hongkong. Taking the next best step, Chiang Kai-shek's ambassador to the United States demanded the *Herald Tribune* publish an apology and retraction. The newspaper stood by Snow, running a supportive editorial several weeks later when his report was verified. Chungking canceled Snow's press privileges.[48]

Several months later Snow commented caustically that the Nationalist defeat of the New Fourth Army was its greatest single "military success, from the standpoint of the numbers of casualties inflicted and prisoners taken" since the battle of Taierchwang. The attack on the Communists left Snow bitter and depressed. General Han Ying, whom Snow had so greatly admired when they met in Hankow, was dead, "allegedly . . . murdered in cold blood." The destruction of the New Fourth Army was a symbol of Snow's failure. Hard as he tried to support a political, military, and economic united front through his foreign correspondence, through *democracy* magazine, through Indusco, unity had not come. Hard as Snow tried to draw Americans' attention to the Far East and to the need to intervene before war forced them to, his countrymen only withdrew.[49]

Those failures colored his feelings about his personal accomplishments. He had less than two thousand dollars to show for his nearly thirteen years in Asia. After the routine of long separations from Peg, he felt his marriage had failed too.

Snow cabled the *Herald Tribune* that he had decided not to take the assignment through South Asia after all. He also turned aside Mme. Sun's suggestion that he stay in China. Instead he left for Manila, where the Babcocks found him so distraught he could barely string coherent sentences together. After telephoning Peg, he boarded a sleek four-engine Pan American Clipper, the fastest way home.[50]

People on Our Side

5

Edgar Snow could not have come home at a better moment. The United States sat precariously on the edge of a world war. Like it or not, Americans had to think internationally, and they looked to journalists who knew their way around a world taking such ominous shape. Steeped in Asia for so many years, where he predicted the coming conflagration, Snow stood in the front ranks of his profession. In the coming years he became so well known that one St. Petersburg, Florida, lady confused Edgar Snow's wintry name with Robert Frost's.[1] At the high point of public acceptance, he had freedom to pursue stories on new as well as old horizons, and he had his greatest opportunity to reach Americans. The question was: would they pay attention?

Snow's spirits rose as the Pan Am China Clipper skipped across the Pacific to the California coast. During an overnight stop on Wake Island, the pilot, sensing Snow's depression, tried to buck him up with a story of a failed love affair that had prompted him to crash his one-seater mail plane. Afterward the flyer fell in love with his nurse. Snow liked the off-beat tale of risk and recuperation. Besides, he had things to think about apart from himself. At Guam, Wake, Midway, and Hawaii he inquired about military readiness for war.[2]

Snow's plane landed in the evening at the San Pedro docks, outside Los Angeles. Peg, busy raising money for Indusco, sent a young man she had met through radical journalist Anna Louise Strong to pick him up. Richard Nickson, an aspiring poet recently out of college, took Snow to his family's hotel, the Brevort in Hollywood, where the young man worked as a clerk. In Nickson's apartment at the rear of the hotel, they talked into the night, Snow asking question after question about the country he had been away from for so long. The next day Peg joined him, and they rented an apartment of their own at the Brevort. Centrally located and comfortable, with a swimming pool ringed by banana trees, the hotel made an ideal base for Indusco fund raising. A steady stream of famous guests passed through during the next weeks. Many were movie stars, a fact that may have inspired Snow to collaborate with radical journalist Anna Louise Strong on a movie scenario set in wartime China. (Nothing came of "Judgment Seat," as the movie was tentatively titled, after they sent it to Orson Welles.) Actor John Garfield and Snow's literary acquaintance from China, Lin Yutang, became vice-chairman and chairman of the Hollywood Indusco committee. Harvard-educated Lin wrote a favorable review of *The Battle for Asia*, released shortly after Snow reached California.

In writing the book, dedicated to his father and mother, Snow used a formula that became standard for him. The major part of the volume contained eyewitness reporting, in this case the brutal Japanese attack on China. The concluding sections forecast subsequent developments—particularly the social changes that would bubble over in China—and recommended what the United States should do to address them.

Only one major reviewer criticized the book, Freda Utley writing in the *New York Times*. The Englishwoman had been a member of the Communist Party, which she forsook following the disappearance of her Russian husband during the Moscow purges. Snow met her shortly afterward, during the siege of Hankow in 1938, where she was a correspondent for the *London News Chronicle*. Moved by her story, he arranged for her to interview Chou En-lai. Utley thought Chou the cleverest man she ever met and disputed Snow's view that the Chinese Communists should really be called Communists. In step with popular front thinking, she considered them "social reformers and patriots." Her enthusiasm waned the next year when Mao rationalized Stalin's pact with Hitler. She feared that Moscow might sign a similar pact with Japan and instruct the CCP "to turn against Chungking." Utley devoted half of her review to criticizing Snow for misunderstanding that Moscow directed CCP policy and for suggesting that the Soviets might make good wartime allies against fascism.

These concerns aside, Utley concluded, "The criticisms that Mr. Snow's political chapters provoke do not, however, detract from the essential value of his exhaustive account of the situation in China, nor from the truth of his argument that Britain must abandon the undemocratic concept of Empire if India and China and the other Asiatic people are to be saved from Fascist tyranny, and the British Empire preserved from the Nazis and the Japanese."[3]

A review in the conservative *Chicago Tribune* was more nearly typical. The piece did not allude to the Communists; it mentioned that Snow visualized "China's future" but didn't explain what he saw. The reviewer concentrated instead on "Japan's effort to force China to her knees." Reviewers who noted Snow was "a sympathetic observer of communism" did so without recriminations. Not one warned readers away from the book. With remarkable frequency reviewers said that it was better than *Red Star over China*. Although *The Battle for Asia* was at the time an extraordinary attack on the Nationalists, the *Detroit News* reviewed it together with Mme. Chiang Kai-shek's *China Shall Rise Again*, both favorably. The book sold briskly by early April. "I want to tell you how deeply indebted I feel to you for that masterly book," Henry Luce, a fervent supporter of the Generalissimo, wrote to Snow.

After Hollywood and a rest at a dude ranch near Tucson, Arizona, where he regained lost weight, Snow and his wife headed east. Wherever he went, it was the same: Snow was a celebrity. When he stopped in Kansas City, family and friends threw a party for him at the grand Muehlebach Hotel. They had to move back the furniture to make room for the people who crowded in. The *Saturday Review of Literature* put Snow's picture on the cover. On March 21, the day after he arrived in New York City, Random House held a press conference to introduce him and promote *The Battle for Asia*. Kelly Graham, in whose bank Snow had kept his money since leaving New York City in 1928, had a dinner party for him; Charlie Towne, who had been a strong source of encouragement in the 1920s, took the Snows to gourmet feasts. Harrison Smith, president of the *Saturday Review* and a partner in the Smith & Haas publishing house that handled Snow's first book, *Far Eastern Front*, visited the couple. The editors at the *Saturday Evening Post* in Philadelphia wanted to meet Snow. In Washington, D.C., he had access to political leaders. Eleanor Roosevelt mentioned meeting the Snows in her nationally syndicated "My Day" column. At a Dupont Circle tea party people "collected around Snow," according to an item in the *Washington Post* society pages.[4]

Requests for articles rolled in. *Publishers' Weekly* wanted a piece recommending the best new books on "the Asiatic Front"; the *Saturday Evening Post* ran his article, "Showdown in the Pacific"; *Fortune* asked for a long essay on "How America Can Take the Offensive." So seriously was Snow taken that daily newspapers often ran stories on his stories.[5]

In China Snow had referred to Kansas City as home and the family's simple brick and wood frame house on Charlotte Street as the "root, of which I am but a stem." Back on American soil he found that while the years in the Far East filled his life in one way, they left a gap in another. The United States had become an unfamiliar land. His family had become strangers. He had not yet met his brother- or sister-in-law, let alone their school-age children. While he lived an itinerant existence, his siblings settled into business-oriented lives far different from his. Claude Mackey, Mildred's husband, worked in the advertising department at the *Kansas City Star*. Howard, in Boston, was development manager for the National Association of Manufacturers.

Everything seemed "speeded up by about thirty miles an hour." Snow could scarcely believe the food heaped in markets and the junk yards full of things that would have been luxuries in China. In Hollywood he and Peg saved piles of "paper bags, lovely brown wrapping paper, fine twine, rubber bands, advertising folders, fancy jars, tin boxes and cans." When Snow reached California he called Henriette Herz, his agent, with whom he had never spoken before. She thought he sounded nice, young, and uncertain.

Snow realized his journalism had not penetrated very deeply in this land of plenty. "You could convince Americans that pyorrhea, body odor, halitosis, constipation and pimply skin threatened the security of their homes," he thought. "But wars were an Asiatic disease or a European disease." Opinion surveys taken in 1941, when war had come to look inevitable, showed a large majority still hoped to avoid direct involvement. Americans were far from agreeing with Snow as to what the war, when it did come, should be all about.[6]

Nothing illustrated this better than the attitude of President Franklin Roosevelt, a man Snow mistakenly considered one of his key allies. On a trip to Washington in February 1942, Snow asked for a meeting with FDR to interview him and to discuss "two or three matters about the Far Eastern situation." After Roosevelt's weekly press conference, presidential assistant Wayne Coy ushered Snow into the Oval Office. Roosevelt said *he* wanted to interview Snow. In the next forty-five minutes Roosevelt worked his magic.[7]

FDR said he didn't approve of United States extraterritorial rights in China, in fact he tried to give them up in 1933 but Secretary of State Cordell Hull's advisers wouldn't hear of it. "Snow," FDR said, "it almost seems that the Japs were a necessary evil in order to break down that old colonial system, to force the reforms that have to be made." Expressing sympathy for the Indian independence movement, he asked Snow to do him a favor when he saw Nehru again. "Tell him I would like to have him write me a letter and tell me exactly what he wants us to do for India."

Emboldened, Snow gave the president *his* plan to facilitate decolonization. "To conduct effective political and psychological war in Asia,"

Snow wrote, "it is necessary for us to convert the defensive have-got and mean-to-hold strategy of the Western colonial powers into an offensive war of liberation, promising the colonial peoples full participation in a post-war democratic world—and giving them all possible immediate aid and arms." He proposed a Federation for Asian Democracy made up of Chinese, Koreans, Filipinos, Annamites, Burmese, Indians, Javanese, and other Asiatics living in the United States. Such an international organization would generate stronger anti-Japanese propaganda than any U.S. agency could and would educate Americans and Europeans on conditions abroad and the necessity of supporting Asiatic democracy.

Roosevelt seemed to realize "that Chiang's oligarchy lacked enthusiastic popular support" and asked how aid could be used to help the people of China. Snow suggested the president ask Chiang to earmark U.S. credits for Indusco. FDR couldn't act that heavy-handedly, he said, but he promised to "let Chiang know that this is the kind of thing we would like to see develop there. I'll ask Chiang to keep me personally informed of progress. In that way won't he see the point of personally supporting it?"

"Write me now and then if you hear anything interesting," Roosevelt asked at the end of the meeting.

The interview, Snow told his sister, "gave me a much more secure feeling about the future of our country in war and peace." In the coming months Snow made no secret of his sentiments. Shortly after arriving on the East Coast, the Snows bought a pre-revolutionary farmhouse in Madison, Connecticut, a Republican town a short drive north of New York City. During the next presidential campaign Snow nailed a big Roosevelt poster to his front door.

Roosevelt, writer John Dos Passos commented, "could play on a man like a violin. Virtuoso." In his hands regular meetings with reporters, "delightful family conferences" he called them, became a powerful instrument. Snow was not the only journalist to become a personal informant after an encounter with the charming chief executive. But as readily as Roosevelt tapped into Snow's vision of the world, the president was, as a practical matter, not far out in front of the people who elected him. As historian James MacGregor Burns aptly described him, Roosevelt was a man of lofty dreams and parochial compromises.[8]

Roosevelt loved to regale Snow and others with stories of his forebears who had been involved in the China trade. As tempting as it was to see sympathy for China in these remarks, the most important thing about FDR's reminiscences was the shallowness they revealed of his sympathy for China. Like most Americans, he did not know much about

China and cared little about its fate. Whatever he might say about disliking extraterritorial rights, the reality was that he had kept them throughout the pre-war years. When a U.S. silver-purchasing program adopted in 1934 seriously disrupted the Chinese economy, Roosevelt thought the outflow of silver from China was "China's business and not ours." United States defense considerations, not a desire to put flesh on his sympathies for China, drew his attention to the country in the 1940s.

Shortly before coming home in 1941, Ambassador Nelson Johnson ruminated on policy differences with Snow in a letter to Stanley Hornbeck, chief of the State Department's Far Eastern Division: "Snow says [in *The Battle for Asia*] . . . that American munitions and money should not be given to the reactionaries at Chungking but to the armies in the field among which he includes the communist forces. Snow would be horrified, I suppose, if I were to accuse him of being an imperialist in that he advises us to do just what the Japanese are doing, namely, set up an American puppet to fight the Japanese controlled Chinese puppet. How else could we prevent the arms and munisitons [*sic*] and finance from reaching the constituted Government of what Snow calls reactionaries."

Johnson recognized the gulf that already existed between administration policy in China and Snow's views, though he misunderstood the essence of the issue that faced Americans. To be sure, the United States must meddle in Chinese affairs in order to force aid past Chiang Kai-shek's government to other organizations in the country. But support for Chiang Kai-shek also amounted to intervention in Chinese internal affairs.

"[I]t is urgently necessary for Americans not only to realize how important and progressive a role their economic aid to China can play but also to understand the dangers to be avoided," Snow wrote after returning to the United States. "American help to Chiang means intervention not only in the Sino-Japanese war but in the internal political equation of China. Washington must decide what kind of situation it desires there—a major enlargement of civil war, to the exclusion of further resistance to Japan, or a democratic development which can assure internal cooperation and continuance of national revolutionary struggle."

By 1941 the United States had made its decision. It was well on its way to creating precisely the proxy Johnson abhorred, only the object of American largesse was not the Communists but the Nationalists. Fearful that the Nationalist government's resistance to Japan might collapse, Roosevelt and his administration supplied the Nationalists with nearly $200 million in economic aid between the end of 1938 and passage of Lend-Lease legislation in March 1941. The administration passed funds through a front, the Chinese-owned Universal Trading Corporation, and gave China wide latitude in spending them. Despite a prohibition against it, the Chinese used some of the money to buy military supplies. As concern about America's Asian flank grew, the administration used another front to supply China with American pilots. The American Volunteer Group, as it was officially called, became better known as the Flying Tigers. Well on his way to creating an image of the Nationalists as staunch allies, Roosevelt left himself little room to maneuver in changing his policies or Chiang's policies. The Chinese, Roosevelt proclaimed, "have been, in thought and in objective, closer to us Americans than almost any other peoples in the world—the same great ideals. China . . . has become one of the great democracies of the world."

Snow also assumed too much about the priority Roosevelt gave postwar decolonization.[9] The Atlantic Charter, signed with Great Britain in August 1941, spoke high-mindedly of self-determination, but like the Open Door Notes it was just talk. In a press conference the day he met Snow, Roosevelt vaguely suggested that he and Churchill had a large number of situations in mind when they drafted the Atlantic Charter. In private Roosevelt teased, never confronted, Churchill about British colonies lest disagreement get in the way of agreement on military issues. The declaration of war signed in January 1942 summed up the prevailing wartime agenda. The document promised only to "preserve human rights and justice . . . in other lands." Snow wanted change.

Far from adopting Snow's propaganda plan for educating Americans about Asian aspirations for freedom, Roosevelt worried about public opinion and the Congress getting away from him the way it had from President Wilson after World War I. FDR used liberal Vice-President Henry A. Wallace as a stalking horse, giving him the latitude to think and talk about programs promoting social and economic development overseas after the war. At the next election FDR ditched Wallace for a more conservative man in the main stream, Missouri Senator, Harry S. Truman.

Roosevelt evidently wasn't impressed with a pair of reports Snow sent on India and Burma within several months of their first meeting. The Burma report was based on a young Burmese's account of the harsh Japanese takeover of his country. Snow's accompanying observations—which Roosevelt did not save and thus are not available to historians—probably paralleled his news reports at the time, stressing the "imperative" of putting the war in Asia on the same footing as the war in Europe and the "imperative" of supporting Asian independence movements, the "only way of retaining a following in this part of the world." FDR noted privately that Snow's comments on India were "very amateurish"; those on Burma were "very interesting but even there there is a very high percentage of sweeping, all-inclusive statements which make one pause."[10]

Mainstream Americans' differences with Snow went much deeper than their win-the-war-first attitude, which relegated post-victory issues far down the list of priorities. The differences were nowhere more clear than with perceptions of democracy and capitalism.[11]

Snow's views grew out of an experience far outside the orbit of other Americans. Very few came to Asia for any length of time. Virtually no other serious journalist combined Snow's long experience in China with the same degree of personal freedom. Not beholden to an American employer, Snow had an opportunity to see the Chinese perspective and came to believe, as many Chinese did, that traditional *laissez faire* capitalism threatened democracy. The relentless search for profits spawned the imperialism that subjugated Asians; it led American business to sell scrap iron to the Japanese, who used it to make bombs to drop on the Chinese. It put profits before people. Which was the "greater atrocity," Snow asked, "to sell war materials to Japanese morons who think that machine-gunning civilians is good sport, or to sell machines of production to other morons who will feed the precious lives of boys and girls into them, in exchange for exorbitant profit?"

Snow's Asian experience colored his view of American capitalism. Long before returning to the United States he was "all for Roosevelt" and FDR's domestic policies "of public works construction which should bring about some fundamental increase in production of consumers goods and raise the level of purchasing power." His concern was "whether we can carry this program to its logical conclusions, to socialism, without reactionary minority elements mobilizing for a last stand and staging a Franco or a Hitler or a Mussolini on us."

In its abundance America entertained no doubts about the fruits of capitalism—or the role of the American political system in bringing about prosperity. Roosevelt, who had little patience with economic theory, did not challenge these beliefs. Contrary to Republican criticism, the New Deal saved the capitalist system and, in effect, made it safe for big business to get bigger.

Snow seriously overestimated the potential for the United States to act out a new socialist economic vision. "[T]he old type of imperialist loan is as dead as the prewar status quo itself," Snow wrote after returning to the United States. "Further exports of capital can perhaps no longer be made to private individuals, corporations, or comprador groups within national states without strengthening potential fascism. If international democracy is the goal, loans ought to support democratic organizations in those countries." Snow was as realistic in believing that Americans would reorder their system to help other countries as Americans were to assume that their version of capitalism could surface in China.

"Mr. Snow may know China," said a favorable and perceptive reviewer of *The Battle for Asia* in the *New York Daily News,* "but he is out of touch with his Uncle Sam."

For all these differences, Snow was anything but a wild-eyed radical.[12] When asked to describe him, the first thing contemporary acquaintances thought of was his credibility. "One of the most honest men I ever knew," was the way diplomat Edmund Clubb put it. Young Richard Nickson was embarrassed when he brought young Leftists around to meet Snow in Hollywood. The younger people presumed to lecture Snow, not ask for his views. Snow did not take offense. He was content to listen. One night twenty people, including novelist Theodore Dreiser, gathered in his apartment at the Brevort. The beefy, white haired author pressed Snow over and over. "Yes, but what about the Communists? Do you feel they have the answer there in China?" Snow kept skirting the blunt question. Finally, reluctantly, he replied, "Yes, I think they do."

"Fine!" Dreiser said, bringing down a big fist. "They have the answer here, too!"

Dreiser desperately wanted to join the Communist Party but, as he told Snow, "They won't have me." Not until 1945 was he "considered good enough." Not surprisingly, Snow could not understand Dreiser's feelings. By nature Snow was not a joiner. He was too much a journalist to take the route of contemporary Leftists in the United States who sought the strength and solace of organizations and paid the price of subjugating their views to group orthodoxy. In *The Battle for Asia* Snow criticized the Soviet Union and ridiculed the American Communists, whose "ability to put themselves out on limbs to be sawed off by the Soviet foreign policy seems to be inexhaustible."

The American Communist Party understood Snow did not fit in its ranks. Shortly after arriving in California, Peg Snow and Pat Tobin, a radical young seaman on her ship, visited a Left-wing bookstore in San Francisco. "Why aren't there any Edgar Snow books here?" she asked. "He's a Trotskyite," the old Frenchman behind the counter replied.

Snow's independence created a confrontation when he agreed to address the June 1941 American Writers Congress in New York. In a draft speech, which he sent the organizers beforehand, Snow said that the United States should aid Britain and China in the fight against fascism. He foresaw a time when the Soviet Union would fight Germany. With Stalin in league with Hitler at the moment, that view was heresy to American Communists. Representatives of the congress wanted Snow to drop the offensive lines. Snow refused. That was too much for the organizers. They rescinded the speaking invitation.

Two weeks later Germany invaded the Ukraine. Snow's prediction came true. Stalin reoriented Moscow's line again, joining forces with the Allies. Snow was delighted to see the cause against fascism strengthened. He delighted, too, in teasing seaman Pat Tobin, who had opposed "bundles for Britain," about the sharp shift now required of party members.

Snow believed that others should be as free to speak out as he was, but he recommended curtailing civil liberties in one instance. He had been shocked to find Japanese workers in military shops in Hawaii and subsequently proposed banning Japanese propaganda in the United States, disarming Japanese and other Axis nationals, and disbanding "Japanese and Axis-controlled political clubs and subversive organizations." Snow's proposals smacked of the same reasoning that underpinned the shameful massive relocation of Japanese-Americans during the war. That men like Snow, Walter Lippmann, and the future liberal chief justice of the Supreme Court, Earl Warren, enthusiastically supported measures abridging the rights of people on the basis of race underscores the fragility of constitutional guarantees. The widespread anti-Japanese sentiment at the time went a long way toward explaining apparent American acceptance of Snow. Preoccupied with their fears of fascism, Americans did not seriously consider his other observations. Significantly, his proposals to deprive Japanese-Americans of their rights sat side-by-side with his comments on the death of "imperialist" loans in an article he wrote for that bastion of capitalism, *Fortune*. The article was reprinted in a slim volume with articles by two other journalists. The book was entitled *Smash Hitler's International.*[13]

At a June 1941 book-signing party for *The Battle for Asia* in the Gimbel's Philadelphia store, Snow, puffing reflectively on his pipe, predicted the United States would be at war with Japan in four months, almost certainly within the year. During that summer he collected material for *Saturday Evening Post* articles on the state of the U.S. armed forces. He listened to foot soldiers and generals, among them George

Patton and Omar Bradley, "in the swamplands and sweat of the Texas-Louisiana maneuver area, at Mary's Place in Georgia, in the roadhouses of Phenix City, Alabama, and along the hitchhike belt from the Carolinas to New England." His conclusions were as steeped in American tradition as a Norman Rockwell painting.

In his youth Snow had two brief encounters with the military. The first, drilling with an ROTC unit in college, he disliked. The second, a brief stint with the New York National Guard, he enjoyed because he was given useful work grooming a horse in Brooklyn. He found the same practical tendencies among the American boys he watched training. These citizen soldiers were "potentially the finest fighters on earth." Enlisted men in tank forces were "more impressive than their commanders—as is always the case whenever the latter are really good." They were prepared to die for their country—they simply didn't "want to be bored to death" waiting for political leaders to get the war under way. With great relish Snow concluded one article with the story of Luke Fields, who had owned the Snow farmhouse in Madison, Connecticut, during the Revolutionary War. Fields joined the rebels and fought well. As soon as the war was won he deserted.[14]

Polly and Will Babcock, back in the United States from the Philippines, were visiting the Snows in Madison when the call to arms was sounded on December 7. En route to the bus station, they heard a radio report on the bombing of Pearl Harbor. The act of war confirmed in one shocking stroke Snow's ten years of prophecies. The *Kansas City Star*, which often cited Snow's views on its editorial pages, noted his sagacity and Americans' "ignorance and wishful thinking."

More than ever Snow was in demand. Radio journalist Lowell Thomas approached him at the end of the year to go into broadcasting; NBC radio invited him to become a news analyst. The *Saturday Evening Post* wanted to make Snow its first accredited war correspondent. Meanwhile, the government courted him. At one point in December he felt obligated to work for the "Donovan committee," unless they could get someone else. This referred, no doubt, to "Wild Bill" Donovan's fledgling intelligence organization, later to become the famed Office of Strategic Services (OSS), which aggressively recruited journalists for propaganda work. Later, apparently, Snow was offered a captain's commission in the Army Air Corps as an intelligence officer.[15]

Snow enjoyed telling how, during his interview with Roosevelt, the president directed him to take the job offered by the *Saturday Evening Post*. It was a good story, spawned by Snow's instinct for the dramatic, but FDR's opinion was not decisive. Before meeting Roosevelt in February 1942, Snow wrote presidential press secretary Steve Early that

"I am going abroad as war correspondent for the *Saturday Evening Post*." Snow had little sympathy for Donovan's "synthetic propaganda." Although Snow may have been uncertain he made the right decision in working for the *Post* and therefore was interested in Roosevelt's opinion, it is virtually unimaginable that he would give up his freedom in favor of an intelligence or military bureaucracy.

The most significant thing about Roosevelt's advice was his motives for giving it. FDR was not shy about pressing reporters into government service. About the time FDR and Snow met, Roosevelt's live-in White House assistant and alter ego Harry Hopkins unsuccessfully urged CBS reporter Edward R. Murrow to join the Office of War Information. But Roosevelt had good reasons to want Snow at the *Saturday Evening Post* rather than in a military billet. Roosevelt's file of the "dirtiest" attacks against him and his family bulged with articles from the *Post*. With Snow, he had an ally on the conservative magazine.

Though Snow did not fit the *Post* stereotype, no job in the world better suited him.[16] In the 1930s the magazine, located on Independence Square in Philadelphia and owned by the Curtis Publishing Company, was as pro-isolationist as it was committed to capitalism. People sometimes called the *Post* America's largest trade journal. That tradition, however, did not prevent it from getting the best writers in harness. George Horace Lorimer, the editor who bought Snow's free-lance articles in the 1930s, summed it up when he said, "Write me a good story and I don't care what your background is." At the end of 1941 the *Post*, concerned that it had paid too little attention to foreign affairs, wanted all the good stories Snow could find overseas.

The *Post* went through a major upheaval between the time Snow was hired and the time he was supposed to begin work. Wesley Stout, Lorimer's successor and the man who recruited Snow, ran an article called "The Case against the Jew." The story was not as objectionable as the headline suggested, Snow thought, but as a result of intense criticism Stout vacated the editor's chair anyway. The man picked to replace him was Ben Hibbs. Raised in Pretty Prairie, Kansas, Hibbs graduated from the University of Kansas with a Phi Beta Kappa key, edited a state newspaper, and later went to work for Curtis's *Country Gentleman* magazine, eventually ascending to the editorship. He was only four years older than Snow and carried himself in the same relaxed way, hanging around the *Post*'s wood-paneled offices in shirt-sleeves. Hibbs was determined to rejuvenate the magazine, redesigning everything from its antiquated type faces to the subjects it covered. Convinced the war was "the greatest news story of our time," he rapidly assembled a corps of talented correspondents around foreign editor Martin Sommers, a Missouri-born former foreign correspondent who understood what Japanese aggression in China meant to Main Street. Under Hibbs's stewardship, half of the nonfiction articles in a given issue could be devoted to international subjects; fiction and cartoons depicted men in uniform; even the ads showed leggy women toiling at some defense job. Though as Republican as the *Post*, Hibbs was not afraid of people who had different ideas, as Snow quickly discovered. Thinking it might be awkward for Hibbs to inherit him, Snow offered to give up the position. Hibbs responded by upping Snow's already generous salary.

The *Post* job, governed by a year-to-year contract, gave Snow financial security for the first time in his life and a regular opportunity to reach an extraordinarily large audience. "Who reads the Post?" a writer asked rhetorically. "Everybody—highbrow, lowbrow and mezzanine; the hard-boiled businessman and the soft-boiled leisure woman; the intelligentsia, often as a secret vice. . . . You read it—and I." John Gunther reported that Mme. Chiang Kai-shek read it, too.

The *Post* job did all of this and did not ask Snow to relinquish his freedom. His contract required him to complete ten or so articles a year, though he and other reporters often did more. He had sufficient time off to write books. He had a voice in choosing what he wrote about and where he went, and the *Post* didn't want him to stay in one place too long.

Being distanced from Peg again and for longer periods did not seem a drawback. Their new home in Madison had its charms. Snow remodeled two corncribs to make a private writing studio next to a pond behind the house. A *Boston Traveller* profile of Peg commented that the couple alternated cooking meals in the rustic old house: "It works out well, they say." Nevertheless, the marriage disintegrated after they returned to the United States. Perhaps Snow and his wife were too far removed from China, the glue that earlier held them together, and could not find a new reason to join forces, say around children. One of the most vivid impressions people had of the couple was Peg's scolding. Still, in the spring of 1942, Snow was not prepared to break with Peg. The *Post* assignment, marked by long absences and fitful correspondence, made it possible to put off the final, inevitable decision.[17]

Snow wanted to cover the Soviet Union, a plan the Russians did not welcome. Moscow disapproved of his writing, said Maxim Litvinov, the Soviet Ambassador in Washington, and refused to issue him a visa. Snow asked FDR aide Harry Hopkins to plead his case and decided to cover India while awaiting the outcome. Several weeks later Snow secured a scarce seat on an eastbound aircraft.

Snow reached India in late April. His feelings about the country were the same as they had been during his first visit, twelve years earlier. Poverty and backwardness were everywhere. The average peasant lived on five pennies a day, while Indian princes ate on gold plate. The British ruled from the splendid red sandstone viceregal lodge in New Delhi, "where the stink of the excrement carts never penetrated from the streets of the lower castes."[18]

An American communications officer with the 10th Air Force in Delhi thought Snow wasn't like many other correspondents who hung around comfortable quarters waiting for press handouts. Snow showed up from time to time, looking scruffy, filed his story, and was gone again.

During his stay, Snow interviewed peasants, socialists, Communists, gaunt Moslem leader Mohammed Ali Jinnah, and the British viceroy, who said during a two-hour interview he didn't think the Indians were ready for Indusco-like cooperatives. With his old friend, the beautiful Sarojini Naidu, Snow toured Calcutta settlements holding two hundred thousand refugees from Burma. He and Foreign Service Officer John Paton Davies, a friend from China days, were the only two outsiders at the final session of the Gandhi's Congress Party meeting in Allahabad. Snow delivered Roosevelt's message to Nehru, with whom he often talked. As before, Snow liked the sophisticated, practical leader, who did think cooperatives made sense in India. As before, Snow wished that Nehru, not the enigmatic Gandhi, ran the country.

Gandhi's anti-British stance tore Snow in two directions. Gandhi refused to cooperate against the Fascists unless the British promised complete Indian independence. Snow sympathized with Gandhi's objective. In *The Battle for Asia* he had called for linking the war effort to Asian independence. But he considered fascism a worse evil than British imperialism. With Churchill's adamant refusal to preside over the downfall of the empire, Snow thought Gandhi naive not to direct his energies at the Fascist enemy first.

Snow and *New York Times* reporter Arch Steele visited the toothless old messiah at his ashram in Sevagram. Gandhi talked about his plans for "open rebellion" through a mass civil disobedience campaign. He had a copy of *The Battle for Asia* with him and wanted Snow to stay behind to discuss it. After waiting a few minutes while Gandhi performed some duties at a hospital, Snow abruptly left. It seemed fruitless to talk to the obstinate leader.

In *Post* articles Snow tried to explain Gandhi's mass appeal, rooted in the hatred of "nearly two centuries of British domination." He also conveyed his exasperation with "the average Indian's profound conviction that every cause of his distress is named British imperialism." Wrote Snow: "Any colonial subject who believes he can win freedom for his country by appeasing or collaborating with Japan is a tragic figure." Snow precipitously concluded that the Mahatma's "quasi-religious political theories" were coming to the end of their usefulness.

During his stay, Snow took a quick trip by plane to Chungking. The visit convinced him that the flow of American aid was not likely to strengthen Chinese resistance. He told *Post* readers that inflation and its stepchild, hoarding, wracked Nationalist controlled areas. He didn't point the finger at Nationalist officials nor did he mention the rampant government corruption. He did say that Chiang "immobilized and hoarded [his military strength] for purposes which will benefit neither China nor her Allies"—isolating the Communists. Snow foresaw a day of reckoning "when acute internal political contradictions must somehow be resolved."

Snow almost had his own day of reckoning coming back to India over the Hump, the treacherous air route over Himalayan mountains. His C-47 skirted a swarm of Japanese Zeros. Snow clutched a tommy gun. Wondering about the possibility of bailing out he counted the parachutes. There were five . . . and six passengers. This was his second close call. When he flew over North Africa en route to India, the plane made an emergency landing to repair a faulty propeller. Back in the sky, darkened by approaching night, the pilot lost the radio beam guiding him to the air base. In addition to the prospect of a crash landing, the passengers had something else to contemplate during the three hours the plane wandered aimlessly: Luftwaffe planes patrolled nearby. Finally, the pilot found the beam. The plane landed with only four gallons of fuel left. The pilot was impressed that Snow remained "perfectly calm and delightfully pleasant" during the ordeal.

Snow used the Hump episode to add a splash of drama to a *Post* article. (The headline read: "A Post correspondent risks his neck with the Himalayan ferry.") When he and Bob Barnett crossed paths in Calcutta, Barnett confided that he never boarded a plane without feeling it was his last ride. Snow related his North Africa adventure as if it were an everyday train trip.

Snow seemed to dislike the time he spent on the ground in India more than in the air. The worst spot, appropriately, was hot, dusty Wardha, near Gandhi's primitive ashram. "The difference between Wardha and a hairshirt," Snow said, "is the latter is removable when you want to scrub your back." He came down with dengue fever there and was no doubt relieved when word came at the end of the summer that the Soviets would allow him into Russia. Snow flew by the well-traveled route through Teheran.[19]

As a key ally, the Soviet Union commanded American respect and attention. It also dominated Snow's wartime reporting. His first tour, from October 1942 to April 1943, came at a time of widespread Russian uncertainty. During Snow's first weeks in Moscow, when the long winter nights left only a few hours of light and shop windows were boarded up, the Red Army faced a brutal German attack at Stalingrad. Although the heroic defense proved the turning point in the war, peasants and generals alike pressed Snow and other Americans on when the Allies would open the promised second front in Europe and relieve Nazi pressure on them. When he returned to Moscow in the summer of 1944, Snow could hardly believe he was in the same place. Russians had scrubbed camouflage off the buildings. People wore "new faces full of hope and confidence."[20] By the time he left, that December, the end of the war was only a few months off.

News dispatches written from one side of a battle line are as complete as stories on a tennis match that describe play on one side of the net. Coverage of the eastern front was especially bizarre—"the most poorly reported part of the Second World War," according to one student of the period. All of which was fine with the Soviets. Officials kept reporters in a tight herd, centered in the cavernous prerevolutionary Metropole hotel and living off scraps of information about action at the front. The local telephone book was a military secret and unavailable. A story repeating something from the Russian press might not pass unscathed through censors who sometimes knew little English. Travel was so restricted that Snow and colleagues weren't able to cover the Battle of Stalingrad at close quarters until two days after the German forces capitulated.[21]

Such restrictions were a new experience for Snow. In Asia he traveled more or less at will; he enjoyed exclusive access to leaders like Mao and Nehru. In Russia only a small group of senior Soviet officials showed up at cocktail parties and rarely said anything important. Snow's old friend Archibald Clark-Kerr served as ambassador to the Soviet Union during the war. During their frequent meetings the British diplomat complained he always felt a stranger, unable to talk to more than a handful of Russians.

During his first tour, Snow wrote four letters asking Stalin for an interview. He never received a reply. At the beginning of his second tour, Snow thought things might change. He had just published an enormously popular book that called for better understanding of the

Soviet Union. The Soviets would realize that he was not hostile and that he had a tremendous impact back home. But as he grumpily complained to John Melby at the American embassy, the Kremlin didn't seem to care. The closest Snow came to Stalin was at the Bolshoi Theater. Apparently by mistake, Stalin entered the lobby where Snow was standing. They did not speak.

Being a reporter on the eastern front, Churchill said to Snow and other reporters during a visit to Moscow, was "rather a case of making bricks without straw."

Correspondents complained loudly about Soviet press treatment, Snow not least of all, but they did not see the Soviets in a them-and-us way. The Soviet Union fought the common enemy. Trips to pulverized cities, interviews with teenage survivors who lost their entire families, the sight of Russians walking on shoes with paper soles—these told reporters of terrible human and material sacrifices. Soviet measures to promote national unity, meanwhile, softened the government's image. Stalin eased up on restrictions over the church and minorities. Anxious to rebuild Russia's population, he took a Vatican-like stance promoting big families and made divorce, which once required a simple postcard, far more difficult. Preoccupied with domestic defense, Stalin made formal what was already fact and abolished his international revolutionary arm, the Comintern.

Russia exuded "a fresh awareness of herself, not as the citadel of internationalism, but as a nation with a destiny," correspondent Maurice Hindus wrote in *Reader's Digest*. "I don't believe there has ever been a time when the people have been so deeply conscious of themselves as Russians, as staunchly permeated with love of their own land as now."

Journalists hesitated asking permission to make reporting trips. "Conditions were so bad in Russia" United Press correspondent Harrison Salisbury admitted at the time, "that we disliked to propose something which would utilize badly needed food and transportation." Reporters were easily tempted to censor themselves. "It was imperative," recalled Alexander Werth representing the British *Sunday Times* and the British Broadcasting Corporation (BBC), "not to play into the German's hands." Snow agreed. "I was not unaware of [Soviet] shortcomings," he said later, "but to emphasize them during the war could not but aid a declared enemy."

Snow liked the Red Army soldiers he interviewed in Cossack settlements, the youngsters he encountered on crowded Moscow buses, the hearty milkmaids he met on collectivized farms. He especially admired Russian determination and energy, the way people regarded national defense as a personal responsibility. His reporting skills powerfully romanticized people like Zina. With the need for able-bodied men at the front, women assumed great responsibility for wartime industrial and agricultural production. Zina, a classic example of these Amazons, worked in a munitions plant. Snow described her wide grin, her arms like pistons, and her patriotism. "Her husband was at the front, and every time she finished a shell she felt he was nearer her."[22]

Contrasting Nazi brutality touched Snow as much. Children told him of asking German officers for food and getting the boot instead. The worst barbarism, etched like acid on Snow's mind, came at the German death factory at Maidanek, just outside Lublin, Poland. Snow visited the liberated camp with other correspondents in August 1944. The Nazis sent untold numbers, mostly Jews, to their deaths at Maidanek. By one estimate, more than seventeen thousand died on one day. The human ashes fertilized cabbage patches at a model farm. Snow spent several hours going through rooms filled with victims' belongings. One building measuring fifty feet by one hundred feet contained nothing but shoes, everything from babies booties to old women's high laced boots.

The BBC thought Alexander Werth's report too unbelievable to use. The *Post* ran Snow's prominently. "Here at Lublin you got a complete perversion of the historical genius of [the German] race, with method and means becoming everything, action completely dominating imagination, and the end itself losing all significance for the automatons who bring it about," Snow wrote. He talked about Maidanek frequently and in the same terms as he did the withering famine he witnessed on the Saratsi plains in 1929.

Snow could do nothing for the people who passed through Maidanek. For the living he responded the same way he had in China. In the wake of the Battle of Stalingrad, Snow and a fellow correspondent bunked with a family in a recently liberated village. Finding their hosts living on meager rations of flour, they smuggled food from the mess set up for foreign correspondents. Snow could not invite Russians to eat with him in the correspondents' private dining room at the Metropole, but he could invite them to dine in his room. He ate in his quarters as often as possible "with a Russian—any Russian I could lure into the hotel!"

Warm personal bonds developed, not least of all with the women who kept Moscow running. Strong women like Zina always attracted Snow, and the pull was all the greater amid the communal loneliness of the Metropole. The warm descriptions in Snow's articles of engaging, full-figured women hinted of wistfulness. In his second tour, he became romantically entangled with an azure-eyed Moscow university student who worked as his courier.

In this, Snow was hardly out of the ordinary. Reporters commonly shared food with their Russian staffs and developed steamy romances. One day in the Metropole an AP reporter knocked down a British tobacco buyer standing with a young Russian beauty. The journalist slung the girl over his shoulder and took her to his room.

What set Snow apart was the quiet way he went about his work. Unlike many reporters, Snow studied Russian language and history. Not writing spot news removed him from the type of intense journalistic rivalry that erupted one night at the regular eleven o'clock briefing. After government spokesmen released information on movement of the battlefront, three tightly-wound agency reporters fought with fists over a map. At the end, two were out cold, the map in shreds.[23]

Snow's colleagues remembered him, as *Chicago Daily News* reporter David Nichol put it, "for an even temperament which was a blessing in our frustrating surroundings." Snow didn't complain when he and Nichol rode all night to reach Stalingrad "in a broken-down ambulance with no glass in the rear window and an outside temperature of about 40 degrees below zero." Snow concentrated on his work and didn't regularly join in the long bull sessions and cut-throat hearts games that dominated life among the self-described "inmates" of the Metropole.

Reporter John Hersey thought Snow stood out during the distribution of supplies, sent at regular intervals from the United States embassy commissary. The divvying out took place in room 373, belonging to *New York Times* correspondent Bill Lawrence. Most things came in small cans easily passed out, but peanut butter came in gallon cans and had to be spooned out, around and around. The clamor from politically committed reporters like Anna Louise Strong, Ella Winter, and Freda Utley "for their exact share of this communal goody was extremely loud," Hersey recalled. "Not Ed; he was so collected, when it came to peanut butter, that he was often chosen to do the spooning."

Snow differed from others in another way—his extensive Asian experience. Others had worked in that region. None had lived there the way Snow had. Asia had given him his standard of comparison. As Snow commented later, he was inclined to judge the Soviet Union as an advanced Asian nation rather than as simply a backward Western one. His Asian years also taught him to pit fascism against socialism and to treat the latter as a liberating force. Snow considered that Asian experience "part of the special equipment a foreign student ought to take with him to Russia."[24] In reality it was both a plus and a minus.

Snow did not believe in the perfection of the Soviet Union when he arrived. In China he had talked with friends like Jim Bertram for hours trying to puzzle out why Soviet policies seemed to thwart the Chinese revolution. All the same he looked hard for evidence that socialism worked in the Soviet Union, a quest easily sustained by the we-are-all-in-this-together spirit of the time.[25]

Russia had made advances. Tsarist rule and its gross inequities had beaten down large segments of the Russian population. Snow had only to look on Moscow's streets to see the leveling that had occurred since the revolution. As shabby as people were, no one was very richly dressed or "in obvious beggary either," as was the case in Asian countries. But Snow was altogether too positive about how well communism had performed. While he recognized "the cost in human anguish" of agricultural collectivization begun in the 1920s, he overstated the benefits those policies reaped. Notwithstanding the positive figures he cited for agricultural production, harvests from 1933 to 1937 stayed consistently below the inadequate levels of 1928 to 1932. Although it was possible to find collectives with well-stocked larders and enthusiastic workers, as Snow did, farmers generally began the war with a long list of grievances. Altogether collectivization marked, in the words of one latter day economic historian, "a painful period, of which many men in high places must feel ashamed in their hearts."

Before going to Russia, Snow saw a parallel between Chinese guerrilla tactics and the Soviets' *"mobilization of the genius and resourcefulness of the people."* Once there he concluded "the triumph of the Red Army is the triumph of Soviet socialism and, above all, Soviet planning." In contrast to Chiang Kai-shek's pronounced reluctance to fight the enemy, the Soviet government carefully nurtured patriotic feelings. Snow portrayed the Red Army as a democratic army. Many in the officer ranks were the sons of illiterate peasants or workers; "racial barriers are not permitted to block individual advancement"; "Russian officers and civilians alike have no economic investments that could conflict with their single-minded devotion to the interests of the nation as a whole."

As late as mid-1945, when he better understood internal repressive policies, Snow still talked in such terms. "Whatever one may say about the lack of personal freedom and individual liberty under this regime—and very much indeed can be said against it—there is no doubt that realization of the principle of racial and national equality inside the Soviet Union is in line with the best traditions of democracy."

Unfortunately, Stalin's effective tactics for enlisting the people in his cause were not so democratic as Snow supposed. The composition of the officer corps was not only a function of social mobility. The Great Purges of the 1930s had depleted the ranks of twenty to twenty-five thousand officers, maybe many more. There was plenty of room for people to move up. Moreover, the new men who rose to the top in civilian and military capacities were ideologically committed but remarkably indifferent to the welfare of the people. Beneath the government's wartime strategy calling for a strong unified defense lay great capacity for racial discrimination, if it suited the state.

Snow also erred when, inspired by visions of Soviet energy and planning, he predicted that the *Pyatiletka* or five year plan, "will by the middle of the twentieth century make Russia an industrial power capable of producing everything her citizens need, as well as many of the luxuries they want." In ten years, he predicted, Russians would enjoy "a higher living standard than any nation on the continent of Europe or Asia." But despite impressive industrial advances, queues for goods persisted as a postwar way of life for consumers.

Harrison Salisbury placed Snow "among the most sympathetic" reporters to the Soviet Union and considered his China experience a handicap in covering the eastern front. This notwithstanding, he compared Snow's reports favorably with other professional journalists.[26] Salisbury was correct. Snow's worst mistakes occurred early in his tenure in the Soviet Union. One thing fellow reporters remembered him for was working hard to get facts and to understand. Snow became more temperate as he learned more. More important than that, Snow and all other reporters faced the same set of problems, no matter what their personal perspectives: the overwhelming dynamic to be positive about the Soviet allies; the difficulty of getting negative information past censors; the lack of good information. Reliable economic statistics on collectivization, for example, did not become available for years. Neither was it possible to know about, let alone understand, the dimensions of harsh policies toward Asian minorities on Russia's southern border. In areas where Snow expressed dislike for Soviet policy, he could find few sources who openly agreed with him. He loathed the personality cult built around Stalin in the same way he hated Gandhi's demi-god status. Because they had suffered and because they were articulate, intellectuals might have been expected to criticize Stalin's strong-arm tactics, but they did not. They tended to put Stalin on a pedestal and blame other officials for his excesses.

Reporters projected overwhelmingly positive images of the Soviet Union when they had a chance to write at length. Russia, AP's Henry Cassidy wrote in a wartime book *Moscow Dateline*, "is showing its benevolence in many ways, some small, almost intangible, but all sig-

Edgar Snow, interpreter, and Mao Tse-tung on T'ien An Men Gate during October 1, 1970, celebration of the founding of the People's Republic of China.

Edgar Snow, about age four.

Edgar Snow's Westport High School graduation photo, Kansas City, Missouri, 1923.

Edgar Snow on the deck of the *Radnor,* en route to Hawaii—the first leg of a journey that would keep him in Asia until 1941. On the back of the photo Snow wrote of his moustache: "I grew it in two weeks—and cut it off at Honolulu in two seconds."

Edgar Snow, 1928, shortly after he arrived in China. "Strange, isn't it," he wrote home only three days after landing in Shanghai, "that this, the most progressive, the wealthiest port in China should be controlled by foreigners! Yet the British and the Americans say it is all right; doubtless it is—for them."

Edgar Snow, 1929, with elderly Korean "of noble ancestry," Snow wrote on the photo, "though that means little now that the Japanese have abolished their throne."

From right to left, Ministry of Foreign Affairs official, Reuters reporter, Japanese reporter, Chinese reporter, Generalissimo Chiang Kai-shek, J.B. Powell, Randall Gould of the Shanghai *Evening Post & Mercury*, Edgar Snow, Japanese reporter, Victor Keen of the New York *Herald Tribune*. Powell, Snow, and Keen were all members of the "Missouri News Monopoly."

Snow wrote on the back of this photo that the fourteen-year-old Chinese boy supported his mother: "One of the reasons why one does not believe in the 'superiority of the white race.' "

Edgar Snow with his first wife, Helen Foster Snow ("Peg"), in Peking during the mid-1930s.

From left to right, James Bertram, Edgar Snow, Peg Snow, Rewi Alley, and Evans Carlson, at a Baguio, Philippines get-together. Snow is modeling an Indusco banner.

Edgar Snow meets Chou En-lai in 1936, shortly after breaking through the Nationalist blockade of the Communists in Northwest China.

Edgar Snow sat for hours in primitive caves interviewing Red leaders during his 1936 trip to Red China. The second man from the left is Huang Hua, the Yenching student leader who accompanied Snow to the Northwest as his interpreter and subsequently rose through the Red ranks.

Edgar Snow with Red Army soldiers. During his travels in Chinese Communist areas Snow assembled material for his monumental book, *Red Star over China.*

Edgar Snow, 1942, as a war correspondent for the *Saturday Evening Post*. Snow put in two long tours in the Soviet Union and was the first American reporter to reach Soviet-occupied Vienna after the war.

Edgar Snow with Mao Tse-tung and Kung P'eng, Peking, 1960.

Edgar Snow with Chou En-lai and Teng Ying-ch'ao (Mme. Chou) at Miyun Dam, 1960. Snow was the first American journalist with previous experience in China to visit since the founding of the People's Republic in 1949.

Edgar Snow and Mao Tse-tung, 1965. Snow was the last American reporter to visit China before the Cultural Revolution.

Edgar Snow with a duck farmer in 1965.

Edgar Snow and his wife, Lois Wheeler Snow, standing on T'ien An Men Gate during the 1971 National Day celebrations.

Edgar Snow, a few months before he died of cancer in early 1972, pointing to a popular Chinese poster of Mao. The poster is based on a picture Snow took of the leader in 1936. Mao wore Snow's Red Army cap for the shot because he didn't have one of his own at the moment.

nificant. The days of purges, for example, have ended." Convinced of the popular support for the regime, *Collier's* Quentin Reynolds said "there is not one Fifth Columnist, not one Quisling at liberty in Soviet Russia." Writing from the United States, *New York Times* reporter Walter Durranty, who covered the Soviet Union sympathetically for years, observed that "the Bolshevik Revolution has ostensibly—and perhaps genuinely—renounced its international aspects"; while it believed in socialism, the government had "adopted capitalistic *methods* to a very large degree," for example awarding extra pay, decorations, and comforts for meritorious service. *Life, National Geographic,* the *Rotarian,* and all but a handful of major American dailies were similarly upbeat. According to one survey of the period, "the most relevant and immediate accounts of wartime Russia were all favorable."

The last word on Snow's reporting of the Soviet Union does not, however, end there. While his China experience may have been a liability in one way, it also made him more clear-headed in another way. Many reporters saw the Soviet Union in strictly American terms, giving rise to images that suggested it was headed for a system like their own. Unafraid of socialism and having developed a capacity to see the world though the eyes of others, Snow was relatively better attuned than many others to Communist motivations and outlook.[27] For many Americans, as one reporter pointed out, Stalin's meeting with church dignitaries, "was as sensational as would be the news that the *Chicago Tribune* was backing Earl Browder for President." Snow understood that the Kremlin used the church to develop support among "the last islands of opposition left in the populace" and later to compete for loyalty in other European countries. Nor did Snow think that dissolution of the Comintern meant the end of "the international character of the Communist movement, nor its adherence to doctrines enunciated at Moscow." Indeed, Snow excelled in forecasting Soviet Union actions after the last shots of the war were fired. While he was not as good a reporter in the Soviet Union as in China, Snow made a contribution that contemporaries and historians overlooked.

As early as mid-1943, the end of his first tour, Snow concluded that the Red Army would bolster Communist forces in the Eastern European countries it entered and that the Soviet Union would have "the main influence and responsibility there for at least a generation ahead." He foresaw Russia's determination to reach Germany. By the end of the following year, still months before Allied leaders met at Yalta to discuss the map and character of postwar Europe, Snow divined more explicity the shape of Eastern Europe under Soviet influence: strong central governments backed by "stable police power"; state owned and controlled industry so that "capitalism as we have known it in America will not exist"; governments operating "on the principle that respect for and collaboration with the Soviet fatherland are not only the best policy but the central policy of their security." The Soviets would extract heavy reparations. Despite promises of freedom of the press, speech, assembly, and worship, "wrong-minded people" had been warned that "democratic liberties would not be allowed to serve the enemies of democracy."[28]

All of that applied to Germany, where the Soviets would operate their own occupation zone in their own way. "It must be remembered that there has been no renunciation here of Marxist Philosophy in general or of the Marxist analysis of the causes of German reaction in particular."

He was equally prophetic about Russian participation on the Asian front. In early October 1943, before Stalin began to discuss the subject informally with American diplomats, Snow predicted that Russia would not turn its forces against Japan until it defeated Germany. When Moscow did agree to turn eastward, it "would make maximum use of the bargaining value of its strategic position in the Far East" and then not actually enter the war until "the moment when she can do so with the least possible risk commensurate with the great aims at stake, not till Japan is near collapse."

At the Yalta meeting, a year and a half later, Stalin won secret agreement from Roosevelt almost precisely along those lines. In exchange for going to war with Japan within "two or three months" after Germany fell, the Soviet Union was to receive the Kurile Islands and lower Sakhalin from Japan and control over Outer Mongolia as well as over the principal ports and railways of Manchuria. The final part of Snow's 1943 prediction would play itself out later: when Soviet "intervention comes, it may not conform to any preconceived patterns imagined for it."

Snow thought the Soviet Union might, after so many years of shunning the Chinese Communists, begin to throw real support to them. "There was a lot of lazy thinking by Americans before the Red Army began moving into Europe, and, consequently a lot of people are now 'disillusioned' to find that the Kremlin has its own ideas about how to make friends and influence people in Eastern Europe," Snow wrote just before Yalta. ". . . These people will probably even pretend to be shocked to find out that Moscow has some very concrete ideas about the kind of good neighbor it wants in China. . . . I see nothing but trouble ahead, if we do not candidly face the known facts right now about Russia and China."[29]

At the end of his first tour Snow reported overhearing a young Russian woman say that the United States would flood the country with "goods of all kinds" after the war. Her idea was "possibly closer to the government's expectations than many realize," Snow commented. Not long afterward Snow offered a strong corrective. A glittering Russian market was a mirage. "Note this carefully," he wrote in the *Saturday Evening Post*, "not what the individual Russian consumer or particular region or group may want to buy from us, but what the State plan requires for its fulfillment, will determine the size and nature of the Soviet market."[30]

The mix of Snow's romanticism about socialism and his realism about socialism showed themselves in an August 1944 conversation with Averell Harriman, United States ambassador to Moscow. Snow said he saw the Red Army as a liberating force. The army might not make much difference to Czechoslovakia, "the only truly democratic government in Eastern Europe," which had developed an ability for living alongside the Soviets, but people in other countries would welcome Soviet troops. In the Soviet wake "organized peasants and organized workers, rather than the land barons and capitalists, will dominate." If Snow forgot a fundamental point he learned in China—that effective social revolution had to come from within a country and could and should not be imposed from the outside—he understood other Eastern European realities clearly. He realized American-style democracy was not irrelevant. "The people in these countries who understand what we mean by democracy are very few," he said. "Democracy in our sense can't exist here because there hasn't been complete overthrow of feudal tradition. The Russians also cannot understand it." In addition, the Soviets would tolerate little opposition, he told Harriman. They would eliminate within these countries "those opposed to the idea of Soviet domination."[31]

Snow once suggested to Harriman that they had similar jobs: both of their reports had to hold up for months. It was a revealing remark. For while Snow realized Harriman had some of the same problems as a journalist, he also saw himself as an unofficial envoy, the eyes and ears of average Americans whose attitudes shaped official diplomatic relations with the Soviet Union. He agonized over the responsibility, asking people as diverse as Secretary of State Cordell Hull and Soviet diplomat Maxim Litvinov what a writer could do to help keep things from "getting worse and leading to more war." The conclusion he reached in Russia was that Americans needed to understand not only what the Soviets would do after the war but why.[32]

The Soviet Union, Snow thought as the war ended, was tired and insecure. The fighting devastated the country beyond anything most Americans imagined: more than twenty million soldiers and civilians dead or missing (as compared to 322,000 American casualties); millions more homeless, many living in holes in the ground. Twenty out of twenty-three million pigs lost; sixty-five thousand kilometers of railway track lost; factories, dams, bridges, tractors—all lost. As Snow recognized, this was only one in a series of blows during the century. The German attack during World War I and the humiliating peace of Brest-Litovsk cost lives and territory. After that war, United States and British forces added weight to White Armies and launched operations on Soviet soil. Poland invaded the Ukraine and actually held Kiev for six weeks in 1920. The two-year delay in opening the second front during World War II, which cost the Soviets dearly, did not allay Soviet suspicions of the West. Some Westerners argued that Soviet Communists and the German Nazis had much in common; both were totalitarian. From Stalin's perspective, however, the Nazis and Western Allies had much in common, constituting a capitalist encirclement of the Soviet Union.

Snow viewed Soviet activities on its border not as expansion for expansion's sake, but rather as an effort to regain lost territory and protect itself against future attack. "As far as I can see, what Russia wants after this war more than anything else is a breathing spell, a chance to make up lost ground," Snow told Litvinov. The United States could not exploit this weakness, he thought, to force the Soviet Union to back down. The Soviets had a natural reach and interest in Eastern Europe, much as the United States had in Latin America. During the war American leaders paid scant attention to postwar issues, never stating their "political aims with clarity and conciseness in a manner which the Russians could consider as a serious alternative to their methods of establishing stability." The solution, therefore, was to recognize the inevitability of a Soviet *cordon sanitaire* in Eastern Europe and, rather than arouse traditional Soviet suspicions of the West, provide financial assistance and seek areas of cooperation. "Once the Kremlin feels reasonably secure in a peaceful world," Snow concluded, "it may become possible for the Russian people to enjoy the freedoms of political democracy—a democracy more in line with our own best traditions—side by side with the Soviet system of economy."

A private talk with Litvinov in October 1944 did not inspire Snow with confidence about the future.[33] Rotund, emotional, and open, Litvinov was a favorite of the foreign community. Once foreign minister and later ambassador to the United States, he was now on the back shelf, as he put it, as Soviet vice-commissar for foreign affairs. Virtually alone among officials, Litvinov met privately with reporters. They entered by a side foreign office entrance. His views were often at odds with the government's. In the conversation with Snow, Livinov agreed that Soviet hostility to the Western press thwarted efforts to develop better American understanding of Soviet aims and aspirations. The Soviets had erred in not making their views clear on why anti-Soviet Polish leaders located in London could not resume power. At the same time he believed that the West was continuing its old ways, trying to isolate Russia. "Poland has got to be friendly toward this country and must abandon the idea that she can be a springboard against Russia and in that way get back her 16th century empire." Likewise, the Soviet Union could not countenance a unified Germany unless it was small and governed by a reeducation program ensuring its people were "harmless and peaceful." Litvinov predicted that "we won't be able to agree on a common program for Germany." It all seemed too difficult. Diplomacy might have been able to circumvent the problems at one time, "but now it is too late, suspicions are rife on both sides."

The conversation lasted three hours. Litvinov had never been so candid with Snow before. His pessimism contrasted sharply with the upbeat rhetoric that prevailed. Snow wanted to convey Litvinov's remarks to Harriman. Litvinov, who at one point did tell Harriman that the Soviet Union simply could not permit another bloodletting, said Snow could only pass them on to Roosevelt. Three days after Christmas, when Snow was back in Madison, Connecticut, he wrote a private letter to the president relating his conversation with Litvinov.

Snow had corresponded with Roosevelt during the war, sending, among other things, a plan for improving Soviet-American understanding and a paperweight bust of Gandhi. To this most recent letter, Roosevelt responded that he found Litvinov's remarks "tremendously interesting"—though FDR soon made it clear he did not consider them particularly important.

In early March FDR reported to Congress on the Yalta meeting with Churchill and Stalin, asserting that the United States had "to take responsibility for world collaboration." Snow, in Washington, sent Roosevelt a note of congratulations. Word came back that Snow should stop by the White House. Continuing a theme from their previous meeting, when Snow was between his two assignments in Russia, Roosevelt claimed he was making progress explaining the United States system to Stalin. Snow found Roosevelt's "optimism so contagious that it dispelled most of my fears."[34]

"Obviously the Russians are going to do things in their own way in areas they occupy," Roosevelt said. "But they won't set up a separate administration (independent of the allied Control Commission) to rival any arrangement made for all Germany. . . . I got the impression that the Russians are now fully satisfied and that we can work out everything together. I am convinced we are going to get along."

The conversation, reflecting the glow of Yalta, masked the uncertainty in FDR's thinking about Europe after the war. On occasion Roosevelt worried about Russian fear of encirclement and the possibility that the British might aggravate that paranoia by carving out traditional spheres of influence in Europe. He seemed at times to have little sympathy for Poland and other small Eastern European countries. But it was far from certain that Roosevelt was reconciled to Soviet hegemony in Eastern Europe. Only a few weeks after meeting with Snow, he and Churchill lodged a protest with Stalin over violations of the Yalta accords in Poland. Stalin had demanded that Soviet-sponsored leaders decide which Poles should consult on establishment of a provisional government. Roosevelt expressed worry over Stalin's unwillingness to send his foreign minister to the United Nations founding conference in San Francisco.

Roosevelt's ambivalence was to prove costly for U.S. foreign policy. No one knew for certain what American policy would be after the war—not Stalin and not the American people. With military objectives monopolizing his time, Roosevelt left tomorrow's problems for tomorrow. Perhaps Stalin's actions would not have changed had the United States given clear signals on its expectations for places like Poland. But realistic U.S. assessments of the Soviets were essential for developing policies to cope and for preventing overreaction by an American public taken by surprise later. Litvinov's remarks to Snow were a warning of the dangers inherent in an approach that glossed over tough issues. Although the Soviet diplomat fruitlessly tried to send his message to FDR through others besides Snow, it was already too late.

Snow believed that Roosevelt would have "left nothing untried, within the limits of his power and his imagination as a great politician," to make and sustain some kind of entente with the Soviet Union. He may have been correct. Roosevelt had a genius for finding solutions to immediate problems. He might, as Snow believed, have worked out an "orderly but speedy attainment of equality" for colonial nations. But Roosevelt, who overrode democratic traditions limiting him to only two terms in office, could not deny the forces of nature. Less than five weeks after talking to Snow, he died at his retreat in Warm Springs, Georgia. Men who did not seem larger than life took over a task for which they had little preparation. For too long Roosevelt had put the future the same place Kremlin bosses had put Litvinov—on the shelf.[35]

Excessive hopefulness about Russia permeated America. Officials who worked closely with the Soviet Union complained of bureaucratic delays and Moscow's refusal to exchange military information. The public heard little of this. As Hull told Congress on the eve of the Teheran conference, "there will no longer be need for spheres of influence, for alliances, for balance of power, or any other of the special arrangements through which, in the unhappy past, the nations strove to safeguard their security or to promote their interests." Roosevelt's unsuccessful opponent in the 1940 presidential race, Wendell Willkie visited "our ally, Russia," in 1942. He wisely hoped for mutual understanding after the war but chose an unwise strategy for achieving it. As he told his Russian hosts, he would not talk about anything that might create an unfavorable impression in the United States.[36]

Willkie's book, *One World*, was the number one best seller in bookstores in 1943. At the same time, public attitudes toward the Soviet Union turned decidedly positive. An opinion poll in early 1945 showed that more than twice as many Americans thought the United States would get along better with the Russians than in the past. When asked what the United States had most to gain from this friendship, the number one response, by far, was "trade, commerce, a market."

Snow wrote two books during the war, one after each tour in the Soviet Union. *People on Our Side*, relating his experiences and impressions of India, China, and the Soviet Union, appeared in late summer 1944. *The Pattern of Soviet Power*, devoted entirely to the Soviet Union, came out in mid-1945. Both books, printed on cheap off-white paper, had the feel of other wartime volumes with eyewitness reporting that glorified the Allies. Both books, like the *Saturday Evening Post* articles from which they were derived, were too hopeful about the good the Soviets might do. But the volumes did not belong among the class of books which fit the description poet Archibald MacLeish gave to wartime movies, "escapist and delusionist." Both talked concretely about the likely harsh realities of Soviet policies in Eastern Europe. As widely reported, the working title of *The Pattern of Soviet Power* was *Russia Invades Europe*. In addition, Snow outlined a realistic program for encouraging decolonization after the war.[37]

A remarkable number of reviewers commented that Snow honestly tried to understand the facts behind events. More remarkable was the way they treated his predictions on Soviet behavior. Although reviewers brought varying degrees of sophistication and points of view to their task, a typical pattern was to note Snow's unpleasant predictions, then discount them. "Some of Mr. Snow's facts will confirm the worst fears of those who doubt the benignity of Soviet intentions," a reviewer in the *Columbus Dispatch* wrote of *The Pattern of Soviet Power*. "But there is also encouragement and comfort both for those who are reserving judgment and for those who sincerely believe that Russia will be a constructive force for the keeping of the future peace." Concentrating on the war, Americans didn't dwell on the accommodations that Snow said were also necessary to maintain peace.

The same present-mindedness applied with regard to *People on Our Side*. In it Snow reported Indians' relative indifference to the Japanese threat and Chiang's squandering of precious resources in the civil war. "That part of the book which deals with the Soviet's singleness of purpose . . . gives us what we want to hear of our allies" a *Chicago Sun* reviewer wrote, "the sections on India and China reveal a weakness in our camp which, had it not been counterbalanced by American, British and Russian unity, could have seriously endangered the victorious outcome of this war." Almost no attention went to Snow's brief proposal for using Anglo-American capital to create independent, prosperous nations out of colonial states after the war. Snow considered it the thesis of the book.

The books did fabulously well. The reviews were the best Snow received in his entire career. Roosevelt said he stayed up half the night reading *People on Our Side* en route to Yalta. (Ironically, considering FDR's reluctance to challenge Churchill, his only criticism was that Snow pulled his punches on the British.) The Book-of-the-Month Club selected *People on Our Side* as a book-dividend; the Council on Books in Wartime chose it as "imperative" reading, a distinction it also gave to Willkie's *One World*. A special printing of two hundred thousand copies was made for distribution to U.S. armed forces. Snow calculated it sold more than half a million copies. *The Pattern of Soviet Power* became a Literary Guild selection. Random House's Bennett Cerf gleefully sent Snow a picture of Shirley Temple "dandling" a copy of one of Snow's books on her knee.

Snow, "one of our era's best political reporters," was a hot property. Though still a terrible speaker, audiences packed Maple Leaf Gardens in Toronto to hear him; he was a sought-after radio guest. Requests for his time poured in at such a rate that, he commented at one point, he was waiting for an offer to give a testimonial for Smith Brothers Cough Drops.

More than one commentator noticed that Snow "represents the farthest Left views on that conservative publication," the *Saturday Evening Post*. But the Snow-*Post* relationship was happy on both sides. Snow wove larger issues into his stories without straying from the flesh and blood portraits of people that the *Post* relished. (The editors billed one story: "A Post Correspondent who has lived with the Red Army paints a vivid picture of the vodka-drinking, warmhearted generals who won't be licked.") The readers liked what they saw. According to *Book-of-the-Month-Club News*, a *Saturday Evening Post* poll of its readers' favorite war reporters placed Snow "first and way in the lead." In January 1944, the *Post* named him an associate editor.

The *Post* editors happily announced in "Keeping Posted," a regular feature about the people who worked for the magazine, that they often didn't know where Snow was. Indeed, they were eager to keep him on the move. Between tours in the Soviet Union, they sent him back to India for a spell, whence he took another short hop over the Hump to China; afterward they briefly posted him in London, where he wrote a story on the aerial war. Snow dedicated *The Pattern of Soviet Power* to editors Ben Hibbs and Martin Sommers, "who gave me this assignment and full freedom to report it."

Snow finished *The Pattern of Soviet Power* in his corncribs studio in Madison, Connecticut. Not long afterward he and Peg agreed to a formal separation, another step toward complete estrangement. The *Post* put Snow back on the fly before his new book was in type. In April he left for Western Europe to cover the end of the war. The day after the Germans surrendered, May 7, he was in Salzburg, where he interviewed Nazi prisoners, among them Hermann Goering. Snow had no sympathy for the tears of "little dark men" like Fritz Sauckel, who as head of the Reich's manpower mobilization had millions of forced laborers under him. Driving a German Ford he scrounged from the military, Snow was the first to reach the Mautthausen concentration camp.

The Red Army had moved into Austria and sealed off Vienna. Armed with a map and an introduction to the Viennese anti-Nazi underground provided by a former prisoner at Mautthausen, Snow and Jack Bell of the *Chicago Daily News* headed for Vienna. They lubricated their way past a Russian outpost with whisky toasts to Allied brotherhood. Russian occupation forces treated the Austrians harshly. In Allied territory, Snow reported "peasants and newly freed prisoners tilled the fields and peacefully tended their herds of cattle. On the Russian side, when you passed cows at all, they were being driven off under guard, to fill meat-craving Bolshevik stomachs." The Russians loaded every east-bound train with reparations. In Vienna Snow interviewed members of the interim coalition government, all of whom seemed hopeful about reviving democracy. He and Bell found four American flyers at the University of Vienna hospital. After wheedling precious petroleum out of a Red Cross representative, the reporters loaded the weakened airmen in the car and headed back to American-held territory. Snow and Bell gave details of their trip to U.S. military officers. The trip was in the best tradition of American journalistic enterprise, producing a scoop that even survived his extended magazine deadline.[38]

Snow kept the Ford. He spent a "wonderful" month driving through Europe, from Marseilles to Brussels. The carefree spirit of the road caught up with him in Paris, where he cemented his reputation as "the worst driver in history," in the words of fellow *Post* correspondent Collie Small. With Small in the car one Sunday, Snow had three accidents in twenty minutes. In the large square of the Place Vendome he managed to ram the only car in sight. Snow eventually sold the Ford to help pay off an eight hundred dollar poker debt.[39]

At the end of July Snow left for Russia by way of Stockholm and Finland. He was hopeful about the future. Harry Truman's most difficult job, he thought, would be to replace "Roosevelt in the relationship which the departed chief established with Joseph Stalin." Yet, Americans would get along with Russia, Snow wrote Saxe Cummins, his editor at Random House. Practical considerations would force Americans to accept Stalin's need for security.[40]

Snow could not have been more wrong.

Legitimate historical debate would later center on whether America's efforts to isolate and pressure the Soviet Union fed its anxiety and destroyed the basis for accommodation after the war. About one thing, though, there was no debate. Americans were utterly unprepared for the events that unfolded. The fault lay not with political leaders, not with the press, and not with the American public generally. The fault lay with all of them together, products of a country that had never learned to look outward. Faced with their failure, Americans did not honor Snow, who for all his idealism had supplied a powerful dose of realism. Acting out of the same historical imperative that drove them to isolationism before, Americans went on a binge of internal recriminations that revealed how superficial Snow's fame had been all along.

In the Path of the Storm

6

The war years were hard on Snow's friends. Evans Carlson, to whom he dedicated *People on Our Side,* was seriously wounded while commanding a Marine raider battalion in the Pacific. The injuries forced the heavily decorated officer to retire. He died of a heart attack in 1947. He was 51. The Japanese interned Jim Bertram in Hongkong. For nearly four years he did coolie work there and in Japan. At the beginning of the war Snow renewed his friendship with *PM* correspondent Ben Robertson, a University of Missouri classmate and author of *Red Hills and Cotton,* the story of his southern boyhood. In 1943 Robertson died in a plane crash off Lisbon.

In the mid-1930s, the Nationalists had shunted aside *China Weekly Review* founder Tom Millard. His inflammatory anti-Japanese feelings ran counter to Chiang's policy of appeasement. Unmarried, in his late sixties, and feeling he belonged in China as much as any place, Millard hung around Shanghai until, on the eve of Pearl Harbor, he broke his shoulder in a fall in front of the American Club. He went to Seattle to recover with relatives and never returned. He died of cancer in the summer of 1942.

J. B. Powell stayed in Shanghai despite threats and a failed attempt on his life. (The assassin didn't pull the pin completely on the grenade.) Rejecting offers from a Japanese front to buy the *Review,* he secretly operated a radio station until December 1941 when the Japanese imprisoned him along with a number of other Missourians, including Victor Keen of the *New York Herald Tribune* and Morris Harris and Jimmy White, both of the Associated Press. Powell first shared a 12′ x 18′ cell with forty other prisoners at the infamous Bridge House Prison. Beaten regularly, deprived of nutritious food, forced to sit for hours on his feet

Japanese-style, and without proper warmth during the winter months, Powell's health deteriorated until his weight dropped to one-half normal. Gangrene set into his feet, parts of which were amputated before the broken journalist went home in late 1942 on the exchange ship *Gripsholm.*[1]

Snow could consider himself lucky. There were hardships: his dengue fever in India; a bout with malaria when he reached London in 1943; a mild case of scurvy as a result of the inadequate diet in Russia. But he kept working. He left the Soviet Union in 1943 weakened from influenza and, according to an amateur military dentist in Karachi, a sergeant, suffering from trenchmouth. Snow headed home for dental treatment. When he reached West Africa a bona fide dentist diagnosed the problem as an abscessed tooth, which he pulled. Snow got on a plane for India.[2] All those years Snow had access to the *Post*'s audience, so enormous that the magazine had trouble during the war finding enough boxcars to haul the weekly print run across the country.

The postwar years, not the war years, brought real hardship for Snow. Americans were not prepared for the events he forecast in Eastern Europe and Asia. At heart they remained isolationist. Although public interest in foreign affairs rose during the war, according to one estimate nearly one-third of the American people paid no attention at all to international events. The *Saturday Evening Post* inaugurated its "The Cities of America" series with an article on Kansas City in August 1945, the month of the Japanese surrender. The author inadvertently summed up the national mood when he observed that Kansas City was "probably the most typical of America's big towns" and that it "was as far from the war as you can get in the United States." Traveling through the country, journalist John Gunther listed midwestern hallmarks: church suppers and country clubs; the worship of vitamins, golf, and Frank Sinatra. "Mr. Willkie's 'one world' idea simply did not exist," he observed, "rather, there *was* only one world, and it was the United States."[3]

Thus, when events overseas took turns they never expected, Americans fell into a funk of bewilderment. Where before they conjured benign views of the Communists, they now saw only evil. Snow, one of those they blamed instead of themselves, survived the war only to become a casualty of the peace.

Snow was back in the Soviet Union when two United States atomic bombs hammered Japan into submission. With peace secured, the key motivation for self-censorship by American correspondents vanished. Despite the old problem of getting Soviets to talk about themselves and their political opinions, Snow was able to penetrate further than before. A Communist-hating Ukrainian acquaintance helped him find a typical Moscow family coping with life after the war. In the resulting article, which he filed outside the country, Snow described hardships under Communist rule: the family's tiny living quarters and the shared kitchen; their long hours standing in line to buy groceries; their despair of having adequate food or clothes any time soon; their worry over a relative sent to Siberia because he "had the misfortune to work in a tractor plant which was alleged, during the purge in 1938, to contain traitors and saboteurs."[4]

In another article Snow reported the murmurings of American discontent picked up from people like diplomat George Kennan, who argued for cutting off assistance to the Soviets, and General John Deane, head of the military mission in Moscow. The Soviets, Snow reported, had only cooperated when it was to their benefit to do so. They did not accredit military observers or foreign correspondents to their military and restricted American use of airfields. Soviet officials routinely stymied Americans with " bureaucratic obstacles and procrastination." As one sign of the lingering suspicion of Americans, Snow noted the potential "disastrous consequences" for ordinary Russians who dared make friends with an American. Worse, it seemed to him that the Soviet leadership favored an offensive posture toward the United States, whose strength seemed menacingly accentuated by the atomic bomb.

When General Dwight Eisenhower visited Moscow, Snow asked him privately about the impact of the atomic bomb on Soviet-American relations. "I don't know," Ike responded. "People are frightened and disturbed all over."

Still, the sight of Ike watching a parade shoulder to shoulder with Russian generals on a podium over Lenin's tomb offered a hopeful sign. Snow's article outlining American frustrations pointed out the "genuine regard" average Russians had for Americans as a result of United States aid and limited cultural exchanges.

"Such trivial gains as have been made hardly seem to have justified the faith which animated Roosevelt's policy, when months before Pearl Habor, he decided to extend Lend-Lease aid to Russia," Snow summed up. "But taken together with other events on an international scale, they leave room for hope that in time the Soviet government will widen the crevices in which it now permits its citizens to meet the family of nations."[5]

Snow's stay coincided with the visit of the first congressional delegation to the Soviet Union since 1939. He spent several days with the four legislators in Moscow. Their report called for an "immediate abandonment of any semblance of appeasement in our own negotiations and relations with Russia." Although the report did not mention Snow, it also emphasized his point on the need for the "increased exchange of people, products, and publicity" between the two countries and a Truman-Stalin conference as soon as possible "to dispel Soviet suspicions of American purpose and intent."[6]

When leaving Moscow in September for Saudi Arabia, the delegation offered to take Snow along. He had an extraordinary open-ended visa to Saudi Arabia, acquired several years before from an acquaintance who worked as a mining advisor to King Ibn Saud. Only one other reporter had entered the secluded desert kingdom. Snow, who planned to return to Asia anyway, eagerly accepted the congressional invitation.

During the first leg of the trip Snow breezed along in the delegation's C–47, helping Republican congressman Karl Mundt of South Dakota with the spellings of names and places for his report. A jittery American Foreign Service Officer greeted them in Teheran. He was to accompany the legislators to Saudi Arabia and didn't like the idea of a woman, Representative Frances Bolton of Ohio, or a reporter going along. Both might offend the King. The delegation refused to drop either. Mundt appointed Snow honorary press attaché.

The delegation spent three days in the country, one of them in Riyadh with Ibn Saud, six feet four inches tall and truly majestic in his robe and hooded cloak. Dinner with the king consisted of mountains of lamb, fish, vegetables, and fowl, eaten under a starry sky. Afterward, he asked for financial help to feed his people until oil wealth materialized. When the legislators filed out, the king took Snow aside for a private talk. Holding Snow's hand in his own, Arabian-style, he reiterated another point he made at dinner. Western nations must recognize the complete independence of all Middle Eastern countries and not try to impose a solution on Palestine. The Europeans, not the Moslems, had persecuted Jews; Palestine should not now have to receive all Jewish refugees.

"Not only is uncounted wealth hidden here but future history potentially full of international dynamite sleeps beside it," Snow concluded. "Before that history is fully written Americans are likely to become as familiar with the map of Arabia as with one of their own states, and Arabs will drop their veil of seclusion, to be assimilated by the industrialized world, for better or for worse."[7]

Snow left Riyadh with an Arab costume, a gold watch, and a jeweled sword, gifts the king bestowed on each member of the delegation. Breaking off from the delegation, Snow went to India for three weeks, with a side trip over the Hump to Kunming, then on to Bangkok and

Saigon to see how Western powers intended to spend the influence and moral capital they had gained by defeating fascism. He quickly concluded they would squander it.[8]

Thailand, the one independent country in southeast Asia at the beginning of the war, had become an unenthusiastic Japanese ally for reasons of self-defense. While Snow accepted that Thailand should pay reparations, he objected to British demands for control of Thai commodity exports and military base rights. It sounded to Snow like the old colonial way of doing things. Likewise, he disliked the British policies in Indo-China. Invited by the provisional Annamite government to help restore order, the British reinstated the French in their original colonial positions. As if that weren't bad enough, they rearmed Japanese troops in order to keep the country out of the hands of the native population.

The United States took little interest in these episodes. American acquiescence contrasted sharply with its wartime broadcasts overseas about freedom, Snow wrote ruefully. "This is one of the reasons why some observers out here keep saying that America ended the war with greater prestige than any nation in history—and is losing it more rapidly than any nation in history."

Snow reported that one member of the small staff of American officers and noncoms in Indo-China perished in a crossfire of Annamite and colonial bullets. A new conflict had begun, Snow wrote. Independence will be "determined, as issues of slavery versus freedom have always been settled in the past, by the sum of armed force the slaves are able to mobilize, by the degree of fanaticism with which they resist, by the moral and political strength behind their struggle, and, in the last resort, by the preparedness of the revolutionaries not so much for self-government as to be machine-gunned, bombed or perhaps atomized in defense of their inalienable rights as free men."

Snow's next stop was Manila, so disfigured by the war he could hardly find his way around. He stayed with a Chinese friend from his days raising money in the Philippines for Indusco. While waiting for *Post* foreign editor Marty Sommers to join him for a trip through East Asia, Snow continued his usual peripatetic wanderings, part of it with a young naval officer he met one Sunday afternoon after giving a talk at the YMCA.[9] Darold Beckman, who had taken an interest in political and social movements in the islands, offered to introduce Snow to Luis Taruc and other leaders of the Hukbalahap, a Communist guerrilla organization of workers and peasants that had resisted the Japanese. Snow's interviews with the Huks at San Fernando, in Pampanga Province, dwelt largely on political theory, Luis Taruc later recalled.

Snow invited Beckman to join him and *New York Post* correspondent Darrell Berrigan for a trip to Baguio. Beckman's memories of the trip formed a vivid picture of Snow's personality and outlook. Snow seemed utterly unselfconscious about his stature or prestige. While traveling in a chauffeur–driven army car, he played chess with Beckman on a pocket-sized board and talked about the skill of peasants who terraced the mountains to make farms. In Baguio he and Beckman shared a room with twin beds, each of which had a thin mattress on a set of springs. When Snow turned out the lights and climbed into bed, there was a metallic twang and Snow landed on the floor. Opposite corners of his bedspring had turned up. With the lights on once more, he and Beckman tried to make the bedsprings lie flat. When they pressed one corner down another popped up until they were hysterical with laughter. "Now," Snow said, "I know why they call them bed springs."

Shortly after arriving, Snow sent Beckman with a twenty dollar bill to get a bottle of whiskey. They took the liquor on an interview with a former Japanese puppet official. They became too loosened up themselves to get the details straight how the puppet president "escaped" from the Japanese and made contact with MacArthur. Snow and his companions returned the next morning, hangover and all, to repeat the interview.

Snow located the fine old Baguio cottage where he and Peg had lived. Igorots had torn out the nara wood paneling and built six native huts inside the dwelling. Snow viewed the episode philosophically as a symbol of native ways replacing Western influence. After watching an Igorot family work together to carve wooden figures, Snow commented on their cooperation. This quality, more than competitiveness, made mankind an advanced animal, he told Beckman.

In a *Post* article, Snow addressed the same question he faced in Bangkok and Saigon: what the United States should do. Snow did not believe that U. S. responsibility ended with Philippine independence, set for July 4 of the next year, 1946. "Political independence is only an illusion for small nations unless economic and military security go with it," he observed. ". . . [T]hese islands are destined to remain a *de facto* dependency of the United States for decades to come."

In suggesting specific steps, Snow did not challenge the policy of maintaining military bases in the islands. But he wanted the United States to combine those strategic interests with policies supporting land reform and extending economic and financial help to the Filipinos. "Unfortunately," he concluded, "our Philippines-rehabilitation program offers little scope for anything but a return to things exactly as they were." The situation could spawn another guerrilla movement.[10]

That important message did not register in Washington. Ultimately, Snow had more influence on the Huks.

Shortly after being elected to Congress in 1946, Taruc was unseated. According to the charges, he, along with other Huks, used terrorist tactics to gain power. Taruc vehemently denied this. His "crime," he said, was to oppose odious government policies, including "the Military Bases Agreement imposed by the United States." The Huks returned to the hills. While Taruc disavowed any direct links with China or Russia, he acknowledged that the Chinese Communist struggle provided an important source of inspiration. The Huks, he said, used *Red Star over China* as a textbook for their guerrilla activities.[11]

Red Star's tale of Chinese Communist resistance had an impressive reach, as Snow reported in an update of the book for Random House's Modern Library series in 1944. Indians, Burmese, and Malayans, as well as a trio of Russian women guerrillas he stumbled upon in Smolensk, told him of using the book as a guerrilla manual.[12]

Conversations on Red China appealed to Snow, Beckman noticed. Indeed, China was on Snow's mind throughout the war. One day in Paris he came across one of his former Yenching students, now a correspondent in Europe. They spent the afternoon in the hotel bar talking of the old days in Peking; more than once Snow said China was his second home. Moreover, Snow worried that the war had not resolved China's problems any more than it had Thailand's, Indo-China's, or the Philippines's.[13]

After Snow's 1939 visit to Yenan, Chiang Kai-shek closed the door to the Red capital so tightly that no Western reporters entered. Ironically, that tactic kept reporters from learning details of Mao's tough rectification campaign, a political tool for tightening discipline during a time of growing party membership and intense pressure from the Kuomintang and Japanese. In a preview of later Chinese Communist campaigns to control intellectuals, writer Ting Ling, whose work appeared in Snow's *Living China*, came under heavy attack. She lost her editorial position and—after confessing her errors—went to the countryside for two years to "study" with the peasantry. But even if reporters had witnessed the rectification campaign, which was nothing like Stalin's bloody purges, the Communists' civic honesty and steps to improve living standards in their region remained their outstanding feature at the time. Of the handful of nonjournalists who visited Red territory, American banker G. Martel Hall came back with a familiar story. Though predisposed to dislike the Communists, he concluded that they created the most nearly democratic government in China. However much real journalists might doubt such reports, they knew Chungking. The daily displays of corruption and inefficiency sickened most of them.[14]

Snow did what he could to stay in touch with China, making brief visits there in 1942 and 1943 and developing contacts with people like Hall. Chou En-Lai wrote to him that China had "changed a great deal since you left us" due to disintegration of the united front. Snow realized that while civil war damaged anti-Japanese resistance it did not necessarily hurt the Communists. As he predicted in 1938, they strengthened their "hold on rural China . . . each day of the war's prolongation." Infiltrating behind Japanese lines, carefully avoiding pitched, open battles, and offering Chinese peasants a life free of oppressive taxes and rents, the Communists steadily enlarged their sphere of influence and conserved their strength. Between 1937 and 1943, the area under Red control increased five-fold; the population jumped from 1.5 to 54 million. Snow and other observers came to see three countries in China—one ruled by the Nationalists, one by the Japanese, and one by the Communists.[15]

Snow remained personally involved.[16] In 1942 he took the trouble to write an introduction to the English-language edition of a patriotic Chinese novel about anti-Japanese resistance. In a characteristic gesture, he sent a one thousand dollar check to Chinese orphans through Evans Carlson. Snow disliked the demands Indusco made on his time and "became very pessimistic" as the war wore on, recalled Peg Snow who worked avidly on the cause. Snow, nevertheless, did what he could from afar to promote Indusco as "the key to China's future." Acting as a bridge between warring factions, he argued, Indusco could head off bloody internecine warfare and "create a solid economic foundation on which to build the future of China along democratic, peaceful lines." He also thought the cooperatives provided a useful framework for democracy elsewhere. "It is necessary for Americans to begin to realize that Indusco offers us a real alternative to participation in the exploitation of slave labor in the colonial countries through continuation of present trends of economic intervention."

As it turned out, 1940 proved the high point for the cooperatives. Americans' contributions reached fifty thousand dollars a month, but the organization was as fractured as the united front. Chungking wanted to corner Indusco's funds, not only for its own purposes but to deny possible support to the Communists. Alley and others who wanted money directed straight to the field for practical, nonpartisan projects, could not overcome Nationalist pressure. In 1942, the government limited Alley's clout by terminating his appointment as Indusco's Technical Advisor. Alley continued as best he could in a more limited role, but

Indusco faltered. Only three to four hundred units survived after the war, less than one quarter the 1940 level.

Snow believed that Indusco did much better in Communist areas. By his estimate, the Yenan depot became in 1942 "the largest regional headquarters in the country with as many workers as all the others in China combined." Years later Snow suggested that independent Communist support for Indusco "became a decisive factor in their final triumph." That claim was excessive. Snow was much closer to the truth when he observed that the Nationalists' failure to use the movement to build popular support went a long way toward explaining why Chiang did not succeed.

As stark as the contrast between the Communists and the Nationalists was, the tension didn't make its way into the American public's consciousness during the first years of the war. In the same way reporters in Moscow confined their complaints to the dinner table at the Metropole, journalists in Chungking held back negative news. Pearl Buck and a few others expressed mild criticism of the Nationalists in 1943, hardly enough to erode confidence in Chiang. Though Snow was among the most vocal critics of the Nationalists, he, too, curbed his comments in hopes of avoiding a rupture that would hurt the war effort.

Robert Barnett summed up the prevailing attitude in an "off the record" talk at an Institute of Pacific Relations meeting in August 1942. In relating a recent trip to China, Barnett complained that censorship and superficial inquiries by editors produced a great shortage of important news from China. He went on to say that he was not about to buck the tide. "Little of what I will say is secret in Chungking. Little of it, however, is for publication."[17]

Under these circumstances, Americans had little reason to doubt Nebraska Senator Kenneth Wherry, who proclaimed to a cheering crowd at the outset of the war that "we will lift Shanghai up and up, ever up, until it is just like Kansas City." Americans thought of the Chinese as truly American in their fighting spirit and aspirations—"our loyal ally China," as the *New York Times* editorial page put it. When Mme. Chiang visited the United States for half a year in 1942–1943, Congress gave her thunderous applause; seventeen thousand Americans crowded into Madison Square Garden to hear her. "The economic aim of the leaders of modern China is to develop their country much as we developed ours," affirmed Willkie, who spent several days with the Generalissimo during his *One World* swing. Willkie recounted that "quiet, sincere" Rewi Alley had Indusco "difficulties when I saw him." Willkie didn't elaborate what they were.[18]

Determination to play down differences of opinion on China muted snippets of criticism directed toward Snow.

In 1941, Ambassador Johnson complained in a cable to Washington that the Chinese Communists were more skillful propagandists than the Nationalists. He singled out Snow as "perhaps the one American who has done more than any other to portray and to explain the Chinese Communists and their principles and objectives in a favorable light." Not long afterward Ernest Hemingway visited China. Upon returning he wrote a letter to Secretary of the Treasury Henry Morgenthau relating his impressions. He thought the United States should not put such a high value on the Reds' war effort. "They have had such excellent publicity and have welcomed writers of the caliber of Edgar Snow to their territory so that America has an exaggerated idea of the part they have played in the war against Japan."

John Paton Davies, who worked in State's Division of Far Eastern Affairs and had little respect for Johnson, easily turned aside the ambassador's criticism. In a note attached to Johnson's cable, Davies said the Communists had strong advocates because of the "crusading appeal" of their movement and Nationalist corruption. Improved press techniques by the Nationalists would hardly help even with more neutral reporters. Hemingway buried his opinions himself. Having been informed "that our policy was to discourage civil war between the Communists and the Central Government," he told Morgenthau that he wasn't writing anything that "would encourage a possible war between the two parties."[19]

Like water building up behind a faulty dam, American grievances accumulated quietly alongside the flawed assumptions about the Nationalists. From the beginning the United States case for helping Chiang rested on strategic military considerations, the need to strengthen anti-Japanese resistance. Although the Roosevelt administration did not accord the same priority to the Asian theater as to the European front, it gave substantial financial and material aid to the Nationalists, which it supplemented with moral support bolstering Chiang's prestige. Roosevelt surrendered U. S. extraterritorial rights in China, at long last, and invited Chiang into talks with Stalin and Churchill. On Christmas Eve 1943, Roosevelt declared, "Today we and the Republic of China are closer together than ever before in deep friendship and unity of purpose."

As it became clear that Chiang had no intention of using his enhanced power against the Japanese, but rather to dissipate his strength through corruption and civil war, profound worry set in. "What I am trying to find out," Roosevelt said plaintively, and privately, "is where is the Chinese army and why aren't they fighting because the Japanese seem to be able to push them in any direction they want to."

In 1944 the Roosevelt administration began to pressure Chiang to reunite with the Communists, who seemed willing to fight the Japanese and controlled territory important for a contemplated invasion of Japan. To facilitate this, FDR urged Chiang to put General Joseph Stilwell in command of all military forces in China with the power to arm and employ the Communist army. Chiang dragged his feet on implementing the request while his representatives worked behind the scenes in Washington to unseat Stilwell. The Generalissimo succeeded in October. Euchred by his campaign to boost the Nationalists' image, Roosevelt could hardly begin to deal independently with the Communists. And he could not force "Vinegar Joe" Stilwell down Chiang's throat. FDR recalled the feisty general.

During a weak moment before Stilwell's recall, the Nationalists had succumbed to reporters' constant demands to visit Yenan. The journalists formed positive impressions of the Communists, who unlike the Nationalists actually had Japanese prisoners to show for their efforts and possessed well-cared-for soldiers who talked enthusiastically about winning the war. With Stilwell's ouster, all the frustration, so long suppressed by the press, burst forth in a way that surprised Americans. *New York Times* correspondent Brooks Atkinson spoke out first on Chungking's transgressions. In a story filed outside China, away from KMT censors, he described Stilwell's recall as the "political triumph of a moribund anti-democratic regime." Other reporters followed with stories contrasting the Communists and the Nationalists. Chiang again forbade press trips to Yenan, but it was too late. Where before harmony seemed the norm, now extreme polarization set in.[20]

Ambassador Clarence Gauss, no more beguiled by Chiang than Stilwell and weary of being by-passed by Washington policymakers, resigned. Major General Patrick Hurley replaced him. Hurley was a World War I hero, oil company lawyer, Hoover's Secretary of War, and most recently a special envoy for Roosevelt. He came to China initially to help Stilwell with Chiang. Hurley knew little of the country and, as ambassador, quickly became entangled in Chiang's web of flattery and promises. He violently disagreed with subordinates exploring openings to the Communists. When these disagreements played themselves out in Washington, Hurley—and Chiang—won. American officials considered by Hurley part of a conspiracy against him went home. "The fault lay squarely with FDR," Snow commented years later.

During 1944 Snow put himself on the side of the foreign service officers who recognized the valuable strategic potential of the Communists. In his update to *Red Star* and in a *Saturday Evening Post* article, Snow argued that the United States should forge direct links with these "lost allies." Like the recalled foreign service officers, Snow faced sharp attacks. The first to take him on was an old friend, Lin Yutang.[21]

Lin had praised *Red Star* and *Battle for Asia*. A quote from Lin appeared on the jacket cover of the latter work. Despite Snow's criticism of Chiang (and of Confucius), Lin considered him "always objective." By 1944 Lin was no longer tolerant of positive pictures of the Chinese Communists. In *The Vigil of a Nation*, released that year, he portrayed the CCP as guilty of atrocities and as a minion of the Soviet Union. He pointed to Snow as one of the chief CCP propagandists and argued that most Chinese abhorred the Communists. Chinese, he said, learned about "the Chinese Communist regime, not by reading *Red Star over China*, but through a hundred lives and a thousand deaths. The truly totalitarian regime and really thorough one-party dictatorship in China is in Yenan, and not in Chungking."

"When two writers forget themselves in a moment of anger and put down their sentiments in black and white," Lin once wrote in another context, "they cannot always get out of it gracefully."[22] So it was with Snow's review of *Vigil* in the *Nation*. He charged Lin with libeling "some of our best allies among the Chinese people" and using unreliable, secondhand sources without paying adequate attention to KMT failings. "Lin's anti-Red tirade," he worried, ". . . will be exploited by ignorant and reactionary groups here which ordinarily take no interest in China's welfare." Lin sent off a heated reply, which Snow rejoined with another missive. Both appeared in the *Nation*.

The exchange became nasty. In an ad hominem aside, Lin observed that Snow misspelled the Chinese name Pang, dropping the "g" the same way a Russian would. In his reply, Snow said that the *Nation* left out the "g" inadvertently. If one were looking for sinister signs, he added, Lin dropped aspirates in Chinese names, including his own "yu-t'ang," the way the Japanese did.

Lin had insight into the totalitarian nature of the CCP. (He reported something of the Communist rectification campaign against intellectuals.) But never having been in Red territory and possessing liberal American values and a lingering respect for aspects of ancient China (which Snow didn't share), he didn't understand that the CCP had a mass following among Chinese. Said Lin in a telling remark, "I doubt if Mao Tse-tung were a Harvard Ph.D. or General Chu Teh were a West Point graduate, either of them could have fallen so hard for Marxism as the newest gospel of Western 'science.' " Lin, who had a master's degree from Harvard, a doctorate from the University of Leipzig, and knew how to tap the American literary market, was more an exception among the Chinese than most Red leaders.

The debate did not go entirely to Snow. Snow stepped in a trap he began setting for himself some months before, and Lin took advantage of it. For years Snow struck a delicate balance on Chinese communism, distinguishing between Red programs and Red objectives. Although he called the Chinese Communists equalitarian, he ridiculed those who said the CCP was merely interested in agrarian reform. He carefully pointed out that Chinese Communists were not democrats in American terms. Distinctions became particularly subtle on the question of Communist timing. Thinking in theoretical terms, he said establishment of communism was a distant goal, at best. Speaking practically, he noted that the Communists wanted power as quickly as possible. While Snow realized that the Communists rode the crest of history, he thought acquisition of undisputed power problematic in the near term. That was also the view of many Communists in Yenan. Snow talked of Chiang responding to events, gaining some control over them, and perhaps working with the Communists in a way that checked each other's strength.

In 1944, Snow shifted his stance in a way that threw off this balance. With fewer qualifications, he began to describe Communist China as a democratic "free China." "What they are now in practice," he said in a speech that concentrated on the here-and-now, "is agrarian democrats." The Communists were willing to share power. In the *Post* article describing the CCP as an important potential ally, he painted a picture of guerrilla partisans; revolutionary Communist objectives receded into the background. Angered over Lin's charge that the Communists were unresponsive to Chinese aspirations, Snow went even further in the *Nation* emphasizing the Chinese Communists "happen to have renounced, years ago now, any intention of establishing communism in China in the near future."

Snow did not explain the reason for his changed thinking, and in fact it is not clear how much his thinking had changed. In his epilogue to the new edition of *Red Star*, Snow wrote that "victory of the physical, the spiritual, the intellectual forces which first lifted the Red Star over China, was not far off—if not the ascendancy of the disputed symbol itself." Just days before Lin's attack, he told Roosevelt that the Communists were not agrarian reformers. The loss of balance may simply have resulted from Snow's own present-mindedness: overeagerness to convince Americans that the Communists were more democratic than the Nationalists and that the United States should press the Nationalists to agree on a unified war effort. Perhaps, too, Snow was mindful of the inability of the Soviets to install thoroughgoing communism in their country after several decades.

In any event, the slip offered a large target for Lin, who used Snow's own earlier writing about Communist objectives against him. In a final reply to Lin, Snow kept up the level of invective, calling the Chinese scholar "somewhat neurotic." All the same he acknowledged that the CCP had "not abandoned its ultimate aspiration to complete the revolution in China and establish socialism there."

In a piece for the *Saturday Evening Post* several months later, as well as in *The Pattern of Soviet Power*, which appeared about the same time, Snow clarified his views even more. The Communist program, he wrote, was "a moderate agrarian-reform platform with a Marxist coloration. . . . But here a word of warning. It is wrong to suppose that these people do not aspire to ultimate complete power. It is also wrong to suppose that they, any more than the Kuomintang, would establish a liberal democracy in China in the American sense, although they would probably bring about a kind of democratic equalitarianism such as is now practiced in areas they control."

Snow described why the Communists appeared more democratic than the Nationalists. The Nationalists stayed in power by "keeping the peasants out of politics . . . whereas the Communists perforce have had to find methods of getting the peasants actively into politics, of enlisting the mass of the people behind them, in order to sustain and strengthen themselves."

The United States, he stressed, as he had before, should support the Chinese Communists as well as the Nationalists. That would strengthen the Communists, he admitted, though not nearly so much as the United States had fortified the Soviet Union in Europe. But by pressing for power-sharing based on the Communists' popular programs, the United States and other allies, including the Soviet Union, could prevent a fragmented, partly bolshevized China after the war.

A great many middle-ranking foreign service officers held the same view, realizing this approach might counterbalance Soviet influence after the war. The success of that stratagem, had policymakers actually tried it, is dubious, at best. As Snow realized, "the irreconcilability of the internal forces presented by the two parties seemed to be deepening." But it was more realistic than the current course and showed that Snow continued to think in terms of saving the Nationalists, rather than ousting them.[23]

In forecasting the growth of communism in China, Snow had overestimated the Nationalists' ability to stay in power. The error of the great majority of American leaders, however, had been to underestimate the Chinese Communists, whom they typically viewed as some other shade than Red. "The Communists," Hurley said as late as 1945, "are not in fact Communists." Stilwell described the Communists as "agricultural liberals." Roosevelt called them "so-called Communists." During the conversation in which Snow told the president that the Chinese Communists were real Communists, FDR said the Communists aimed for an agrarian reform program and not communism. As the Chinese civil war became more visible, disillusionment with the Communists set in. Snow's brief lapse in the contretemps with Lin Yutang gave a false scent to those on the trail of culprits who misled America about the Communists—as Snow found when a second attack came, this one from his old friend J. B. Powell.[24]

Before the war, Snow regularly saw Powell when visiting Shanghai and sometimes stayed in his home. Obvious mutual affection notwithstanding, they argued about the Nationalists and the Communists so intensely that an outsider could not get a word in edgewise. Powell's status as a kind of father figure may have prompted Snow to be more aggressive in personal conversation than otherwise. After his imprisonment, Powell went through a prolonged recuperation at New York's Columbia Presbyterian Hospital Medical Center without losing any of his populist sentiments. When a banker's group asked him to speak, he refused. They just wanted to see him hobble up the stairs, he said. Nor did he lose respect for Chiang, who sent him a ten thousand dollar personal check, one of many contributions at the time. Powell was as quick to argue about Chinese politics as before. His son, Bill, remembered that Agnes Smedley, another old friend, visited often. She would give J. B. a bottle of brandy or some other gift; within five minutes, they would be yelling at each other about Chinese politics.

Smedley concluded fights by asking Powell, "Is there anything I can bring you when I visit tomorrow?" By the end of the war, it became impossible to bridge the differences of opinion. Powell helped found the American China Policy Association, which was to become an active player in the pro-Nationalist China Lobby taking shape. With former Communist Max Eastman, Powell also wrote a *Reader's Digest* article arguing that Americans faced a choice between the Nationalists, who represented democratic America, and the Communists, who represented totalitarian Russia. Itemizing the deceptions perpetrated on Americans about the Chinese Communists, the authors harked back to Snow's exchange with Lin. Snow, they wrote, was the "best-known popularizer of the pro-Communist view, with the remark that the Chinese Communists and their leader, Mao Tse-tung, 'happen to have renounced, years ago now, any intention of establishing Communism in China in the near future.' "

Powell's son revived the *China Weekly Review* after the war. J. B. planned to take over later. It was not to be. Powell testified at the 1946 war crimes tribunal in Tokyo but did not go to China. Back in Washington on February 28, 1947, he delivered a luncheon address to a University of Missouri alumni group. Just after taking his seat, he collapsed and died.[25]

In the months after the Japanese surrender, Nationalist and Communist forces moved to occupy areas held by the Japanese. The Truman administration remained steadfastly on the side of the Nationalists. In September and October, United States planes flew Chinese Nationalist troops to Manchuria in hopes of heading off the Communists. Some fifty thousand United States Marines moved in to hold ports and airfields for the Nationalists, at some points actually clashing with Communist troops. These new developments were one of the chief reasons Snow wanted to return to China after *Post* foreign editor Marty Sommers joined him in the Philippines.[26]

Edgar Snow was the last reporter the Nationalists wanted to see in the country. During his 1942 visit to Chungking, Snow complained to journalist Israel Epstein of the obstacles the Nationalists put in the way of his getting interviews. The story he filed afterward reported the Nationalists' unwillingness to engage the Japanese and their squandering of U. S. aid. Mme. Chiang Kai-shek, who considered Snow a member of the Comintern, had him banned from the country. He became so much a symbol of the kind of reporting that the Nationalists didn't like that when they finally let the handful of reporters visit Yenan in 1944, officials worried they would have to cope with "eleven Edgar Snows." His name was among those singled out in a secret Kuomintang report examining the causes of bad attitudes toward the KMT. Snow's 1944 edition of *Red Star*, which echoed the views of those wanting to funnel aid to the Communists, only confirmed Snow's status as a major foe—and an influential one. It went through six printings with a total sale of twenty-seven thousand copies, an extraordinary performance for an "old book." "To its credit," Smedley happily wrote in a review of the new edition, "it is still a thorn in the side of the ruling Kuomintang."[27]

By late 1945, the Nationalists had banned reporters, among them Brooks Atkinson, Vincent Sheean, and Snow's traveling companion to Baguio, Darrell Berrigan. If they needed added justification for blocking Americans, Patrick Hurley supplied it with his surprise resignation as ambassador in late November. Hurley charged that "a considerable section of our State Department is endeavoring to support Communism generally as well as specifically in China." In the wake of Hurley's allegations of sinister American behavior, the Nationalists informed Snow that he could not have a visa to cover Marine operations or anything else.

"It is a serious violation of elementary freedom of the press," Snow protested, "by an Allied government which has claimed our sympathy with the promise of such freedom, and by the government of a country in the cause of whose independence many Americans have died and hundreds of millions of dollars of our taxpayers money has been contributed. . . . It is ironic that I who for many years advocated abolition of extraterritoriality should now be among the first excluded as a result of full restoration of sovereignty under the Chungking government." *Post* editors lodged protests with President Truman and the State Department. The episode received considerable press attention, with *Time* stating the increasingly popular refrain that Snow "had done more than any other man to sell [the Communists'] case to the U. S."[28]

According to official word from Chungking, the decision on banning Snow was not final. In February, former Army Chief of Staff General George C. Marshall, who went to China to continue mediation efforts between the Nationalists and the Communists, succeeded in lifting the ban.

By that time Snow's travels had diverted him to Japan and Korea, and he developed second thoughts of his own. In a letter to Hibbs and Sommers several months later, he ruled out a China visit. "Civil war seems looming large on a grand scale there," Snow wrote. "If we are to remain and back the Kuomintang with armed forces then it would be necessary for me, if I went there, to take sides in support of a regime and a policy with which I would be out of sympathy." The *Post* should send someone else, he concluded.[29]

Shortly after arriving in Japan in mid-December, Snow stumbled on Jim Bertram at the Correspondents' Club, a happy reunion after the long war years. Snow was less enthusiastic about his encounter with General Douglas MacArthur, head of the occupation forces. MacArthur called his program in Japan "practically revolution." Snow had doubts. Women's suffrage and other political reforms, disarmament, policies promoting land reform and breakup of the large *zaibatsu* industries, and the willingness of some peasants to voice their opinions were positive signs. The problem was just how far the restructuring of Japan would go.

Snow learned from a Japanese industrial cooperative association, to which he gave advice drawn from his Indusco experience, that lack of credit prevented workers from buying capital equipment. Peasants related their difficulties acquiring land when compensation was required. Snow felt sorry for Emperor Hirohito, with whom he toured dilapidated buildings full of refugees. All the same, like the Communists he interviewed, Snow considered the "rather pathetic little figure whom the peasants still call Son of Heaven" part of the problem. The failure of sweeping economic reforms went hand-in-hand with steps to save the emperor and the traditional power structure around him. "So far, there has been no transfer of power from one class to another, and thus, in a historic sense, there as been no economic revolution," Snow thought. Under those circumstances the *zaibatsu* companies would reemerge, a view that Bertram and Owen Lattimore shared. Seeing a world clearly demarked between capitalists and workers, Snow predicted that political changes in Japan could produce a Left-wing coalition of Socialists and Communists at the helm of the government within the planned five year occupation by the United States.[30]

Korea also troubled Snow. He had been delighted when Roosevelt misleadingly told him in 1942 that he had no plans for a Korean trusteeship after the war. What actually emerged was far worse than Snow imagined—two trusteeships that split the country. On one side of the 38th parallel, where Snow spent New Year's eve, were the Americans; on the other sat the Soviets. A unified country, marked by equitable distribution of goods, seemed as distant as when Japan ruled Korea.[31]

General John Hodge, with whom Snow and Sommers dined, headed an occupation force totally unprepared for the assignment. Rather than support Korean Leftists who, Snow believed, had a strong following in the country, the United States backed people who had no deep popular support. The United States forces did not promote land reform or the redistribution of other assets, which would have been easier than anywhere else in Asia since the great majority of land and capital did not belong to Koreans but to the Japanese.

"When everything has been said about our occupation of Korea, probably the most significant thing is that we stopped a revolution here," Snow wrote in the *Saturday Evening Post*. The Soviet occupation force, Snow added, "was no better prepared to govern Korea." It eliminated the "owning class" from power but also brought a large measure of chaos. Among other things, the Soviets helped themselves to whatever they wanted and "kept supreme directive authority in their own hands."

Snow worried that the division of Korea would harden unless both sides withdrew their forces and let the Koreans hold national elections. "The longer the bargaining is prolonged," he wrote, "the more the two zones draw apart, the more each tends to reflect the social pattern typified by its occupying power." Ten years later, after the Korean war shattered any hope for reunification, Snow placed the greatest blame on the Soviets. Socialism would have triumphed, Snow thought, if only they had let Koreans seek power through political means. "They could not learn any game but their own. They could not believe that the rules of parliamentary chess could here be played straight, to their own advantage. They lost because they could not believe that America wanted to leave, not to stay and build a colony. They insisted we were 'imperialists,' and they knew all about imperialists."

"We ask it in Manchuria. We ask it in Eastern Europe and the Dardanelles. . . . We ask it in the Baltic and the Balkans. We ask it in Poland. . . . We ask it in Japan. We ask it sometimes even in connection with events in our own United States. What is Russia up to now?"[32]

Republican Arthur Vandenberg's questions on the Senate floor in early 1946 were questions many fearful Americans had begun to ask. The Soviet Union was so much on Americans' minds that using "Russia" or "Soviet" in an article title, Hibbs noted, "produces phenomenal readership," sometimes boosting it by half a million people.

In March, with Truman at his elbow, Winston Churchill provided what became a standard answer about the Soviets' intentions. During his famous Fulton, Missouri, speech he described "the Iron Curtain that has descended across the Continent." Moscow, he said, wanted "indefinite expansion of their power and doctrines." Perceiving an anti-Soviet Anglo-American alliance taking shape, Stalin countered that Churchill's remarks were "a call to war with the Soviet Union." In the following weeks the Soviets evacuated Manchuria in such a way that the Chinese Communists picked up Japanese military equipment left behind. At home Stalin worked all the harder to close the country to foreign ideology. Giving up hope of resolving issues with the Soviets, the United States took steps to unify the three western zones of Germany into an independent industrial center. Polls taken a few days after the Fulton speech showed that a clear majority of Americans thought the United States was "too soft" on the Soviets. The U.S.-Soviet standoff in Korea was fast becoming the global norm, each side frozen in place, each side feeding on each other's fears and aggressions.

Anxious Americans were no less interested than Stalin in rooting out foreign ideology. In July the House Civil Service Committee launched an investigation to hunt for disloyal civil servants, by which the committee meant those with purported Red leanings. Having chafed for years under Roosevelt's New Deal, Republicans saw their chance to attack and presented the upcoming mid-term election as a choice between "Communism and Republicanism." Richard Nixon, aspiring to a House seat, and Senatorial incumbent Joseph McCarthy from Wisconsin built their campaign platforms with anti-Communist planks. They won. Just as nineteenth-century politicians established their American credentials by portraying themselves as rail-splitting frontiersmen, politicians of all stripes were learning to substantiate their Americanism—and the Americanism of their policies—by proving that they, too, abhorred communism and the insidious Red evil that infiltrated the government. Within days of Republican congressional victories, Truman created a Temporary Commission on Employee Loyalty to ferret out Reds. He and other establishment figures became far more responsible for what became known as McCarthyism than the petty demagogue from Wisconsin who gave the era its name.[33]

MacArthur's Japan previewed how fears of foreign and domestic Communists mutually reinforced each other—and how they would involve Snow. Proconsul MacArthur stood firmly on the side of the Nationalists in China and warily watched for signs of Russian influence in Japan. Censors monitoring news printed in Japan used their broad mandate to kill negative stories about the United States. MacArthur often managed to distance himself from the day-to-day obstructions his staff tossed in the path of American correspondents, many of whom considered the public relations team "bigoted, insolent, uncooperative and dictatorial." Privately, MacArthur railed against reporters. In a secret cable telling Washington why he opposed a U. S. press tour of Japan, he lumped reporters from the *Christian Science Monitor* and the *New York Herald Tribune* with a representative of the Communist *Daily Worker*. When Secretary of the Navy James Forrestal visited Japan, MacArthur complained that the Left-wing reporters promoted communism against the interests of their own country.[34]

During Snow's 1945–46 stay in Japan, he discovered intense local interest in him. Jim Bertram rarely saw Snow in the Tokyo Press Club when he wasn't surrounded by Japanese publishers asking for rights to his books. Snow returned to the United States in the spring of 1946. Several months later the issue of Snow's royalties became entangled in MacArthur's capricious censorship operation. A *Chicago Tribune* correspondent in Tokyo reported that Communist propagandists took advantage of a "copyright tangle." Forbidden to remit funds outside the country, Japanese publishers found it difficult to buy rights to American books. The Soviets met this problem by simply foregoing royalties. Using the kind of non sequitur that would become an art form under Red baiters, the *Tribune* reporter noted that only two American books had been published, *Guadalcanal Diary* and *The Pattern of Soviet Power*. The first had been pirated, apparently absolving the author of any bad intentions; Snow, "known as the foremost press agent for the Chinese Communists," personally had arranged publication of his book. No one mentioned that Snow had earmarked some earnings for an orphanage in China.

Snow's publishing troubles continued. He learned from a Japanese friend that MacArthur's Civic Information and Education section held up publication of the second part of a two volume edition of *Red Star* for more than three months. Later the Author's League of America reported that MacArthur's staff blocked publication of four of Snow's books, as well as John Hersey's *Hiroshima*. MacArthur protested that this was untrue, part of "a maliciously false propaganda campaign." These reports aroused little public concern about threats to freedom of speech. On the contrary, they seemed to confirm in many minds the perniciousness of Snow's writings.

As his Japan problem simmered, Snow thrust himself more centrally into the domestic debate over communism and the Soviet Union. He did little writing in mid-1946, other than a highly laudatory profile of Archibald Clark-Kerr, who left Moscow to become British ambassador to the United States. In the fall, Hibbs encouraged him to write a series on the Soviet Union. The topic appealed to Snow, worried deeply over the increasingly uncompromising United States attitude toward the Soviet Union. The problem was that the *Post*, which once held a view of the Soviet Union compatible with Snow's, was in the forefront of those Americans concerned about "our inane surrenders at Yalta." Snow thought it unlikely that the *Post* would want to print his views on the subject. But with Hibbs's assurance that he could write as he pleased, Snow assented. He spent the last weeks of the year working on the series at his New York City apartment an East 56th Street and among the small lakes and wooded groves of the Yaddo writing colony in Saratoga Springs, New York.[35]

The result constituted an act of extraordinary courage. At a time when the Americans did not want to see the Soviet point of view, Snow made "lifting the lid from Ivan Ivanovich's skull" a central theme of his articles. Equally daring, Snow used heavy doses of irony, sometimes bordering on sarcasm, and delved into Marxist theory, hardly standard fare for an American family magazine.

Snow did not make a case for socialism or try to vindicate the Soviets. He noted Soviet transgressions and ignorance, and that "I wouldn't like to spend my life under the Russian system." Rather, he pointed out that the Soviets saw the world through their own history and experience and that the United States should not expect Kremlin acceptance of the American system or its agenda. Snow added that Americans had contributed to misunderstandings because they had been so unclear during the war about *their* postwar priorities.

"Our generals and politicians never assumed that any Allied agreement required us to sponsor communist parties in our occupied areas," he wrote in one passage. "Why should the Russians have assumed the same agreements required them to support capitalist parties in theirs?"

As earlier, Snow identified insecurity as the dominant factor in Soviet foreign policy. Smarting from the war, the country wanted time to rebuild; its policies in Eastern Europe were aimed at insulating the country from future attacks, not spreading communism. Stalin most of all wanted peace. The World War showed that cooperation with the Soviets was possible, no matter what the Communist rhetoric might be about capitalism. "The Kremlin is not open to persuasion or conversion but it *is* open to bargaining." In Snow's mind the idea was to find out what the Soviets wanted and what they would take in exchange for lower reparations in their zones, political cooperation, and disarmament.

Unfortunately, he said, Americans chose a policy that made the Soviets feel less secure and, in any event, was unrealistic in assuming that the United States would really go to war in Eastern Europe. "Owing to his congenital myopia, [Ivan] does not perceive that the American power outside every Soviet window is intended to give him an enhanced sense of security," Snow wrote, directly challenging the "containment" policy taking shape. "Hopelessly muddled, the poor dope begins to think that he is surrounded."

Picking up a theme that would eventually become a keynote in his discussion of Communist China, he argued that the United States bore more responsibility for creating the climate of accommodation. Although Snow couched this in terms of America's greater military might, he was saying something else, too, something that bespoke his feeling about the superiority of American political institutions. "There is considerably less excuse for our mass ignorance about elementary facts concerning Russia, if public opinion is to play an intelligent role in determining policy toward our gravest problem in foreign affairs."

When Snow sent the series to the *Post* offices in Philadelphia, editors became locked in disagreement. Some liked the stories; others counseled killing them on the ground that any tolerant articles about the Soviets damaged United States interests. As was the rule in such cases, Hibbs made the final decision. After working out some editorial changes to Snow's satisfaction, he decided to publish. The first installment of the three-part series appeared in February 1947. "I feel that the American people, who are traditionally fair-minded, are entitled to look at all sides of any issue as critical as the Russian question," Hibbs wrote in an accompanying open letter "to Generalissimo Stalin and Other *Post* Readers." ". . . Secondly, I think it is barely possible that these articles may constitute something toward an understanding with Russia and the winning of the world peace for which we all so devoutly hope."

A few weeks after the series appeared Random House published *Stalin Must Have Peace,* a slim volume containing the articles. An introduction by Martin Sommers gave a qualified endorsement of Snow's "provocative material." Snow added a concluding chapter stating more explicitly his vision of a new American foreign policy that did not use nuclear weapons to bully allies and that abandoned the old "hit-or-miss, muddling through policy of improvisation" that had so often failed in the past. "I mean a policy which recognizes, as the significance of isolationism abandoned, the explicit lesson that external peace and the prosperity of other nations are inseparably linked with our own domestic peace and internal prosperity." The United States should find ways for the discussion and the exchange of ideas with the Soviet Union and for the provision of loans and credits to help the Soviets rebuild their economy and to regain mutual trading opportunity and trust.[36]

Snow acknowledged that people would call his approach soft on Russia and unrealistic. "No one could guarantee in advance it would work," he admitted. "All we know is that the only alternative is quite certain to fail."

About the time he finished the articles, Snow requested an interview with Truman. By way of making a case for the meeting, Snow noted that he was from Missouri, a Democrat, knew "one or two things" about the Soviet Union and China, and "would like to volunteer my services to the President" on the next trip overseas. Snow apparently had the meeting soon after, though the Truman Presidential papers make no record of when or of what was said. In any event, Truman was set on a course that Snow could not sway.

Within a few days of the appearance of Snow's *Post* articles, Truman proposed an assistance program for Greece and Turkey. Rather than stressing economic and humanitarian reasons for such a program, Truman advertised the aid as a way of combating communism. The Truman doctrine fit neatly with Americans' anti-Communist mood at the time and reinforced it. Snow told Sommers that Truman's plan was "small-town thinking" and revealed that "the administration had no real plan after the war, had no scheme anticipating the obvious, does not have any plan now, cannot be depended upon not to jump in another direction tomorrow."[37]

Snow recalled Truman's parting remarks after the interview. "I didn't ask for this job, you know. Roosevelt knew when to die. You have to die at the right time to be a hero. If he had lived he would have found himself in exactly the same mess I'm in."

In the prevailing climate Snow's *Post* series produced spontaneous combustion. The volume of letters pouring into the *Post* was among the highest in the magazine's history. Mail initially ran four to one in favor of the articles. "As letters from the unreconstructed hinterland began coming in criticism increased," reported the *New Republic* in an article on the series. Within a couple of weeks, almost half the letters disagreed with Snow. Some letters included a recent speech by J. Edgar Hoover to the American Legion in which he said "Communist influence has projected itself into some newspapers, magazines, books, radio and the screen."[38]

One letter stood out from the others.[39] It came from Patrick Hurley. Snow had used the former envoy as an example of American misunderstanding of the Soviet Union, noting that Hurley came away from an April 1945 meeting with Stalin believing that the Soviet Union would follow the United States lead in China. Hurley reacted angrily to the reference, sending Hibbs an open letter protesting falsehoods in Snow's "pro-Communist article." He alleged that Snow's distorted account came from confidential reports "given or sold to Communists by State Department officials."

Hibbs stood by Snow, "a careful reporter who rarely makes a mistake." Only after Hurley distilled his windy objections in a shorter letter did the editor send them to Snow, by then in France. Snow wrote a reply, which Hibbs decided not to forward to Hurley because of the former envoy's threats, never carried out, of legal action. In it Snow had offered to take out references to Hurley in the book version of the articles. He refused to repudiate his account—and for good reason.

Historical research would show Hurley's gullibility in dealing with the Soviets. Significantly, during the meeting with Stalin, the diplomat had recalled the Communist leader's earlier statements that the Chinese Communists were not authentic Communists (something Stalin probably held as at least theoretically true). Afterward Hurley reported back to Washington that "Stalin agreed unqualifiedly to America's policy in

China as outlined to him during the conversation." Ambassador Averell Harriman, George Kennan, and other officials knew of the episode and disagreed with Hurley's interpretation. In conversations with people who personally knew the details of Hurley's conversation with Stalin, Snow had carefully pieced the story together.

Stalin Must Have Peace became a selection of the Book Find Club. Harrison Salisbury, writing in the *New York Times*, called the book "the most penetrating analysis of the Soviet which has yet appeared in the press." But if some thought the book required reading for legislators, as the *Trenton Times* did, others like the *Chicago Tribune* breathed "a sigh of thankfuless" that Snow's policies would not find a welcome reception in the halls of Congress. As Snow told a friend, only a book entitled *Stalin Must Have War* could be a best seller.[40]

About the time of the *Post* articles, Snow received two letters that charted changing attitudes. One, from Marty Sommers, carried news that the War Department awarded Snow a certificate for "patriotic and outstanding and conspicuous service with our armed forces" as a foreign correspondent during the war. Through Random House, Snow learned that the National Council of Jewish Women dismissed a highly commended social worker for allegedly diverting the council along Communist party lines. As proof of her sympathies, the council noted that the social worker had recommended, among other books, Snow's *The Pattern of Soviet Power* and *People on Our Side*.[41]

Although Hurley's open letter to the *Post* did not circulate widely, one organ saw a big story behind it: *Plain Talk*, a virulently anti-Communist organ of diehard conservatives who pleaded the Nationalists' cause. Six months after printing the letter, it delivered a promised "exposé" on Snow, "Red Star over Independence Square: The Strange Case of Edgar Snow and *The Saturday Evening Post*." The author was Freda Utley, who had completed her march to the right. In addition to attacking Snow's *Post* series on the Soviet Union, she mustered an elaborate critique of his China reporting. Using the same half truth and innuendo of which she accused Snow, she capitalized on his statements during the time of his debate with Lin Yutang, pointed to changes he made in *Red Star* as examples of his subservience to Moscow, and generally reduced his complex thinking about communism to a grotesque caricature of a sinister fellow traveler.

The message was clear: Snow had tricked the public into thinking the Communists were not Communists at all; he even managed to fool the good conservative *Saturday Evening Post*. Snow, she summarized, "is, without a doubt, one of the cleverest, smoothest, and most subtle advocates the Kremlin has ever had on its side." Why should anyone doubt Snow's reporting, she asked, when "Mr. Ben Hibbs himself vouches that what Snow tells them is based on 'months of painstaking research.' "[42]

An anti-Snow campaign ensured that Utley's article was not confined to *Plain Talk*'s limited circulation. Rose Wilder Lane, who had once written fiction for the *Saturday Evening Post*, sent reprints of the article to prominent people across the country. In a personal letter she asked that recipients pressure the *Post* to "get rid of this Communist." Hibbs and Sommers spent months answering the mail that came in.[43]

The strangest happening of all, however, was not on Independence Square in Philadelphia, as Freda Utley suggested. It was on Red Square in Moscow. The Kremlin refused to give Snow a visa to return to Moscow. Snow learned from Soviet officials that his *Post* series had been "positively unsatisfactory." Snow was not certain why. He subsequently guessed it may have exposed Soviet weakness or the possibility of Communist revisionism in Yugoslavia.[44]

Snow was in Western Europe when Utley's article appeared and knew only a little of the attacks against him or of his staunch defense by the *Post*. But he, too, wondered if his association with the *Saturday Evening Post* made sense. He felt on unfamiliar footing in Europe. He complained to Marty Sommers of his frustration in not speaking much French. The beat was all the harder because other *Post* correspondents had staked out claims in the region long before. In addition, he was ill with recurring kidney troubles that dated from his days in China when he had a stone removed cystoscopically. By July the *Post* had rejected his first two articles from Europe, and, as Snow told Hibbs, he "had a feeling the next will also prove a dud." Worried that he no longer carried his weight at the *Post*, Snow offered to resign.[45]

"Definitely do not want you resign," Hibbs cabled back instantly. In a letter he said Snow should take a rest. The *Post* would drop the yearly payment guarantee but keep his name on the masthead and pay expenses until he could get back into production. When Snow sat in front of a typewriter again, Hibbs counseled, he should humanize his stories rather than deal "so heavily in abstractions and broad political trends" as in the series on the Soviet Union.

"You have been so valuable to us, and you are such a swell guy and such a good friend," Hibbs concluded, "that I want to do everything possible to keep you in our stable. Please believe that I mean every word of this."

Snow was on the verge of having his kidney removed in a Paris hospital when a fellow reporter advised against it. Snow put on his street clothes and went to Bern, Switzerland. The doctor there prescribed six weeks hospitalization, drugs, and no surgery. By the end of the year Snow was on his feet and had produced publishable material on Switzerland, France, and England. In mid-December he relocated to India. He, Sommers, and Hibbs hoped that familiar terrain might prove more fruitful. But as Snow put it a few years later, he was in the path of the storm.[46]

Ishmael in His Native Land

7

The strange case of Edgar Snow and the *Saturday Evening Post* was one chapter in a dark saga that turned a period of extraordinary American prosperity into living hell for many decent Americans. "Strange" could have been the byword of the era. *U.S News & World Report* used it in detailing "The Strange Case of John P. Davies: Investigated since 1945, He's Still a Diplomat." "Strange" conveyed suspicion but avoided taking responsibility for leveling a direct accusation. The word left Americans wondering what unknown treason lurked in the shadows. The absence of evidence made the treason all the more insidious. The author of one book of the period, *While You Slept*, promised "to describe this strange experiment in mind control," carried out by "friends and agents of Stalin" to hide the truth about Communist intentions. "Strange," and the thought behind it, easily smashed careers.[1]

Domestic Communist activity fit into a perceived worldwide plot. "The Communist conquest of China, now dangerously near completion, long has been planned as a major milestone in Moscow's road toward creation of a Soviet America," Louis Budenz, formerly a Communist party member and managing editor of the *Daily Worker*, wrote in *Collier's*.

Frightened Americans turned on themselves, on everyday people: librarians, teachers, scientists, maritime workers, electricians, New York City Transit Authority employees. A nineteen-year-old Seattle potwasher lost her job in a hospital kitchen when her husband and father were named during a hearing of the House Committee on Un-American

Activities. In 1952, Henry Willcox, president of the Willcox Construction Company, visited Communist China for two months. While he was gone the board of directors voted him out for fear of losing a contract with the New York Housing Authority. The New York Guild of the *New York Times* and the *New York Daily News* elected not to defend reporters who lost their jobs for taking the Fifth Amendment before congressional investigating committees.

Americans and their representatives generated more public confusion and did more to wreck fellow Americans' lives and to subvert American values and institutions than Stalin, in his country's weakened state, could ever have hoped to achieve through Soviet actions. They did it all in the name of patriotism.

The real tragedy of Edgar Snow was about to come into the open: not the tragedy many proclaimed, that Snow had misled Americans about Communist intentions, but the tragedy that Americans, who had not paid close attention to what Snow wrote before, decided to ignore him altogether, precisely at a time when his insights, experience, and contacts were so desperately needed.

In late spring 1946, entering the revolving door of the Waldorf Hotel, Snow became tangled with a dog. At the other end of the leash he found the wife of journalist Vincent (Jimmy) Sheean. Diana Sheean invited Snow to an after-theater party given to raise money for Russian relief. Snow accepted and that evening met Lois Wheeler. The attractive young actress had arrived in New York from California five years before with a scholarship to the Neighborhood Playhouse. She helped found the Actors Studio and in 1946 was appearing in the play "Dear Ruth." A role in Arthur Miller's "All My Sons" was just around the corner. Lois had read *Red Star* as a girl and had just finished *The Pattern of Soviet Power* when she met Snow. That first night he asked her out, and she accepted.

During the rest of 1946, which Snow spent in the United States, he continued to see Lois. The next year she joined him in Europe. When Snow was hospitalized in Bern with kidney problems, she stayed. John Carter Vincent, a friend from China days, was ambassador to Switzerland. His wife, Betty, sensed the couple was in love.[2]

This improvement in Snow's personal life occurred against the dark backdrop of Cold War. Lois picked up the implications for Snow the night they met. Though familiar with Snow's books, she had not followed his career closely and was surprised to learn that he was on the staff of the *Saturday Evening Post*. Why, she asked, did he work for such a conservative publication?

"The *Post*," Snow replied huffily, "prints any article I want to write. They don't change my material. They pay me very well and they send me places I want to go. And the magazine gets into many houses."

That answer still made sense to Snow in late 1947 when he headed for India. Despite his troubles covering Europe in 1947, the *Post* editors had stuck with him. In South Asia his comparative advantage as a reporter could shine. But Snow soon discovered that East-West hostilities overwhelmed everything. Lois's question became one that Snow asked more and more often.[3]

Events in South Asia seemed tailored for Snow. The British raj, so long odious to him, ended in August 1947. In its place rose Hindu India and Moslem Pakistan, the latter an oddly split nation carved out of India's east and west flanks. Just after the new year Burma declared its independence as well. The country, where nearly twenty years before Snow had his first glimpse of agrarian revolt, proclaimed a socialist government—one that was also independent of the Soviet Union.

Snow liked what he saw in the three fledgling nations. Although recognizing the precarious national unity that existed in Burma, Snow wrote approvingly of land reform, nationalization of foreign-owned industry, and obvious Burmese interest in the Chinese Communists. He visited Karachi and concluded that bifurcated Pakistan could survive. In Bombay he took perverse delight in the fact that waiters served Indians first in the elegant, high ceilinged Taj Mahal Hotel next to the Gateway of India, the haughty waterfront arch the British had built long before to commemorate their own imperialism. Snow happily reported Nehru's vision of a nonaligned Indian nation concentrating on domestic reforms.

Snow thought Great Britain had acquired moral capital by relinquishing its hold on Asia. But he thought British and American responsibility in the subcontinent was not at an end. "It would be a grave mistake to underestimate [Pakistan] or to refuse to Pakistan the friendship and technical aid which its more progressive people expect from the United States," he concluded.[4]

The problem of maintaining national unity, which was to plague Burma, India, and Pakistan, came shockingly to the fore when Snow was in New Delhi. On the evening of January 30, Gandhi made his way to the prayer garden at Birla House. En route a Hindu extremist, distraught over the partition of India to create Pakistan, stepped forward and pumped three shots from his Beretta pistol into Gandhi's bare chest. Word of the assassination swept through the city and reached Snow at the Imperial Hotel. Snow immediately headed for Birla House, where he met Jimmy Sheean, who had been ten feet from the tragic scene.

Sheean and Snow could see Gandhi's body lying on a straw mat inside his bedroom. The next day Snow sat at the edge of Gandhi's cremation platform on the banks of the Jumna river and threw sandalwood on the pyre.

Sheean, who rejoiced in letting his emotions course through his work, claimed to have developed stigmata on his hand at the time Gandhi died. He holed up in his hotel room. Though Snow was not prey to such emotional outpourings, the assassination confirmed a feeling that he had been too hard on Gandhi. Shortly after arriving in India, Snow had called on Gandhi. "You were not very kind to me in your last book," the venerable old leader rebuked. He took Snow's hand in his own. "You are more ready to listen to me now, I know," Gandhi said. The comment struck Snow. "I understood that he was talking about the atom bomb and the far worse bacteriological weapons, and a world arbitrarily 'divided into two irreconcilable camps,' that we had all got as our answer in the war [against Japan] he wouldn't fight."

In recounting the assassination in a *Post* dispatch, Snow was far from launching a full-fledged panegyric. He didn't "pretend to have understood Gandhi or to have moved upon the stage where I could take in the metaphysics of his philosophy or his personal dialogues with God." But in the overwhelming emotion of the moment, he finally saw in Gandhi's spirituality a form of activism. "On this visit to India he made me see clearly that he was always and everywhere with the oppressed and the downtrodden," Snow wrote of Gandhi's fight against racial and caste discrimination, of his devotion to the sick and helpless, of his efforts to win "national independence for more millions of people than any other leader of men, and with less bloodshed." Snow summed up, "This small man, so full of a large love of men, extended beyond India and beyond time."[5]

Newsman Bill Shirer thought Snow's dispatch "one of the classics of American journalism." When the published article reached Snow in Bombay, he reacted differently. Snow had written that Gandhi "was a practical socialist in that he never opposed the state as a necessary instrument in achieving social democracy." The *Post* editors added that "democracy as [Gandhi] understood it is certainly not to be confused with the kind of police state ruled by the Kremlin."

"Thunderstruck" that the *Post* "put words in my mouth that I did not write," Snow shot a letter off to Ben Hibbs. He resigned as associate editor. If the *Post* insisted, Snow said, he would fulfill his contract. The issue was not merely that the added line "defiled the integrity of the individual," as Snow put it. The impact of the words promoted anti-

Red rhetoric in line with the *Post*'s policies. In a calmer follow-up letter from Rome, he confessed disillusionment with brutal Soviet foreign policies. A few days before, Moscow had carried out a stunning coup in Czechoslovakia, crushing the sole democratic government in Eastern Europe. Snow agreed that the Soviet Union was a police state and worried that Moscow policies were inflaming hostilities. All the same, he said in the letter, he did not want to contribute to the tension by using a "worn and banal expression" that put him in "the category of people like the Alsops," brothers who wrote tough anti-Communist articles.

"It takes me out of the category of reporters trying to do an objective job and seeking facts on both sides, without imposing a hostile point of view in the selection of facts in such ways as always to find the other side completely wrong."[6]

Hibbs, equally upset, also felt betrayed. His initial reaction was to accept Snow's resignation. In his reply he let his feelings tumble out. Snow, Hibbs accurately said, didn't realize the extent of the anti-Communist attacks against him or the efforts that the magazine had devoted to defending him. The *Post* had a right to edit copy, which Snow often needed when he used "scholarly terms and references which the rank-and-file does not understand." That was the case in this instance when the general public would not understand the difference between Gandhi's perception of socialism and the Kremlin's. The editors liked to show changes to authors, Hibbs added, but this was difficult in the case of foreign correspondents, and nearly impossible with Snow. "You are not as careful about informing us of your whereabouts as most of our other correspondents. For example, Marty [Sommers] had been trying unsuccessfully to reach you by cable in India for many days prior to the time we found you had gone to Rome."

Nevertheless, Hibbs proposed they continue the association. When Snow returned, he said, they could discuss the whole thing. Snow was somewhat chastened by Hibbs's stiff response and news of "the attacks against me which I had not known existed on such a scale." He defended his point on the editorial change but acknowledged the happy years he had spent with the *Post* and its support. He thought the anti-Communist attacks might be reason for Hibbs to let him go; otherwise he would stay. The relationship was salvaged once again.

Sharp exchanges can be part of normal editor-foreign correspondent tension: Snow, the craftsman, laboring over the fine points in his copy; Hibbs, respecting that but keeping his readership in mind. The bigger issue, the one that moved the disagreement beyond the normal, was the political climate in which it occurred and the fact that the *Post*, however willing to give a voice to Snow, did not see the world the way he did. Significantly, Hibbs was far more comfortable with the views of Joseph and Stewart Alsop. He paid them a five hundred dollar quarterly retainer to supply article ideas and to give the magazine preference on their magazine-length articles.

The *Post* and the Alsops fit into a distinct class of anti-Communists. McCarthyite tactics outraged them. When McCarthy criticized the *Post*, Hibbs criticized back, telling the senator that the magazine was "against wild, unsupported charges such as you have been making." Hibbs added that McCarthy's "conduct ill becomes a United States senator." Although a staunch supporter of Chiang Kai-shek since his military service in China during the war, Joe Alsop despised "the obscene Utley" and former Communist Louis Budenz. In an *Atlantic Monthly* article fittingly titled "The Strange Case of Louis Budenz," Alsop exposed Budenz's charges against foreign service officers as blatant lies. As much as he disagreed with those who had counseled closer ties with the Chinese Communists, Alsop never doubted "the loyalty of Stilwell and the men working with him."

Like the great majority of Americans, however, Alsop believed that "the challenge of Soviet power is our real problem" and considered Stilwell and Davies "victims of the then fashionable liberalism which idyllically pictured the Communists as 'democratic agrarian reformers.'" The Communist threat existed right inside America. He and his brother pondered in the pages of the *Post* if the CIO "could shake the Communists loose." The *Post*, hungry for such pieces, paid the phenomenal price of seventy-five thousand dollars for a ten-part series by ex-Communist Whittaker Chambers in 1952. As courageous as they were, journalists like the Alsops and publications liked the *Post* fanned the fires of the witch hunt at home. They obscured the complicated nature of communism abroad and did not facilitate the development of realistic policies to deal with it.[7]

After returning to the United States, Snow wrote two articles that made the fine distinctions about communism he considered important.[8]

On the way home Snow had reassessed his view of Soviet policy in Eastern Europe. He cultivated excellent sources during a stop in Soviet-dominated Czechoslovakia, Sommers noted, and came home with "his perspective considerably changed on Russia." Snow was primed to criticize Soviet policy in Eastern Europe, and events in Yugoslavia that summer gave focus to his article. Yugoslavia under independent-minded Marshal Tito had resisted Soviet domination. When Stalin failed to topple the government as he had in Czechoslovakia, he charged Tito with the sin of nationalism and in June expelled Yugoslavia from the

Eastern Bloc. Unchastened, Tito countered with a similar charge of his own: The Soviets used rhetoric about worldwide Communist unity as a cover for achieving its national objectives. Snow agreed. Tito's defiance offered "the first effective frontier against *the expansion of world communism as an extension of Russian nationalism.*" Snow did not predict that other Eastern Bloc countries would break away soon. Those nations did not have Tito's "independent military and police power." As the perceptive article pointed out, the Soviet Union could not let other weaker countries go their own way without calling into question the infallibility of the Communist line abroad and therefore the legitimacy of its rule at home. The Soviet system had become tripped up in its own robes. It could no longer claim to be a liberating force; more than ever it had to worry about maintaining security rather than expanding its control. That, Snow carefully noted, did not mean "disintegration of socialism and communism as a world force." The foundation of communism was nationalism, independence from other countries—a point that Snow made in his second piece, on China.

The end of the Nationalist government was near. In early 1949, Chiang Kai-shek resigned and a few weeks later retreated to Taiwan. In an April *Post* article Snow summarized the view he had presented of the Chinese Communists over the years: They were Marxists, and they strove for communism, though real communism would take time. Although they considered the Soviet Union an ally, they would not be bossed by Moscow, which had not foreseen, let alone directed, the revolution in China. The impending Chinese Communist victory rested on the foundation of national liberation and the promise of domestic social reform. China, Snow wrote, was an example of political changes in Asia that marked the end of the colonial system.

These articles were as lucid as any Snow had ever written. They recognized that communism, however it might flourish, was not a monolithic global movement. Americans had room to maneuver. But public opinion moved inexorably in the other direction. Hibbs and Sommers, who had reservations about Snow's perspective in the China article, published it with a disclaimer that the *Post* "was by no means as hopeful as Mr. Snow is that a Communist China can remain outside the orbit of Soviet Russia."

The China article was the only one by Snow the magazine published in 1949. The next year Snow's production was higher, though far below what it had been during his peak years and largely on subjects that didn't interest him. He wrote for the *Post*'s cities of America series—really glorified travel pieces—on Flagstaff, Arizona, Mexico City, and Acapulco. In two other pieces Snow wrote about the building of the

United Nations headquarters in New York City and an acting troupe that toured the country. Only one *Post* article dealt with a political subject, a profile of Soviet foreign minister Andrei Vyshinsky. And that story came hard for Snow.

Soviet actions increasingly irritated Snow. When the Soviets arrested Anna Louise Strong and shipped her out of Moscow as a spy in 1949, he resigned from the Left-wing Committee for a Democratic Policy in the Far East, which hadn't defended her. Along with a small group of others, he signed a letter of protest to the Soviet ambassador. While not exonerating the United States from its contributions to Cold War tension, he held the Soviets more responsible. As Snow told an inquirer asking about his changing views in 1951, he thought "U.S. sins have been largely sins of omission as contrasted with Kremlin sins of commission." As such Snow had no love for Andrei Vyshinsky, the chief architect of Soviet foreign policy and, in Snow's eyes, the "cynical genius" who helped mastermind Stalin's 1930s purge trials. But an article attacking Vyshinsky seemed hypocritical to Snow. "If an opportunist of the McCarthy type can, with complete immunity, slander, libel and assassinate the character of faithful and brilliant public servants, and ruin honest scholars and loyal citizens," Snow told Sommers, "why should I choose this moment to denounce the same kind of behavior Vyshinsky carried to its logical conclusion?" After considering scrapping the piece, Snow went ahead. The first draft he sent to the *Post* apparently contained a few lines articulating his concerns about Soviet parallels with McCarthyism. In any event, the *Post* editors kicked it back for a rewrite and the reference to McCarthy did not appear in the published version.[9]

In October 1950 Snow tallied up the past year's boxscore. He had proposed twenty-five stories, of which the *Post* accepted three: a 0.115 batting average, he said. In contrast, the *Post* had suggested five articles, of which Snow agreed to write two.

Snow's suggestion that he was more flexible than the *Post* was misleading. True, Hibbs and Sommers purposely steered him away from political topics and they objected to his Leftist point of view. They also wanted to save him from himself. But Snow was hardly a willing subject. When Harrison Salisbury came down to lunch at the *Post* to discuss possible free-lance story assignments, Sommers confided his difficulties protecting Snow.

Salisbury, who had a "hero worship of Ed," simply couldn't understand Snow's stiff-necked attitude. Salisbury's considerable energies were flexible. When he came back from a tour in the Soviet Union for the *New York Times*, his editors decided to cut him down a notch and told him to write a story on New York trash and garbage. Salisbury produced the most complete treatment of the subject in the *Times'* history. "If Snow had gone out and written for a couple of years about baseball," Salisbury thought, he could have saved himself and his relationship with the *Post* for the big stories that would come up later.[10]

For his part, Snow confided to a friend one evening, he couldn't understand old China Hands like Theodore White. White had trouble renewing his passport, as did many who had covered Chinese communism. After clearing himself with the State Department, White did not write about China again for years and, he ashamedly confessed much later, "deliberately ignored the dynamics of foreign policy and defense because too much danger lurked there." Snow regarded that approach as out of the question. He prided himself on his ability to anticipate the course of political events, especially those involving the Left. That was what he cared about and that was what he was determined to write about, whether in Western Europe, where he investigated the potential for communism after the war, or in South Asia where independence opened the prospect of sweeping economic changes. In 1950, when the *Post* was trying to keep him on safe ground, Snow wrote a piece proposing a new United States foreign policy, a "Tru-Deal," which accepted the fall of China to the Communists, refused to subsidize "the French war in Indo-China," and proposed liberal assistance for colonial and newly independent countries. He sold it to the liberal *Nation*. Snow, who had developed his expertise because of his independence, wasn't going to write stories on garbage, no matter how prestigious the publication for which he worked. When the State Department balked at renewing Snow's passport in 1953, he submitted an affidavit stating "I am not now and have never been a Communist" and kept speaking out.[11]

For Snow the issue became less whether the *Post* could live with his point of view than whether he could live with the magazine's outlook. In the same way that Hibbs considered it his duty to moderate Snow's "extremism," Snow believed that *Post* editorials and articles compromised *his* reputation. "I can't tell them anything any more," he told his brother. He thought it a personal embarrassment to have his name on the masthead as associate editor.

The tension broke in February 1951. With differences of opinion looming in Snow's mind, he submitted his resignation a third time. Hibbs hated to let people go, even with cause, and he had developed affection for Snow, who often stayed overnight at his house on visits to Philadelphia. Others on the staff felt the same way. Sommers had a reputation for defending the correspondents under him. When told that a story by one of his reporters was not up to par, one correspondent recalled, Sommers's "face would turn red and swell up like a bullfrog." Everyone knew that Sommers was Snow's best friend on the *Post*. Managing editor Bob Fuoss, perhaps the toughest of the bunch, considered Snow "the most perfect gentleman" he knew among foreign correspondents and thought Snow had the best contacts in the Far East of any reporter in his generation. But if Fuoss and Sommers were not as conservative as Hibbs, they were not as far to the Left as Snow either. All three thought Snow would stay if they reassured him that he was an important part of the *Post*. All three were worn down by the friction, which came on one side from conservatives, who tried every kind of pressure including leaning on newsstand proprietors, and on the other from Snow, so uncompromising in his point of view. All agreed that Hibbs should accept his resignation.[12]

Bob Fuoss remembered the painful final gathering with Snow at the Down Town Club, the top-floor restaurant in one of the Curtis Publishing Company's twin marble towers overlooking Independence Square. Each day the editors took their mid-day meals there, often with visiting correspondents. Normally the luncheon talk looked ahead to what the reporter would cover in the coming months, where he would carry the *Post* colors. This time, with memories of past friendship weighing on their minds, the lunch was tense and tearful. The end had come.

Even at that, Hibbs hoped that the connection could be saved in some form. He offered to take free-lance articles. Hibbs thought Snow accepted rather grudgingly and later decided that, too, was a mistake. Snow showed "little glint of his great abilities in these articles." Snow's complaints continued. A tough profile of cold, calculating Georgi Malenkov, Stalin's right-hand man, came off alright. But not Snow's balanced profile on Chou En-lai. Snow thought in terms of a title like "Mandarin in a Red Hat." *Post* headline writers, often carried away by their own creativity, entitled the piece "Red China's Gentleman Hatchet Man." Snow worried that the misleading title would ruin his standing as an objective reporter between China and the United States.[13]

Snow's break with the *Post* came at an awkward moment. He was now a family man, with a family man's responsibilities.

In mid-May 1949, he and Peg had finally divorced. The proceedings had entangled them in months of expensive, acrimonious wrangling with numerous lawyers until the marriage seemed to him an "intolerable incubus." At one point Peg hired detectives. Nine days after the divorce, the soonest Snow could obtain a license from city hall, he married Lois Wheeler in an old Georgian home belonging to friends of Agnes Smedley at Snedens Landing, a community across the Hudson from New York City. With her usual gusto Smedley arranged the small ceremony, filling the house with mock orange blossoms. Snow's brother, Howard, stood up as best man.

By the time Snow left the *Post* nearly two years later, he had a son, Christopher, and the birth of his daugther, Jennifer Sian, was just a few days off. Snow no longer had his *Post* expense account or the fat two thousand dollar checks the *Post* paid him for each article. Meanwhile, he had alimony payments to Peg, who kept the house in Madison and never remarried. Snow walked the streets of New York City with his brother, worrying aloud about how he would support his family.

Yet, the lonely years drifting emotionally, without regular warmth and affection, were over. "It seems to me that life has suddenly become good again after a long darkness," Snow wrote to his sister shortly after the wedding.[14]

After their marriage, he and Lois had headed for California, she to appear in a movie with Susan Hayward and Dana Andrews, he to work on his Flagstaff, Arizona, article. They moved from an apartment at 47 West 9th Street in New York City to Snedens Landing about the time Snow left the *Post*. Initially, they rented the Captain John House, as the venerable house was called, overlooking the Hudson. The next year they used assets acquired during his *Post* days to buy a larger, awkward-looking stone home, originally a Dutch farmhouse but now transformed, with thirty foot columns, a wrap-around porch, and a green tile roof. The house, across the road from Snedens Landing, in Rockleigh, New Jersey, sat on three acres of land, with a barn and a brook.[15]

Snedens Landing, less than a hundred homes set among stately trees and stone fences, and the Rockleigh community with large stretches of woods, provided a congenial setting for raising children. Lois could commute to New York to appear in stage productions and television productions, including a long stint on the soap opera *The Guiding Light*. The community also offered a haven from McCarthyism. The residents included actors, artists, writers, and musicians. The clackety-clack of typewriters issued audibly from houses on days warm enough to warrant opening the windows. It was a place where children grew up hearing intense political debate. "You, McCarthy, you," young Christopher blurted out in a snit of anger at his father one day.

Though fifteen years younger than Snow and impressed with his experience, knowledge, and objectivity, Lois was her own person. An accomplished actress, she had her own views on domestic and foreign policy, and she advanced them with conviction and a sense of humor.

"I am against capital punishment. I have been against capital punishment for a long time," Lois said once, adding with a laugh, "But I would like to see Henry Kissinger hanged." It did not bother Snow that Lois stood in the back of a truck on a New York street corner to speak on behalf of a congressman or that she criticized him roundly for letting a friend give Christopher a toy gun. Snow liked outspoken, independent women. Although Lois's passions bubbled to the surface more readily than his, the underlying convictions were the same. Their obvious warmth and complementing personalities made them an attractive couple.[16]

Snow, approaching fifty years of age, lost none of his charm or appeal. Age made his visage more rugged and highlighted the small dimple on his chin. His hair was gray, though still thick and curly, with hints of red. Bushy eyebrows accented his brown eyes. Despite his short stature, Snow looked robust, outdoorish. Friends imagined him picking his way through Nationalist lines to visit the Chinese Communists. If there was any change in his persona, it was a certain dignity that comes with seasoning and accomplishment. He still had a winning way with people. His junior colleagues "adored" him, as one editor put it, because he seemed to care so much about them. When Lois put on a cast party for young people with whom she performed, many didn't seem to appreciate Snow's accomplishments and treated him glibly, older friends thought. It didn't faze Snow. "Ed never thought about himself," mystery writer and Snedens Landing resident Dorothy Salisbury Davis reminisced. "It never bothered him to be in a room where no one knew him." As much as she criticized Snow, Freda Utley thought he was a nice guy.

Sprightly, pretty Betty Vincent, a woman who knew her own mind, said later Snow was the one man besides her husband she could marry. That was a common refrain from women. "He was an intellectual and a man," said Madeleine Gekiere, a Swiss artist married to an actor who worked with Lois on *The Guiding Light*. One evening during a large party in Rockleigh, Snow took the baby sitter home and invited Gekiere along. When they returned to the house, they sat in the car and talked for an hour. The discussion, carried largely by Snow, was on the Yugoslavian Communist philosopher Milovan Djilas. It seemed romantic to Gekiere. It was the way Snow had about him.

Snow always did better in small groups. The dramatic flare he brought to his writing vanished when he stepped behind a microphone. No amount of coaching from Lois cured his slow talking delivery or general discomfort. He was too earnest for clever give-and-take, and never a wit, a master of the *bon mot*. He had a Mark Twain sense of humor, liking stories that cut through cant and sophistry. One anecdote he particularly enjoyed occurred in India. During an interview with Gandhi, Jimmy Sheean's watch stopped; it stopped again at the moment Gandhi was killed. The phenomenon, which appealed to Sheean's mysticism, repeated itself during a press conference with Nehru when *both* Sheean's and Snow's watches stopped. After the conference, Snow asked Nehru how he explained the odd event. "What you need," Nehru observed, "are new watches."[17]

Snow had the absent-minded quality that people had seen in his father. He left coffee cups stashed under sofas and failed on one occasion to notice that he had set the curtains on fire. Actor Norman Rose once lent his New York apartment to Snow; when Rose returned it was as hot as a jungle. Snow had forgotten to turn off the oven. After visiting his brother in Boston, Snow arrived late at the Back Bay train station and jumped on a car as it pulled out of the terminal. Unfortunately it wasn't a New York bound train, but one heading for Chicago. He couldn't get off until Springfield. Snow drove his beat-up green Plymouth station wagon, one friend thought, as if "he were going to give it away."

Lois commented often that her husband never bothered to ask about the possibility of maintaining his health insurance when he left the *Post*. Publishers often wondered just what he was doing and when it would get done. He didn't pay attention to taxes, sometimes filing when he didn't need to and other times carelessly throwing letters from the government into a drawer. Big-hearted Harry Davis, an actor who lived in Snedens Landing, put Snow in touch with an accountant who admired Snow's work. The arrangement, frustrating for both Snow and the accountant, soon ended. Snow, a friend said, should have been born holding a lawyer's hand. Before moving to Snedens Landing, Snow had built a home along the Connecticut River. The contractor took the money, leaving behind a pile of unpaid bills and a half-finished job, done so poorly that the foundation had to be poured again. The house was still not completely built when he and Lois sold it in the early 1950s.

In his youth Snow had been lucky, reaping a profit on the stock market in 1927 to finance his world travels and, in Peking, winning at the horse races so he didn't have to take a job with the Associated Press. He saw no real reason why that should change. Snow remained a risk taker. He liked to test himself against the unknown. A stable neighbored his Rockleigh home, and he rode the horses fearlessly, jumping over fences. One afternoon, while relaxing with friends along the banks of the Hudson, he jumped into the river for a swim. Ignoring Lois's protestations, he swam far out—so far that he had to struggle back against the stiff tide. Mary Heathcote, an editor at Random House in the 1950s, thought Snow had an internal gyroscope so that he walked close to danger without falling off.

Snow liked working around the house, doing carpentry or gardening. He could build an expert-looking cedar-lined closet or knotty pine kitchen cabinets one day and the next come up with a thoroughly whimsical idea. One of his most notorious schemes was buying sheep to eat the grass, thereby saving himself the trouble of mowing. The Tom Sawyer-like idea backfired because the sheep ate everything, including the fruit trees.

Snow was proud of his family. He had a young, attractive wife who juggled her acting career with elaborate birthday parties for the children, dances in the barn behind their house in Rockleigh, and canning preserves and knitting. Some thought she must never sleep. Snow always liked children. When, in the 1920s, he interviewed the allegedly lineal descendant of Confucius, a pre-teenager, Snow promised to send the young sage movie magazines. Snow was an uncle who wouldn't hear of his five-year-old niece staying with a baby sitter while the older people went to a French restaurant. She would go along! As a father himself, he seemed tolerant and didn't talk down to his children. Christmases, he commented to Howard after his children were born, were among the "best I've had in my life."[18]

But there was an intensity to Snow, too. Friends sensed a gap between the outer absentminded, easy going Snow and the inner intellectual Snow. He chewed the ends off his pipes and had trouble sleeping. He sat before his typewriter twisting at his hair in deep thought and spent long hours reading, making notes in the margins of books. This was as it had always been, the two sides of Snow's personality working together. He was so good a journalist because he brought so much concentration to his work. But there were new pressures in the 1950s. Being a gray-haired father was one. He realized that he had not become a family man by the book. "Thank God," he told a pregnant friend, "some friends are going to have children younger than ours." While other fathers his age were at their peak earning years, he struggled along doing "piece work." The income Lois earned was crucial. They weren't starving, but they decided to rent the barn, which Snow had hoped to use as a studio. After years of living at the center of breaking news, he was sidelined. Dorothy and Harry Davis watched Snow during a party one evening as he talked to an old colleague from China. The conversation animated Snow and showed poignantly, they thought, that he was out of his element in Snedens Landing.

Before and during World War II, when Snow's stature was at its height, parts of official Washington quietly built the scaffolding on which his reputation would be hanged in the 1950s.[19]

The Dies Committee—so called because of its chairman, Texas Democrat U.S. Representative Martin Dies—maintained its interest in Communist subversion in the years leading up to the war. Snow's name came up briefly in hearings. One woman testified that the Washington Committee for Aid to China was "Communist dominated." As evidence she recalled that someone associated with the committee recommended she read *Red Star over China*.

Meanwhile, on orders from Franklin Roosevelt, the FBI investigated "subversive activities in the United States, particularly Fascism and Communism," and perfected its surveillance and record keeping techniques. Although the Dies Committee faded in importance during the war, the Federal Bureau of Investigation, under J. Edgar Hoover, kept the bit between its teeth. In 1941, just after Snow returned from China, the FBI noted in its files that Snow received an allegedly Chinese Communist periodical in the mail. In January 1944, seventeen months before the war ended, the FBI staff compiled a twenty-three page, single-spaced typewritten report on Snow, which it sent to the New York office. A covering memo, written over Hoover's signature, explained, "This is being supplied for your general information concerning Snow in the event an occasion should arise when background information regarding Snow would be desirable."[20]

After the war, agents in the field monitored Snow's activities. One reported that the day after Snow arrived in Tokyo in late 1945 he visited "the headquarters of the Communist Party of Japan where he interviewed Central Committeemen and asked them various questions of the present and future of the Communist Party of Japan." Snow's name appeared in connection with investigations of others like Anna Louise Strong and Agnes Smedley. The Shanghai Municipal Police Department reports that followed Snow around Asia beginning in the late 1920s found their way to his FBI file. In the 1950s agents questioned him at Snedens Landing and in Rockleigh. Snow came across as "cordial, cooperative, and apparently frank"—and loyal to friends and acquaintances about whom he was quizzed.

The heft of the FBI file amassed on Snow was deceptive. Much of the file consisted of lists, for instance of Snow's passport renewals; background from *Who's Who* and other general distribution publications; long excerpts from Snow's articles, speeches, books (including the dust jackets), and articles by others. In effect, the bureau continuously recycled—and retyped—that first 1944 report, from time to time adding a new fact or two. Though devoid of social imagination, conservative J. Edgar Hoover created jobs for platoons of secretaries in those days before photocopying machines.

In the final analysis, the case against Snow boiled down to this: his name appeared in the address books of other suspects; alleged Communists read his books; he supported organizations during the war that promoted Soviet-American peace; he was the object of dubious observations by a handful of informants. One of the earliest informants said cryptically that Edgar Snow was not actually a party member but the party "knew just how to use him." A former Communist said Snow was a "concealed communist," working under "communist discipline." He admitted never having met Snow, only having heard about him from others. Another informant noted that during a 1950 trip to Mexico, Snow rented his New York apartment to some "longhairs" who appeared to be Communists.

FBI interest was shallow. Agents made little attempt to explore leads. The files noted that Snow had been billed as a speaker at the 1941 American Writers Congress. No one apparently found out that the congress revoked the speaking invitation when Snow refused to revise his remarks to suit the current Soviet line colored by Moscow's alliance with Nazi Germany.

Judging a person's politics by whom he knew or who read his books set in motion a nightmarish circular argument. If alleged Communists read *Red Star,* Snow must be a Communist sympathizer; and if Snow were a Communist sympathizer, then others who read *Red Star* must be Communist sympathizers as well. Likewise, a favorable or even neutral comment by the *Daily Worker* implied Communist sympathy, while a positive book review in the conservative *New York Herald Tribune,* if mentioned at all, "proved" how crafty the author was.

As thin as all this was, the FBI knew its man. An FBI official prepared an analysis of a 1945 article by Snow in the *Saturday Evening Post.* Snow's conclusions, the analyst wrote, did "not appear to be well-founded" because they deviated from stated U.S. policy and remarks by Ambassador Hurley. This was a litmus test for journalism akin to the abhorrent Soviet system of assuming that only the state knows the truth. After reading the report, one of Hoover's top aides wrote in longhand at the bottom, "Snow is an ingenious fellow-traveller."

Such "evidence" had no place in a court of law (although the courts were not immune from the Red Scare). But most cases never went to court. Trials, such as they were, took place in the media and in congressional hearing rooms, without formal accusations, juries, or other legal safeguards. Indeed, simply mounting a defense was reason enough to assume guilt. As Senator Joe McCarthy boasted to a group of reporters who made their regular rounds to his office one evening, "If you are against McCarthy, you are a Communist or a cocksucker."[21]

Many of Snow's friends and acquaintances had to defend themselves.[22] Diplomats Edmund Clubb and John Carter Vincent were forced into retirement. John S. Service, dismissed from the foreign service, went to work in the steam trap business in New York until he was reinstated in a low ranking post six years later. John Leaning, the Englishman who was managing editor of *democracy* magazine, had subsequently worked for the Institute of Pacific Relations (IPR) in the United States, where he started a family. When the IPR came under attack, so did Leaning. Snow helped him find temporary work; Leaning ended up heading a classics department at a private Massachusetts boys school, Wilbraham Academy. J. B. Powell's son, Bill, kept the *China Weekly Review* alive until 1953. Under him the *Review* criticized U.S. Far Eastern policy and highlighted reports of American use of germ warfare in Korea. When Powell came home, he, his wife, and an associate were indicted for sedition. The government gave up the case in 1961 but Powell's journalism career was finished. After renovating homes for a time, he and his wife opened an antique shop in San Francisco's Mission district.

In early 1949, General MacArthur's staff released a fifty-four-page report declaring Agnes Smedley part of a Soviet spy ring in China before the war. To escape the intense attention, Smedley secreted herself out of Snedens Landing, lying in the backseat of a car covered with a blanket. Snow helped her find a hotel room in New York City and defended her in an article in the *Nation*. Although the spy charges were retracted, Smedley went to England where she waited for a visa to China. She died suddenly in May 1950 following surgery for stomach ulcers. Smedley was buried in the National Revolutionary Martyrs Memorial Park outside Peking. Snow guided her last book, a biography of Chinese general Chu Teh entitled *The Great Road*, to posthumous publication and served as an executor of her estate. The royalties went to Chu.[23]

The China Lobby, a network of Chiang Kai-shek supporters including such people as textile importer Alfred Kohlberg, founder of *Plain Talk*, put Owen Lattimore at the top of its list of people who sold out China. Easily egged on, Congress investigated Lattimore twice; after that the Justice Department charged him with perjury, a common tactic to corner victims on some obscure misstatement made during protracted testimony. FBI agents questioned Snow about Lattimore. Just before Christmas 1952, Snow was called to appear before a Washington,

D.C., grand jury considering the Lattimore case. The grand jury handed down an indictment before Snow was called to the stand. The indictment was so weak that Lattimore never went to trial, though the Justice Department tried to force the issue for three years.

Snow never appeared before any of the congressional committees investigating Communist activities. His name, however, came up time and time again.[24] Witnesses were asked about Snow's views on the Soviet Union; about Indusco and *democracy* magazine, which McCarthy called a Communist periodical; about helping Philip Jaffe reach Yenan in 1937; about the Army's use of *People on Our Side* as an educational tool during the war. The Senate Subcommittee on Internal Security, chaired by Democrat Pat McCarran, had a special interest in China Hands like Snow. When it published an index of its hearings and reports during the 1950s and 1960s, more than 120 citations appeared under Snow's name, many of them including multiple pages. During its investigation of the Institute of Pacific Relations, the McCarran committee established two categories of China Hands: group A for "anti-Communists" and group P for "pro-Communists." Not much was required to be a member of the latter group: One witness had to testify under oath that an individual had been affiliated with one or more of "the Communist-controlled organizations" cited by the committee. Among other things, Snow had written an article drawn from *Red Star* for IPR's publication *Pacific Affairs*. He was a member of group P.

Testifying before the Senate Foreign Relations Committee, former Communist Louis Budenz included Snow in a list of people who had been Communists. Snow's Red affiliations might have changed, Budenz implied, since divorcing Peg, who was also under suspicion. Later, during IPR hearings, Budenz dredged up Freda Utley's old canard. Snow he said, "amended one edition of [*Red Star*], as I recall, at the request of the Communist Party." Budenz couldn't quite recall if he was involved in party discussions to get Snow to revise the book "or in subsequent discussions in which the matter was reviewed." The Senate subcommittee thought enough of Budenz's testimony to reiterate his main point in its summary: "Edgar Snow obediently altered later edition of his book" to obscure its message that the Chinese Communists were "genuine Communists." The subcommittee also noted the 1937 criticism by Asiaticus of *Red Star* in *Pacific Affairs*. This, the subcommittee concluded, was evidence that the Comintern "used the pages of IPR's *Pacific Affairs* in order to communicate to world Communist circles the orthodox Communist line on China."

Snow was also implicated in the strange case of John Paton Davies and "Tawny Pipit."[25] Tawny Pipit was the code name for a scheme concocted by Davies in 1949 while working under George Kennan on the State Department's Policy Planning Staff. The idea, which Davies presented to the Central Intelligence Agency, involved "using" Snow, Agnes Smedley, Anna Louise Strong, Harvard professors Benjamin Schwartz and John Fairbank, and Fairbank's wife Wilma in "the Cold War." The CIA rejected Tawny Pipit at an early stage. The idea lived on in congressional hearing rooms.

Appearing before the McCarran committee, a CIA official to whom Davies broached the scheme testified that Davies wanted these so-called Communist sympathizers to provide "material and guidance" to the government. On orders from his superiors, Davies refused to discuss the plan during the hearings because it "touched on an operation only slightly less sensitive than that of atomic energy." He did deny categorically recommending Snow and the others for employment in the CIA. Unable to pin down Davies, the committee engaged in wide-ranged questioning that at one point touched on Snow's "girl friend" in Moscow during the 1940s. Davies described her as "a cute dish," someone the NKVD, the political police, might have been "trying to use on us." Davies also insisted that her relationship with Snow was strictly "apolitical."

The committee pressed the Justice Department to charge Davies with perjury because his remarks differed from those of the CIA witness. Charges were never brought. Shortly afterward, Davies, cleared on four previous occasions by the Loyalty Review Board, underwent another investigation, which this time included muddled testimony by Patrick Hurley. The board recommended—and Secretary of State John Foster Dulles carried out—Davies's dismissal from the foreign service. The board had found no evidence of disloyalty but concluded Davies "lacked judgment, discretion and reliability."

Sources later told Teddy White that Davies's scheme had been "to plant in Peking Americans considered 'friendly' by the Chinese Communists and then milk them for intelligence we needed." Whether or not that was the plan, it is doubtful that Snow would have cooperated in anything other than straight reporting—which may be all Davies had in mind anyway. Nor was it likely that a "cute dish," even if thoroughly political (which she apparently was not), had any more impact on Snow's reporting than Davies would have had. All the same, the effect of wild speculation was damning, made all the worse by intemperate witnesses encouraged to engage in any manner of speculation.

In this regard, Dr. Karl August Wittfogel was a prize witness. Like Freda Utley and Budenz, Wittfogel had gone from the Marxist Left to the McCarthyite Right; and like them he had something to say about Snow's revisions to *Red Star*, something quite novel indeed. The German-born professor testified on his acquaintance with Snow in Peking during the 1930s. At the time, Wittfogel was becoming disillusioned with the Soviet Union. "I am partly responsible" Wittfogel said, "for the unfriendly remarks about the Soviet bureaucracy which appear in the first edition."

It was a preposterous statement. Although Wittfogel never mentioned it in his testimony, Snow had in fact sent draft sections of *Red Star* to him for comment. But the draft had the "unfriendly remarks" in it already—the reason being that Snow picked them up among his travels with the Chinese Communists. Such were the times that Congress, like the FBI, was satisfied with comments like Wittfogel's, and witnesses came to see themselves as omnipotent. Thirty years later in an interview with this author, Wittfogel revealed how he arrived at his conclusion that Snow followed his lead: He and Snow took a short walk during a picnic with a group of friends. Wittfogel related his concerns about Stalin. And that was that—or so Wittfogel argued in a neat bit of egocentricity.[26]

Snow's name and the bogus tales about his writing became a regular feature in conservative books like *How the Far East Was Lost*, in pamphlets like *America Betrayed*, and in articles in the *American Legion Magazine*. Time after time writers dredged up the agrarian reform myth, and Snow's "strange" association with the *Saturday Evening Post*. John Flynn's *While You Slept* observed that "one pro-Communist article in the *Saturday Evening Post* can do more damage than ten years of the *New Masses* or the *Daily Worker*."

In *The China Story* Freda Utley introduced a new theme when she criticized Snow's anti-Soviet article on "The Venomous Dr. Vyshinsky." Feeling the pressure of public opinion, she said, Snow had reversed himself "without a word of apology" to his readers. Snow, she wrote, was a "careerist." That line of criticism did not catch on generally, though Utley did not abandon the notion. "I don't think he was a Communist," she said in an interview twenty years later. "He was a careerist."[27]

Suspicion of Snow penetrated establishment journalism circles. Arch Steele, a careful, objective reporter who respected Snow's work, learned from a "source I regarded as absolutely reliable" that Snow was a member of the Socialist party. Although Steele did not regurgitate any of this, others did. A *Chicago Tribune* writer, discussing "foreign 'isms' " in the press, brought up Snow's name. He reported that a fellow journalist, "who produced exposés of communist infiltration into trades unions," was convinced the *Saturday Evening Post* turned down his articles because Snow was an editor. When the Tawny Pipit incident came to light, Snow issued a statement saying "There is no basis for any statement that I am a Communist or pro-Communist." The *New York Times* reported the denial. Several months later *Times*man James Reston, in a front page story, identified Snow and the others whom Davies thought of using in Tawny Pipit as "a mixed crew of Communists and liberals."

Lois thought her husband should sue. Snow, who respected Reston and approved generally of *Times* editorials on McCarthy, protested in a letter to the editor. Who, Snow asked, were the Communists to whom Reston referred?

Publisher Arthur Hays Sulzberger wrote Snow an apology; Reston called Snow personally and wrote a reply in the *Times* regretting the ambiguity. Reston said he had no reason to believe that Snow, the Fairbanks, or Schwartz "ever had any connection with the Communist party." Reston did not answer Snow's point that Agnes Smedley was not a member of the Chinese Communist party. But he addressed the larger problem: If a reporter simply related what people said, he gave "currency to Senator McCarthy's implication that Mr. Davies tried to put 'Communists and espionage agents in key spots in the Central Intelligence Agency' "; if a reporter passed judgment on the charges, he became more than a reporter.

The dilemma Reston identified provided an acute irony as far as Snow was concerned. Much criticism against him centered on the fact that he reported what the Chinese Communists said. Yet McCarthy and other Red baiters thrived precisely because the press reported what *they* said, without commenting on the absurdity of the charges. In later years reporters often blamed the journalistic convention of "objectivity," which put them on a short leash. Charles Seib, who covered Capitol Hill during the 1950s and later became ombudsman for the *Washington Post*, recalled that reporters who went beyond the convention did so at the risk of hearing from publishers, many of whom were McCarthy supporters. Whatever their feelings about communism, editors at the *Saturday Evening Post* did not minimize the ability of media moguls to promote their point of view for ideological and self-interest reasons. Although admittedly without proof, they suspected one source of rumors against Snow was Henry Luce, at the helm of their competitor, *Time*. Luce had turned hostile toward godless, anti-free enterprise Chinese communism.[28]

Knowing Snow became a liability for old friends and acquaintances. In 1950 the State Department Office of Security collected material on Snow from official diplomatic files. His name and activities came up in the course of have-you-now-or-have-you-ever-been-a-Communist questions asked in the course of loyalty investigations.

Harry Price, the Yenching economics professor who helped the Snows start *democracy*, needed a security clearance to serve as a UN economic advisor in Nepal. Ten months passed before his clearance came through and then only after he explained adverse comments in his file, including his association with Snow and the magazine.

Mac Fisher, Snow's old UPI reporter friend from China, had headed Office of War Information operations in China during the war. Afterward he continued on as a State Department information officer. In January 1951, the Loyalty Security Board gave Fisher an eighteen-page interrogatory with forty-nine questions. Among the questions were these:

- "Are you acquainted with Edgar Snow?"
- "If so state the nature and frequency of your contacts giving the date and occasion of your most recent contact."
- "To what extent, if any, have you been aware of his alleged pro-Communist sympathies and activities?"
- "If you have been aware of such alleged sympathies and activities what has been your attitude toward them?"

The same questions were asked of Fisher's relations with other Americans and with Chou En-lai and Mao Tse-tung. ("To what extent, if any, are you aware of [Mao's] alleged pro-Communist sympathies and activities?")

Diplomat John Allison, who arranged Snow's Tokyo marriage to Peg and eventually became ambassador to Japan, "often wondered how I escaped [McCarthy's] attention and what he would have said if he had known that I had once shared an apartment in Shanghai with Edgar Snow."[29]

The questioning process forced a negativism on many under investigation. Fisher told investigators that during the 1930s he "formed a high opinion of [Snow's] journalistic ability and acumen" but had to admit that he did not share Snow's positive assessments of the Communists in the 1940s. "My attitude today is that while I would not necessarily go out of my way to avoid seeing Snow as an old personal friend I would refrain, as I have consistently since the war, from discussing matters touching on U.S. policy." John Paton Davies admitted that in Moscow he had wondered about Snow's relationship to the party but thought he was more balanced with his comments on Tito. John Carter Vincent, also under attack, stood solidly by Snow.[30]

On every flank, it seemed, Snow had a problem. In early 1953 two McCarthy staffers traveled through Europe, looking for pro-Communist books in United States government-sponsored libraries. Operating under broadly defined department directives, intimidated diplomats burned some volumes and removed many more from overseas libraries. When the *New York Times* reported that Snow was among the authors whose books were removed, he protested in letters to President Eisenhower, Senator Karl Mundt, and the *New York Times*. Mundt, with whom Snow traveled as unofficial press secretary to Saudi Arabia, denied that McCarthy's Subcommittee on Investigations, on which he served, singled out Snow's books for such treatment. The State Department denied that it proscribed his books but admitted that "in some posts your books were withdrawn from the shelves." Snow was assured that his books would be reinstated. Opinion surveys during the period showed that book banning enjoyed considerable popular support.[31]

In the mid-1950s Lois Snow ran for the Rockleigh Board of Education. Referring to the Reston article on the Tawny Pipit affair, the chairman of the borough council advised people not to vote for the wife of a Communist. She lost the election by a narrow margin. A local attorney, Charles Joelson, considered Snow unflappable, even laconic at times. But after the vote, Snow was blistering mad. He wanted Joelson to sue. Joelson had trouble convincing Snow to settle for a verbal retraction at a town hall meeting.[32]

Lois had a taste of network television blacklisting that was unrelated to her husband. Through actor Harry Davis, who also suffered blacklisting problems, she managed to see the network hatchet man. When Lois pressed, the executive asked if she ever lived in Brooklyn, if she ever used an assumed name? Her stage name was Lois Wheeler, she said.

"Are you not Miriam Oppenheimer," he asked?

No, not really, she replied. That was the name of the Brooklyn character she played in "The Fifth Season." As had happened to Davis, the network blacklist was a case of mistaken identity.

Snow was no longer a hero in Kansas City, "a man who knows his stuff," as the *Star* put it in the mid-1940s.[33] Snow's father, who died in 1958, was feeble and not always lucid, and thus apparently was spared embarrassment. Mildred and her husband, Claude Mackey, heard plenty, which no doubt stung all the more because of their political conservatism. "Say, I hear Ed is a Communist," volunteered a boyhood friend of Snow, a vice-president of a life insurance company. A local judge approached Claude Mackey at a party. "I went to school with your brothers-in-law," he said. "Howard is OK. As far as Ed is concerned, I have no use for him. He's turned Communist." When Claude disagreed, the judge stomped away.

When Bob Long, with whom Snow traveled to California as a boy, visited New York, he looked up his old friend Al Steen. Steen was editor of the high school fraternity newspaper that Snow helped found. He graduated from the University of Missouri journalism school and in the 1950s was East Coast editor of the movie magazine *Box Office*. Long thought they should call on Snow for a sort of reunion. Steen refused. He didn't like Snow's political beliefs.

Howard Snow was acutely aware of his brother's problems.[34] Howard worked in the National Association of Manufacturers' (NAM) Boston Office. He regularly saw Robert H. W. Welch, Jr., an ultra-conservative Massachusetts businessman, who served on the NAM board and founded the John Birch Society in the mid-1950s. The society kept its own files on Edgar Snow and the first issue of its magazine, *One Man's Opinion*, noted that the most serious mistake by the *Saturday Evening Post* in the last twenty years was "a series of articles on China by the now notorious Edgar Snow . . . . [T]hose articles helped mightily in the brainwashing of the American people which enabled the Communist influences in our midst to manipulate the sell-out of China to agents of the Kremlin." Welch didn't know Howard was related to Edgar Snow.

Howard, who forwarded Welch's invective to his brother, thought McCarthyism "a hateful force that has been let loose in the world." But like the NAM, which invested millions each year on anti-Communist rhetoric and had a committee (chaired for a time by Welch) to promote free market philosophy in schools, he had conventional views on the virtues of capitalism. This injected rancor in the brothers' relationship. When Howard told his brother "your never said anything critical about Communists in your writing," Snow shot back a letter the next day. Snow was "a bit sore because I hear my own brother parroting the baseless remarks of some of my worst enemies."

"The next thing I know," Snow added, "you will be telling me that *I* said the Chinese Reds were 'only agrarian reformers' and 'were not real Communists.' "

"I hear from Howard occasionally," Snow told his sister. "He writes me long letters telling me what a wonderful thing the American system is and how grateful I should be to Mr. Eisenhower and Mr. Dulles, who seem to be occupied mainly in putting their feet in each other's mouths, when Mr. Dulles is not writing directives about what books should be burned."

Snow's life became an endless round of fighting back. He wrote directly to Welch threatening suit. When Budenz referred to Snow as a "Soviet espionage agent" in his book *Techniques of Communism*, Snow demanded the publisher amend the volume. The publisher put errata slips in the book, which effectively served to draw more attention to Snow.

As much as Snow was "sick to death of idiots writing in to the [*Saturday Evening Post*] or anywhere I publish to repeat this old canard" of the agrarian reform myth, he felt forced to deal with it. When FBI agents arrived in Snedens Landing, he assumed they came to question him about his statements on Chinese communism. The agents inquired instead about another journalist who worked in China, Gunther Stein. Nevertheless, as the agents recorded in their report, Snow volunteered that he wasn't a Communist and "that in his writing concerning China for the past 15 years, he has stated on numerous occasions that the Chinese Communists are not agrarian reformers but are Communists in every sense of the word."[35]

Before 1950 Snow did not check page proofs on one of his books. It simply wasn't possible, he was so steadily on the move. All that changed in the 1950s. He had plenty of time to read page proofs. The problem was finding something to write about, somebody to write for.

Snow's journalistic output dwindled to a trickle in the 1950s: a handful of articles in the *Saturday Evening Post*, none after 1956; a book review in the *Saturday Review of Literature* in 1959; publication of a talk on China in the *Annals of the American Academy of Political and Social Science*. If he wanted to say something about the Eisenhower administration's belligerent and counterproductive China policy in a mainstream American newspaper like the *New York Times*, he had to say it in a letter to the editor. *Asahi* in Japan and publications in India, England, Switzerland, and Indonesia were far more interested in his work than were Americans. The Modern Library edition of *Red Star* never seemed to be on bookstore shelves.

The one exception was the *Nation*. The editor, crusading Carey McWilliams, abhorred McCarthy and the Cold War—and admired Snow, "a great reporter, perceptive, canny, with rare social imagination." One of Snow's efforts for the *Nation*, a three-part series on the significance of decolonization in 1955, won fifth prize in the Second National Peace Contest sponsored by Lawrence S. Mayers. McWilliams offered Snow a job as foreign editor. Snow turned it down, perhaps realizing the magazine could not open the world to him. The *Nation* had a limited circulation and a tight budget in the best of times. In the 1950s

McCarthyites purged the weekly from school libraries in New York City and Newark. The stories Snow produced for the magazine entailed virtually no reporting. Mostly, he wrote book reviews and, like the award-winning series on decolonization, editorial comment.[36]

Unable to acquire new information, Snow mined his past work. He wrote up his interviews with Franklin Roosevelt in a two-part series for the *Monthy Review*. John Fairbank at Harvard hired him as a research associate, during which time Snow assembled his unpublished notes on the Chinese Communists. Snow sent the material to Random House, which recognized that it was not a mass market book. Harvard published it in 1957 as a paperback monograph, *Random Notes on Red China, 1936–1945*, intended for scholars.

Public speaking was equally difficult. Stephens College, a women's school neighboring the University of Missouri in Columbia, offered Snow expenses and a five hundred dollar honorarium if he would speak in 1951. He turned down the offer. When Snow wrote to the college in 1954 to revive the idea, he complained it did not reply. Agents who previously wanted Snow in their stable of speakers said he was too controversial.[37]

Snow's creative energies always ranged beyond reporting. He had regularly thought about writing fiction since *Liberty* magazine published his callow tale in 1930. But for the same reasons that he didn't have time to read page proofs on his books when he was a reporter, he rarely did much about the non-reportorial ideas that constantly occurred to him. In the 1950s, with no regular work and worries about making money, he had time to pursue his creative impulses, which came to seem like real opportunites. Unfortunately, they met with little success.

In 1951 he wrote a short story that appeared in the *Post*. Based on an experience in Peking during the 1930s, it told the tale of an American's attempt to save a Chinese girl from her miserable surroundings. The story was his only fictional success. He shopped another piece to the *New Yorker*, thought about working with a literary agent, considered turning some of his work into television scripts, and talked to mystery writer Dorothy Salisbury Davis about collaborating on a spy thriller. Nothing came of these ideas. His fiction writing, Snow confessed to Random House editor and friend Saxe Commins, was simply a form of exercise.

Other ideas died at one stage or another of development. He couldn't interest *Holiday*, a Curtis publication, in a travel piece on Missouri. It had published one. The Crane family, with whom he became friendly, commissioned him to write a biography of Charles Crane, an American plumbing manufacturer and an envoy to China who had been close to

Thomas Millard. Snow worked on the project without much enthusiasm. The manuscript was never published. Snow finished a children's book, "Where the Blue Sky Begins," which was to be illustrated by artist friend Madeleine Gekiere. For a while it seemed that a publisher was serious. But for reasons no one could remember years later, it never went beyond manuscript form. For a time Snow thought about capitalizing on inventions "worked out with an ingenious young man and now being patented."[38]

One of Snow's best friends at Snedens Landing was Sam Zimbalist, a fun-loving, accomplished musician whose interests had turned to composing. They spent hours together. Joining creative forces they cooked meals jointly and made wine; they thought about a floating restaurant and theater on the Hudson. Zimbalist wrote music for Snow's children's story and together they wrote a musical based on Voltaire's *Candide*. Snow felt a kinship with Candide, the hapless, peripatetic idealist who learned to doubt it was "the best of all possible worlds" and decided, simply, to tend his garden. For hours Snow sat in Zimbalist's tiny living room, the musician playing the black piano and Snow working on the lyrics. When Zimbalist died in the mid-1950s, Snow cried.

The one avenue for Snow was books, and that was complicated, too. Random House gave him a contract for a biography of Mao Tsetung after the Communist takeover of China in 1949. Snow needed to gather new material on China's leader. A first he could not get an invitation from the Chinese, who as Mao later explained were preoccupied with the Korean War. When the Chinese invited Snow in 1952, he could not accept. He was no longer with the *Saturday Evening Post*, which had financed his travels as part of his regular writing assignments. And Snow refused to come as a guest of the Chinese for he felt that would compromise his writing. The project became more problematic when the United States government restricted travel to China. Meanwhile, Snow had turned to a semi-autobiographical account of his life.

When Snow started thinking about the autobiography in 1951, he miscalculated that "the writing won't be difficult if I can get a few months of uninterrupted work."[39] Snow was reluctant to make himself the center of the story, at first trying to write in the third person. By October 1952 he had written well over a hundred thousand words but felt uneasy about the draft. Saxe Commins agreed. He thought the book wasn't right, too diffuse and unorganized. "I feel stuck with [the book]," Snow told his friend Darrell Berrigan, "having spent the advance and having, now, nothing else anywhere near ready, to offer as a substitute; so I have to get on with it." Not until 1958 did Snow finish the volume, working on the last stages with Commins, who helped cut material. Part of the trouble was captured in the constantly changing titles, which included *In the Path of the Storm* and the defensive title *The Rest Is Hearsay*.

Despite Snow's early problems, *Journey to the Beginning*, as it was finally called, was well written. The subtitle was *A Personal View of Contemporary History*, and the accent was on history, not Snow's life, which he casually telescoped in some sections to make the story move along. The book avoided excesses of self-defense against McCarthyist charges. Snow defended his past reporting; he wove Utley into the 1930s portion of the narrative to point out, accurately, that she as much as anyone created the agrarian reformer myth with her early positive reporting on the CCP. Rather than bitterness, the book reflected remarkable objectivity given the era. Snow described why the Chinese Communists won, conveyed his disenchantment with the Soviet Union, and counselled that the United States had to find ways of working with both regimes. Much of the prose was lyrical, among Snow's very best. All in all, *Journey to the Beginning* demonstrated the best of personal history journalism.

The death of Saxe Commins shortly before publication dampened festive feelings about the book. Random House arranged a small lunch on the day it came out. Mary Heathcote and Donald Klopfer of Random House and several journalists, including Annalee Jacoby, attended. Heathcote thought the small, relatively insignificant group symbolic of Snow's status.

The book appeared at an unpropitious time. As usual Americans had a steady diet of secondhand reports on Chinese Communist atrocities. In addition, the Communists had begun shelling the Quemoy islands, which along with the nearby Matsu group held one-third of Chiang's ground forces. Eisenhower pledged to defend the islands. When Snow appeared on the Dave Garroway morning television show to talk about the book, he thought the interviewer asked loaded questions. On the positive side, the interviewer's final word was ". . . a book we highly recommend."

This pattern seemed to prevail. Notices were by no means entirely negative. Nor were they as enthusiastic as with previous books. In the *New York Times*, the *New York Herald Tribune*, and the *Saturday Review*, Annalee Jacoby and other colleagues of Snow told people to read the book but gave tempered endorsements, criticizing the writing as uneven and sometimes uninteresting. Snow had carefully hedged judgments about the Communists' current policies, saying he simply hadn't seen them close up since they took power. Reviewers criticized him for not being "a good deal more explicit on the less savory aspects of Chinese communism." The *Washington Post* reviewer, foreign cable editor Philip Foisie, thought Snow "ceased to practice his trade" when he discovered the Red Bandits in 1936. Reflecting a common view that Snow's career was behind him, Foisie added that Snow had lost his reporter's legs: "He will probably never be able to do a 'follow story' on the 'new China.' "

At a dinner at the Overseas Press Club in New York, where Snow appeared to promote the book, Charles Van Doren walked over to him. The Columbia University professor, a whiz kid, had rung up impressive and, as was soon to be revealed, fraudulent winnings on television quiz programs. He told Snow how much he liked his books. "Well," Snow replied without irony, "I'm glad to see that the books haven't handicapped your career. I wish I could say the same thing for myself."

Journey to the Beginning barely discussed Snow's life after 1949. Except for the dedication, he did not mention Lois and the children. It was tacit admission of the peripheral position he held in America in the 1950s. His opinions fell like stones into a deep well and landed without a splash.

American foreign policy ran in precisely the opposite direction Snow recommended. In the book as well as his other writing, Snow pointed out the impossibility of defeating Red China, the high economic costs of containment, and the corresponding need to recognize the country diplomatically. Secretary of State Dulles refused even to shake Chou En-lai's hand when the two accidentally met at an international conference. A New York columnist gasped that Edgar Snow could appear on a New York radio show arguing for knowledge and understanding of "Red goons, gangsters, and murderers" before "judgments are made."

Snow argued against seeing the world in strictly East-West terms. Although the scores of newly independent countries making up the Third World would not copy the United States, he said, Americans should support self-determination among those countries. Instead the United States looked to the military strength of NATO. It offered minimal foreign aid, and then in the negative context of fighting communism, not in the positive sense of promoting economic development in accord with the recipient country's own history and aspirations. The United States did not strengthen United Nations-affiliated institutions responsible for decolonization and economic development.

"American policy," Snow observed in 1957, "has offered little to countries whose primary pre-occupation or problem is not military defence against hypothetical Communist aggression from without but internal defence against the political consequences of profound poverty, industrial and scientific backwardness, and lack of capital and technique."

When the French began to negotiate their withdrawal from Vietnam in 1954, Snow counseled against the folly of American intervention in their place. The United States did not know how to fight a guerrilla war against Ho Chi Minh and his Vietminh insurgents; the United States did not have "reliable bases in the hearts of the people." All Americans had to look forward to was the "prospect of tremendous additional waste of material and life in vain." Within three months the Eisenhower administration declined to agree to the international accord signed by France, China, the Soviet Union, Britain, and the Vietminh. By 1959 the United States had given more than a billion dollars in aid to an American proxy government that seemed determined to alienate rather than inspire the Vietnamese.[40]

Dr. Charles White, who went with Bob Long and Snow on their boyhood California trip, came to New York in 1958 for a medical convention. It was the first he saw Snow since the 1920s. White told Snow that a Kansas City church put out information that he was a "Red." What did Snow think, White asked? Snow laughed. "I'm not a Communist," he said. "I feel philosophically that I am a world citizen."[41]

That was a typical response for Snow. Snow was part of an informal group of authors who gathered occasionally to discuss media strategies for countering McCarthy. Carey McWilliams, also a member, marveled at "the philosophical way in which Ed put up with the unpleasant consequences the tacit blacklist had imposed." Snow kept his personal problems, including financial difficulties, largely to himself and close friends.

Yet, Snow thought hard about his place in America. In writing *Journey to the Beginning*, he explored his family's roots. He read history with a fresh eye and troubling insights and, likewise, reread Mark Twain, discovering the Missouri author's dark side—especially his "To the Person Sitting in Darkness," a brilliant satire on how Christian America civilized the heathen Chinese for its own gain. More than before Snow realized the United States had become a country he neither understood nor entirely approved of. Years before, when working overseas, Snow came to think of himself as an outsider, "an Ishmael in a foreign land." In the 1950s, John Service observed, Snow became an Ishmael in his own land. When he described himself as a citizen of the world, Snow revealed his sense of estrangement as well as the world view he had developed since leaving Missouri.[42]

"It is the country and the times that have changed, not myself," Snow told his brother.[43] Edgar Snow's America was the agrarian Missouri of his school days, the Missouri of individual farmers and entrepreneurs. America had become the Missouri of NAM business boosterism. And business—big business—towered, like a skyscraper, over the country in the 1950s. During that decade the 500 largest corporations absorbed 3,404 smaller companies. From 1939 to 1964 General Motors, U.S. Steel, and Du Pont increased sales 5, 12, and 900 percent respectively. Payrolls typically doubled or tripled. Howard fit this change into his Missouri value system. "No corporation (or government for that matter) can push the INDIVIDUAL citizen around for very long and get away with it," he insisted in a typical exchange with his brother. Ed Snow saw in Howard's remarks the "old slogans of individualism now captured in material substance by the great monopolies, trusts, corporations." The corporation broke the back of the individual and the country.

"It is not the Corporation which has made this country great," Snow told his brother idealistically, "but men like Jefferson, Thoreau, Lincoln, Roosevelt and others who placed man above property and human values above corporate values."

Influenced by Texas historian Walter Prescott Webb, whom he quoted in letters to Howard, Snow perceived the rise of the corporation as paralleling the end of the American frontier. Prescott had observed that the frontier offered men a rich store of resources to exploit, if only they had the wit. Frontiersmen responded by creating institutions appropriate to individual activity. But with the closing of the frontier, those institutions no longer made sense. Corporations, Snow summed up, did not compete against nature as frontiersmen did, but against each other. The corporation "became something above and apart from the individuals who make it up."

Snow did not discount economic enterprise and progress any more than his brother devalued individual rights. But as he saw it, the spectacular prosperity of the 1950s, with the proliferation of television sets and washing machines, was partly illusion. The gross economic figures told of real incomes increasing 29 percent between 1947 and 1960; of disposable income increasing three and a half times between 1939 and 1955; of the stock market bouncing to the level it had attained when Snow set out for China in 1928. But this prosperity did not wash over everyone. Social ills persisted—racial discrimination, inadequate education, 40 percent of the population living below the minimum levels set by the federal Bureau of Labor Statistics. The individual could not move ahead on his own because the corporation sapped individual initiative at the same time it offered man cradle-to-grave security. On the open-land frontier a man owned his means of production. When the frontiers shifted from developing land to developing new technology, a man could not easily compete with massive corporate investment. "For the mass of people," Snow told his brother, "these 'new frontiers' mean at best new wage-salary situations, or greater dependence on the Corporation."

Snow described his own troubles making a living in corporate America when he noted that the "great Prosperity continues, with increasing numbers of friends and acquaintances desperately hunting for employment—most of them admittedly of the brain-worker variety, who lacked the foresight to perpare themselves for careers as engineers, chemists, accountants and, above all, as salesmen, occupations which require brains but are generally immunized against thought."

As much as Snow understood why other countries might choose communism, he "did not suppose that Russian communist methods would work in this country nor that it would be in the least desirable that they should." He wanted government to plan the economy and its benefits, to keep the corporation at bay. Instead the general mood, summed up by Ike's Secretary of Defense, was "what was good for our country was good for General Motors, and vice versa." The government, Snow complained, paid landowners not to till soil, created markets for government-purchased armaments, and "turned over to private power companies all the results of an enterprise developed at the expense of the consuming public." With more than a little insight he observed the paradox that, despite the rhetoric, " 'free enterprise' exists in this country, and can only exist, by virtue of heavy state subsidy." It was, actually, "state-supported capitalism, controlled for private profit."

Snow accepted Webb's prediction: "We are now in the stage of realizing that a little corporateness is a dangerous thing, dangerous to those who resist or remain outside it." McCarthyism seemed part of this new fabric. As Snow told his brother, "The sense of freedom and liberty we know or thought we knew or were taught we actually had, as boys, the feeling that one could express an opinion or could openly discuss any idea with immunity, seems to be gone from this country." "We are forced more and more to become all of a piece, as like as peas in our politics, nobody daring to contradict the conventional views expressed in the great conservative or reactionary press, and in this respect becoming more and more like automatons in Russia."

Snow addressed these issues publicly in two articles for the *Nation*. One talked about "foreign aid" for America, which he viewed as a necessary precursor for convincing other nations of the benefits of the free market system. In the other, a satire, Snow wrote in the voice of Colonel Beriah Sellers, the feckless businessman in Mark Twain and Charles Dudley Warner's *The Gilded Age*. In that book the upbeat Sellers had tried to build commercial success on government largesse. Snow, tongue in cheek, made Sellers's case for "unrestricted private enterprise" in which business owned roads, libraries, national parks, and the military. "Liberated from the bondage of socialistic or federal ownership—or practically any ownership at all—99 per cent of the people will have absolute freedom to enjoy absolute equality in the absolute antithesis of the atheistic Russian system."

Snow's one positive article about business proved misguided. He was an early believer in the value of commercial nuclear energy. In 1947 he bought stock in uranium producing companies, though he had to sell before steep price climbs came. Snow thought developing nations could benefit from this new source of power. Through Howard, he learned of John Jay Hopkins, chairman and president of General Dynamics and a believer, too, in putting atomic energy at the service of developing nations. Although Snow could not accept Hopkins's belligerent anticommunism, he wrote a favorable profile of the self-made, energetic executive for what turned out to be his last article for the *Saturday Evening Post*. "The important fact," Snow concluded in the piece, "is that America hasn't much time left in which to seize the initiative in a dynamic assault on world poverty by taking the lead in atomic industrialization."

Time would show that commercial power in most countries was uneconomic and dangerous. Like Mark Twain, for whom hopeful investments repeatedly petered out, there was a touch of Colonel Sellers's great expectations in Snow.[44]

If that came with Snow's Missouri upbringing, so did his stubborn refusal to relinquish his independence. He left the *Post* because he could not submerge his views in a giant media organization. Though constantly worried about money, he did not owe anyone. Thus free, he had developed a perspective that combined his American idealism with what he learned overseas observing countries seek independence from Western domination. The resulting amalgam offered hope. In an August 1949 interview with the *Kansas City Star*, when the Chinese Communists were just a few days from proclaiming their control over the country, Snow speculated that free market and Communist systems were moving "toward a synthesis of the best workable principles in both regimes." In 1954 he told his brother that "we are now living though a process of regional unification of nations which is preliminary to gradual unification of the world—as nationalism as the main form of organization of power is unable to cope with the problems of men any longer without leading to his final obliteration."[45]

After finishing *Journey to the Beginning*, Snow thought "the wasted decade" over. His fortunes improved slightly with the book, which was also published in Europe. McCarthy had died, removing a piston in the Red scare machine. Snow seemed to have more positive visibility at home and was surprised to find himself "billed as the chief attraction" at an Institute of World Affairs meeting at Washington State College in 1957. He received $750 for the address, "the best I've done so far," he told his brother.[46]

In 1959 a big break came with a call from Karl Jaeger.[47] Jaeger, the adopted son of a wealthy Columbus machinery manufacturer, was a creative, eccentric dilettante. When he once thought about creating a model educational community, he chose a site near a nuclear power plant on the San Andreas Fault. While studying for a masters degree in education at Ohio State University, Jaeger learned of an experiment in the 1920s to take students on a year of travel and study around the world. Undeterred by the fact that the experiment went off the rails, ending with a mass marriage ceremony in Paris, Jaeger decided to create his own school-on-wings for college-age and near college-age students, the International School of America. He called Snow to ask if he would go as the social studies professor on the five person faculty. After flying to Columbus to talk with Jaeger, Snow agreed to a September 1959 to May 1960 contract. He had no other real work on the horizon and the trip would give him a chance to renew contacts overseas, perhaps even to find a way into China. Snow and Lois had been thinking of visiting Europe for some time and decided that she and the children would stay in Switzerland. They rented a house on Lake Geneva belonging to the physician who had treated Snow's kidney problems in 1947.

Jaeger's itinerary was not unlike the one Snow drew up when he left for his around-the-world cruise in 1928: New York, Washington, D.C., San Francisco, Honolulu, Tokyo, Hongkong, Bangkok, New Delhi, Cairo, Istanbul, Rome, Florence, Geneva, Berlin, Paris, and London. And just as that trip eventually led Snow to Mao Tse-tung and his Red bandits, so this excursion resulted in Snow rediscovering the Chinese Communists. Only this time, Snow's reports brought enmity, not even shallow fame.

The Long Perspective

8

In 1943, Snow visited Kunming aboard the *Gulliver II*. He unsuccessfully tried to get pilot Eddie Rickenbacker and his crew into town for a Chinese meal. No one wanted to leave the poker games and "the sound of Yankee talk."[1]

It was thus in 1960. Fundamentally, Americans didn't care much about China. The hysteria over Chinese communism was a by-product of traditional isolationism. For Truman, China constituted a major domestic political problem. He might have accorded diplomatic recognition to the Communist regime had the Chinese not intervened in the Korean War. Afterward Truman did nothing. The Eisenhower administration declaimed against the evils of Red China and swore to defend Quemoy and Matsu, but it had no intention of taking any action against China. When it came to foreign policy, both administrations viewed relations with Europe as the axis of real importance.

Both presidents were in step with public opinion. In early 1950, when Americans worried that the Chinese Communists might overrun Taiwan, polls showed a mere 18 percent of the public willing to give Chiang Kai-shek financial and military aid; only 13 percent favored using American forces to defend the island. Congress, a barometer of public attitudes, allocated more than twice as much money to the House Committee on Un-American Activities as to the Foreign Affairs Committee. Not hinged to any practical imperative, American perceptions of China swung on emotions. With Americans receiving no firsthand news on China, half-truths and domestic fears about communism whipped those emotions around wildly.

In his 1960 visit to the People's Republic of China (PRC), Snow recreated his dramatic discovery of the Chinese Communists in 1936, except this time the climate in the United States was radically different. In the 1930s Americans wanted positive stories about their Chinese Communist allies; in the 1960s they wanted bad news. The worse the report, the more welcome it seemed to be. Snow swam against the tide of public opinion. His defiance made him as unacceptable as his message that all was not evil in China.

"I have always said that if the Kuomintang itself contains the seeds of self-destruction, then it will certainly be defeated without waiting for opposition from others," Chiang Kai-shek prophesied when he governed China. "Otherwise, no opposition or obstruction to it can be effective."

Snow agreed. "Revolutions are not caused by revolutionaries or their propaganda," he said in a 1955 speech. "Revolutions are caused by intolerable conditions under bad, incompetent and corrupt governments. In China the Communists also won because they convinced more people that they had something worth fighting for and dying for than Chiang Kai-shek was ever able to convince."[2]

But tearing down an old corrupt order and building a new, just regime are different tasks. The progression from an idea to a thing produces inequities of its own. Out of force of cultural habit leaders revert to type, repeating the idiosyncrasies of those from whose hands they wrested power. This time-honored pattern appeared in China after 1949, but it was overlaid by Mao Tse-tung's determination to stand history on its head. Anxious not to see his revolution course through traditional channels, Mao wanted to be ruler and revolutionary. He tried to institutionalize chaos. Disorder was a tool to cap traditional Chinese bureaucratic elitism and to maintain his grip on power. As time would show, Mao's lust for chaos imposed its own kind of order and its own corruptions.[3]

The pace and depth of the Chinese Communist revolution exceeded anything the Nationalists likely could have achieved, even with the stability that came with the end of civil war. Free of beggars and prostitutes, of filth and unchecked disease, China overcame past scourges. Bloody repression of the landlord class, as well as of enclaves of Chinese who resisted the new regime, remade the countryside. Land reform, which began with freehold farmers, quickly led to agricultural producers' cooperatives and, in 1955, collective farming. The old gentry no longer ruled China.

The Communists instituted a marriage law that provided a strong theoretical base for putting wives on a par with husbands. Mass education programs tripled primary school enrollments between 1949 and

1958 and increased secondary school enrollment sevenfold. (By 1980 literacy had jumped from 20 percent of the population to 66 percent.) Health care improved. Between 1949 and 1957 life expectancy rose from thirty-six to fifty-seven years. China's national income grew 8.9 percent annually between 1953 and 1957. "The spread of rural electrification, local industry, technical training, and publishing has brought modern science and technology to the doorstep of most of China's 200-odd million households," experts later concluded. "China's most remarkable achievement . . ." the World Bank also observed later, "has been to make low-income groups far better off in terms of basic needs than their counterparts in most other poor countries."

Mao pursued the revolution relentlessly, impetuously, ruthlessly, and often stupidly. He initiated the Hundred Flowers campaign in 1956–1957 to "let a hundred flowers bloom together, [to] let the hundred schools of thought contend." The idea was not to promote individual expression so much as to bring intellectuals into the system and use them as a flywheel moderating entrenched party bureaucrats. Mao had not fathomed the depth of intellectuals' disenchantment. They had not become so thoroughly Red as to limit their complaints to the bureaucrats. They criticized party doctrine. With the help of leaders like Teng Hsiao-p'ing, Mao turned the criticism campaign on the intellectuals. The flowers withered as quickly as they had bloomed. Ting Ling, a victim again, went back to the countryside to tend chickens.

Despite its economic success, the CCP foolishly pursued Soviet-style emphasis on heavy industry. Rewi Alley, who stayed in China, recalled "a long lugubrious Russian" advisor who came by his out-of-the-way Indusco-like school in the early 1950s and turned up his nose at the idea of training people for small industries. Chinese farmers could not finance this heavy industry strategy and produce enough food for themselves and their urban comrades. Eager to promote "permanent revolution," unleashing the creative energies of the peasant masses, Mao compounded the problem by launching the Great Leap Forward in 1958. Populist in outlook, the leap shunned expert advice. Chinese peasants, organized into some twenty-four thousand communes, plowed deep into the soil and made their own steel with local pots and pans. The program damaged the fields and produced low grade steel. When traditionally fickle weather came in 1959, and again in 1960 and 1961, the country faced a dire food shortage. Estimates of deaths ran into the millions.

Mao's mistakes helped push former revolutionary comrades-in-arms into opposition. In late 1958 he gave up his post as chairman of the republic to Liu Shao-ch'i, though he kept his position as party chairman. The next year Defense Minister P'eng Teh-huai, the popular commander with whom Snow traveled on the Northwest plains in 1936, criticized Mao for the mistakes of the Great Leap Forward. Though P'eng's underlying loyalty to the chairman and the government was unshakable, Mao had him dismissed as head of the army. P'eng shuffled off to an austere life in the outskirts of Peking. The stage was set for Liu and Teng Hsiao-p'ing to line up against Mao's economic strategies, promoting instead "individual responsibility" and reliance on experts.

Not only did bad weather exacerbate problems. Sino-Soviet disagreements had festered for some time and were a point of contention between Mao and P'eng, who thought the Chinese military needed Soviet support. Defying common convention among Communist leaders, Mao had not attended Stalin's funeral in 1953. He later irritated Premier Nikita Khrushchev by claiming that China would achieve communism before the Soviet Union and by antagonizing the United States at a time when the USSR wanted to explore accommodation. In mid-1960, the Soviets withdrew technical advisors.

The revolution was difficult to judge under any circumstances. But Americans took precisely the wrong tack. Throughout the 1950s they asked "Who lost China?" instead of objectively inquiring "What kind of government had the Communists created in the place of the old regime?"

The common American perception was that the Chinese built a bamboo curtain around themselves. But China alone was not responsible for the barrier between the two countries. After toppling the Nationalists, Mao declared from the top of T'ien An Men square that "China has stood up." No longer willing to suffer the indignities of imperialism, his regime excluded foreign correspondents who represented media from countries with which China did not have diplomatic relations. Showing how tough it was on communism, the Eisenhower administration restricted all travel to Communist countries in 1952. William Worthy, a reporter with the Baltimore *Afro-American*, defied the travel restrictions in 1956. The State Department dissuaded CBS from airing Worthy's broadcasts from Peking. Late in the year the administration had a chance to rethink its policy. The Chinese offered to admit American reporters, providing the United States would reciprocate. Dulles drew up a list of American news organizations that could send a correspondent. At the same time he refused to let any Chinese Communist reporters enter the United States. The protracted stalement continued.

News organizations, as well as the State Department, set up listening posts in Hongkong or tried to cover China from elsewhere in the Pacific, if at all. Establishing *sub rosa* links with non-American diplomats and others inside China hardly compensated for not seeing the country firsthand. Julian Schuman, who worked on Bill Powell's *China Weekly Review,* which continued after 1949, lamented that disgruntled Chinese refugees became one of the most important sources of American information about China.

Unedifying American news coverage paralleled extravagant Nationalist reports on the Red Bandits in the 1930s. (It also paralleled U. S. reporting on the 1917 Communist revolution in Russia.) From the early 1950s, and through the period of the First Five Year Plan (1953–1957), when Chinese farmers reaped record harvests, news media routinely reported mass starvation. Supposedly the Chinese were adopting the Russian alphabet. Word spread that Mao was dead or that the regime was about to topple. Scripps-Howard prepared a series on the "Chain Gang Empire." A 1956 *Time* article reported on the "greatest planned massacre in the history of mankind." "The terrorist with the twisted mouth," *Time* wrote of the Chinese Minister of Public Security, "knows better than most that there will never be peace—can never be peace—in Communist China." Schuman and Powell read a U.S. report on a Shanghai herb dealer who poisoned himself, his family, and seven employees and their families. Not long afterward the two men spotted the merchant and his entire staff at work.

Reporters are obliged to address issues on the public's mind, and intense popular suspicion of China channeled reporters' stories into narrow discussions of anti-American Chinese rhetoric. John Strohm, a farm editor and publisher, was the lone reporter to visit China with State Department and Chinese permission in the 1950s. His series of articles, syndicated by the Newspaper Enterprise Association in 1958, emphasized that "Communist China is a nation organized to work and to hate." "The searing blast of hatred" Strohm witnessed overshadowed glimpses he offered of the new China, for instance that he did not feel the need to lock his hotel room because of the honesty that seemed to pervade the country. He never explained the motives for the hate-America campaign, let alone that the belligerent sentiments were akin to those many Americans felt toward the Chinese state.

"I get impatient with the newspapers," a perceptive Californian told newspaperman Arch Steele. "One day China is collapsing and the next day it is a threat to our security. What can you believe?"[4]

Snow became a long-distance China watcher himself. From his listening post in suburban New York, he worked hard to keep up. He traded ideas and information with other uprooted China Hands, read translations of Chinese press reports, examined new books on China, and tried to pull information out of people like his old friend Rewi Alley. He talked to a woman who had been arrested in China as a spy and underwent thought reform (he thought she was remarkably objective considering the experience). When *Time* magazine came up with its report on Communist "massacres," he tracked down the source, "an aging Kuomintang diplomat," and sent a letter of protest to the editor.[5]

"This was a revolution and revolution of a violent nature with plenty of repression and bloodshed," he said publicly. In his *Saturday Evening Post* piece on Chou En-lai, he depicted the urbane leader as capable of dissimulation and having "an adroit, ruthless, efficient, coldly analytical and resourceful brain." Yet, Snow did not think a policy that ignored the existence of China made sense. The Chinese had a long tradition of authoritarian regimes. And as Rewi Alley had written to him, "There is a new stability and confidence everywhere now." The question for the United States was whether it would explore avenues of peaceful cooperation with the country or delude itself that the Chinese Communists would fall of their own weight. In a paper published in *The Annals of the American Academy of Political and Social Science* in 1959, Snow called for U. S. recognition of the PRC. That step, he argued, would admit that past United States policy was flawed and that the only way to compete effectively with communism in the Third World was to formulate positive policies to help those developing nations.[6]

Although willing to take strong stands on broad issues relating to China, Snow wrote cautiously about the country. As Alley had also said, Snow needed to see the country for himself. Unfortunately the winds, as Snow put it, always seemed to blow the wrong way. He hadn't been able to visit China in the early 1950s to collect material for the Mao biography and had to decline an invitation in 1957, because he had not finished *Journey to the Beginning*. Later Snow tried again. In the search for financing, he considered working out some arrangement with the British Broadcasting Corporation, to whom he sold movie film he had taken in 1936, or with his old employer, the London *Daily Herald*. He delicately raised the question with the Chinese of receiving back royalties for the Chinese editions of his book, a step that could give him adequate financial resources to visit China without making him an official guest. Simply getting word from the Chinese was problematic. Alley said he could not really do much to help. Snow hoped the stint with Jaeger's around-the-world school might be his ticket inside China.

Tutoring the young students was hardly prestigious. Snow liked the students well enough, the faculty less so. He was not a brilliant teacher, Jaeger thought, and student evaluations did not portray him as a commanding lecturer. Though perhaps too sophisticated for the students, Snow did offer a perspective not widely available in American schools. One typical question with which he challenged the youngsters was to discuss the nature and evolution of colonialism and the challenge of social and technological revolution for the West. The demands of teaching frustrated Snow's hopes of writing along the way. But he was able to renew foreign contacts, including with Nehru, who also agreed to meet with the students, and he saw parts of the world he had not seen before, among them the ancient city of Troy. Entrance to China remained a question mark. In Hongkong, one of the first stops, he explored the possibility of visiting to gather material for a book. No reply came back from China before he had to move westward with the students. No doubt concerned about how he would keep busy once the trip was over, Snow thought about writing a novel based on the school. Then, toward the end of his trip, when he was in Europe, Snow's fortune changed. He received word of a Chinese invitation.

Since the Chinese did not admit American "correspondents," Snow had to apply for a visa as a "writer." (Chou En-lai later insisted on calling Snow a historian.) The only way to get State Department approval, however, was to travel as a "correspondent" representing one of the media approved for sending reporters to China. Snow first approached the *Saturday Evening Post*, which was accredited. It was a chance for a "spectacular," thought Ben Hibbs, who had been trying for some time to get a correspondent to China. He was tempted. But Hibbs, as well as Fuoss and Sommers, felt Snow's approach would not suit the *Post*. The old arguments would surface again. Hibbs considered his turndown the "final unhappy end of my relationship with an old friend, whom I admired greatly in many ways." With the help of Bennett Cerf, who paid an advance for a book based on the trip, Snow made contact with *Look* magazine. When *Look* agreed to sponsor Snow, the State Department balked. As a senior official in the public affairs office put it privately, "Snow is no good"; they should tell *Look* he was a "foul ball." "When we instituted this program," a department spokesman said publicly, "we wanted objective reporting in depth, and now [*Look* editor and owner Gardner] Cowles comes along with someone we feel cannot be objective." The department, as well as senators, tried to talk Cowles out of the decision. *Look* editorial director Dan Mich told Snow that Cowles alienated lifelong Republican friends when he stood by the decision to sponsor Snow. *Time* magazine wrote a piece on the planned trip in its media section. The headline read: "Snow Job."

State Department approval came through in mid-June. Early on the morning of June 28, Lois and the children, who were staying in Switzerland, saw Snow off at the Geneva airport.[7]

Snow had every reason to feel exhilarated as his plane touched down on the Peking runway. For the first time in a decade he was embarked on a sustained period of reporting. For the first time in twenty years he was back for a long stay in China.

His arrival had a festive quality to it. The greeting party at the airport included old friends: Rewi Alley; Israel Epstein, editor of the Foreign Languages Press in Peking; George Hatem, the physician who went to the Communist Northwest with Snow in 1936 and stayed after 1949 to work on venereal disease eradication; Huang Hua, the student leader who served as Snow's translator in 1936 and was about to become ambassador to Ghana; and other Chinese, including a former official with the Chinese Industrial Cooperatives. Driving into Peking, Snow noted they drove on an improved road bordered by greenery and new buildings—houses, schools, research institutes, and factories.[8]

Snow used his first two days in Peking to get his bearings and, supposedly, to rest. He took everything in as if it were the first time. The schedule he finally drew up was encyclopedic in scope. His inquiries ranged over the arts, health care, the machinery of the government, the personality of leaders, education, marriage (and divorce), the military, children's reform schools, industry and agriculture, recreation. He attended Catholic church services. Though he had never paid attention to traditional Chinese medicine, he looked into acupuncture. He met Liu Shao-ch'i for the first time and learned that it was Liu who had authorized the invisible ink letter to Mao in 1936. Snow also met the man who wrote the letter, the current mayor of Shanghai.[9]

During the next five months Snow got up early to conduct interviews and visit Chinese facilities. He worked late into the evening assembling and reviewing his notes. To Chinese who accompanied him, he was a thorough professional. He was comfortable interviewing peasants, squatting as they did and making small talk over tea. When it came time to get facts from officials, his questioning was intense. He often asked the same question many times over, each time putting it slightly differently. He took elaborate notes, wrote down detailed biographies of people he interviewed, and spent hours poring over criticism written during the One Hundred Flowers movement. When he became fatigued, his old kidney problem flared up. His visit to the Peking Medical Institute gave him material for a chapter in the book. Altogether he visited fourteen of China's twenty-two provinces, nineteen major cities, and eleven communes.[10]

Snow had two long conversations with Chou En-lai and spent a day traveling with him by train to the Miyun Dam, north of Peking.

In their conversations, Chou emphasized the door was open to negotiations with the United States, though not without conditions.[11] The United States first had to agree that disputes "should be settled through peaceful negotiations, without resorting to the use or threat of force" and it would "withdraw its armed forces from Taiwan and the Taiwan Straits." The tough second proviso underlined China's worry that the United States might eventually begin to think of Taiwan and the PRC as permanently separate countries. But Chou also revealed flexibility. He did not utter threats about liberating Taiwan and said specific steps on "when and how" the United States withdrew its forces could be left to subsequent discussion.

Chou described the departure of Soviet experts as "a natural thing. Having come to China, they are bound to return some day." Reviewing his notes back in the hotel that night, Snow realized that the important part of the interview was not Chou's glossing over disagreements but his admission that there were any disagreements at all. The premier had given him Peking's first "official acknowledgement of any differences or dissimilarities between the two major Communist leaderships."

On October 1, nearly four months after arriving in the country, Snow came face to face with Mao Tse-tung on a terrace overlooking T'ien An Men Square. The occasion was the eleventh anniversary celebration of the founding of the People's Republic of China. Half a million Chinese paraded through the square. Snow reminded Mao they had not talked since 1939, twenty-one years before. Mao said they should have a meeting, and in the next weeks Snow saw Mao twice for a total of nearly ten hours.[12]

At the first and longest meeting, the evening of October 22, Mao greeted Snow in the courtyard of his home in the old Imperial City. The pair at first talked of their early meetings. Mao seemed genuinely happy with the reunion and told aides to fetch Alley and Hatem. The chairman was familiar with Snow's article in the *Annals of the American Academy of Political and Social Science* calling for U. S. recognition of China. He was out of touch on other matters. He didn't know Snow was divorced and thought Snow's daughter, Sian, had actually been born in that Chinese city to Peg. He had not talked at length to Rewi Alley since 1954 or George Hatem since 1952, and seemed surprised to learn that Hatem had been in the vanguard of the VD eradication campaign. Snow took careful note of Mao's health ("good but not too good"; he couldn't ride a horse any longer) and habits (he ate simply). Though not wanting to exclude Hatem and Alley from the conversation, Snow realized he dominated the talk. "There were so many questions and so much ground to cover in so little time!" he wrote in his notes.

Mao said that China had a long way to go before it achieved modernization. It was still poor. That was a standard refrain by Chinese officials, one in keeping with traditional Chinese modesty. More revealing was Mao's apparent concern with keeping Chinese revolutionary instincts keen. "He thought it doubtful that increasing creature comforts beyond reasonable basic needs was a good thing," Snow noted. "What happened to the inner man was more important than all his comforts." Mao said, "We want to maintain world peace, we don't want war." Snow repeated a suggestion he had made earlier to Chou. If the Chinese were serious about fostering good will with the American people, their press should draw broadly from the American media, not simply repeat anti-Chinese Communist comments that served to deepen hostility and suspicion. Mao agreed and asked an aide to follow up.

In 1937 Chou En-lai had told a journalist in Wuhan that "to us Snow is the greatest of foreign authors and our best friend abroad." While no doubt meant to compliment Snow, who was present, he did have a special, privileged relationship with Communist China.[13] He was the first of the American correspondents who knew China before "Liberation" in 1949 to return. His other special ties were manifest. It was he, after all, who spirited Mme. Chou out of Peking in 1937. The 1936 picture that Snow took of Mao, who posed in Snow's cap, had become famous. The Chinese reproduced it in books and posters. While in Peking, Snow donated movie film and photo negatives taken during the 1930s to the Revolutionary Museum. This donation contained the first movie footage ever taken of Chou, Mao, and others. Snow also brought a gold watch for Chu Teh, purchased with money from Agnes Smedley's estate.

The airport greeting party had represented only a tiny fraction of the old friends and acquaintances who now occupied positions in the government. The other Chinese woman he had escorted out of Peking with Mme. Chou was chairperson of the Peking Women's Federation. Her husband, Hsu Ping, the professor who brought the invisible ink letter to Snow from Mao in 1936, was a senior bureaucrat for the Central Committee. Liao Ch'eng-chih, whom Snow knew from his days working with Mme. Sun's China Defense League, headed the Overseas Chinese Commission. Others worked in foreign trade promotion and the State Planning Commission's Research Bureau. People whom Snow interviewed in the Northwest in 1936—Lin Piao and Teng Hsiao-p'ing, for instance—had become ministers and vice-ministers. A teenage orderly in P'eng Teh-huai's camp was a physician, a cancer specialist, working with Dr. Hatem. Snow was too late to see David Yu, the lean young Chinese student who played a role in getting him to Paoan in 1936. Yu, who became mayor of Tsingtao, died of a heart attack in 1958. Yao I-lin, who had come to Snow's house as a student in 1935, became Minister of Commerce in 1960. Kung P'eng, who along with her sister was a Yenching student leader during the December 9th period, had become Chou En-lai's first secretary and, later, director of information at the Foreign Office. She sat in on Snow's conversation with Mao. In addition to the fact that Snow knew many people, many more Chinese knew about him from reading *Red Star over China*.

His interview with Mao was the first by an American reporter since 1949. In 1959 Anna Louise Strong, living in China, sat in on a conversation between Mao and black radical scholar W. E. B. Du Bois. But Mao told her pointedly she was there as a hostess, not as a journalist. Although initially insisting that his remarks to Snow were strictly off the record, Mao allowed him to quote some of them and tacitly agreed that Snow could draw from the others without attribution. When Snow complained to Mao that he could not get permission to visit military installations, Mao intervened. Ordinarily the Chinese did not let correspondents see or photograph the army, Mao told Snow, but military officials had forgotten that he was a special case. Snow was the first Westerner permitted to take photographs and movies inside military installations in years. He was the first foreign visitor to return to Yenan since it had served as the Communists' Northwest headquarters in the 1930s.

Although a strong authoritarian central government existed in Peking, it was often local officials who actually circumscribed foreigners' travel in the country. Not wanting bad news reported about their region, cadres would limit reporters to model areas. But having ties to senior Peking leaders gave Snow a special cachet. Some rank and file cadres called him Comrade Snow among themselves. In 1960 the mayor of Shanghai explicitly ordered that Snow see the poorest places in the city, as Mao had directed.

It troubled Snow when Chou En-lai and Mao Tse-tung said his visit was no precedent for visits by other reporters. Snow thought China should facilitate visits by American journalists despite United States policies. But in truth Snow was a special case.

By the time Snow's trip ended he was in a familiar quandary. Should he stay to gather more material or should he get home and start writing? He toyed with the idea of traveling by bus from Kunming, his last stop in China, to Rangoon. That way he could retrace the journey he made in 1931 with Dr. Rock. The argument for leaving without delay won out. Snow faced competition from British journalist and filmmaker Felix Greene, whose visit to China partly overlapped his own. Though Snow had an overwhelming edge over Greene, who was not a China Hand and did not have wide contacts, Greene had interviewed Chou for a television program, was bent on writing a book for the American audience, and was already back in the United States. "It seems funny after so many years of no interviews [by Chinese Communists] at all that this should happen in such a way just now," Snow said in a note to Chou while he was still in the country. Snow boarded an airplane for Rangoon in mid-November. His luggage, he estimated, held about half a million words of notes, interviews, and diary entries, four thousand feet of movie film, and about fifty rolls of Kodachrome.[14]

Snow had not seen his old friend Mme. Sun Yat-sen when he visited Shanghai. In a letter explaining she was too ill to receive visitors, Mme. Sun underscored her feelings about how far China had come under communism. "Write the long perspective as well as for the moment," she advised Snow.[15]

Snow did not need prodding. This was his natural inclination. "The character of the nation was more important than the politics," he commented to a friend in the 1950s. The Chinese were on a long march of modernization that would be peculiarly Chinese. It was mandatory, Snow said in his book-length report, "to see China today as a point in time and space reached by a great people who have traversed a long, long road from antiquity."

Beyond this there was the matter of Snow's personal long perspective. The trip resembled his path-breaking journey to the Communist Northwest in 1936. As before, he broke a blockade. As before, Mao was at a crossroads with the Soviets and competing with comrades for control. As before, Snow was exhilarated by what he found. As before, he was eager to get his story out before the competition did. As before, the news he bore shed light on issues so murky that the wildest speculation had been possible. But one thing was different. This was the second time Snow discovered the Chinese Communists.

Snow painted on a canvas crowded with memories. When guides took him to the Peking jail, he realized he had been there before—in 1935 to visit December 9th Movement student demonstrators. Snow wanted to see places he knew previously. When he arrived at a familiar spot, his mind immediately gauged differences with the past. What struck him about Mao's old cave in Yenan was that it now had electric lights. Manchurian steel production did not particularly impress him.

The Japanese had developed heavy industries there in the 1920s. Kunming did impress him. In that city, "where no motor of any kind was produced before the war," Chinese now made jeeps, buses, and generators. In Kunming children no longer sucked on sugarcane laced with opium; they licked popsicles. Formerly putrid Chungking had paved streets, not muddy alleys, and 250 miles of sewers. In Shanghai Snow visited the Chapei slums. Some old shanties stood, but they had "roofs, glass windows and dry floors." There were trees along the clean paths and piped water. He stayed at Shanghai's elegant old Cathay Hotel, now called Peace Hotel. Out of nostalgia he rented the penthouse suite the first night. The lavish room was as it had been during the days of the foreign concessions. Snow could hardly sleep, his mind teeming with recollections of his earlier life there.[16]

With Snow's long perspective came a personal stake in China. When he rode into Paoan in 1936, he was young and relatively uncommitted. He had been anti-Fascist but undecided about the benefits of socialism for countries like China. By 1960 he was linked to the Chinese Communists. He had forged personal bonds with many of them. His extraordinary access to senior leaders had contributed to his early success. Like any reporter, maintaining those contacts weighed on his mind. Snow's predictions about the Chinese Communists also constituted a part of his personal history. A positive picture of China validated his past reporting.

Yet far more than personal considerations pressed down on Snow. If his prior experience forged emotional and intellectual ties, it also gave him a valid standard for measuring China's success. And China had progressed greatly. Shortly after arriving in China, Snow met Felix Greene. Greene's impression was not of a man who knew what he would find in China but of a man who was surprised at how well China had done. If personal considerations had driven Snow forcefully, he would have fared much better professionally in his own country had he written a book decrying the Chinese Communists.

Snow saw his extraordinary access imposing extraordinary responsibility. He had always tried to understand why other countries acted as they did, especially in China where he had come to develop a Chinese perspective on history while keeping his American values. The situation in 1960 seemed to demand this approach all the more. With Americans seeing China through the miasma of hate and fear that thwarted realistic policy toward the country, Snow felt he had to use his access and years of experience to go beyond reporting Chinese errors, though he certainly saw and reported those, to explaining China. Snow addressed individual chapters in his book, which he called *The*

Other Side of the River: Red China Today, to questions on Americans' minds, such as the existence of Chinese slave labor. In a letter from China he told Bennett Cerf how much he worried about overcoming American skepticism about the immense change in China. The desire to tip the scales of American perception into balance drove Snow. It was a difficult position for a journalist, and his approach to his reporting was by no means infallible. But it provided a perspective Americans desperately needed.

Snow had long before resolved the problem of personal involvement in events he reported, although that involvement troubled him. Neutrality, he wrote shortly after giving information on the Battle of Stalingrad to the American embassy in Moscow, was a myth. "In this international cataclysm brought on by fascists it is no more possible for any people to remain neutral than it is for a man surrounded by bubonic plague to remain 'neutral' toward the rat population. Whether you like it or not, your life as a force is bound either to help the rats or hinder them. Nobody can be immunized against the germs of history."

As in those earlier involvements, Snow did not skirt the hard issues in 1960 China. He still reported what he saw. A sense of honesty suffused the book. He carefully dropped warnings and qualifying statements into *Red China Today* to illustrate the limits of his knowledge and research. His Chinese speaking ability was serviceable, he said, but not what it once was. With the simplification of written Chinese, he did not recognize many Chinese characters. He told readers that officials or interpreters were generally present at interviews and that "nobody bares his soul to either one, especially with a foreigner around." He wandered about as he wished but only saw pieces of the country. Education by travel had its limits, he reported; he said he visited an exceptionally prosperous commune as "a tourist." Officials put up a wall of positive statements that was difficult to penetrate. "I can't recall visiting any mine or factory where 'underfulfillment' [of production quotas] was predicted," he observed. He admitted thinking of questions he should have asked but overlooked at the time. He told of giving up his questioning because he didn't want to embarrass a woman prisoner about the specifics of her efforts to seduce men.[17]

Israel Epstein noticed that Snow was frustrated with Hsinhua, the government press agency. Everything was formal, not like the old days when Snow could "walk in and out of Mao's cave." Officials told Snow how it was in Yenan. In his book he described listening "for hours to the usual outpouring of facts, figures, dates, tributes to Mao Tse-tung, the 'general line,' the 'eight-point charter for agriculture,' and praise for the communes" before he got a commune leader to open up about himself. He noted, "It was difficult to get a well-trained Chinese Communist to answer a question which hypothesizes a situation he knows to be the incorrect outcome of reform." Snow was especially irked with an official who escorted him and Alley to the Northwest. The guide was a "martinet," condescending, mouthing Communist platitudes the way Snow had seen bureaucrats in the Soviet Union do. Snow described the official as wearing a "tight-fitting blue serge suit buttoned to the chin and the brain . . . full of bowdlerized history, misinformation, the general line, misquotations from Mao, and with three fountain pens in his right breast pocket."

Snow chronicled his frustrations figuring out the Hundred Flowers Movement and the backlash against intellectuals, with whom he felt an affinity. He sent letters to former students, who did not reply. Hsiao Ch'ien, whose work Snow had translated in the 1930s, had edited a Chinese literary journal that stridently criticized government policy toward the arts. When Snow inquired what had happened to Hsiao, another artist said he was "happily working in a commune" and "no longer much interested in writing." That, Snow wrote, was "a change of character which I could not at all imagine." Mao Tse-tung told Snow he didn't know what happened to Hsiao or to Ting Ling, though her alleged crime dated to the 1930s when, while under loose house arrest, she supposedly collaborated with the Kuomintang. "If what I was told by a Very High Official is true," Snow reported without making a judgment himself, "her exile from Peking may have had little to do with her writing and is a much more serious affair."[18]

For all his supposed deference to the Chinese Communists, Snow questioned and criticized. During a visit to a Shanghai park, he spotted a child with severely blackened teeth. He asked the nurse why. She replied that it was from too much sugar. Snow investigated and learned that large quantities of sugar were not available due to rationing. He reported the incident in his book and his conclusion that the child really had vitamin deficiency. He thought the protests that erupted during the Hundred Flowers Movement "did not sound like people seeking 'unity' but people fed up with unity too long imposed by censorship." He said the Chinese decision to keep out correspondents was "unwise." He stressed more than once that Chinese officials exaggerated statistics on the Great Leap. Seeing the world through Marxist-Leninist lenses, Snow observed, caused the Chinese to misunderstand the West. Snow speculated that the Chinese may have held off giving him a visa at one time in the 1950s because his views on the origins of the Korean War did not jibe with Peking's. But he did not back off from those views. Said Snow in *Red China Today*: "The Peking government maintains—and most of the people of China seem to believe—that South Korea started the attack at American instigation. I have seen no convincing proof of that, I do not believe it, and most of the world does not believe it."

Despite evidence of vitamin deficiency, Snow thought, as he told Bill Powell in a letter, "There is no question that the material and cultural condition for the great mass of the *poor* people of China has been vastly improved." He wrote vividly of women studying engineering alongside men at the Iron and Steel Institute. He explained that contrary to popular impressions, the Communists had not destroyed idyllic family life. For one thing, the Nationalists had passed many decrees, for instance abolishing ancestor worship, which started the process. More to the point, the old family was often a maelstrom of evils, marked by wife beating, child brides, child selling, polygamy, arranged marriages, mother-in-law tyranny. The Communists elevated the role of the state, but, Snow commented, the commune system "may actually come nearer to achieving the ancient ideal of family 'mutual help and mutual benefit.' " The loss of the traditional Chinese theater was no big loss, for the stage had catered to elites, not to the common man who could neither afford nor understand it. In modern China every factory had a drama club. "While contemporary themes are usually handled in crude distortion of black and white (with little of the gray nuances of traditional Chinese painting) they are at least filled with vigor, youth and affirmative hope for man (Socialist man)." Snow saw positive benefits in rectification campaigns checking the development of a new bureaucratic elite in Red guise.[19]

The workers' share of profits remained small, he reported. The government invested surplus back into the economy. Even so, the government provided education and health benefits that came only later in the development process for countries under private capitalism. In addition, "the worker and peasant, who understood very well how, and to some extent why, they are being relieved of the profits of their toil, have some satisfaction in knowing that no individual or owning class is getting rich on their efforts and that capital is being collected and invested for the benefit of society as a whole and especially for their children."

Snow educed an important point in making a comparison with the past. At the time, mass enthusiasm for the Communist regime ran high. Although the Communist government was as authoritarian as Chiang Kai-shek's, Snow said, it was different too. The Kuomintang was organized to protect the interests of a small group. "The Communist dictatorship has organized its bases among the have-not peasants and working people and deeply *involved* them in the revolutionary economic, social, political and administrative tasks of building a socialist society." Chinese willingly threw themselves into campaigns to build roads, dams, and bridges.

Snow stressed that Chinese did not have American-style freedoms. Lu Hsun, the revolutionary writer he admired, would not be able to write in modern China the way he did in the 1920s and 1930s, Snow confessed. Lu might not be killed, but he would undergo thought remolding. The state controlled the unions; the military was no longer so egalitarian as in guerrilla days. Snow did not visit Tibet, but he knew the Tibetans must "adapt or perish" to Communist rule.

Snow's "long perspective" enthusiasm for improvements in China plus his desire to explain could take the reader into a semantic thicket. In describing greater Chinese equity, Snow talked of "democratic dictatorship." At the least the oxymoronic phrase was confusing. Taken in combination with other statements it seemed downright tendentious. While acknowledging that peasants had no say in the choice of senior officials, Snow said Chinese participated in choosing local administrations. Participation was a fact, a new fact, in China. But local elections were ornamental with a slate of candidates uniformly similar in outlook and allegiance to the party. It was enough to argue that China, which had no democratic tradition, made advances in creating a government more responsive to individual needs.

Snow made comparisons throughout the book that gave an apologetic air to the narrative, though his points were often important.[20] Thus: While the Soviets killed the Romanovs, the Chinese Communists let the Manchu boy ruler, who had collaborated with the Japanese, work in the Academia Sinica botanical gardens. Thus: "Nearly everybody in China *is* obligated to do some kind of manual labor, from the professor to the coolie"; but "there were no more child slaves in China." Thus: Chinese surveillance of foreign residents "was smooth, unobtrusive and probably efficient"; but America had its own techniques. "I never got a letter from China that had not been obviously opened and delayed." Thus: State control reached deep into society; but it had advantages, for instance, sharply curtailing prostitution and crime. Back "in rich and brain-free New York," Snow observed, crime was a way of life. Thus: the Chinese leadership knew little about the United States, except what it saw in the movies; but Chou En-lai spoke English. "Has the United States ever appointed a Chinese-speaking Secretary of State?" Snow asked.

The cult of Mao had become a permanent fixture since the victorious Red Army marched triumphantly into Peking in 1949 waving placards emblazoned with Mao's likeness.[21] Snow hated the cult, just as in his first days in China during the 1920s he hated the deification of Sun Yat-sen. One of the early attractions of the CCP for Snow was the simplicity of Mao and other leaders, who ate with their men and wore the same plain, patched clothes. The glorification of a ruler ran counter to Snow's view that common men stood at the center of events. Snow's irritation with the cult spilled out regularly. Over breakfast he complained in front of Chinese officials about Mao's ubiquitous presence. He told Epstein he was concerned about the development of a new generation of leaders. Snow raised the issue of the cult with Mao, which by Chinese standards was a daring line of questioning. After leaving China Snow conveyed the same concerns over Mao's exalted status in his speeches.

Snow devoted many pages to the cult, a sign of his preoccupation with it, and he conveyed his dislike of it. "In so far as the Mao 'cult' is reminiscent of the synthetic beatification of Stalin when he was alive," Snow observed gingerly, "it is to any Westerner nauseating in the same degree." More directly, he reported that Mao had power and used it. For "a man who had made a career of nonconformism," Snow observed insightfully, Mao "demands from the nation a degree of conformism unsurpassed anywhere. He is as aggressive as any civilized leader alive." But seeing his book as a vehicle for explaining, Snow withheld condemnation. Deification of leaders was not new in China, he said. "Nations which for centuries have been ruled by authoritarianism may cast aside one skin and pick up another but they do not change chromosomes, genes and bodies in a generation or two." On the positive side, Mao put his authority in the service of common men, for he recognized that the common man was the route by which he rose to power. Snow went out of his way to note Mao's simple dining habits and that his socks drooped.

Snow spoke to a small group of faculty and graduate students at Harvard after his trip. The journalist, one student thought, seemed disturbed about P'eng Teh-huai's fate. That would not have been surprising. Snow developed affection for the rugged commander during the 1930s, and P'eng's dismissal is today considered one of the greatest injustices of the Maoist era. In *Red China Today* Snow went out of his way to describe P'eng as able, intrepid, and loyal to Mao "in every test." One passage, describing how expelled party members had their constitutional rights abridged, may have been a veiled criticism of P'eng's ostracism. The comment seemed directed to the Chinese as much as his American readers. Still, Snow reined in his feelings in print, describing P'eng's disgrace as part of a process of political pulling and hauling, and speculating that P'eng might assume an important role again if relations with the Soviets improved.[22]

In this compromise, Snow's long perspective revealed its soft underbelly. Time had changed some of the rules that guided his earlier judgments. Whereas he previously criticized Chiang's one man rule, he now used it as a precedent to explain Mao's dictatorial rule. The perspective was valid enough. China had a history of glorifying its leaders. The problem was that the approach diluted Snow's intuitive powers. Snow should have listened to the nagging voice inside him about the cult of Mao. Mao had not "shot his opposition" in the party, as Snow noted. But, as Snow also knew, mass adulation leads to massive abuse of power. He was too hopeful about Mao having learned lessons in the 1950s. The worst had yet to come. Although some leaders were interested in rehabilitating P'eng, as Snow hoped, it never happened—at least not until 1978. By then the Cultural Revolution had come and gone, and P'eng, like many of Mao's revolutionary comrades, had died as a result of beatings and other brutalities.[23]

One of the major issues while Snow was in China was the food shortage. The long perspective helped him assess the problem, though it did not save him from errors.[24] Snow did not parrot the Maoist line that the failure of the Great Leap was only a function of bad weather and Soviet treachery. He understood there had been planning errors, including overhasty implementation and failure to use expert advice. The party "made the egregious mistake of placing 'politics in command' of rural statistical field workers." Snow thought Mao was, at least in part, to blame. He estimated that the decline in agriculture was so steep that China's total output value for 1960 was "less—and possibly considerably less—than in 1957." That meant severe malnutrition and setbacks that "applied a brake on the entire economy."

Snow went to great pains to calculate food production, reckoning the 1960 grain harvest at 152 million tons. That figure turned out to be only 6 percent over the lowest generally accepted estimates assembled in subsequent years and much better by some other impartial calculations. Yet, he underestimated the impact of the food shortfall. He read too much into what he saw, such as on the trip he and Alley made to the districts where they first witnessed the brutal famine of 1929. The absence of beggars or stick thin figures and the newly planted shade and fruit trees along the road, which in past famines would have been stripped of bark for food, did not tell the complete story. "One of the few things I can say with certainty is that mass starvation such as China knew almost annually under former regimes no longer occurs." Snow was correct that people did not wither so obviously as before, nor was the death rate so high as in the past. Malnutrition, rather than outright starvation, accounted for many deaths. Still Snow missed the reality of *mass* death. Travel, as he said, had its limits.

Snow's faulty perception paralleled the Communist leaderships' errors. Depressed farm output did not fully explain the famine. Another important factor was food distribution. Uplifted by the revolutionary aspirations of their leaders, local party cadres aimed to please their glorified leaders in Peking, not only in the goals they set but also in the inflated yields they reported. Not realizing the first mistake of creating excessive zeal among their followers, the leadership made a second grave mistake. They based government procurement decisions on these inaccurate food statistics and pulled too much grain from the countryside to support their industrialization campaign in the cities. The resulting starvation occurred quietly among pockets of the population. Alley traveled extensively. After leaving China, Snow continually pressed him for information on the food situation. In letter after letter Alley reported food shortages but no famine. "Around Peking yesterday," he noted of May Day celebrations in 1961, you never saw a healthier looking populace." The most obvious explanation for the inaccurate figures Chou gave Snow was not that he lied. Chou probably didn't know.

Snow had enormous handicaps as one of the first outsiders to wrestle with the food issue after the Great Leap. He had virtually no reliable data. The difficulty was so great that scholars did not understand the calamitous results of the Great Leap for years afterward. As late as the 1970s respected historian C. P. FitzGerald argued that the food shortages in 1960–1962 were less significant than the lives the Communist government saved. "The Commune system, clumsy though it was, and resting on the more effective cooperatives, saved the lives of millions, simply because resources were centrally controlled, and rationing made possible." Although much more is known today and many scholars put total death at 20 million, the debate over how many died continues, with estimates varying wildly.

If Snow's reporting on the Great Leap showed how difficult it was to cover China from the inside, it also showed how impossible it was to cover the country from the outside. It hardly proved anything that other reporters were at the time reporting famine. Journalists had passed along such cataclysmic tales when food production was at record levels. In 1960 some predictions became outlandish in their exaggeration. In a *Saturday Evening Post* article, Joseph Alsop reckoned that Mao's policies would cost 150 million lives, one-fourth the entire population—provided Mao stayed in power. Alsop thought the regime or the entire Communist system might break first. About the same time *Time* magazine ran a cover story on China. Out of the nine-plus pages of text and pictures, one paragraph described advances under the regime.

The American press missed the big story that Snow, from his long experience in China, understood. The Communists were not about to topple. Mao, for all his power, was not Stalin. It was more complex than that. Stalin wantonly brutalized peasants during collectivization. Mao could and would abuse his power. But when he realized that procurement patterns hurt the peasants, he backed away from bad policies. The food shortage derived from Communist errors but not because the leadership turned its back on peasants. Over the long haul the Communist Chinese were on the way to advances, not least of all in the area of food security. As noted in a 1983 report by the World Bank, "No large developing country has done as well as China in this regard."

China's food crisis was not, Snow understood, "the sum total of the revolution." Behind all the anti-Chinese propaganda "stand millions of unknown and unsung men and women who have successfully and devotedly carried out the real work of releasing half a billion people from a heritage of dense ignorance and superstition, widespread disease, illiteracy and universal poverty. The task is far from accomplished, but the *foundations* of a modern civilization have been laid with little outside help, and against handicaps to which Americans have made heavy contributions."

This progress, plus his conversations with Mao and Chou, fit with his own sense that China would not give itself over to Moscow. "What recent years have revealed is that *nationalism inside the Communist system of states* threatened to be at least as powerful a factor as the bonds of class solidarity which socialist power would thoretically make unbreakable." Lack of Soviet help, which had been minimal, would not hold back China's development, even in nuclear arms. China had its own foreign policy and, Snow accurately predicted, could have its own bomb by 1964.[25]

In the end Snow remained as philosophical about China as when he came. After talking to several Chinese Catholic priests, he confessed to his guide that he had little use for Christianity. "I share every man's profound ignorance and his lonely fear of oblivion after death," Snow said. "The organized church exploits both for its own glorification and a power often misused." He felt equally uneasy about Marxist dogma, he explained in *Red China Today*. As ardent as some believers might be, time worked its way on all religions. The central point was progress toward something better, something beyond rigid rules of church and state to a recognition of the brotherhood of man, an ideal imbedded in both Christianity and Marxism. The feeling manifested itself in Snow's belief that time would smooth the rough edges. China, he thought, would again produce great literature.

"Seen in perspective, end events are always more complex than any plan can foresee," Snow wrote, "and the synthesis is certain to be a compromise quite different from, and sometimes the very opposite of, anything consciously desired by even the most powerful nations which set in motion forces to contain or direct history."[26]

Without denying the problems China created by blocking visits of American jounalists and broadcasting anti-American propaganda, Snow thought the Chinese open to improved relations, provided the United States moved first. "For what seem to me good reasons I have stressed American more than Chinese responsibility for the present isolation from each other of two nations whose peoples total nearly a third of humanity. The United States is far richer and more powerful. In 1949, American government and society existed in stability and maximum security. The United States had not just emerged from a century of invasion climaxed by a revolution and an acute sense of persecution. The United States initiated the formal cut-off in communications. Being an American, I have an incurable tendency to expect the United States to grow slightly up."[27]

Snow thought the time was right for an American step forward. While he was in China, Americans elected young, liberal John F. Kennedy president. The defeat of Red baiter Richard Nixon and the arrival in Washington of "some men of competence and imagination," as Snow put it, promised a new era. The United States could "be tall," Snow thought. It could agree to withdraw the fleet from Quemoy and Matsu, cancel the trade embargo and travel restrictions, invite Chinese visitors such as Mao Tse-tung to the United States, extend longterm commodity credits to the Chinese, and declare its desire "to see a peaceful conclusion to the Chinese civil war through direct negotiations between Taiwan and Peking."[28]

Eager to make an impact, Snow hurried to New York City after a short reunion with his family. Bennett Cerf arranged a meeting with Dean Rusk, president of the Rockefeller Foundation and just named by Kennedy to be the next Secretary of State. A heavy snow fell the night before Snow's 8 A.M. appointment. Unable to get a taxicab, Snow walked from Edmund Clubb's Riverside Drive apartment, where he was staying, to Rusk's New York office. For a change Snow arrived on time. Rusk was late. While Snow talked, Rusk bolted down breakfast and took telephone calls. Within a few minutes, the Secretary of State-designate abruptly ended the interview with no suggestion of scheduling another. The new architect of American foreign policy said he was sorry, but he was pressed for time.

Snow frequently repeated the incident to friends. John Service, who saw Snow in Switzerland not long afterward, thought "it was the closest I have ever seen him to anger."[29]

Snow completed his first *Look* article in New York in December. He regarded the fifteen thousand dollar payment for the piece "unexpectedly generous" and believed he resolved a misunderstanding over the editing of other articles: he would approve all changes in the copy. Snow told friends he admired *Look*'s "guts and support for me." The first piece, twelve pages devoted almost exclusively to his interview with Chou En-lai, appeared in mid-January 1961, when Snow was back in Switzerland. In a self-protective preface, the *Look* editors said the Chinese Communists "still considered [Snow] their friend" and it was "equally obvious that large parts of what they say can be easily labeled 'Red Chinese propaganda'. . . . Yet we feel that it is vitally important for the American people and its government to know as much as possible about these men and their attitudes." *Look* also ran an article by China expert Doak Barnett to give the appearance of balance.

Even so, *Look* faced heated criticism for giving space to a Chinese official when the Communist press would not publish comments by an American. The Kuomintang government fueled the fires. "No one," the Nationalists said in a statement "could more properly be called a fellow traveler than Edgar Snow. One must take Snow's observations on China with a grain of salt." Barnett thought Chou's statements singularly unbelligerent and deserving "careful scrutiny." According to the AP story in the *Kansas City Star*, the Nationalists portrayed Chou's remarks as "a message of intimidation," not compromise.

Three days after the article appeared the Senate Committee on Foreign Relations, spurred on by Republican members, set out to determine if the new administration had a different view. The occasion was the confirmation hearing of Chester Bowles, nominated as Rusk's deputy. Bowles was a bona fide member of the liberal wing of the party, a man who favored a United Nations-oriented approach to world problems and had begun to understand the complexity of communism. Before the election he wrote an article for *Foreign Affairs* calling for a reappraisal of China policy. Bowles challenged the myth that Chiang Kai-shek ruled all China. There were two Chinas, one under the Nationalists, one under the Communists. So as not to get too far out in front of the public, Bowles hedged his position by emphasizing that Chinese intractability made immediate negotiations unlikely. Kennedy saw the article in draft. He thought the schema Bowles proposed a useful way of reshaping policy. After the election, when Bowles went up to Capitol Hill for his confirmation hearings, the president gave him a new signal. Kennedy asked Bowles to emphasize how his position was like that of most members of Congress, not how it broke new ground. A distressed Bowles did as he was told. Although he might have used Chou's statements to Snow in *Look* as a sign of conciliation, Bowles used them as proof of how difficult the Chinese could be. Testifying in the hearing room, which overflowed with spectators, Bowles noted that Chou had criticized his two China policy because the policy failed to recognize China's claim on Taiwan. This "attack," as Bowles characterized Chou's comment to Snow, showed that no discussions were possible. "We should not, under any circumstances, retreat under fire," Bowles said.

Snow's relationship with *Look* deteriorated. He was unhappy about the magazine's prefatory disclaimer on his article. For several months he and *Look* editors haggled over editorial changes in his subsequent reports. While Snow thought the compromises erased nuances important to a balanced picture, *Look* took an entirely different view. In June Dan Mich wrote that *Look* had decided not to publish the other two articles from Snow's trip. "Frankly," Mich said, "we are now too skeptical about many of the facts and figures, and too concerned about the obvious slant." Snow thought the explanation puzzling, especially in view of the investment the magazine had made. With grace and, perhaps, a touch of irony, Snow dedicated *Red China Today* to Cerf and Klopfer of Random House, Rewi Alley, Chou En-lai, Mao Tse-tung, and Gardner Cowles.[30]

Look's decision dashed Snow's hopes of scooping competitors like Felix Greene. Greene had started right to work on his book, and work on the *Look* material put Snow further behind on his own volume. By May 1961, when Snow was pondering his notes and deciding what he wanted to say, Greene's volume was in type. Snow realized not only that Greene's book might draw attention from his but also that the pace of events could outdate his material. Feeling the competition, Random House pressed Snow to finish. In August he forwarded as much as he had written to New York. He suggested how, with some patching, the manuscript could be published quickly—if that was what Random House really wanted. Snow hoped they didn't. Rather than adhere to his original idea of writing a short book, 200 to 250 pages long, Snow preferred to write a longer book, even if it came out much later. The lesson of the *Look* fiasco, he thought, was the need to document facts and figures as fully as possible. No doubt realizing it was too late to catch up with Greene anyway, Random House agreed.[31]

The job of spanning "the ocean of prejudice and lack of interest at home," Snow wrote to friends, was "terrible." In more than one letter to his publishers, he told of routine ten and twelve hour stretches in front of the typewriter. He came down with a sinus infection and accompanying headaches, which put him briefly in the hospital and cost him more time. He was a glutton for information. Within a few weeks of leaving China he was writing Kung P'eng, the former girl student who worked in the foreign ministry, for more details on food production. He telephoned his Random House editor, Mary Heathcote, from Switzerland to ask her to find out how many calories were in a sweet potato. He used the information to address the question of famine, which continued to dominate news stories. In early 1962, when he had completed a draft, Snow worked his way through an exhausting fifteen-week U.S. speaking tour. By the time that was done, the book was in bound galleys—a time when major revisions are discouraged. Snow added more material and rewrote sections to answer questions raised by audiences he had addressed. He wrote to Israel Epstein:

> Anything you can send to me to explain the current situation would be most valuable. Even a single national figure on crop output, steel, industry generally, whether agricultural middle schools have been abandoned (as reported), whether urban communes have all but disappeared (as reported), whether it is now a common sight to see children with swollen tummies, blackened teeth and rickety legs, whether P'eng has definitely been kicked out of the [Central Committee] as well as the Politburo because he opposed communes and argued with [Mao] and sided with [Khrushchev], whether militiamen are among the refugee exodus into Hongkong, whether cadres are becoming demoralized and corruption is now widespread, whether foreigners are now barred from travel to [certain cities] . . . whether industrial output had declined by two-thirds (Alsop), and if not then how much *is* the decline, and so on. . . . Do try to get me a few FACTS.

After the book dustjacket was printed Snow changed the title from *Red China Today* to *The Other Side of the River: Red China Today*. The line from Blaise Pascal appealed to Snow: "A strange justice that is bounded by a river! Can anything be more ridiculous than that a man should have the right to kill me because he lives on the other side. . . ." (In later editions Snow reversed the title, a step that made marketing sense and, as Mary Heathcote observed, drove librarians crazy.)

Snow received his first bound copy of *Red China Today* on November 13, 1962. Hoping to cash in on the Christmas rush, Random House aggressively promoted the book. "My first edition of unusual size (13,500) was out of stock a week before [official] publication and a second printing was hastily ordered," Snow wrote his sister of Random House's efforts to get the volume in book stores.

The timing, which initially looked so good, quickly came to seem "unfortunate," Bennett Cerf confessed. A printers' strike beginning in early December shut down nine New York newspapers for four months and curtailed the planned advertising campaign. In addition, the book's debut coincided with Indian-Chinese hostilities. Although time would show that the Indians provoked the brief conflict over the ill-defined border, common American presumptions about Chinese belligerence made Snow's predictions look stupid: that "neither India nor China can seriously plan to use major military means to win a 'map victory' in largely uninhabitable wastelands of no real value to either power"; that Mao's China was not bent on military conquest.

Red China Today was a difficult book to review.[32] The first problem was its size. This was the biggest book Snow ever wrote, eight hundred pages long including appendices. Eager to explain everything, he piled facts and figures in the reader's path; he offered hunks of history and quotes from his previous reporting; he allowed himself observations, some gratuitous, that strayed from the main theme, for instance a long facetious passage echoing Mark Twain's "To the Person Sitting in Darkness." Snow's friend John Service thought *Red China Today* did not show Snow's usual spark. Yet, while the book should have been cut, and was in later editions, Snow could not cut too deep without leaving himself open to another kind of criticism—that he was too superficial. One way or the other, size was a problem.

A second problem was that the book's strength—Snow's extraordinary opportunity to see China—was also its greatest liability. With travel to China limited, reviewers generally could not be truly expert. Unable to speak from personal experience and always mindful of the flow of anti-Communist propaganda that poured forth, no one really knew where Snow was right and where he was wrong. Favorable reviews had to admit a certain skepticism. Snow offered "a huge accumulation of facts," the *New Yorker* said, "if we could only guess which they are." A reviewer in *Book-of-the-Month Club News* put it another way: *Red China Today* "underscores our misfortune in not having many correspondents free to visit Red China to provide more firsthand information for assessing a government that rules nearly one quarter of humanity." The club gave a nice notice to the book but did not make it a selection.

Considering these problems, a remarkable number of favorable reviews, some in unlikely quarters, appeared. Although a weekday review in the conservative *New York Herald Tribune* was negative, the better-read Sunday book review section raved about the book. Like many other scholarly journals, the *Annals of the American Academy of Political and Social Science* called the book "Snow's second great 'scoop' . . . unquestionably a must for all who wish to understand mainland China today, whether layman or specialist." But unmitigated criticism came easily, too. In the 1930s no one complained that Snow used long quotes from the Chinese Communists, in essence giving them a chance to make their case. That technique in 1962 was akin to treason. The *Chicago Tribune* called *Red China Today* "little more than very clever and skillfully written propaganda." *Commonweal* called the book "so biased and naive as to constitute a public danger." *Time* happily ridiculed Snow's Mao as a man with "old cotton socks that droop charmingly around his ankles."

The most damaging review came in the *New York Times*. As Snow understood it, the *Times* book review editors turned down Harrison Salisbury's request to review *Red China Today*. Salisbury had given Snow the impression he was "enthusiastic" about the book. The assignment went to Michael Lindsay instead, who was at the time a British professor at American University in Washington, D.C., and hardly a man suited to an objective appraisal. Lindsay—Lord Lindsay of Birker—had taught at Yenching University in the 1930s and, during the war against Japan, served as an advisor to the Communists, setting up radio stations and training Chinese. This gave Lindsay an extraordinary inside view of the CCP in the 1940s. Like many he was impressed with Communist reforms and, like many, discounted the Red's revolutionary intentions. Also like many, Lindsay became disillusioned with the Communist regime after 1949 and militantly critical. Lindsay had met Snow in Chungking in 1940, a cordial occasion when they shared positive views on the Communists. But in later years he developed a grudge against the journalist. As the Englishman blurted out years later during an interview for this book, he thought Snow had rejected a story he submitted in the 1940s to the *Saturday Evening Post*, predicting why the Communists would win in China.

Lindsay's review was as much a review of China as it was of Snow's book. He excoriated both. Though an objective reviewer had to point out Snow's sympathy for the Communists, balance required at least a recitation of what Snow saw and some acknowledgment that he had, after all, gone where other visitors to China had not. Instead, Lindsay said, Snow "offered very little to accounts given by other foreign observers." Rather than see Snow's long interviews with Mao and Chou as a plus, Lindsay portrayed them as a minus. The Communists could not be serious about improving relations with other countries, Lindsay wrote, because they would spend three times as much time with a sympathetic person like Snow as with Clement Attlee and "other British Labor party leaders," who had also visited the country. He did not give the slightest indication that for all Snow's sympathies, the book contained considerable balance—indeed, far more than Lindsay's review.

Times' reviews carried a great deal of weight with book sellers and with book buyers. In hopes of redressing the damage, Snow wrote a long rebuttal to the Lindsay review, which Mary Heathcote condensed and forwarded to the *Times* book editor. Snow criticized Lindsay for failing to report "my own listing of many [Communist] weaknesses, including the regime's inability to accept criticism of itself." He also pointed out Lindsay's bias, among other things noting that Lindsay's complaint about Attlee's short interview with the Communist leaders was more than of academic interest to Lindsay. Lindsay had been a member of the Attlee group. As good as these points were, Snow's characteristic desire to square the record was a mistake. Along with Snow's letter, the *Times* book review section ran a rebuttal from Lindsay that was nearly twice as long and only left the reader confused, provided he bothered to read the letters to the editor section at all.

Snow's letter was one of many attempts to clear the record. He protested to the *New York Herald Tribune* regarding the negative review in the daily paper. He protested to the *Kansas City Times* regarding its reporting of a talk he gave locally. In hopes of ensuring accuracy, Snow had beforehand written out the answers "to ten common questions" about China. Nevertheless the local reporter misunderstood his comments. "I said there was no real famine in China but that there is a serious *food shortage and an agricultural crisis.*" Snow made a second speaking tour in early 1963 to promote *Red China Today* and sent more than one letter to Random House suggesting advertising copy and strategies for countering bad reviews.

By early 1965, when all the reviews were in and all of Snow's speeches delivered, Americans had bought more than twenty-one thousand copies of *Red China Today*. That was a respectable sale, especially since the fat volume cost ten dollars when nonfiction typically sold for five dollars. Early on, *Publishers Weekly* thought the book a candidate for the best sellers list. But neither the book, nor anything else, had moved American policy on China. Snow was destined to talk about the

1960s, the way he talked about the 1950s, as "a decade of lost effort to penetrate the lofty realms of policy making with a few pieces of useful information."[33]

Snow attributed Kennedy's uncompromising policies toward China to the "military-industrial complex," which thought in terms of force, not compromise. An even deeper reason lay in the parochial vision that guided the United States foreign policy throughout the century. Americans saw the world in uncomplicated black and white terms. They refused to examine their faulty assumption that a Communist regime could not develop support among its citizens. Americans thus convinced themselves that Chiang was not only the rightful ruler of the mainland, but also that he could return victoriously. Bowles's "two China" policy was a creative exit plan from this morass. But because the Communist Chinese could not concede that Taiwan was an independent nation, the idea required that policymakers look for artful ways for each side to save face. And as Bowles's testimony revealed, it was easier to avoid China policy than to change it. The task offered no political rewards and plenty of political risks. Snow summed up the problem in a sarcastic observation in a special abridged edition of *Red China Today,* completed after Kennedy had been in office for two years. The statesmenlike leaders needed to change policy toward China were to be "found only in the pages of John Kennedy's *Profiles in Courage.*"[34]

The lack of firsthand reporting about China could not explain the depth of American ignorance about the country. A mid-1964 survey showed that 28 percent of the public did not know that a Communist government controlled China; of those who knew who ruled the PRC, 39 percent could not recall that there was another Chinese government on Taiwan. Americans cared little about China. They had a hazy notion, fed by fears of China's potential nuclear might and the brief conflict with India, of a Red menace. Between 1961 and 1963, according to opinion polls, the threat from China surpassed the threat from the Soviet Union in the public mind. A negligible percent of the country—10 percent, according to a 1964 poll—favored helping the Nationalists attack the Communists. But political leaders could lead the public gradually into a Southeast Asian war which they justified, in large part, as stopping the spread of Chinese Communist influence. During his 1962 speaking trip Snow thought most people were open to his views. They just didn't seem much interested one way or the other in forcing a change in China policy.[35]

With public opinions ill-formed and confused, well-organized groups exercised extraordinary influence on political decision making. The death of Senator McCarthy had not eclipsed pro-Chiang Kai-shek stalwarts who made up the China Lobby.[36] When a critical book appeared on the China Lobby in 1960, partisans pressured the publisher to destroy more than four thousand copies. Of the eight hundred copies that circulated, many were stolen from libraries and replaced by a favorable volume called *The Red China Lobby*. In 1961 the Committee of One Million acquired more than a million signatures on a petition opposing admission of the PRC to the United Nations or any other steps that might open communications with the regime. A majority of members of Congress, representing both parties, signed the petition that year and again in 1965.

Pro-Chiang groups remained decidedly anti-Snow. John Birchers harassed him on several occasions during his speaking tours. Three dozen members of the Committee for Truth picketed his 1962 talk in Fresno, California. "No Snow Job for Fresno," said one sign. Birmingham Southern College withdrew an invitation to speak when the Pan-Hellenic Council spread rumors that Snow was a card-carrying Communist. The FBI, concerned that the information allegedly came from its classified files, found the source of the rumors, a woman who said she used public information, including the library. The FBI continued to build up its files on Snow, watching his comings and goings throughout the 1960s, though not always with a sense of urgency. In April 1966, more than three years after *Red China Today* appeared, FBI headquarters in Washington, D.C., directed the New York office to "discreetly obtain one copy" and forward it to the Washington research unit. (Less concerned with public opinion, the American-supported Korean Central Intelligence Agency came down hard on an editor who published a story by Snow explaining why the Chinese revered Mao.) The rightwing press in the United States had no interest in discretion. "Well, the belief that Mao was an agrarian reformer has reaped a whirlwind which swept 600,000,000 Chinese into slavery, and Edgar Snow—in all decency—should now keep his mouth shut," said *Human Events*. "But, alas, not so." In 1968 Snow was given more than a full page in the John Birch Society's *Biographical Dictionary of the Left*.

Kennedy's request that Bowles avoid making an issue of China policy fit into the larger picture. Kennedy defeated Nixon by a whisper, a mere one hundred thousand votes. If that weren't enough to make him back off from the politically volatile issue of China policy, Eisenhower swore to come out of retirement if he did. Equally important, China policy did not trouble Kennedy deeply. Not that he didn't hint, from time to time, that policy revisions were in order. But Kennedy thought within a narrow set of options. He was, like politicians of a far more liberal stripe, a full-fledged member of the Cold War consensus. As a young congressman, JFK had joined in criticizing Lattimore and Fairbank; during the election, he made an issue out of Republican "loss" of Cuba to communism. Once in office Kennedy did not see the Sino-Soviet spilt as a chance to develop an opening to China. Like the great mass of Americans, Kennedy viewed China as all the more dangerous, a Red rogue threatening all of Southeast Asia. About the time *Red China Today* appeared, Kennedy increased the number of advisors in Vietnam from five hundred to ten thousand and authorized them to engage in combat.[37]

People with whom Snow could talk worked in the State Department during the Kennedy administration. Robert Barnett, vilified by the right during the 1950s, served as deputy to several Assistant Secretaries of State for Far Eastern Affairs. He wanted a thorough overhaul of China policy. For a time Averell Harriman headed the Far Eastern bureau. In Moscow during the 1940s, Harriman questioned Snow on the Chinese Communists and, Snow observed in his notes, "did not seem too friendly disposed toward them." Still, Harriman was willing to listen to others' ideas. Before he took charge of the Bureau of Far Eastern Affairs, he spent part of a Sunday in Snow's Swiss home discussing China. Harriman and Snow met again in the State Department, thanks to Barnett. When a junior foreign service officer wrote a note to Harriman criticizing *Red China Today* as a disappointing "polemic," Harriman asked Barnett's opinion. Barnett said he disagreed. Harriman thought Snow a too-hopeful but useful source. In 1963 he appeared with Snow, and others, on a television documentary, "China and the Bomb." Harriman said the administration welcomed "public debate" on China policy.

But the man who ran the State Department had no such agenda. An uncontroversial, solid, dedicated public servant, Secretary of State Rusk had earned impeccable Cold War credentials as Assistant Secretary of State for Far Eastern Affairs under Truman. In 1951 he labeled Peking a "colonial Russian government" that is "not Chinese"; John Foster Dulles recommended him for the job as president of the Rockefeller Foundation. In the 1960s Rusk easily conjured up the image of "a billion [united] Chinese, armed with nuclear weapons," threatening the world. Rusk knew how to get along with Congress, and he was not the kind of person to challenge the White House. According to the word Barnett heard floating around after the election, Kennedy told Rusk, "I will listen to your advice, but for Christ sake don't tell me what to do about China." Rusk didn't want to alienate Kennedy any more than Kennedy wanted to alienate Ike.

One of the great triumphs of those foreign policy experts who wanted to break with the past was the loosening of restrictions on travel to China. But it took them five years to persuade the administration to validate passports for doctors and public health officials. Roger Hilsman, Harriman's successor, bravely made a speech at the end of 1963 acknowledging the inevitable permanence of the PRC. Though seen by many as a major breakthrough, one insider later observed, the speech "was an accident of bureaucratic politics." Hilsman's superiors, including Rusk, had been too busy to read his remarks carefully before clearing them. The ice began to flow down the river, as Harrison Salisbury wrote to Snow in 1966, but slowly.

Immediately before becoming Secretary of State, Rusk chaired a panel which concluded that "the need for complete knowledge of what is going on in China is so paramount that lesser interests and concerns should give way to insure full reporting by Americans on the spot." Several months after Rusk became Secretary of State, he happened to sit next to Larry Houstoun at a luncheon. Houstoun, a young man who first met Snow in Rockleigh and became a fast friend, coyly asked if Rusk didn't think it was useful to have Edgar Snow's views on China. No, Rusk said. The United States already knew everything it needed to know about those aggressive people.[38]

Lyndon Johnson did not make any sweeping change in China policy after the Kennedy assassination. He willingly inherited Kennedy's Secretary of State and his policies. "This President," National Security Advisor McGeorge Bundy said in an oft-told story, "will never take the steps on China policy that you and I might want him to take unless he is urged to do so by his Secretary of State. And this Secretary of State will never urge him to do so."

Chou En-lai's comments to Snow in 1960 proved prophetic. First, Chou's formula for negotiation with the United States became the framework within which Sino-American rapprochement would occur—a decade hence when Nixon went to China. Second, Chou thought the Kennedy administration fit into a national consensus preventing any serious revision of Eisenhower's policy toward China. "In our view," Chou had said, "the two U.S. parties have no basic differences on China policy."[39]

Unexpected kudos came Snow's way after *Red China Today*. Ed Sullivan, New York columnist and television emcee, wrote to say the book was "a brilliantly rendered service to the world." Sullivan personally brought the book to the attention of George Woods, president of the

World Bank. Delighted as he was with the attention, Snow did not consider his standing high.[40]

A new generation of journalists was on its way up. "I rarely see more than one person I know on the few occasions when I get involved in any press conferences," Snow told his old friend Martin Sommers. The old critics continued to ignore him—or worse. In 1965 Alsop dismissed *Red China Today* in a column as "a woolly eulogy." "All the useful evidence we have about rural China," Alsop said, came from Hongkong refugees. A 1964 survey asked ninety-one correspondents representing American news organizations in South and East Asia to name the outstanding academic or journalistic specialists in their area. Perhaps one or two respondents listed Snow. The published results only listed the journalists mentioned more than twice. There were ten on the list; Snow was not one of them.[41]

On a summer afternoon several years later, Snow and an editor friend, Trudie Schafer, sat in a little Greenwich Village restaurant talking about China. A young man next to them said he couldn't help overhearing the conversation.

"Are you a China expert?" he asked Snow.

Snow shrugged. He knew something of the country.

"Are you Doak Barnett?" the boy asked.

No, Snow said without elaborating.

Snow continued to have financial problems. He complained to Random House of investing sixteen hundred dollars of his own money in *Red China Today* for maps, index, and endpapers, plus more for the photographs. By December 1962 when the book came out he had spent virtually all the advance from Random House and most of the money paid by *Look*. Snow's hopes of making money from book sales diminished when Random House could not pay out royalties. Snow had not been able to keep up alimony payments to Peg. Thinking that he was making money now, she attached his earnings with Random House. Legal wrangling started, with Snow suing Peg for profiting from photos and films he took in the 1930s. Not until the end of 1964 did Snow work out a new settlement with her. Under its terms she got a lump sum payment against the bulk of the royalties built up on *Red China Today*; he no longer had to pay alimony. Peg returned the pictures. Snow needed most of the remaining royalties, he complained, to settle legal fees.[42]

Snow slipped into the same pattern of thinking about the United States that kept him in Asia during the 1920s and 1930s. He planned to return, perhaps in a few months time, but not now. Lois enjoyed Switzerland at first, learning the language and spending time with Sian and Chris, teaching English in a small private school, traveling in Europe, hosting visitors who passed through. Later she came to miss acting so much she could not bear to go into a theater. The children settled into school routines. Their French grammar, Snow thought, was better than their English. Lois and the children visited the United States during the summer of 1966. The Vietnam War was raging and newspapers reported grisly murders by Richard Speck in Chicago and by a college student sniping from a University of Texas water tower. America, rather than the peaceful Switzerland, felt alien.

Living was cheaper in Switzerland than in the United States, and Snow was closer to audiences that wanted his work. The BBC used film from his 1960 trip. *Red China Today* appeared in Israeli, German, Swedish, French, British, Japanese, and Italian editions. Foreign periodicals solicited articles from him not only on Asian subjects but also on racial tension in the United States. The translations could be frustratingly inaccurate but at least the reports were welcome. That was more than Snow could say about the United States. Between 1960 and 1964 he wrote one article that qualified for mention in *The Reader's Guide to Periodical Literature.* That was the *Look* piece.

On the one hand Snow professed faith that "in the long run the American people will reach a more mature understanding of events in the impoverished lands of this world now in various stages of social revolution." On the other he complained that American media generally "refused to publish any reports by eyewitnesses of the China scene except those which confirm their own wishful thinking and self-deception."[43]

The year-by-year sojourn took the family through a succession of homes: their first place along Lake Geneva; a year in a mountain villa built by French philosopher Henri Bergson; a lease on another big old home in the same village, St. Cergue; in the fall of 1965 an apartment in Nyon, closer to the children's school. Snow often talked about buying a remote place in New Hampshire or Vermont. On one visit to Washington, D.C., he and Larry Houstoun drove out to West Virginia to look at a valley property. Snow walked over the twenty-five acres, imagining how they could divide it into lots. Nothing came of the idea. After renting out their Rockleigh, New Jersey, home for several years, the Snows sold it. While visiting the United States in 1967 Snow found another house near New York City. He called Lois about it and sent her pictures. She was enthusiastic.

"Did you get the house?" she asked as soon as he returned to Switzerland.

"Let's discuss it," he said. "Do you really want the house?"

Lois did. They made a transatlantic call. The house was sold.

In 1968, the Snows finally bought a dwelling of their own outside the village of Eysins, an old farm house that they restored. "This is our Swiss home," Snow said to Lois, "but we will go back to the United States eventually."

Though Snow was to become welcome again in America, the Swiss farm was to be his last home.

With Honor

9

Edgar Snow's Swiss home was a lonely outpost between two countries unable throughout the 1960s to meet each other half way. Forty-nine hundred miles to the east, Peking's leaders gripped their nation around its throat with the Great Proletarian Cultural Revolution. Forty-two hundred miles west, Washington leaders masterminded a war in Southeast Asia that aimed to promote American values but instead plunged their own nation into profound self-doubt. An observer from another planet might wonder what kind of logic subsequently drove these two self-absorbed nations to long overdue rapprochement—or what kind of justice decreed that the new beginning should mark the passing of the man who virtually alone bridged the two countries for so long.

Snow considered his position delicate. His contacts with the Chinese Communists made him suspect among many Americans. As an independent reporter he risked offending the Chinese, possibly increasing their distrust of the United States. He was careful about being interviewed because, he told one Filipino friend who misquoted him, "I feel responsible about what is attributed to me."

Maintaining his independence was always on Snow's mind. Anna Louise Strong knew the problem too well. She stayed in China until she died in 1970 and was quite capable of making up her own mind on matters such as the "Thought of Mao Tse-tung." At the same time she felt a certain ambivalence about breaking confidences, especially when she was a guest of the Chinese. Apparently out of courtesy, the Chinese solicited her advice before giving Snow a visa in 1960. She approved but told Snow's friend Liao Ch'eng-chih, head of the China Peace Committee and the Overseas Chinese Commission, that Snow had a "disquieting tendency to quote historical figures like Litvinov and Soong Ch'ing-ling verbatim about things that they certainly did not say for the public." Strong did not want Snow to know how much "I get for free here, for he is not discreet with facts that seem to him to make a good story."[1] Because she was willing to stay in China, Strong was even less successful than Snow at reaching Americans.

Although at one point in the 1950s Snow had considered selling his old film to the Chinese to help finance a trip to the country, he ultimately dismissed the idea. During his 1960 visit the Chinese insisted on paying him for the film, which he gave to the Revolutionary Museum. Just before getting on the plane to leave Kunming, he handed a package wrapped in newspaper to a Chinese official. It was addressed to Rewi Alley. Inside was the money with instructions to return it to the museum.

In the absence of formal Sino-American links, Snow became an obvious go-between for those Americans who wanted to see China for themselves. "I am constantly pestered by VIPs who want to visit China and solve matters—everybody but the president has written or long-distanced me," Snow told Alley. Snow considered his influence with the Chinese marginal, if not precarious. He used it sparingly. Despite protests that he could not be of much help to those who asked him to intercede with China, Snow could make a difference. His name opened doors. He advised his friend K. S. Karol, an ex-patriot Pole writing for the British *New Statesman*, that he could not get him a visa to China. Karol happened to be at a dinner in Algiers later, which Chou En-lai also attended. Karol got the premier's attention by dropping Snow's name and on the basis of the resulting conversation soon had a visa to China. But Snow was fundamentally correct about the limits of his influence. When he used his cachet for something he considered important, it often made no difference. As the Karol episode suggested, making a connection at either end of the Sino-American equation was problematic at best and almost always frustrating.

One of those who appealed to Snow was Grenville Clark. Clark, a wealthy New York lawyer, was a perennial public citizen who, among other things, spearheaded imaginative schemes to give military training to Americans privately before United States entry into World War I and later to promote the formation of a world federal government. In 1963 Clark asked Snow to help secure an invitation to China for Paul Dudley White, Eisenhower's distinguished personal physician. In addition to writing George Hatem, Snow sent a five-page single-spaced letter to Mao Tse-tung. Writing as a man who felt "responsibility to both China and America," Snow urged Mao to admit private American scientists, doctors, and businessmen who could act as a counterweight to negative press. A good place to start, Snow said, was with Dr. White. White, Snow assured Mao, had agreed to go without State Department approval. The Chinese did not admit White in 1963, though he became instrumental in engineering the State Department's modification of travel restrictions to China two years later. In 1964 Snow unsuccessfully made the case that Clark himself should visit China.

George Pratt, an international engineer and boyhood friend from Kansas City, asked Snow to help senators Edmund Muskie, Frank Moss, and Ernest Gruening tour Chinese water projects. When Snow first called on the senators during a stop in Washington in 1963, he couldn't get past their secretaries. He was eventually encouraged enough to raise the issue in China. Snow sensed the Chinese were suspicious. He told Senator Moss over lunch that China needed absolute assurances that the senators would accept an invitation if given. Moss promised to write a letter to that effect. The letter never came. Pratt guessed that "some place along the political and bureaucratic mazes of Washington the feeling was that the time wasn't right."[2]

Snow lent his name to groups like the Committee for a Review of Our China Policy, co-founded by former Democratic Oregon congressman Charles Porter. But he preferred writing about China to formal mediation between Americans and China. With completion of *Red China Today*, Snow explored the possibility of a return trip. A State Department passport was one problem; money to finance a trip another. Still another was Chinese willingness to let him in. No American reporter visited China after Snow's 1960 visit, and the Chinese did not reply to *his* request for an invitation. Snow suspected that his critical remarks about the Communists, perhaps regarding their treatment of intellectuals, was the cause. Rewi Alley wrote in the summer of 1963 that Snow might have to wait as many years to return as the last time. That was fifteen years, Snow wrote to his old Yenching student friend Kung P'eng at the Foreign Ministry. "I fear I may not be around by then."[3]

Chou En-lai started a ten-country Africa tour in December 1963. Sponsored by the Paris weekly *Le Nouveau Candide*, Snow traveled to Africa and met the premier in Conakry, Guinea. The rare five-hour interview one evening became the envy of other journalists, including one whom Snow suspected of rifling through his hotel room. The *New York Times*, among others, subsequently purchased Snow's interview. In talking to Snow, Chou admitted that Peking and Moscow had agreed to negotiate disagreements over their mutual border. China, Snow observed, had not before acknowledged that there were border disputes. Chou reaffirmed that China was "unshakably" opposed to any "two

China policy," a statement of immediate importance. The interview came less than a week before Peking and Paris formally announced normalized relations, bringing to nearly fifty the number of nations recognizing the PRC. Snow "surmised" that full Franco-Chinese diplomatic ties might not preclude the French from keeping a representative in Taiwan. He pointedly reported that some Washington policymakers considered such a device "an eventual exit for the United States from an intensified dilemma."[4]

As it turned out, France broke all relations with Taiwan—and the United States remained at the same impasse as before. Snow's situation, however, seemed to have moved ahead. In the Africa interview, Chou indicated that Snow's reporting after the 1960 trip had not made him unwelcome in China.

Snow had to delay making arrangements for a visit when a blockage of his bladder required surgery in early April. A postoperative infection kept Snow off his feet until June. The next month he went to the United States. In Washington he spoke at length to Harriman about State Department travel authorization to China. After a prolonged wait, permission came through. (To Snow's chagrin, permission for Lois to come along was not granted until the day he left China.) Macmillan, where his friend Mary Heathcote now worked as an editor, gave Snow a book contract. Although no American periodicals seemed interested in sponsoring a trip, French *Le Nouveau Candide*, German *Stern*, and Italian *L'Europeo* advanced Snow money. He entered China through Hongkong in late October 1964.[5]

After all the delays, Snow felt he arrived at "an opportune moment." Evidence of China's economic recovery since 1960 was "everywhere apparent and dramatic." He abandoned the idea of gathering materials for a history of the Long March, deciding to write a short book bringing his reporting on China up to date and to gather film for a documentary.

Although good statistics were not available and the trip was relatively short and confined to urban areas, Snow accurately concluded that food production was clearly back to high 1950 levels. Officials appeared confident and realistic. Without denying the harshness of Chinese Communist rule or the prospect of more mistakes, he expected that within twenty years Chinese youth would "reach an average level of scientific education, cultural and physical fitness not inferior to any in the world." Indeed, rather than wilting without Soviet aid, China flourished. This self-reliance made Snow think of a Missouri phrase he used in one of his first articles for the *China Weekly Review* in 1928, when he precipitously found "a spirit, or at least the hopeful semblance of a spirit, of 'Lift China out of the Mud!' " Snow entitled a draft chapter in his book "Up from the Mud."[6]

"Perhaps if I had just come over from my country the encounter might have produced a different effect . . . ," he wrote in a rough draft reminiscent of his arguments in *Red China Today*. "I did not judge the Chinese Reds against my American background but against the background of poverty, filth, brutality, oppression and general hopelessness which I had seen and felt in Eastern Asia."

Snow formally interviewed Chou twice in his residence and, before leaving in mid-January, spent a long evening with Mao in the Great Hall of the People. Kung P'eng and her husband, also a senior Foreign Affairs Ministry officer, attended the dinner-conversation. Mao surprised Snow when he said their talk was on the record. Snow believed that this was the first time since 1949 that Mao spoke to a foreign journalist for publication.[7]

Mao spoke philosophically, though apparently with a purpose. He said Chinese youth had no revolutionary experience; they "had never fought a war and never seen an imperialist." The personality cult, by now built into a towering structure, was very much on Snow's mind. He saw his 1936 photo of Mao blown up to a thirty-foot high monstrosity. Snow asked Mao if there was a basis for criticizing the cult. Mao replied that Khrushchev, who had recently lost his position, did not have a cult at all. Khrushchev might have survived if he had had one. Taking a different tack, which hinted he believed his days of power were limited anyway, the seventy-two-year-old leader said he expected to see God soon.

Mao and Chou's intense questioning on the United States puzzled Snow, he confessed later to State Department China watcher Allen Whiting. Both men reminded Snow how wrong he had been about a change of China policy under Kennedy. But despite their obvious doubts about his insights, they pressed harder than ever for his opinions. That might have suggested they were looking for an opening to the United States. But when Snow asked Mao if he had a message for President Johnson, Mao said no. Mao thought relations might improve over time, though he didn't seem to be in a hurry. As for Vietnam, Mao noted, Rusk had said the United States didn't intend to expand the war into North Vietnam. For its part, China had no intention of fighting outside its borders. China would only fight, Mao said, if the United States attacked it. The North Vietnamese were holding their own. Chou had told Snow that China would oppose a Geneva conference unless the United States withdrew its forces. Mao, however, thought withdrawal was not necessarily a precondition for negotiations.

Mao sent Snow home with the first statement by a Communist official that Chinese troops would not intervene in the Vietnam war. The statement countering widespread American perceptions of deep Chinese Communist involvement in Vietnam came at a moment when United States policy seemed fluid. The previous August, Congress had passed the Tonkin Gulf resolution, giving Johnson legal authority to increase the military commitment in Vietnam. But in the presidential campaign several months later, Johnson portrayed himself as the peace candidate and decisively defeated Barry Goldwater, who had acquired a mad bomber image. Johnson pledged not to send American boys into an Asian war.

Snow believed Mao had directed his Vietnam remarks chiefly at Americans and only secondarily at the rest of the world. As usual, however, Americans were a difficult target for news on China. His interview with Mao, Snow told Epstein, appeared prominently in journals "from Britain to Australia, in France, Italy, Netherlands, Scandinavia, Africa, Canada, Mexico, etc., everywhere, I believe, except the USSR and USA." After failing twice at the *New York Times*, Snow had queried the *Saturday Evening Post*. The *Post* had a new editor and in recent months had editorialized about beginning to trade with China. Nevertheless it declined, too. Concerned about American newspapers like the *Times* excerpting misleading portions of the interview as it appeared in foreign publications, Snow authorized his agent to sell it to the *Washington Post* on condition that it would not be syndicated or cut. As a result of a mix-up, the *Washington Post* did a major rewrite *and* syndicated the story. The *Post* described Snow's interview as a "conversation between two old friends." Still hoping to get the interview out in one piece, Snow next sold it to the *New Republic*. He decided not to release his Chou En-lai interview in the United States, hoping to "reserve it for intact publication in the U.S.A. in book form only." Bound by no such constraints, American newspapers picked up the Chou material from *Le Nouveau Candide*.

Mix-ups characterized the entire process. Harrison Salisbury, *New York Times* national editor, later told Snow that the paper declined the Mao interview because the price was too high. In making a second offer, Snow had failed to clarify that he didn't care about the money. He concentrated instead on explaining why the piece was important. The Japanese caused Snow trouble when *Asahi* jumped the release date. Only when Snow agreed to write additional filler material did *Asahi* agree to interrupt publication. *Stern* complained about being four days behind *Le Nouveau Candide*.

But the problems went beyond tenuous long distance communications and an apparently lax literary agent. In other times, when Snow had no trouble finding outlets for his reports, having other publications pick up his stories was a mark of success. As Harrison Salisbury said, the *Times* paid a high compliment "by taking up the report as it was published in other papers and carrying it on Page 1." Being the sole direct American link with China added a difficult diplomatic dimension to Snow's journalism. It forced him to place conditions on his stories to ensure that no distortions occurred. Snow bypassed *Life*, which expressed an interest in material from his China trip, because he felt he couldn't trust it. He rejected a *Newsweek* offer to buy one frame of his film of Mao for use on the cover. They wouldn't let him approve the title placed on it.

"You have made China practically a monopoly!" Salisbury congratulated Snow. The phrase, suggesting financial success, hardly seemed apt. Snow complained that he did not make enough money from U.S. sales to pay for his transatlantic telephone calls. Whereas exclusive contacts were supposed to create a golden opportunity for journalists, unique links with a perceived enemy were expensive—and useless. Snow could not compete with columnists like Joe Alsop, who goaded President Johnson into expanding the war.[8]

By the time the Mao interviews appeared in February, LBJ had decided, with Rusk's acquiescence, to bomb North Vietnam. In explaining his policy Johnson talked about "the deepening shadow of Communist China." He saw "the new face of an old enemy." Unwilling to "lose" Vietnam as Truman lost China, he refused to betray the slightest weakness. Although he wanted to calm criticism of his belligerent policies, the word "negotiate" was too much of a concession. He would wage war until the North Vietnamese agreed to "unconditional discussions." Johnson held out an olive branch in such a way that it looked like a stick to beat the Vietnamese with.

Meanwhile, China pursued its separate course. Snow had felt that Mao's comments on the cult hinted at some internal tension. What exactly, he didn't know. As he told Chinese friends, all the interest in building Mao up suggested that someone wanted to bring him down. Besides, Snow had his doubts about the proximity of Mao's demise. Mao showed no sign of fatigue and, as Snow also reported, Mao's physician said he was in good health. The import of Mao's remarks became clearer in the coming months, when the Great Proletarian Cultural Revolution burst forth. Mao revealed that domestic, not foreign enemies, were really on his mind the winter night he spoke to

Snow. Possibly wanting to confuse his adversaries about his plans, Mao had allowed the Chinese press to carry the interview.

Snow had returned to Switzerland exhausted. In March he went to the Bern hospital with an infection. He didn't have the energy to face a spring lecture tour and canceled. He planned to concentrate instead on his book, *China since the Bomb*, and a documentary, using film from the 1930s plus material he gathered in 1960 and 1965. A generous investment in the film by Grenville Clark helped offset the cost. Snow told his sister he wasn't worried about writing the book. He planned a short volume this time, and the Macmillan advance was the biggest he had ever had. "So we should coast through this one."[9]

It was not to be. The book was not finished in December 1965, as planned, and he and Macmillan had different ideas about what it should contain. Macmillan wanted a long authoritative account of the revolution, not a short paperback version with his most recent interviews published in total. Work on the film went more slowly than expected. Snow spent large chunks of time in London working with the producer. Costs exceeded his expectations, and he was not entirely happy with *One Fourth of Humanity* when it was completed in late 1966. The seventy-four minute, largely color film picked up technical glitches in the final editing process that irritated Snow.

The Cultural Revolution, which burst into the open the summer of 1966, became the greatest complication of all. Seeking to reestablish the egalitarian revolutionary spirit, Mao exhorted Chinese to "bombard the headquarters." By the end of November some 10 million Red Guards took part in six Peking rallies. The revolution spread throughout the country with youth taking over party offices and challenging entrenched authority. The idea of soft bureaucrats going to the countryside to get in touch with the people had a strong appeal. China had throughout its history suffered tyrannies from entrenched bureaucracies. Michael Lindsay, who violently criticized Snow, thought the Cultural Revolution might be "a hopeful development for China." But egalitarianism became a convenient stepping stone to injustice. Despite the leadership's injunctions against violence and illegal arrests, marauding Chinese went on a spree of public humiliations, beatings, and murder. As many as four hundred thousand may have died from maltreatment, sometimes inflicted by one family member on another. Mao's vision of renewing Chinese revolutionary commitment became a casualty. In the long run, the Great Proletarian Cultural Revolution engendered cynicism. Chinese intellectuals, less inclined than many to favor egalitarianism, lamented that the comradely spirit faded in China as a result of abuses during the terrible years of anarchy.

It was hard to know what to believe when the Cultural Revolution was in full swing. Outsiders knew that Liu Shao-ch'i was out in 1966; the circumstances of his death in 1969 were not publicly known for ten years. Outsiders knew cities were under siege but not what each of the factions stood for. Although the worst excesses occurred from 1966 to 1968, when Mao finally called out the army to contain the monster he had created, violence continued into the 1970s. In 1974, according to one Chinese source, fifteen hundred died in a factional battle in Chengtu. On such a day the streets of Peking and other cities could be peaceful, as if order had been restored countrywide. In 1973 a friend of Ting Ling conjectured that she was alright, living in the countryside; she was actually in solitary confinement in a Peking prison. (In the countryside Red Guards had beaten her and destroyed her draft novel.) During much of the 1960s the confused American press reported that Mao was on his way out.[10]

Alley's letters provided a vague sense of the zeal and confusion that gripped China. "We are all behind Chairman Mao," Alley told Snow shortly after the Cultural Revolution started. In September 1967 he wrote that Indusco had become a target. "It is sometimes the fashion to call Gung Ho [cooperatives] just a tool of US imperialism, trying to get hold of Chinese industry." In September 1968, Alley cryptically told Snow that he could not forward letters to Israel Epstein. Alley did not know where Epstein was. (Epstein and his wife were imprisoned—he for four and one-half years—charged with CIA connections.)

Unlike many other outsiders, Snow did not think the leadership mobilized the Red Guards to enter the war in Vietnam. From the very first he speculated that the Cultural Revolution was the greatest leadership crisis since 1949, a clash between the old revolutionaries and the new bureaucratic elite. In any event, he thought, the Cultural Revolution changed the equation in China. Without knowing precisely what these changes meant, Snow did not want to revise his documentary film or, for that matter, pursue the book. "Too much going on," he wrote to Alley. "And too little reliable information." Shortly before his death in January 1967, Grenville Clark told Snow not to worry about repaying him for the money he gave to help finance *One Fourth of Humanity*. Snow should forget problems with the film and move on to other things.

For Snow, moving on meant getting back into China, an unlikely possibility. Though anchored in domestic tensions, the Cultural Revolution showed an anti-foreign face. Red Guards burned the British and Indonesian embassies and, in an ultimate expression of xenophobia, attacked their own foreign ministry. At one point Huang Hua was the only Chinese ambassador overseas. He was eventually recalled from his post in Cairo for a stint in one of the May 7th Schools set up in the countryside to cure effete bureaucrats. When Snow wrote to Kung P'eng in the summer of 1966 exploring the possibility of returning, no reply came back. "It is just the time I should be there," Snow told Alley early the next year. "Someone who knew the past must connect it up somehow, to avoid the distortions now dominating the running account." Snow unsuccessfully wrote to Chou En-lai, asking if he could return to gather film footage to update *One Fourth of Humanity* or, barring that, if the Chinese could send him some. The next year, Snow stopped in Hongkong at the conclusion of a speaking trip. Although knowing he could not have a formal China visit, Snow thought he might travel home via Moscow, with a quick stop in Peking. That was refused, too. Respected China Hand Allen Whiting told Snow that not since the Opium Wars had China been so cut off from the West.

Snow eventually learned that he was one of those under attack in China. One charge making the rounds was that he was a spy. "Evidently I have made some powerful non-friends," Snow wrote to Epstein. "Several people I am bound to believe tell me that I am 'no longer considered a friend of China' by those who judge such matters. That saddens me because if that were true and I were judged and condemned on the basis of hearsay or slander then I would have to reassess the value of that kind of friendship. In any event my record on China is clear for all to see; though my writing is full of faults in detail, and though it is not the work of a sycophant, it is honest and independent journalism seeking the truth. . . . I am not a writer who changes his political views to suit a weather vane."

Anthony Grey of Reuters, held hostage in his Chinese house for over two years, wrote to Snow after his release. Grey related that Chinese confiscated his copy of *Red China Today*, saying it was "unfriendly to the Chinese People's Republic." An official suggested to Grey that he might want to write a news story to that effect. In an effort to keep such criticism from spreading, Snow wrote to Grey that he was surprised at the suggestion. Chou had said he considered the book "honest" and "highly regarded." Although Snow asked Grey not to use the story in his upcoming book, the British journalist included it as a telling incident.

With his own book *China since the Bomb* "lying around in a half-finished condition while I waited for some resolution to the China turmoil and the VN war," Snow turned "revisionist," as he jokingly put it. Before the 1964 trip, Random House's rights had expired on *Red Star over China,* and Grove Press republished it. With time on his hands in 1967 and 1968, Snow undertook a revision for Grove. He started with modest changes and eventually rewrote portions and added a long section of biographical sketches drawn from his notes. John Fairbank wrote an introduction. Snow dedicated the book "To Grenville Clark, who was taller than his time." Eventually buying out of the Macmillan contract, Snow signed with Random House to do a *Mao Reader,* which was never completed, and to revise the United States edition of *Red China Today,* republished in 1970.

Snow continued to produce for foreign markets. He reworked a small portion of *Red China Today* for a picture book on China put together by a Swiss photographer. He also updated *Red China Today* for European markets. The film did better than he predicted, having showings throughout Europe. In 1968 Snow took a two-month speaking trip to Japan, sponsored by Asahi publications. He spent the seven city tour "interviewing and being interviewed," he told his brother Howard, ". . . was dined by the foreign minister, learned to like Japanese food." His standard speech, with interpretation, took three hours. The first night in Tokyo, ten thousand Japanese applied for the twenty-five hundred seats. *One Fourth of Humanity* appeared on television twice. Asahi published the transcripts of Snow's talks and interviews in a hardback book, for which Snow wrote a concluding chapter.

Snow wrote little on the Cultural Revolution. In an introduction to European editions of *Red China Today,* he intentionally raised as many questions as answers about the upheaval. For the *New Republic* he profiled Lin Piao, Liu Shao-ch'i's replacement as Mao's heir. The story relied heavily on Snow's long interviews with Lin in 1936. In the biographical notes added to *Red Star,* Snow hinted at his concern over Maoist attacks on loyal officials—among them, Liu Shao-ch'i and his wife, "authentic military hero" Foreign Minister Ch'en Yi, and Wu Han. Wu, whom Snow first knew as a lecturer at Tsing Hua University in the 1930s, had become a CCP official and author of the play *Hai Jui Dismissed from Office.* This story of a Ming official wrongly cast out for criticizing the emperor was later interpreted as an attack on Mao's treatment of P'eng Teh-huai. Snow had criticized Chiang Kai-shek in the 1930s for his heavy censorship, which was based on supposed symbolic attacks on the regime. Snow pointed to the same tendency in Communist China, though with less directness. "Nothing better demonstrated the chasm that separates Western China experts from comprehension of Communist China than the fact that not one of them discerned the current political significance of Wu Han's play, and of the published Aesopian literature of the same nature, before these works came under counterattack by the Maoists." Snow also listed the changes in the party leadership in *Red Star*. He marked with an asterisk the names of Liu, Teng Hsiao-p'ing, and others who were "eliminated without open Party procedure."[11]

Snow made enough money to support the family without really getting ahead financially. Apart from small royalty checks, he had no real pension and nothing like a financial nest egg. His teenage children were almost ready for college. Snow felt he had little prospect of building up a cash reserve. He complained to his brother that bond prices fell just after he made a small investment. When *Business Week* called him an "aging and admittedly leftwing journalist," Snow half-humorously picked up the "aging" part in describing himself. Friends like Marty Sommers were dying off. From time to time Snow asked Howard to send tonic to darken his hair, now thoroughly gray. "I am appalled at the short time remaining to us," he wrote his brother in 1969, a few weeks before his sixty-fourth birthday.

The world seemed more complicated, especially with the Vietnam war. "I remember the twenties now as a good time when we were satisfied just to be ourselves without so much preaching with bombs and so on," he wrote. "How did we get to be god so quickly?"[12]

Many Americans saw a link between Vietnam and China, and so did Snow. But the links they perceived were different. The common American perception was one of a Peking-Hanoi partnership that had little to do with nationalism and much to do with international communism. The connection Snow saw was between United States policies toward both countries. The United States repeated in Vietnam the errors it made toward China after the war, failing to recognize the force of nationalism or the way American hostility to nationalism turned countries to communism. The difference in this case—and it was a big difference—was that the United States threw its military might against Vietnam so that it would not lose there as it had in China. "I knew that Harry Truman and Dean Acheson had lost their effectiveness from the day that the Communists took over in China," Johnson reminisced afterward.[13]

Snow spoke out often on the Vietnam-China connection. In an open letter to a U.S. conference on China policy in mid-1965, he noted that the United States demanded that China renounce the use of armed force in the civil war with Taiwan, while "recognizing the legality of American armed intervention in such a war. . . . The Vietnamese are asked to renounce the use of force to overthrow a foreign-supported dictatorship, while recognizing the righteousness of American intervention and its use of armed force in Vietnam as legal."

Such a war could not be won, Snow thought. Americans would only be drawn in more deeply, thus making disengagement all the more difficult. "Perhaps it is America's profound psychological misreading of Asia not to see that the more any foreigner beats and flays any part of Vietnam the easier it must become for a consensus leader there to unite all parts of Vietnam and its people in a common cause of patriotism against the only visible foreign invader."

The supreme tragedy, Snow thought, was that Americans tried to conquer a movement they did not understand with techniques that subverted their own professed values about self-determination. Snow had summed up the problem earlier to Grenville Clark. Clark had asked Snow's opinion on a declaration calling for world disarmament administered by a global federation. "We must not assume," Snow replied, "that what seems true, logical and workable in our country" will appear so to other countries. Moreover, while a federation might prevent war, it should not be designed to head off popular uprisings against intolerable regimes. Snow could not approve of a body that did not "make the world safe for revolutions."

Like Ahab in his search for Moby Dick, Snow said more than once, Americans sought a victory that could only result in their own destruction. If America wanted to win in Vietnam, Snow wrote prophetically in the early 1960s, it could not rely on army rangers trained in guerrilla warfare and "some paltry charities or reforms urged upon the bought army elites in the impoverished lands." The United States could only compete by supporting land reform and other positive programs to promote better education and health. As he wrote in one of several articles on the war for the *New Republic*, Snow agreed with Walter Lippmann that "more than anything else we are fighting to avoid admitting failure."

"Vietnam depresses me daily," Snow said in a personal note that summed up the mood around his home. In one of several outraged letters to appear in the Paris edition of the *Herald Tribune*, Lois said she was "disgusted" by a front page photo of grinning American soldiers who slung a dead body over the hood of a jeep. "Please continue to publish such pictures," she wrote. ". . . Let us continue to be disgusted as long as the bombing and killing go on."

"All well," Snow wrote in a holiday note, "and as happy as any Americans may be who feel ashamed at what LBJ is doing to the wretched Vietnamese in our name this xmas."

Snow's bitterest attack on Vietnam policy came in response to Johnson's portrayal of the war as "careful and self-limited." "Barkinson's Law on Bombing" appeared in the *Columbia University Forum*, an alumni opinion journal. The satire took an obvious cue from D. Northcote Parkinson, who observed that bureaucracies expand to fill the space available. But where Parkinson was humorous, Snow wrote in black despair rather like Jonathan Swift's "modest proposal" in the 1720s to solve the potato famine. (Children would not be a burden to their parents or the country, Swift observed, if they were used as food for the rich.) In the same way that bureaucracies expanded, Snow observed, selective bombing inevitably moved toward saturation bombing. Whatever they might say to the public, enlightened leaders understood that people should be targets. "Here Barkinson in beautifully clear: *it is men that make war, not weapons*. What makes Vietnamese Communists? Men! Where do men come from? They come from children. What is the means of their production? Women!" The sensible thing, Snow said, was to remove irrelevant passages from army manuals enjoining soldiers from war crimes and crimes against humanity. "Anyway, that is what we Barkinsonians believe."

On a visit to Washington in the spring of 1966 Snow met with Senator William Fulbright, chairman of the Foreign Relations Committee. Bill Fulbright felt he got on well with Snow in their few meetings. He was just Snow's age, born in Missouri (though raised in Arkansas); his mother, like Snow's father, had a love of the printed word and ran a weekly paper. Like Snow, Fulbright had a careless way of dressing. Neither of them, Fulbright thought, was part of the eastern establishment. By the standards of the Senate, Fulbright was independent and courageous. After guiding the president's 1964 Tonkin Gulf Resolution through the Senate, which he came to regret, he spoke out more and more against foreign policies that clung "to old myths in the face of new realities" on the threat of communism. Fulbright viewed the meeting with Snow as an opportunity to put one more brick in the wall of opposition he was building against the war. He invited his powerful and respected colleague, Georgia Senator Richard Russell, to join them in his big, dimly lit office cluttered with books. Russell seemed to be wavering in his support for the war. If Russell could be convinced to oppose the president, Fulbright told staff aide Richard Moose, he could take a lot of senators with him.

Snow talked initially about China. Moose was struck by Snow's dispassionate presentation in which he explained the Chinese perspective, without advocating it. Next Fulbright nudged the discussion to Vietnam. He asked Snow to describe the Vietnam leadership. Snow explained that the Vietnamese were determined to reunite the country and remove Western influence. Russell asked if there wasn't some reasonable way for the United States to resolve its differences with Hanoi. Otherwise, the senator said, he was going to have a hard time keeping the enthusiasts for bombing from "dropping everything and the kitchen sink."

"All we want to do," Russell said, "is get out of the situation with honor."

"With honor?" Snow replied, rhetorically.

"Yes, that's all. With honor."

Snow paused. "No, I don't think that's possible."

Snow, Fulbright said later, "came closer to recognizing reality that any of our leaders."

In November 1968, Americans elected Richard Nixon president. Within a few days Peking Radio broadcast for the first time in several years a call for Sino-American discussions on the "Five Principles of Coexistence." Quietly, almost unnoticed, the seeds of rapprochement began to take root in the bitter soil of mutual domestic turmoil.[14]

Both sides had their own reasons. Having sidelined Liu Shao-ch'i and his followers, Mao was ready to end the Cultural Revolution. Though not as damaging to the economy as the Great Leap, the Cultural Revolution had not promoted economic development either. In addition, the leadership was worried about the Soviet Union, which had crushed the dissident government in Czechoslovakia and threatened preemptive attacks against Chinese nuclear facilities. Hostilities sparked along the Sino-Soviet border where Moscow stationed more than a million troops. Wanting to reduce external threats, the CCP's Ninth Party Congress in 1969 talked about "peaceful coexistence between countries with different social systems." "China's door may be open a crack or two now," Snow observed in a *New Republic* article shortly afterward.

The United States was equally unconfident about its place in the world. Nixon's election was a vote against the bankrupt Vietnam policy. The war sent waves of disillusionment through the country unlike anything since the 1930s, when capitalism was called into question and the United States extended long overdue diplomatic recognition to the Soviet Union. For Americans the terms of debate changed from fighting Reds to coming to terms with them, from believing in the American government to doubting it—a shift crudely summarized by antiwar protesters who glorified the Cultural Revolution as a model of grass roots activism.

One sign of the change was the reception of the revised edition of *Red Star over China*. "After sleeping all these years in the US," Snow observed, the book sold well "apparently due to political archaeological research among youths beginning to ask for whom the bombs toll." Received almost as though it were new, not a reissue, the book generated a round of reviews. Although the word "classic" appeared more than once to describe the volume, present-minded reviewers used the book as a springboard to reflect on "a way out of the morass." The lesson of *Red Star*, a California reviewer wrote in words that could have been Snow's, was that "programs to fight poverty, ignorance, injustice may cost money but they will be cheaper—and better—than wars." Young China scholars eager to establish Sino-American relations called Snow "prince of China-journalists." Snow spoke at the U.S. Army War College, Notre Dame University, and the Chicago Council on Foreign Relations in 1967. The *New York Times* covered a talk in Hartford where he said the Chinese Communists would not send troops to Vietnam. In 1968, 750 people turned out to hear him speak at the University of Kansas, not far from his hometown.[15]

In July 1969, Snow wrote to Mao Tse-tung to inquire if he could fit through the small opening decreed by the Ninth Party Congress. "I do not like to presume on an old friendship to write to you, even now," Snow said, but ". . . would it be harmful if I were to be permitted to renew acquaintance and see for myself the results of the Great Proletarian Cultural Revolution?" While Snow waited for an answer, he suffered a series of afflictions that harked to the past. He came down with a bout of malaria, after many years absence, and a 103 degree fever. Lingering fatigue, which predated the malaria, was diagnosed first as heart trouble, then accurately as a recurrence of his bladder infection. Snow traced the blockage to cystoscopic removal of a kidney stone in Peking during the 1930s. He canceled a U.S. speaking tour and the next spring underwent two operations to remove the tumorous growth. Afterward Snow experienced prolonged postoperative problems, including fever.

In June 1970, as he was about to leave for Rome to appear on a television program, the Chinese embassy in Paris unexpectedly called. It wanted to see him immediately. After making his Rome stop, Snow went to Paris where he was told he and his wife could come to China. Snow declined the Chinese offer to pay Lois's way and said he felt too weak to leave immediately. In the next weeks he arranged financial backing from *Epoca*. The Milan weekly—an Italian version of *Life*—advanced funds to cover travel costs "and a bit more" in exchange for non-North American rights for half a dozen or so articles by Snow.

Although the Chinese still insisted on calling Snow a historian, a rule change under Nixon provided automatic passport validation for journalists and members of other special professions traveling to China. Lois was supposed to go through regular request procedures. After years of wanting to visit China, however, she was not about to let the State Department stand in her way again. She decided to go without validation. The couple boarded a Swiss Air DC8 on July 31. Snow arrived in Hongkong exhausted and several days later landed in the hospital with the infection flaring up again. Not until August 14 did he and Lois cross into China. They took the air-conditioned train to Canton past emerald fields of rice and, from there, the plane to Peking.

Snow had been the last American journalist in China before the Cultural Revolution; he was now the first to return. The *Washington Post* China watcher reported that the visit signaled Chinese interest in developing contacts with the United States. The American consul in Hongkong cabled Washington that the visit was a "favorable portent for Sino-US relations."[16]

The familiar collection of friends greeted Snow and his wife at the Peking airport, among them Rewi Alley and Huang Hua. Huang had been brought back from his May 7th School to arrange Snow's visit. Snow had two questions on his mind. He asked the greeting party to give him a resumé of the last five years and to explain why he was there. Two days later, he got an answer to the latter question—an answer he more or less expected.

After dinner at the summer palace with friends, Snow and his wife were taken on a surprise visit to see Chou En-lai. The premier, presiding at a ping-pong tournament, talked with Snow in a side room. First came "family talk." Chou suggested Snow go to the Peitaiho seaside resort to rest, an invitation he declined. Chou questioned Snow intensely about the United States. When Snow asked about the chances of new Sino-American initiatives, Chou replied that they invited him hoping to get the answer to that. Chou acknowledged concern with the Soviet threat. Snow reflected afterward that merely inviting him to the tournament might have been meant "to make an impression on foreign diplomats" also in attendance.[17]

The Chinese soon made Snow a far more visible symbol. After spending much of September in the Northwest, Snow was back in Peking for the October 1 celebrations marking the twenty-first anniversary of the founding of the People's Republic. The Chinese invited Snow and his wife to join dignitaries on the balcony of T'ien An Men, the buildinglike gate where the leadership presided over the festivities in Peking's main square. Below the gate tens of thousands of Chinese paraded past, waving banners, dancing, riding floats. To Snow's surprise he and Lois were seated close to the center of the balcony, not off on the end. When the parade was well along, Snow felt his arm being pulled by Chou En-lai. Chou led him and Lois through the rows of guests to Mao Tse-tung, who stood at the center of the pageant.

After an exchange of pleasantries, Mao said he had received Snow's letter asking if he could visit. "It pays to complain. So now you are here."

"Did I complain?" Snow asked.

"Yes, you did." Mao replied. Mao said a group of "ultra-Leftists" had opposed Snow, the same people who burned the British embassy. "They are all cleared out now." Mao had read Snow's articles, which included criticism of the cult of Mao, and saw "nothing objectionable in these comments. We do not expect you to agree with everything we say. You have a right to your own opinion. It is better to keep your independent judgment."

Since returning, Snow said, he realized he had made mistakes in interpreting the Cultural Revolution. "How does it look to you down there?" Snow asked about the people below who carried statues of Mao and large placards with Mao's sayings.

It was better, Mao said. But he was far from satisfied. During the few minutes left, Mao asked about the United States and the political significance of the the antiwar movement.

The Snows had tea with Chou En-lai after the ceremony in one of the rooms inside the gate. When the Snows returned to their lodging, the hotel staff, who had seen the T'ien An Men performance on television, practically embraced them. The photograph of Snow and Mao, side by side, appeared on the front of the *People's Daily* on Christmas day. Snow was described as a "friendly" American.

The gesture was part of a diplomatic minuet between the United States and China, so secret and complicated that for much of early 1970 it wasn't clear to either side whether the other was dancing. Sino-American talks had resumed at the beginning of 1970 in Warsaw, the site of more than one hundred sterile American-Chinese meetings over the years. In response to a U.S. suggestion, the Chinese had indicated that they would welcome an American emissary to Peking. These first steps seemed to lead nowhere when Nixon enlarged the war into Cambodia, and bureaucrats in the United States and, quite possibly, in China resisted the idea of rapprochement. Only small gestures came. In July, the month Snow left Switzerland for China, the Chinese released an American prisoner, and the United States agreed that an Italian firm could sell dump trucks with General Motors engines to the Chinese.

The Chinese leadership reflected this diplomatic uncertainty in its talks with Snow. In their first brief meeting, Chou said China had not replied to the Nixon overture because of Cambodia. In a November 5 interview, Chou admitted that China had indicated its willingness to receive an American envoy but the United States had not replied. The door to better relations was opened, Chou said, but it appeared "Nixon was not to be taken seriously." When a transcript of the conversation came back a week later, Snow noticed that Chou's remarks about Nixon not being serious had been deleted. During the interim the president of Pakistan, Yahya Khan, had visited China. He carried a message from Nixon reiterating American interest in sending an emissary.

Additional steps were taken in the next weeks. As spelled out later by Nixon's national security advisor Henry Kissinger, Chou replied affirmatively to Washington's new overture. That reply reached Washington, via the Pakistan ambassador, on Dec. 8. On December 16 Nixon relayed through Pakistan that the United States wanted an agenda that went beyond Taiwan. While Nixon awaited an answer to that, he received another Chinese message, this time from the Romanian ambassador, saying Nixon himself was welcome in Peking.

Early on the morning of December 18, while this was unfolding, a Chinese official awoke Snow. Mao was ready to see him. Snow pulled on a sweater and slacks. He arrived in time for breakfast and stayed until about one o'clock. In the wide-ranging conversation, which as usual touched on the cult of Mao, Mao elaborated on his earlier statement that he was unhappy with the Cultural Revolution. The widespread use of force and maltreatment of captives, he said, violated the spirit of revolution. On Sino-American relations, Mao said that messages were going back and forth between the two countries and that an American envoy might be coming to Peking. He said China was considering ways of admitting Americans. In that context Mao would happily invite Nixon, "either as a tourist or as President." Before leaving, Snow raised the plight of Israel Epstein. Mao said he didn't know Epstein was in prison. Snow said that he had never known Epstein to be disloyal to China.

Snow traveled the length of the country, making the only visit to Paoan by a foreigner since 1945.[18] He saw Lin Piao at the October 1 celebrations for the first time since 1939 but wasn't granted an interview with him, perhaps because the army chief opposed the opening to the West which Chou and Mao pursued. Snow dined with Mme. Sun and saw Chou on numerous occasions, twice for long interviews. He and Lois met Prince Sihanouk at the October 1 celebrations. Several weeks afterward, Snow talked for two hours with the exiled Cambodian leader, whom he considered intelligent, emotional, and courageous. Sihanouk said Nixon's bombing of Cambodia was creating Communists. He gave the Snows a silver soup ladle and a smoking set. In November Snow met with a Canadian delegation. One young delegate asked Snow to sum up his impression of China in three words. "Stabilization, Peace, Growth," Snow replied.

Paoan, a poor place full of ragged people when Snow visited in 1936, showed the benefits of a massive public land reclamation program carried out by the people. Rows of trees lined—and held in—the river. Where there had once been one store, many lined the streets. Before there was no industry; now there were thirteen handicraft shops, a machine repair shop, and a power plant. In other places Snow visited consumer goods were more plentiful and cheaper than in 1965. China's rural communes, poor by Western standards, provided opportunities far "beyond the former dreams of the landless and perennially overworked, hungry illiterates who were most of the peasants in prerevolutionary China."

Conflicting thoughts and emotions ran through Snow's mind in interviews. In a visit to a hospital, he interviewed a man burned so badly that one side of his face was gone. The hospital propaganda team had stayed with the patient around the clock for weeks. The man's plight and the humanitarian efforts to keep him alive touched Snow. He wept. Later Snow thought to himself that the Chinese team might have exerted itself not for selfless reasons but to win glory for Mao and themselves. He thought again. What if they did? The result was good.

The leadership, which enjoyed amorous affairs in the revolutionary days, seemed staid, the country increasingly puritanical. Snow was struck by the uniformity of dress. "Mao everywhere you look"—pictures of Mao posted inside the car, along the highways, along the waterfront, in the shops. Snow found the long "canned" harangues from commune and plant leaders tedious. "Chairman Mao saved me and gave me a new life," said a man whom Snow interviewed at a locomotive plant. ". . . Father and mother are dear to me, Chairman Mao is dearer still." One elderly man said that by being ideologically remolded he could compete with youth. While listening to the man declaim his age, Snow noted in his book that *he* was old and "tired and bored." In Sian he composed a ditty: "Mao Tse-tung was a poet of note, who lived by writing things to quote." No one seemed to think it funny.

In interviews Snow could press hard. On one occasion a steel plant official gave production figures that didn't add up. "Figures don't lie,"

Snow said, "but liars figure." Snow asked Mao if those who quoted him the most ardently might not be the ones most opposed to the spirit of the revolution. In his usual way of trying to understand how the other side saw events, Snow came to think the set speeches not entirely bad. It was something new for workers to voice their pride in their shops, factories, and farms. He liked aspects of the interchange between city and countryside—barefoot doctors providing care to people who never before had medical attention; the cadres exposed to manual labor and learning the difficulty of producing food. The military had abolished rank insignia. He thought the Cultural Revolution—which he viewed as demanding self-criticism but promising forgiveness—better than Stalin's staged trials and executions. At the same time, Snow argued with a Chinese friend over the appropriateness of deposing Liu without following consitutional procedures. Rewi Alley later recalled that Snow "was bitter and sad when he heard of treatment meted out to old cadres he admired." He realized that May 7th Schools provided hard, primitive existences and that forced attendance disrupted families. Epstein was not the only foreigner affected, Snow knew. Rewi Alley's quarters seemed more bleak. Both he and George Hatem seemed worried about their Chinese families.

If Snow understood the shape of the Cultural Revolution, he did not realize the depth of hardships. He could not know that. China was too big and too difficult to penetrate. Snow questioned old friends, like Huang Hua and others, about the Cultural Revolution—about the human toll. The answers given Snow were straightforward but not critical. Huang Hua told Snow that he had been in a May 7th School in Hupei, planting rice and loading boats on the Han River; he told Snow that his wife and two children went to three other sites. He also said that the Cultural Revolution was good, a spiritual transformation. That was a common refrain. The Cultural Revolution, people said over and over, "is the greatest thing that ever happened." It wasn't safe to say anything else. When Snow eventually left China, he felt he had not broken through the model scenes he visited with Lois.

Little wonder Snow used an Alice in Wonderland quote to describe stories praising the May 7th Schools: "I can't believe that!" Alice said. "Can't you?" the White Queen replied. "I dare say you haven't had much practice. When I was your age, I always did it for half-an-hour a day. Why, sometimes I've believed as many as six impossible things before breakfast." Not able to summon the enthusiasm of those whom he interviewed, Snow reported what people said, expressed skepticism about the wisdom of wasting experienced professional talent in rice fields, noted that one heard only from the winners, not the losers, and—as usual—explored the reasons for the Cultural Revolution.

Lois relished the chance to work with her husband on China, a subject that had been a central and yet distant part of her life until then. But even though she described herself as "helpmate-secretary," she pursued her own interests, too. She gathered material for the first book she would write, *China on Stage*, as well as for articles. Lois also was not afraid to make her feelings known. She did not like the lace curtains that the Chinese hung over windows in official sedans. It gave the cars the look of a heavily curtained emperors' litter. Lois pulled them down. She told her husband she preferred to travel with the whole party in one minibus, as they did to the Great Wall and the Ming Tombs outside Peking, rather than in a long caravan of official cars. He suggested she tell Chou En-lai. She did. The premier said he agreed. The problem was they had lots of sedans but only three minibuses.

Lois left China on December 20, in time to spend Christmas in the United States with her daughter, a freshman at Antioch College. Her husband stayed on, continuing to research and waiting for another interview with Chou En-lai. He planned to meet Lois in California in a couple of weeks. The all-night interview with Chou came in mid-January. The wait for a transcript of the interview and amplification of his notes dragged on. Snow, who had planned to stay only three months, was still in China at the end of January, more than five months after he arrived.

Snow found his status as a "friendly personage," which conveyed the idea of "be good to this person," partly humorous and partly cloying. When he and Lois were about to travel to the chilly Northwest, Chou insisted they have special coats made. Snow, who in the past was happy traveling in a borrowed Chinese coat, complained of being "guested to death." He had to fight to pay for all his expenses. On a visit to Peking University, formerly Yenching, a woman official welcomed him as "an old friend of Mao Tse-tung." The comment irritated Snow, as if he could not exist without Mao's imprimatur.

It didn't help to know that he held a special go-between role. When Huang Hua informed Snow that he could meet with Mao, Huang added that Mao wanted to interview him, not the other way around. Snow wrote in his diary that he could not give "realistic answers." He didn't speak for the American government; he had avoided power. Yet, Snow added, "No one can entirely avoid responsibility for power. It bothers me greatly that I have not solved this contradiction in my lifetime."

Snow resisted Chinese suggestions that he stay in China to live or write his book. It would force him, he thought, to join the team. As time dragged on in Peking, he felt trapped. Health problems added to Snow's aggravation. He had been sick several times during the trip, once with bronchitis so severe he coughed up blood. By January, the extraordinarily dry winter, combined with the heat in homes, so dehydrated Snow that, with his other medical problems, he had trouble urinating. George Hatem wanted him to see local doctors. Snow resisted. He didn't want to do anything that might keep him in China. He felt a money crisis coming and needed to start writing. He had trouble getting letters to or from Lois in California. No one seemed to understand, he thought. He complained to Huang Hua of the protracted wait—then regretted having made a protest. In early February he left without the Chou material, which was to be forwarded to him in Switzerland.

The press in Hongkong was eager for information on Snow's visit to China. Reporters who tracked him down thought he seemed disturbed to see them. "He at first refused to say anything about his five-month visit to China," a reporter with the *Hongkong Standard* noted, "until he was reminded that as a young reporter he also had to interview people who did not want to talk." When questioned about Sino-American relations, Snow crisply said, "They don't exist." Wanting a sanctuary and a chance to evaluate his health, Snow checked into a Hongkong hospital during the two-day layover. He arrived home in Switzerland tired, somewhat depressed, and worried about how well he understood what he had seen in China. He was glad his son, Chris, was home to help fend off journalists who wanted to talk to him.[19]

The confusing Sino-American diplomatic drama continued while Snow was writing in Switzerland. Nixon was careful not to appear too eager. He did not respond to the Romanian-delivered invitation to visit China personally, deciding instead to wait until the Chinese agreed to the agenda for talks. Nixon's removal of all restrictions on China travel came hand in hand with a South Vietnamese offensive, supported by U.S. air power, into Laos. In early March Snow sent a note to Senator George McGovern, with whom he had corresponded before and who was to face Nixon in the next election. Snow told McGovern of Nixon's approaches to Peking and said McGovern might be able to go first.

While Snow was in China, the *New York Times* asked him to submit a piece on his trip. Although he did nothing for them while he was there, he thought the paper, with its large readership, was the ideal place for his Chou En-lai interviews and the premier's "open door" comments. On her way home to Switzerland, Lois stopped in New York and confirmed the newspaper's continued interest. Snow submitted the article. Not long after, a 2 A.M. call came from the *Times*. Snow, who had been having trouble sleeping, had just taken a sleeping pill and drifted off. He listened groggily while an editor said he was sorry, the *Times* could not use the piece. As a condition of his interviews with Chou, Snow had promised not to cut Chou's answers to individual questions although he did not have to publish all the questions and answers. Snow therefore insisted that the *Times* not edit the story without his approval. The *Times* editor said the paper did not have enough space to run the story. The *Times* seemed uninterested in finding a way to get the interview in the paper.

Lois had never seen her husband more furious. He had been certain he would break through this time. The years of frustration trying to reach the American public gushed out as he told Lois about the telephone call and paced back and forth. He swore. "It meant a total refutation finally on top of all the years of not being accepted, not being the bridge, not having attention in any important way in Washington," Lois recalled later. "All the things he had gone through: the ignominy of the Dean Rusk meeting; simply being tossed aside while the Chinese thought he would be the one who could bring some enlightenment, some thought to Washington based on reality. And then they paid no attention."

This was the last time Snow had any dealings with the *Times*. He told his agent not to approach them again. The paper had accepted an op-ed piece by Lois on the streets of Peking. She withdrew the article. The Chou interviews became the first installment of a five-part series in the *New Republic*, which began in March.

In early April the diplomatic scene changed suddenly. The Chinese issued a startling invitation. The American ping-pong team, competing in an international competition in Japan, could visit China. According to ground rules established with the Chinese, Snow could use the Mao interview piecemeal and without direct quotes. After much hesitation, he decided "ping-pong" was the right time to report Mao's statement that Nixon was welcome "either as a tourist or as President." Although Snow had agreed not to relate what Mao said about messages being exchanged between the United States and China or the possibilities of the United States sending an envoy to Peking, journalism convention allowed him to relate those facts if he could attribute them to other sources—which he could. He approached *Life*, which grabbed the story. It ran the interview as well as twenty-one pages of pictures taken by photographers traveling with the American ping-pong team. The magazine, which before Luce's death in 1967 had been virulently anti-Communist, editorialized that it was time for rapprochement.

Snow's plain statement that the United States and China were drawing closer elicited a "no comment" from some government quarters. Secretary of State William Rogers, who had not been apprised of the secret negotiations, publicly discounted the story. Mao's invitation to Nixon wasn't serious, he said.

On July 16 rumors and speculation ended. Richard Nixon appeared on television to announce that Kissinger had returned from a secret trip to Peking. The Chinese had invited Nixon to Peking. The president said he had accepted "with pleasure."[20]

The morning after the announcement, Snow's telephone started ringing. The Associated Press wanted a comment. The resulting AP story appeared in the *Chicago Tribune*, his old nemesis. Television networks called to say they wanted to interview Snow. They sent crews to Geneva. *Life* ran a second article by Snow in July. *Time*, a sister publication, excerpted part of the story for its next issue. The piece discussed what Nixon should expect in China. A full-page ad promoting the article in the *New York Times* "gave me a bit of soul food," Snow told Alley. "Now the US can't get enough of it. So much for ping-pong." Within two months the new paperback edition of *Red Star* sold 11,500 copies.[21]

Snow naturally wanted to cover Nixon's China trip. He planned to arrive before the presidential party, scheduled to land in Peking in mid-February, rather than with the horde of reporters lining up to make the trip. *Epoca*, which had sent a messenger by plane to pick up Snow's reports in April, wanted him to represent them. So did *Life*. When misunderstandings arose over a contract to represent *Life*, managing editor Ralph Graves wrote to Snow. If Snow's agent said exactly what he wanted, Graves said, "he would get it for you from *Life* at the best price and without difficulty."

The Snow house seemed like a kind of embassy. Joan Jaeger, Karl Jaeger's former wife who lived near the Snows, came over to help handle telephone calls. Letters flooded in from people who wanted to visit China—journalists, medical students, senators, a man who wanted to write a children's book on China. Someone suggested Snow bring Chinese musicians to Switzerland; another proposed to work with Snow arranging U.S.-Chinese sports exchanges. Snow tried to arrange a speaking trip for Hatem before American medical organizations. To most inquiries, he sent a form letter saying that he had no influence.

Snow and Lois had managed a two-week trip to the Italian coast, near Naples, after the ping-pong diplomacy began in April 1971. Upon returning to their home in Eysins, they began work in earnest on their writing. Lois's first article appeared on the front page of *Le Monde*, and she was soon well along in a draft of her book. Snow expected to deliver his manuscript by the end of the year. Random House planned to have the book out in time to capitalize on the Nixon trip. Stalwart friend Mary Heathcote came to help. As eager as Snow was to move ahead, he felt constantly weary. The fatigue turned to intense pain in early October. He could not sit at the typewriter for more than twenty minutes without horrible back pains. He traced the trouble to lumbago or arthritis. Hoping to get the rest he needed, Snow took a ten-day trip to Morocco where he reclined on the beach reading his manuscript and Lois's and playing chess with a young man he met on the beach.

Snow returned home to find he had forgotten the manuscripts, which the young chess partner delivered shortly after. When Snow arrived, Lois, whose own health had deteriorated, was sick in bed. She went to the hospital, where doctors diagnosed infectious hepatitis and prescribed rest. Speculating that his continued fatigue might have the same cause, Snow reluctantly moved into her double room for tests of his own. Impatient with the waiting, feeling constrained by hospital routine, Snow abruptly left one morning before Lois awoke. Shortly afterward he learned of the test results. His liver was gravely enlarged, the result of cancer of the pancreas.

Doctors in Lausanne performed a four-hour operation in December. Snow left the hospital shortly after Christmas. There was talk of recovery, that perhaps chemotherapy would help. The walks from the farmhouse to the village, however, became more difficult. Snow would not travel to China to cover the Nixon visit.[22]

Joe Alsop got into a nasty exchange with Snow before Nixon's announcement of his trip. In a letter to the editor of the *International Herald Tribune,* Snow and his wife criticized Alsop for using secondhand, exaggerated information to report brutalities in May 7th Schools. The schools might not be the best way to break down bureaucratic snobbery, the Snows said, but they met many graduates who were in excellent health. Alsop replied that he read *Red Star* before going to China in 1941 and learned within twenty-four hours of arriving that Snow's picture was misleading and "grossly mendacious." Snow taught him an important lesson, Alsop said in an odd bit of self-incrimination: "no newspaperman can ever assume that there is much real truth in the fashionable view of situations overseas. . . . I would not write about foreign situations that I had not gone to see for myself." If Alsop wouldn't report on what he didn't see for himself, Snow wrote in reply, how could he report on May 7th Schools?

Alsop visited China after Nixon opened the door in 1972. Once inside, he revised himself on the Chinese Communists, if not on Snow. "Everything in China has changed, in truth," Alsop wrote from Nanking, "except the endlessly resilient, hard-working and clever Chinese people. The quality of life has changed, vastly for the ancient ruling class but for the better for everyone else." The Great Leap left a final deposit "that seemed to me to be working very well when I was in China. . . . In the same way the destructiveness of those four years of seeming chaos [during the Cultural Revolution] had been considerably exaggerated." About the same time Alsop called Harrison Salisbury.

"Harry," Alsop said, using a diminutive that Salisbury disliked, "you and I are the only ones who ever really understood China."[23]

Richard Nixon said that when he shook hands with Chou En-lai in Peking "one era ended and another began." So it seemed. Hatred and fear of the Red Chinese, expressed for so long by Alsop and others, vanished overnight. Old China Hands cashiered during the 1950s came to be heroes. In his column in the *New York Times*, C. L. Sulzberger nominated John Paton Davies as a candidate for first ambassador to China. (*The Nation* chose Edmund Clubb.) Edgar Snow's writings were among the briefing materials Nixon "read with exquisite care," as Kissinger put it, to prepare himself for China. Nixon, who had railed against Communist China, prepared himself to make an agreement, which as one historian put it, "essentially endorsed the positions the Chinese had been setting forth since 1949," including the progressive withdrawal of U.S. military forces from Taiwan and acknowledgment that Taiwan's future was an internal Chinese matter.*

It is convenient, reassuring, to see vindication of Snow's policies in his last days. Snow, however, had his doubts.[24]

Nixon had special qualities that made change possible. As a Republican, he was not tainted, as Democrats were, by the "loss" of China. He had a more sophisticated vision of the world than his predecessors, understanding that communism was not a unified movement but fragmented. Henry Kissinger possessed this same outlook. When Chou said initially that Taiwan must be a focal point for discussions, Kissinger

*The U.S. statement on Taiwan in the Shanghai Communiqué is worth stating here: "The United States acknowledges that all Chinese on either side of the Taiwan Strait maintain there is but one China and that Taiwan is a part of China. The United States Government does not challenge that position. It reaffirms its interest in a peaceful settlement of the Taiwan question by the Chinese themselves. With this prospect in mind, it affirms the ultimate objective of the withdrawal of all U.S. forces and military installations from Taiwan. In the meantime, it will progressively reduce its forces and military installations on Taiwan as the tension in the area diminishes."

understood "this was a standard formula." He understood that the big thing was that the Chinese wanted to talk.

Yet neither Nixon nor his staff delineated a sharp break from the past. In a celebrated article, "Asia after Vietnam," published in *Foreign Affairs* before he was elected, Nixon outlined a new policy toward Asia in Cold War terms. Bringing China into the family of nations was a step toward "recognizing the present and potential danger for Communist China, and taking measures designed to meet that danger." It was also a tactic for putting pressure on the Soviet Union. Perhaps Nixon, the supreme realist, wrote with a view toward shaping a new policy that squared with American assumptions. If so, it only proved how small a distance Americans had moved.

Americans, as confused as they were with the failed policy in Vietnam, did not question the fundamental rightness of the war. If they had, a realistic president could have exited from Southeast Asia without ceremony. Nixon expanded the conflict with continued bombing and his "secret war" in Cambodia. "Our insistence on peace with honor," Nixon said at the time of the Paris peace accords in January 1971, "has made peace with honor possible." Peace with honor cost an additional five hundred thousand Vietnamese and twenty thousand American lives, and ended with South Vietnam in precisely the same situation it would have been had the United States departed the day after Nixon was elected. With the end of the war, peace marchers celebrated a victory in Lafayette Park, across from the White House. They talked as if the day had come for wholesale reform in America. Actually the "silent majority," to which Nixon appealed, suffered a defeat of the worst kind. They quit a war they considered morally right because the price seemed too high. They had not learned much.

Snow's prediction in his own "Asia after Vietnam" article in the *New Republic*, which appeared within months of Nixon's, was dead on the mark. The peace process just getting underway, Snow said, seemed headed for the same conclusion as Nationalist-Chinese conflict in China in the 1940s. "Both sides fought it out until US [mediation] efforts were deflated to empty talk in the face of realities of communist victory." "One can see the logic of expectations in Hanoi and Peking," Snow concluded, "that the US may soon be obliged to leave Vietnam unconditionally." Nixon's actions, Snow told Howard, created the most "serious crisis of confidence in the presidency since Hoover."

Chinese articulation of the principle of self-determination was precisely what troubled Americans wanted to hear. Americans did not intend to invest much to ensure that other nations could shape a better future. United States policies toward developing countries remained more or less what they had always been, weak and insignificant. For Americans as well as the Chinese, the appeal of self-determination lay in its justification for keeping the rest of the world at a safe distance. The essential truth of rapprochement was the mutual effort to reduce the prospect of hostilities and only secondarily to create a relationship. As Nixon said, a central motive guiding the trip was his desire to prevent sending Americans to fight in Asia again. Faced with leadership succession crises in both the United States and China, leaders on both sides were in no hurry to climb out of the Taiwan hole they had dug. Formal diplomatic relations did not come until 1979.

Americans' views and Snow's intersected only superficially, as they had in the 1930s. Although Nixon, the realist, came closer to Snow's view than many other recent political leaders had, the White House found Snow a convenient symbol rather than anyone able to give guidance. Nixon said that Snow's *Life* article "confirmed private signals we had received of Chinese interest." Historians called it "an unmistakable signal." But Nixon had made up his mind to explore relations with China long before Snow arrived in China. Nothing would have changed without the Snow article. More revealing was Henry Kissinger's comment years later that the Chinese "overestimated our subtlety, for what they conveyed [by bringing Snow to stand with Mao on T'ien An Men Square] was so oblique that our crude Occidental minds completely missed the point."

Snow did not get caught up in the euphoria.[25] The long, disappointing years taught him to hold back hope. When the Johnson presidency began to crumble and LBJ began to explore peace possibilities, Snow told an audience near Kansas City that it would take time before any real change occurred. In 1969 Snow saw that the United States might return to the concept of self-determination for China, but he cautioned that officials had uttered such statements in the 1930s without backing them up with action. "Miracles are not forecast for tomorrow," Snow said. "Each generation is doomed to learn for itself that the new print cannot altogether obscure the underlying 'old misunderstandings.' "

Before his 1970 China visit, Snow told Owen Lattimore that he used to believe in the idea of American "exceptionalism," that the country was exempt from the trials that toppled other large industrial nations. McCarthyism had not ruined that totally, Snow said, but Vietnam did. "Now millions seem to be waking up in the U.S.—though not necessarily because they recognize and wish to overthrow American imperialism." As for himself, Snow said, *he* had been the exception, "taken in by the establishment, tolerated for awhile."

Snow's comment was not the expression of a man resigned to being different. It was the expression of a man troubled by the great chasm that stood between him and his country. In looking forward to change, Snow really looked backward to the values he acquired in his Missouri youth. No act by Richard Nixon could heal the estrangement.

Trudie Schafer, who had helped Snow revise *Red Star*, ate dinner with the Snows right after Nixon's July announcement of his upcoming Peking visit. The telephone, which had been ringing all day, fell oddly quiet during the meal. When they finished, Lois noticed that the phone was off the hook. Snow said he thought they should have some peace during dinner.

Nixon's planned trip, the vote to admit China to the United Nations in October—these were steps in the right direction, not wholesale change. Snow confessed to a Danish interviewer that he was, at first, astonished that Nixon wanted to visit China. Snow couldn't help seeing Nixon in negative terms. He also thought that the United States would be hemmed in by its past pledges to Taiwan. Snow summed up his feelings about that problem, and in a way about Nixon, in a WCBS radio interview. "In brief, sir, perhaps it is better for Mr. Nixon to go to China with Taiwan in his pocket than no change at all."

He put it another way to his sister. "Now 'they' are all phoning and writing *me*, ha, wanting to go into China and do business as usual. They have a lot yet to learn."

In early February 1972, a letter arrived from Washington, D.C. Snow was feeling particularly ill that day. Lois read to him:

> Dear Mr. Snow:
>
> I want you to know that my thoughts are with you as are my prayers for your recovery. I know how confining a hospital must be for a man of your energy and enthusiasm, and I can only hope that it will strengthen you to know that your distinguished career is so widely respected and appreciated. My best to you always.
>
> Sincerely,
> Richard Nixon

Lois asked if he wanted to answer. Snow smiled ironically. "Don't bother."

Snow had not finished his book before the cancer operation. Afterward he and his wife worked in the study next to their upstairs bedroom, when he could. Branson O'Casey, a friend from London who worked with Snow on *One Fourth of Humanity*, came to give him a hand. Snow never really finished. With the help of Mary Heathcote, Lois later prepared *The Long Revolution* for publication. She was not certain what her husband would have said about Liu Shao-ch'i. Lin Piao, who died in a plane crash over Mongolia in September 1971, presented another problem. Mme. Sun advised Snow not to guess at the facts behind Lin's death, "even the people inside know not the particulars." Informants told Snow that Lin had been involved in a plot against Mao, a version that did not come out until July 1972. Snow figured it climaxed a struggle between those like Chou En-lai, who wanted to rebuild the government, and the political arm of the People's Liberation Army General Political Department under Lin. Snow wrote nothing in *The Long Revolution* about Lin's demise. The interviews with Mao and Chou from his 1964–1965 trip, as yet not published in full in the United States, took up a large section of the book. Some of the chapters were unusually brief, suggesting that Snow would have filled in material—if he had had time.[26]

The book seemed to react against the wave of enthusiasm developing for China, as if he were concerned the scales could become misaligned in the other direction. Although he stressed how far China had come since he knew it as a young man fresh from Missouri, Snow was more skeptical than he had been in 1960. He cautioned that "we may not for many years see *all* the threads or be able to reveal a brief, clear pattern of what happened" in the Cultural Revolution. His final words in *The Long Revolution*, informed by his experience, not only looked ahead in China but also provided warning for Americans:

> The danger is that Americans may imagine that the Chinese are giving up communism—and Mao's world view—to become nice agrarian democrats. A more realistic world is indeed in sight. But popular illusions that it will consist of a sweet mix of ideologies, or an end to China's faith in revolutionary means, could only serve to deepen the abyss again when disillusionment occurs. . . . [A] world of relative peace between states is as necessary to China as to America. To hope for more is to court disenchantment.[27]

Snow fought the reality of approaching death. He scribbled "To the man who saved my life . . ." in the book he gave the surgeon who operated on him. The children came home, Sian from Antioch and Chris from England, where he was studying. Friends, acquired in every part of the world, gathered around, often just long enough to throw a few logs on the downstairs fireplace and slip out quietly. When Lois wrote to George Hatem of her husband's operation, Hatem replied that Snow should come to Peking for treatment. A similar invitation followed from Chou En-lai, with supportive messages from other officials. On January 24 Lois learned that a Chinese medical team—four doctors including Hatem plus nurses and an anesthesiologist—was arriving that day to escort Snow back to China. The Swiss authorities had waived normal visa formalities.

The Chinese act of concern for Snow was extraordinary. China certainly would not have reached beyond its borders in such a way for any other American. But as flattered as Snow was, he did not want to leave. His response to Chou's initial invitation was that he was in the middle of chemotherapy treatments, which could not be interrupted. Snow also wanted to stay near his notes and finish his book. Shortly after they pulled up in front of the Snow home in three black Chinese embassy limousines, the Chinese medical team realized there was no question of going to Peking. Snow was too ill. After a brief discussion among themselves, the Chinese decided to stay and attend Snow in his Eysins farmhouse. As Lois Snow later wrote in her graceful, moving account of her husband's last days, *A Death with Dignity*, the Chinese act of kindness meant Snow did not have to return to an impersonal hospital. He remained at home, surrounded by friends and family.[28]

In early February Huang Hua arrived, too. Appointed the first representative of the People's Republic of China to the United Nations, Huang was en route to New York City. He walked up to Snow's bedroom with George Hatem. "Well, we three old bandits," Snow said in surprise. Not long after he slipped into a coma.

At 2:20 on the morning of February 15, the first day of the Chinese Lunar New Year and sixty-two hours and sixteen minutes before Nixon's plane left Andrews Air Force Base for Peking, Ed Snow died.

Righting the Wrongs?

10

Before President Nixon and his party landed in Peking, the Chinese memorialized Edgar Snow in the Great Hall of the People. It was the first such tribute ever in that building for a foreigner. Mao Tse-tung, Chou En-lai, and Soong Ch'ing-ling sent condolences to Lois Snow. Said Soong, who kept a picture of Show's two children in her home, "Edgar Snow will remain forever green in the hearts of the Chinese people."

With his untimely death, the *Kansas City Star* editorialized, "Edgar Snow had at last become a prophet of great honor in his own country." The *New York Times* called Snow "prescient" for his predictions in the 1930s on Japanese aggression leading to all-out war, on decolonization afterward, and on the Chinese Communist revolution. The *Chicago Tribune*, not long before sharply critical, wrote, "It's too bad that Snow didn't live long enough to give Americans his firsthand impression of Mao and Chou *after* the historic meeting with President Nixon." *Newsweek* said critics had been wrong to see Snow as an apologist. Snow earned his "insuperable advantage over other journalists . . . the hard way," through diligent reporting; he "often was critical of American and Chinese leaders alike." *Time* chimed in sympathetically: "Snow's criticism of Peking's authoritarian excesses sometimes seemed too low key. The reason was, perhaps, that Snow saw himself a contributor to better relations between Peking and Washington. . . . Whatever the charges, Snow never forgot that he was an American." In the euphoria of renewed Chinese relations, the only American criticism came, faintly, from organs of the far Right like the *Cross and the Flag*, founded by racist Gerald L. K. Smith.[1]

Snow's presence hung over the eighty-seven journalists who accompanied Nixon to China. Few had even a smattering of knowledge about the country. "Frankly, in covering Washington and national policies, our foreign policy had very little to do with the problems of Red China in terms of American politics," said Jerald F. ter Horst, who covered the White House for the Detroit *News*. "All you had to do was remember that every President has been against Red China, and that solved a lot of political problems and a lot of thinking on the journalistic side." Before leaving for China, journalists read Snow's books, which had been recommended by China specialists at the pretrip briefings held in the Mayflower Hotel in Washington, D.C. But no amount of tutoring could adequately prepare a reporter for the frustrating assignment. Many came back from the trip saying what NBC newscaster John Chancellor did: they had never worked harder in their lives, and still they had been largely confined by the "scenario made up by men who work either across from Lafayette Park in Washington or T'ien An Men Square in Peking." Nixon's business meetings with the Chinese leadership were so secret that ter Horst could not get a description of Mao's home, let alone its location. A member of Kissinger's staff told him to use the description in Snow's book. The *Wall Street Journal*'s reporter relied on Snow's "keen . . . eye" when describing old Shanghai.

Reporters, as well as editors back home, lamented the superficial reporting that emerged from the trip. Although unable to penetrate the way Snow had, many shared the uneasy feelings he experienced on his ground-breaking visits earlier. The press corps, Charles Bailey of the *Minneapolis Tribune* wrote afterward, "found itself playing an unaccustomed role: it was . . . part of the process of diplomacy and not merely an observer of that process. It was not a comfortable role."[2]

In the months after rapprochement Lois Snow agonized about a family problem with international implications: where to place her husband's ashes. The decision would make a final statement about Snow's life, which not only spanned many countries and much history but also suffered from deep public misunderstandings Lois did not wish to perpetuate. When she consulted her children, her daughter came back with a sensitive reply. "Papa," Sian Snow wrote in a letter, "would probably have come up with an appropriate quotation from Mark Twain" solving the problem. The difficulty, she understood, was that while her father "loved Missouri and the Mississippi River," a traditional cemetery in the United States seemed inappropriate. Her father also loved China, but "I know how uneasy he felt about being honored and privileged and how he wanted above all to remain a simple man. He wanted no favors, especially not from China since that might reflect on his writing."

The solution came in the summer of 1973, more than a year after Snow's death. Lois found a note shuffled among her husband's papers. "I love China," he wrote. "I should like part of me to stay there after death as it always did during life. America fostered and nourished me. I should like part of me placed by the Hudson River, before it enters the Atlantic to touch Europe and all the shores of mankind of which I felt a part, as I have known good men in almost every land."

The Chinese offered to place Snow's ashes in the National Revolutionary Martyrs Memorial Park where Agnes Smedley and Anna Louise Strong were buried. Lois demurred. Her husband, she thought, was neither a revolutionary hero nor a martyr. At her request his ashes were placed on the campus of Peking University, formerly Yenching, where Snow had taught. The site, dedicated in October 1973, was along a frequently trod path that rimmed the lake. Chou En-lai drafted the brief text and wrote the Chinese characters that appeared in both English and Chinese on the white marble marker: "In Memory of Edgar Show, an American Friend of the Chinese People, 1905–1972."

The following year, on a perfect spring afternoon, another small group of family, friends, and admirers placed the other half of Snow's ashes in Sam Zimbalist's yard in Snedens Landing, New York, next to a sheer upturning of ground. Beside a small granite flagstone inscribed "E. S." they planted a dogwood, Missouri's state tree and Snow's favorite.[3]

Edgar Snow's reports survived him. Before he died, *Life* commissioned him to write a just-in-case obituary of Mao Tse-tung. With *Life* defunct when Mao passed away in 1976, *Time* published Snow's brilliant summation of the Chinese leader, a man who "could simultaneously hold in mind contradictory concepts of time and space, of strategy, of right and wrong; he could act out decisions into realities as if they were the only truth, knowing all the while that the opposite was an essential part of it." When speculation mounted that Teng Hsiao-p'ing was a likely successor to Mao, reporters looked to Snow for background. Snow had interviewed Teng on his trip to Paoan in 1936.

Fifty years after it was written, *Red Star*, one of four books by Snow in print in English in the mid-1980s, remained a primer on revolutionary China. The State Department listed the book as useful background reading. On his first visit to China as president of the World Bank, A. W. Clausen briefed himself by leafing through the biographies of Chinese leaders at the end of *Red Star*. When she was incarcerated, black radical Angela Davis found it one of a handful of books in the prison library that "held the slightest interest." A Peace Corps worker in the Philippines, who casually picked up the book, found herself dragged into it. The book was not about communism, she thought. It was "about people doing something." In 1978 the Chinese published a new edition of *Red Star*. By 1982, 1.65 million copies had been released. Something as simple as the photograph of Lu Hsun that Snow used in *Living China* remained relevant. The picture, greatly enlarged, hung inside Lu's European-style house, at the end of a short Shanghai lane. Guides eagerly volunteered Snow's connection to the photo.[4]

There was poetic justice in the belated recognition that came Snow's way. And yet it was not wholly a triumph. Snow's renewed popularity edged into the kind of glorification he disliked so much in the personality cults of Mao and others. The Chinese lumped Snow with Agnes Smedley and Anna Louise Strong in the Smedley-Strong-Snow Society, which they shortened to the SSS Society. They issued a postage stamp honoring Snow and put his picture and the Red Army cap he gave Mao in 1936 in the Revolutionary Museum in Peking. In the United States, the University of Missouri-Kansas City conferred an honorary doctorate on Snow in 1983. It started an Edgar Snow Visiting Professor program and pulled together a collection of his papers, which soon commanded the top floor of a campus building. Snow's name and image were invoked to score political points. Under normal circumstances the Chinese, who put much stock in anniversary celebrations, would have staged an elaborate ceremony to mark the tenth anniversary of Nixon's visit and the signing of the Shanghai Communiqué. Irritated in 1982 over the Reagan administration's plans to sell jet fighter planes and military spare parts to Taiwan, the Associated Press observed, the Chinese leadership put its energies into memorializing Snow's death.[5]

Snow, who sought to remain his own man, became a symbol for others to use. In the years after his death, the question that had surfaced in every turn of his career remained: did America understand him or what he wrote? Did they recognize in their shifting attitudes toward him a metaphor for their own inability to understand the forces loose in the world during the twentieth century?

Snow made an extraordinary odyssey from his Missouri boyhood to citizen of the world. It was not just that he witnessed so much history in the making, the dramatic moment of Gandhi's assassination or the long-term processes that brought revolution to Asia. The way he became involved mattered most. Snow left the United States in 1928 utterly idealistic about his country and its values but with no clear political theory or experience behind him. Asia offered that practical education. And he studied in ways that others, who represented businesses, governments, or churches, did not. Unwilling even to tie himself to a news organization, Snow made no compromises for professional reasons. Free to explore as he wished, he came to see unrestrained capitalism the way many Chinese intellectuals did, as imperialism—an evil negating positive American values about independence and economic opportunity. With this and his natural tolerance, Snow developed a capacity to understand how others viewed the world.

Snow became an unusual American breed. The United States had no real experience with thoroughgoing revolutionary upheaval. Americans who led the fight for independence in the eighteenth century did not seek to change the system, only to confirm their ownership of it. American tradition recoiled from violent change. If Americans remained uneasy about expanding their political control overseas, they were not eager to wreck the stability created in Asia and Africa by imperial powers. As James Truslow Adams pointed out in 1930, Americans wrestled with the question of freedom or empire, naturally finding the latter more appealing once they had achieved the former. Snow, in contrast, was nurtured on American rhetoric, educated about the world in countries that yearned for dramatic political, economic, and social change, and had no vested interest to protect. He became an American truly in search of revolution.[6]

It was as Dr. Charles White, his boyhood friend, had said. Ed Snow "had been raised like the rest of us. He just saw more."

Po I-po, who joined the CCP in the mid-1920s and eventually rose to the rank of vice-premier and minister of finance, met Roy Fisher, the dean of the University of Missouri Journalism School, after Snow's death. "We want our journalists to be like Edgar Snow," said Po, who favored reopening Chinese involvement with the journalism school.

It is unlikely that Chinese Communist reporters will soon find it possible to emulate Snow. The press is meant to serve the party, not check its power. Snow provides more attainable lessons for Americans, though the milieu in which he lived has disappeared.[7]

The world is not what it once was for Americans who fancied themselves acting out Richard Halliburton's romantic voyages. Boys like Snow—and young ladies like his first wife, Peg—easily jumped on steamers, as stowaways, as paid deckhands, or as ticketed passengers. Americans ventured forth with a sense of confidence. If the United States wrestled with the notion of exerting global power, it had not yet committed the transgressions of long standing imperial powers like

Great Britain and France. It was not as brutal as the Japanese. The bloody Vietnam War lay half a century in the future.

The cost of living in treaty ports (a pleasant byproduct of imperialism) was low, and payment for freelance articles relatively high.[8] Outlets for articles proliferated. The process of newspaper consolidation, which eventually saw the demise of internationally-minded papers like the *New York Herald Tribune* and the *Chicago Daily News*, had not begun. Magazines like the *Saturday Evening Post*, *Asia*, *Collier's*, *Literary Digest*, *Saturday Review*, *Life*, and *Look*, also doomed to disappear, courted on-the-spot articles analyzing and forecasting foreign events. The corporate world that Snow abhorred and managed to avoid had only begun to work its way on journalism. In a later era a journalist, like any other worker, had to think hard about the risks of living without a company health insurance policy. Snow possessed an uncommon streak of independence. But in the 1920s and 1930s it was much easier for a young man to live comfortably and freely by his wits.

Likewise, the heady days of exhilarating revolution are virtually gone. In the first half of the century national independence movements took shape in every part of the world. In the forty years after World War II those movements succeeded in creating so many new "Third World" countries that membership in the United Nations tripled. In the wake of independence has come a new complex phase of development, marked by consolidation of political and economic power.

Snow's intimate ties to the Chinese Communist revolution will surely remain unique. Some of his complaints about the Nationalists apply also to the Communists. In December 1986 university students paraded through the streets in several cities. Although the causes of the march were not entirely the same as those of patriotic anti-Japanese students in the 1936 December 9th movement, the young people carried some of the same signs calling for freedom of speech, a goal Snow applauded. A big difference between the mid-1930s and the 1980s, however, is the effectiveness with which the Communist regime governs. The Communists, who won because they developed a base among the great mass of the people in a way the Nationalists did not, not only engineered greater advances but exercised greater control over their own citizens as well as over foreign reporters. In 1986 *New York Times* correspondent John Burns set out with two friends on a motorcycle to travel back roads effectively off limits to journalists in north China. For several hundred miles the trio followed the route Snow took fifty years before through Nationalist lines to Paoan. Where Snow had succeeded, however, Burns failed. Chinese authorities apprehended Burns, said he was a spy, and expelled him from the country.[9]

Snow was a man of his time, shaped by contemporary events he followed so intensely. Though he disliked the idea of great leaders dominating their countries, in practice he was attracted to larger-than-life characters like Mao Tse-tung and Franklin Roosevelt who seemed the vanguard of change. Coming of age at a time when fascism loomed as the chief enemy, he saw socialism as a logical answer to poverty and oppression. Although he came to see Stalin's rule "by knout" as itself oppressive, Snow kept faith in the possibilities of socialism. As he noted in *Journey to the Beginning,* "the mere fact that in Russia Socialism did not at once liberate the human spirit no more proved Socialism a failure than the regression of fascist Italy, Japan, Germany and Spain necessarily proved that the freedoms of dissent must inevitably disappear under capitalism." Like his early mentors and fellow Missourians, Tom Millard and J. B. Powell, who became early supporters of the Nationalists, Snow came to identify his hopes with the Communist revolution.[10]

Yet, Snow transcends his times.

Snow was an idealist about his work. "My view," he once told an inquiring Chinese, "is that writing justifies itself if its results add even a very small net contribution to man's knowledge, and I believe that that cannot be done without advancing the interests of the poor and the oppressed of this world, who are the 'vast majority' of men." Snow was also a realist. In a passage buried in *Journey to the Beginning,* he explained the practical importance of understanding the interests of the poor and oppressed. Many overseas Americans, Snow recalled of his days in the treaty ports, emphasized their own "hard interests" to the exclusion of all others. "The attempt to discover what the 'soft interests' of other people really are, how they feel and think about their own problems and their place in the world, seemed to me mandatory if we were to have any notion of the direction history was taking toward that compromise which we call world society, not to say peace." Snow proved that idealism and realism were not irreconcilable opposites. How well people ate and the importance people attached to attaining independence—these became the barometer by which he was able to forecast history.[11]

Similarly Snow's extraordinary rapport with the Chinese, and the resulting insights into their thinking, sprang from his humanism. One Chinese, who contributed a short story to *Living China,* recalled the modesty with which Snow described his role in assembling the volume. "At a time when most foreigners treated us as cows that could produce milk for them, Snow took us as equal partners who co-operated with him for the cause."[12]

Whatever his sympathies, Snow was above all a journalist. While many visitors came to countries like Communist China in search of Utopia, Snow arrived with hardheaded questions. If he reined in his skepticism in the 1960s to counter hysterical negative American publicity about the Chinese, he did not fall into the trap that so many naive souls did. While others judged the country by the special treatment they received, Snow disdained privilege. Significantly in his last book, he tried to temper the new wave of good will that began to surface as a result of the rediscovery of the hospitable Chinese. He had little patience for those who dwelt on doctrine. His quarrel with Asiaticus and others on the Left after publication of *Red Star* was that they did not understand that the Chinese Communists could be social revolutionaries without mimicking Soviet policies and that ideological purity was unimportant compared with establishing a united front against Japan. As much as Snow disliked British imperialism, he urged Gandhi to accommodate it in order to strengthen anti-Japanese resistance. For good reason Chinese Communists said he was a reliable reporter but not to be trusted as an interpreter of Chinese communism. Snow was too independent.[13]

Many of Snow's insights, considered treason after World War II, are as valuable today as when he first voiced them. He wisely argued that the only sensible policies toward the Soviet Union lay in finding and exploiting common interests, rather than in pursuing the chimera of overwhelming military superiority. Though not widely embraced today, this approach finds its way into "new" strategies for coping with East-West tensions. Snow also realized that military might was not the answer to defeating Communist influence in the Third World; the answer was to support policies that squared with Third World desire for economic and political independence. He understood the internal causes of discontent in developing countries. Snow observed in the 1940s, for example, that land reform was an indispensable prerequisite to stemming Philippine domestic insurgency. The Philippine Catholic Bishops' Conference stated in July 1987, "today we are in danger of being torn apart as a nation on the problem of land reform." Snow was no less acute in understanding the problems that lay before China.[14]

After their War of Independence, one historian has noted, "Americans could have made almost any constitution work."[15] With open spaces, virtually unlimited resources, and little tradition to hold them back, Americans had room to maneuver. Compromises came easily. China, in contrast, often seems like a country in which almost no government can work. The burgeoning population presses down on resources that are already vastly oversubscribed. China's ancient social, economic, and political achievements have become liabilities. Mao and Teng Hsiao-p'ing, men often seen as different, have faced the same problem of how to overcome bureaucratic traditions that hamper modern development.

From the vantage point of his earlier experience in China, Snow recognized the magnitude of Communist progress after 1949. Having seen how far the Communists had come he sometimes exaggerated how quickly they would advance in the future. On the eve of the Great Proletarian Cultural Revolution, which debilitated the Chinese educational system, he erroneously predicted that by 1986 "Chinese youth will have reached an average level of scientific education, cultural and physical fitness hardly inferior to any in the world." Even so, Snow accurately stressed that China was a poor nation; that while it would not abandon its Marxist-Leninist goals, its course was not yet certain. He understood the tension between what Mao called the peasant's "spontaneous desire to become a capitalist" and the regime's need to ensure equity, a goal that stood at the center of the Communists' legitimacy. Wrote Snow, "the road is long and the road is hard, and must be covered in stages. There will be more cultural revolutions to come."[16]

Snow distinguished himself from many Americans in recognizing that the United States enjoyed exceptional advantages that did not apply abroad. He did not believe that other countries could copy the United States any more than they should emulate the Soviet Union. China and others had to find their own way. But the belief that truth did not lie on one side of the river, as Snow liked to say, did not stop him from believing in American superiority in another way. The extraordinary conditions that gave rise to the United States, he thought, should also produce a people more tolerant than others, more magnanimous. Though complaining that he failed to reach the American public with more enlightened policies, let alone with facts, he always wrote as if he could make a difference. While others wisely let criticism or misstatements pass, Snow labored to keep the record straight in wasted letters to the editor, which often highlighted the problem more. "Perhaps," contemporary writer Emily Hahn observed of Snow, "he was incurably earnest."[17]

The irony in the years after Snow's death was that while Americans sometimes talked, as the *Kansas City Star* did in 1979, of righting "some of the wrongs against a courageous writer who wanted what was best for both America and China—peace and friendship," Snow's ideas were out of step with the country.[18] Americans exalted themselves without displaying tolerance toward others. As much as anything they seemed nostalgic for an earlier era when the United States could distance itself from the rest of the world or, if necessary, impose its will forcefully. Leaders lamented the loss of bipartisan agreement on foreign policy without recalling how misguided the one-dimensional postwar anti-Communist consensus had been. Americans continued to see developing countries in Latin America, Africa, and Asia as a murky collection of poor, backward nations. Instead of realistically appraising Third World hopes and aspirations, or the impact their progress would have on the United States economically and politically, American leaders viewed the "South," as these countries were often called, as an East-West battleground.

Visions of Communist China fell into an old pattern. Snow's warning, shortly before he died, of the dangers of recreating the old agrarian reform myth had little meaning for many Americans. The upsurge in warm feelings about China after the Nixon visit in 1972 had another lift when Mao's successor, Teng Hsiao-p'ing, sought to free entrepreneurial forces in the country. Reports about the new reforms drowned out information about aspects of China that had not changed, leaving the impression that China was exchanging the quotations of Chairman Mao for Adam Smith's free market maxims. Hankering as in the past for their friends to become like them, Americans often did not see the fine print showing the government's continued dominance over intellectual and economic activity. Too little was made of Teng's insistence that the Chinese system "is better than the capitalist system" or that "we certainly cannot allow our young people to be corrupted by capitalist thinking." Violently anti-Communist President Ronald Reagan, who confessed to having little time to read about China before his 1984 visit, spoke en route to Peking of "so called Communist China," virtually the same term Franklin Roosevelt and Patrick Hurley had used forty years before.[19]

Long after Snow's death, the United States had yet to pass a crucial test. It had achieved great wealth and power and, despite grotesque episodes like the Red Scare in the 1950s, enviable civil liberties. But could it learn to help others prosper and to apply its ideals in such a way that other countries would rally around them? Could Americans come to understand other countries' perspectives, to anticipate their actions, to work together with them? Or would Americans only see the world through the prism of their hopes and fears, and try clumsily to impose their will unilaterally? If Americans could not retrace Snow's odyssey, could they begin to learn, as Snow did, to see more?

Notes

American research on Edgar Snow has not begun to approach the historical significance or drama of his life. To some extent that may be a function of circumstance and personality. John Reed, with whom Snow is misleadingly compared, was a flamboyant figure who, because he died early, was easily mythologized, especially during the 1930s when the Left was strong in the United States. Snow, a serious journalist whose life spanned six and one-half decades, died on the eve of what has become a conservative revival. Under any circumstances, however, he would be a difficult person to classify in America. For that reason he offers scholars a broad field of inquiry.

Edgar Snow is a good guide to himself. As a writer, he recorded in books and long articles, as well as in newspaper accounts, what he saw. In the fashion of his time, he practiced "personal history" journalism, putting himself in the narrative. At its best, however, "personal history" journalism is not so much personal as reportorial—an I-was-there technique that creates readable and honest reporting. Snow, who mastered the technique, was casual about the details of his life, which he often telescoped into a few lines. In his one attempt at autobiography, *Journey to the Beginning*, Snow conveyed essential truths about himself. But the book aimed chiefly to examine the events Snow covered and, in any event, stopped at the late 1940s.

Among the secondary sources helpful in learning about Edgar Snow is Lois Wheeler Snow's chrestomanthy of his pre-1949 reporting, *Edgar Snow's China*, and her moving account of his last days, *A Death with Dignity*. Helen Foster Snow made Snow a center of attraction in her autobiographical account, *My China Years*. A useful collection of views on Snow is found in Wang Xing, ed., *China Remembers Edgar Snow* (Beijing Review, 1982).

Three good essays by personal friends of Snow are: John S. Service's "Edgar Snow: Some Personal Reminiscences," in the *China Quarterly*, and John Fairbank's "Edgar Snow in Red China," in *China: The*

People's Middle Kingdom and the U.S.A. (Belknap Press, Harvard, 1970), and "Edgar Snow," in *China Perceived: Images and Policies in Chinese American Relations* (Knopf, 1974). Jerry Israel, " 'Mao's Mr. America': Edgar Snow's Images," is an often insightful essay (*Pacific Historical Review* 47 [February 1978] :107–22). Among unpublished scholarly works, there are two theses: Robert O. Boorstin's "Edgar Snow and America's Search for a Better China: The Making of *Red Star over China*, 1928–1938" (B.A. thesis, Harvard University, 1981) and Bruce R. Erickson's "The Reporting of Edgar Snow" (M.S. thesis, University of Kansas, 1976). All of the above contributions have informed this biography. In addition to this book, I have written several articles on Snow and discussed part of his life in my doctoral dissertation. In the cases where those pieces have something to offer beyond this book, I have cited them in the notes, below.

Regarding the notes, I have wanted, on the one hand, to give readers a good guide to the sources used in this biography and, on the other, to avoid cluttering the book with notes every inch or so. The compromise has been, to a large extent, to organize notes around issues as they arise in the narrative. For this reason the reader will find that individual notes often contain references for several quotes in the text as well as for background used in drawing conclusions.

Research for this book involved extensive use of manuscript collections. Personal small holdings from which I have drawn are cited individually in the notes. Below are listed the major collections, with abbreviated citations in parentheses for those papers used most frequently:

Anna Louise Strong Papers, Suzzallo Library, University of Washington, Seattle, Wash.

U.S. Department of State Records, National Archives, Washington, D.C. (DOS).

Edgar Snow Collection, University Archives, University of Missouri-Kansas City, Mo. (ESC).

Edgar Snow file, Federal Bureau of Investigation, Washington, D.C. (FBI).

Franklin D. Roosevelt Library, Hyde Park, N.Y. (FDRL).

Grenville Clark Papers, Baker Library, Dartmouth College, Hanover, N.H. (GCP).

Harry S Truman Library, Independence, Mo. (HSTL).

Joseph W. and Stewart Alsop Papers, Manuscript Division, Library of Congress, Washington, D.C. (JSAP).

Nelson T. Johnson Papers, Manuscript Division, Library of Congress, Washington, D.C. (NJP).

Nym Wales Papers, Hoover Institution on War, Revolution, and Peace, Stanford University, Palo Alto, Calif. (NWP).

Patrick J. Hurley Papers, University of Oklahoma Library, Norman, Okla.

Philip Jaffe Papers, The Robert Woodruff Library for Advanced Studies, Emory University, Atlanta, Ga. (PJP).

Random House Papers, Butler Library, Columbia University, New York, N.Y. (RHP).

Raymond Gram Swing Papers, Manuscript Division, Library of Congress, Washington, D.C.

Stanley Hornbeck Papers, Hoover Institution on War, Revolution, and Peace, Stanford University, Palo Alto, Calif. (SHP).

Charles Hanson Towne Papers, Manuscript Division, New York Public Library, New York, N.Y. (CHT).

Youth: An Introduction

1. Interviews with Charles White.

2. John K. Fairbank, Introduction to Edgar Snow, *Random Notes on Red China, 1936–1945* (East Asian Research Center, 1967), v; Warren I. Cohen, *America's Response to China: An Interpretive History of Sino-American Relations*, 2d ed. (Knopf, 1980), 256. For similar views see Fairbank in "Edgar Snow in Red China," *China: The People's Middle Kingdom and the U.S.A.* (Belknap Press, Harvard, 1967), 83; and Owen Lattimore, Introduction to Jack Belden, *China Shakes the World* (Monthly Review Press, 1970), xv.

3. Interview with Maxwell Geismar.

4. Louis Francis Budenz, "The Menace of Red China," *Collier's*, March 19, 1949, 23.

5. Mary Heathcote, "Edgar Snow: 1905–1972," *University Review* 23 (1972):39.

6. Ronald Steel, *Walter Lippmann and the American Century* (Vintage, 1981), 198; Granville Hicks, *John Reed: The Making of a Revolutionary* (Macmillan, 1936), 70–71; Edgar Snow, *Journey to the Beginning: A Personal View of Contemporary History* (Random House, 1958), 13–14. Interviews with Robert Fuoss, Howard Snow, Lois W. Snow, Mildred Snow Mackey, and Harrison Salisbury.

7. Heathcote, "Edgar Snow," 38.

8. On Missouri and Kansas City see: Franklin D. Mitchell, *Embattled Democracy: Missouri Democratic Politics, 1919–1932* (University of Missouri Press, 1968), 1, 6; Lyle W. Dorsett, *The Pendergast Machine* (Oxford University Press, 1968), 4, 86; *Kansas City Star*, July 23, 1905; Lewis E. Atherton, *Main Street on the Middle Border* (Indiana University Press, 1954), 22, 332; S. H. Wainwright, "Missourians in Japan," *Missouri Historical Review* 15 (April 1921):468; Paul C. Nagel, *Missouri: A Bicentennial History* (Norton, 1977), 81–84, 103; and Henry C. Haskell and Richard B. Fowler, *City of the Future: A Narrative History of Kansas City, 1850–1950* (Frank Glenn Publishing, 1950), 100.

9. Snow wrote about his family and youth in Snow, *Journey*, 11–15, 25; Edgar Snow, "The Heir to Confucius' Name and Fame," *Asia*, Oct. 1930, 179; Edgar Snow, "Missouri Days," unpublished chapter from *Journey*, located in Random House Papers, Butler Library, Columbia University, New York, N.Y.,

hereafter referred to as RHP (sections of this chapter appeared in John T. Alexander, *Kansas City Star*, Oct. 6, 1958); Edgar Snow, "Autobiographical Note," typescript, undated, Edgar Snow Collection, University Archives, University of Missouri-Kansas City, Mo., hereafter cited ESC. On Samuel Snow as ancestor see Edgar Snow correspondence with Eleanor Babcock, Sept. 1, 1951; July 3, 1952; and March 27, 1953, ESC. Also helpful were interviews with Lois W. Snow, Mildred Snow Mackey, Howard Snow, Claude Mackey, Kay Edelman Lyon, and Charles White. *The Classified Buyer's Guide of the City of Kansas City, 1920* lists an Edelman & Fleming Construction Co. Snow spelled his mother's maiden name with two "n"s; he also refers to his grandfather as Harry Edward Edelmann.

10. J. E. Snow, "The College Bred vs. the Self-Educated Man," typescript, Burden, Kansas, Sept, 12, 1893, ESC.

11. Lucy Smoot quote found in a history she wrote of the school, located in ESC. Katherine Edelman, *Shamrocks and Prairie Grass* (Frank Glenn Publishing, 1954).

12. On Boy Scouts, Judson Compton, Associate Director, Public Relations, Boy Scouts of America, to author, July 20 and 31, 1981. Interviews with Mildred Snow Mackey, Howard Snow, and Lois W. Snow.

13. Information on Snow's grades in E. F. Krekel, Dean of Students, Penn Valley Community College, to author, July 8, 1981.

14. The Laski book with Snow's notation is located in the library of Dorothy Salisbury Davis, Snedens Landing, N.Y. Yearbook located ESC. Interview with Kashen Wheeler, Snow's sister-in-law, who thought he was born reading Twain.

15. Details of trip west drawn from: Interviews with Charles White and Robert Long; Snow, *Journey*, 28–29; Snow, "Missouri Days." Snow calculated his age as fourteen at the time. This is almost certainly incorrect given both the details recalled by White and Long and their corroboration in the press during 1922.

16. Robert D. Townsend, "One Law for All," *Outlook*, Sept. 6, 1922, 12–14.

17. Halliburton's Kansas City travel companion was Irvine Hockaday; Richard Halliburton, *The Royal Road to Romance* (Bobbs-Merrill, 1925), 398. Interview with Robert Long.

18. Edgar Snow's Columbia University grades are on file at ESC. Useful background on Snow's time at the University of Missouri found in Edgar Snow to Albert S. Keshen, July 2, 1959, possession of author.

19. John Maxwell Hamilton,"The Missouri News Monopoly and American Altruism in China: Thomas F. F. Millard, J. B. Powell, and Edgar Snow," *Pacific Historical Review* 55 (Feb. 1986):27–48. Also, J. B. Powell, "Missourians in China," *Missouri Historical Review* 15 (July 1921):611–16; J. B. Powell, "Missouri Authors and Journalists in the Orient," ibid. 41 (Oct. 1946):45–51; Wainwright, "Missourians in Japan," ibid. 15 (April 1921):468–86; William H. Taft, "Walter Williams: 'International Journalist,' " *Journalism Quarterly* 36 (Spring 1959):151–57; unpublished, untitled manuscript by Maurice Votaw, copy in possession of author.

20. University of Missouri academic records, University of Missouri journalism school.

21. Otis Pease, *Responsibilities of American Advertising: Private Control and Public Influence, 1920–1940* (Yale University Press, 1958), 11.

22. Interview with Howard Snow; Howard Snow to author, Oct. 1981. Spur tie ad in *Saturday Evening Post*, March 19, 1927, 127.

23. Charles Hanson Towne, *So Far So Good* (Julian Messner, 1945), 207. Towne obit, *New York Times*, March 1, 1949.

24. Edgar Snow to J. E. Snow, Oct. 3, 1927, ESC; Graham obit, *New York Times*, May 6, 1962.

25. Edgar Snow to J. E. Snow, March 2, 1927, and Oct. 3, 1927; to parents, Jan. 9, 1928; and to Mildred Snow Mackey, Aug. 8, 1926, ESC.

26. Edgar Snow to Anna and J. E. Snow, Feb. 1928, ESC.

27. Sara Mullin Baldwin, ed., *Who's Who in Kansas City* (Robert M. Baldwin, 1930), 118.

One: Adventure Bound

1. Harold R. Isaacs, *Scratches on Our Minds: American Images of China and India* (John Day, 1958), 71; Robert Dallek, *The American Style of Foreign Policy: Cultural Politics and Foreign Affairs* (Knopf, 1983), 47–48; William Appleman Williams, *The Tragedy of American Diplomacy*, 2d rev. ed. (Dell, 1972), 34; James C. Thomson, Jr., Peter W. Stanley, and John Curtis Perry, *Sentimental Imperialists: The American Experience in East Asia* (Harper & Row, 1982), 102, 148; Cohen, *America's Response*, 128; Halliburton, *The Royal Road*, 352. On press coverage see Mordechai Rozanski, "The Role of American Journalists in Chinese-American Relations, 1900–1925" (Ph.D. diss., University of Pennsylvania, 1974), 376. For a masterly study of the period see Paul Varg, *The Making of a Myth: The United States and China: 1897–1912* (Michigan State University Press, 1968).

2. For a discussion of the trip from New York to Hawaii see Edgar Snow to Charles Hanson Towne, March 7, 1928, Charles Hanson Towne Papers, Manuscript Division, New York Public Library, New York, N.Y., hereafter referred to as CHT. Edgar Snow to Howard Snow, March 26 and April 5, 1928; to Anna Snow, May 11, 1928; to J. E. Snow, May 23, 1928, ESC. Edgar Snow, "In Hula Land: A Record of a Trip to the Hawaiian Islands," *Harper's Bazaar*, Sept. 1928, 98–99.

3. Details of the stowaway story and trip to China from: Edgar Snow, *Kansas City Journal Post*, Nov. 11, 1928. Edgar Snow to Charles Hanson Towne, June 26, 1928, CHT. Edgar Snow to parents, June 29 and July 9, 1928; to Al Joslin, June 21, 1928, ESC; interview with Howard Snow. In his *Journal Post* article, "Kansas City Boy Stowaway," Snow changed his companion's name to Dan Hopkins to protect him from possible recrimination.

4. For background on Millard's life see Hamilton, "The Missouri News Monopoly," 30–35; Rozanski, "American Journalists," 36–37, 91; Millard obit, *New York Times*, Sept. 9, 1942.

5. Thomas F. Millard in the *New York Times*, June 21, 1908, as quoted in Jerry Israel, *Progressivism and the Open Door: America and China, 1905–1921* (University of Pittsburgh Press, 1971), 39. For similar statements see Millard, *America and the Far Eastern Question* (Moffat, Yard, 1909), 353–62.

6. John B. Powell, *My Twenty-Five Years in China* (Macmillan, 1945), 11; John W. Powell, "My Father's Library," *Wilson Library Bulletin* 60 (March 1986):36; Hamilton, "The Missouri News Monopoly," 35–41; interviews with Elizabeth Hart Woo, Helen F. Snow, F. McCracken Fisher, and especially John W. Powell, J. B. Powell's son. Powell's contemporary comments on China found in J. B. Powell, "The Open Door Is the Monroe Doctrine," *Chinese Students Monthly*, reprinted in *China Weekly Review*, Nov. 5, 1921; *China Weekly Review*, April 30, 1927.

7. Sterling Seagrave, *The Soong Dynasty* (Harper & Row, 1985), chapter 10.

8. For Snow's initial impressions of China and work on the supplement see Edgar Snow to parents, July 9 and July 28, 1928; to J. E. Snow, Aug. 15,

1928, ESC. Interview with Robert W. Barnett. Snow, *Journey*, 4. For example of *Kansas City Star* similarities to *China Weekly Review*, see issue that appeared on Snow's fifth birthday, July 19, 1910.

9. Snow's early travels in China found in Edgar Snow, *China Weekly Review*, Jan. 12 and Jan. 19, 1929. Edgar Snow to Howard Snow, Jan. 17, 1929; Anna Snow to Edgar Snow, Jan. 26, 1929, ESC. Regarding Batson's career see Alfred Batson, *Vagabond's Paradise* (Little, Brown, 1931).

10. The series, by Snow and S. Y. Hu, appeared in the *China Weekly Review* on May 18, Aug. 10, and Nov. 9, 1929, and April 5, 1930; Edgar Snow, *China Weekly Review*, July 20, 1929.

11. Edgar Snow, *China Weekly Review*, Jan. 19, 1929; Edgar Snow, "The Summit of Eternity," *Travel*, March 1930, 17. Edgar Snow to Anna Snow, May 5, 1929, ESC.

12. Edgar Snow, *China Weekly Review*, Aug. 3, 1929; Edgar Snow, *Kansas City Journal Post*, Sept. 11, 1929; Snow, *Journey*, 8.

13. John W. Powell to author, April 18, 1974; Snow, *Journey*, 15; John M. Allison, *Ambassador from the Prairie: Or Allison Wonderland* (Houghton Mifflin, 1973), 9–10; Edgar Snow, *China Weekly Review*, July 13, 1929.

14. Edgar Snow to Howard Snow, Feb. 21, 1929, and to J. E. Snow, April 11, 1930, ESC. Edgar Snow, "Adventures in Chinese Advertising," *Advertising and Selling*, May 1, 1929, 30; Edgar Snow, "Opium," *Liberty*, May 10, 1930, 61.

15. For Snow's political views on China see: Snow, *China Weekly Review*, August 3, 1929; Snow, *Journey*, 10, 26; Edgar Snow, "The Strength of Communism in China—The Bolshevist Influence," *Current History*, Jan. 1931, 523; Edgar Snow, *New York Herald Tribune*, March 16, 1930, and *Kansas City Journal Post*, March 16, 1930. Edgar Snow to J. E. Snow, March 21, 1929; to "family," Aug. 18, 1929; to Anna Snow, Jan. 7, 1930 (misdated as 1929); to Howard Snow, Jan. 13, 1930, ESC.

16. Edgar Snow to J. E. Snow, April 11, 1930, ESC.

17. From diary entry quoted in Lois Wheeler Snow, *Edgar Snow's China* (Random House, 1981), 47; Edgar Snow to Anna Snow, Jan. 7, 1930, ESC.

18. *China Weekly Review*, Nov. 9, 1929; *North China Daily News*, Nov. 12 and 13, 1929; *China Weekly Review*, Nov. 16, 1929; Snow, *Journey*, 25; interview with John W. Powell.

19. Edgar Snow to Howard Snow, May 3, 1929, and June 3, 1930; to Anna Snow, Nov. 22, 1929; to "family," Dec. 2, 1929; and to J. E. Snow, Dec. 13, 1929, ESC. Snow, *Journey*, 31–33.

20. Interview with Lois W. Snow. J. E. Snow to Edgar Snow, May 12, 1930, ESC.

21. Edgar Snow to Howard Snow, May 17 and June 3, 1930, ESC.

22. Edgar Snow, "The Americans in Shanghai," *American Mercury*, Aug. 1930, 437–45; Randall Gould to Donald Gillin, Aug. 16, 1975, Donald Gillin files; British comment on Snow's article by Sir Arthur Willert, Sept. 2, 1930, FO 311/14746 63732, British Public Records Office, Kew Gardens, England.

23. On the first leg of Snow's Asia trip: Horace Epes to Edgar Snow, Aug. 20, 1930; Edgar Snow to J. E. Snow, Dec. 8, 1930, ESC. S. B. Sutton, *In China's Border Provinces* (Hastings House, 1974), 111–12, 211–12; Snow, *Journey*, 38–39, 52–53; *China Weekly Review*, Dec. 6, 1930; Jan. 17, 1931. Letter to Walsh quoted in L. Snow, *Edgar Snow's China*, 44. S. B. Sutton to author, March 26, 1981.

24. Edgar Snow, New York *Sun*, Oct. 20, 1931; Snow, *Journey*, 62.

25. Edgar Snow, New York *Sun*, June 16, July 2, and Sept. 15, 1931; and April 9, 1932. Edgar Snow, *China Weekly Review*, Nov. 1, Nov. 8, Nov. 15, 1930—all reprints from Consolidated Press dispatches. Edgar Snow, "Japan Imposes Her Culture," *Asia*, April 1935, 219–20. For background see Snow, *Journey*, 41-

46. For another example of face slapping see Theodore White, *In Search of History: A Personal Adventure* (Harper & Row, 1978), 106.

26. On Snow's India experience: Edgar Snow to Mildred Snow Mackey, May 29, 1931; to J. E. Snow, June 13 and Aug. 5, 1931; to Horace Epes, Aug. 5, 1931, ESC. Steve MacKinnon to author, Nov. 20, 1981. Edgar Snow, New York *Sun*, June 10, 1931; Edgar Snow, *China Weekly Review*, July 25 and Sept. 19, 1931; Edgar Snow, *Kansas City Journal Post*, Nov. 1, 1931; Snow, *Journey*, 76–79; William Shirer, *Gandhi: A Memoir* (Simon & Schuster, 1979), 226–27.

27. Edgar Snow to Charles Hanson Towne, Aug. 6, 1931, CHT; Randall Gould to Donald Gillin, Aug. 16, 1975. According to Gould, Snow told him the *Chichibu Maru* story years later.

Two: The Second Act

1. Details of Snow's attitude on returning to China: Edgar Snow to Howard Snow, March 26, 1928, and Oct. 27, 1932, ESC. Edgar Snow to Charles Hanson Towne, Aug. 6, 1931, CHT.

2. Lloyd E. Eastman, *The Abortive Revolution: China under Nationalist Rule, 1927–1937* (Harvard University Press, 1974), 214–16; Hung-Mao Tien, *Government and Politics in Kuomintang China* (Stanford University Press, 1972), 6; Barbara W. Tuchman, *Stilwell and the American Experience in China, 1911–45* (Macmillan, 1971), 131–33; Edgar Snow, *Far Eastern Front* (Smith & Haas, 1933), 155.

3. Edgar Snow, *New York Herald Tribune*, Dec. 6, 1931, reprinted in *China Weekly Review*, Jan. 23, 1932; Eastman, *Revolution*, 188.

4. On Japanese advances on North China: Edgar Snow to Howard Snow, Dec. 7, 1931, ESC. Snow, *Far Eastern Front*, 94, 121–28, 187–90; Tuchman, *Stilwell*, 131–34.

5. On Japanese attack on Shanghai: Snow, New York *Sun*, Jan. 25, 26, 27, 28, and 29, 1932, and Feb. 1, 5, 19, and 27, 1932; Snow, *Far Eastern Front*, 227–30, 240–41; Snow, *Journey*, 95–105; Tuchman, *Stilwell*, 136.

6. Snow, *Far Eastern Front*, 91; Snow, New York *Sun*, Jan. 25 and 26, 1932.

7. Edgar Snow, New York *Sun*, Oct. 18, 1932; Edgar Snow, *New York Herald Tribune*, Aug. 6, 1933; Snow, *Journey*, 84–95; Jung Chang with Jon Halliday, *Mme. Sun Yat-sen* (Penguin, 1986), 140.

8. Snow, *Far Eastern Front*, 291–92; Jerome B. Grieder, *Hu Shih and the Chinese Renaissance: Liberalism in the Chinese Revolution, 1927–1937* (Harvard University Press, 1970), 272–79.

9. Foreign Editor, London *Daily Herald*, to Edgar Snow, Feb. 9, 1932, ESC.

10. For details on Snow's labors on this book see Edgar Snow to Howard Snow, March 2 and May 17, 1932, and to Howard and Dorothy Snow, undated (probably July 1932), ESC. For discussion of his evolving political views see Snow, *Far Eastern Front*, 156–62, 164–66, 328–30; Edgar Snow to Mildred Snow Mackey, March 31, 1932, ESC. For an example of his daily reporting on KMT Fascist organizations see Edgar Snow, New York *Sun*, Sept. 30, 1932. On the Nationalists' road building success, C. P. Fitzgerald, *The Birth of Communist China* (Penguin, 1966), 76.

11. Snow, *Far Eastern Front*, 319, 324–25; Edgar Snow, "The Decline of Western Prestige," *Saturday Evening Post*, Aug. 26, 1933, 67, based on last chapter of *Far Eastern Front*.

12. Gertrude H. Applebaum to author, March 11, 1981. Applebaum worked for Snow's agent. Helen F. Snow disagrees that the book met with numerous

rejections before being published, Helen F. Snow to author, no date. Bennett A. Cerf, "A Matter of Timing," *Publisher's Weekly*, Feb. 12, 1938. Edgar Snow to Howard Snow, Sept. 6, 1933; to Mrs. William Brown Meloney, June 1, 1933; to Horace Epes, April 25, 1935, ESC. Edgar Snow to Charles Hanson Towne, Nov. 21, 1933, CHT.

13. O. L. (probably Owen Lattimore), "Far Eastern Front," *Saturday Review of Literature*, Nov. 25, 1933, 298; Herbert O'Keef, Charlotte, N.C. *News*, Oct. 29, 1933. On correspondents' reaction, interview with A. T. Steele.

14. On American attitudes: Charles A. Beard and Mary R. Beard, *America in Midpassage*, vol. 1 (Macmillan, 1939), 107–8; Gerald W. Johnson, "The Average American and the Depression," *Current History*, Feb. 1932, 671–75; Frank W. Warren, *Liberals and Communists* (Indiana University Press, 1966), 32–33; Joseph Barnes, ed., *Empire in the East* (Doubleday, 1934), v; *Cong. Rec.*, 93d Cong., 2d sess., March 22, 1934, 78, pt. 5:5104; Robert Aura Smith, *New York Times*, April 22, 1934; Justus D. Doenecke, *When the Wicked Rise: American Opinion-Makers and the Manchurian Crisis of 1931–1933* (Bucknell University Press, 1984), 48-49, 55, 65-66, 115; Rozanski, "American Journalists," 376; Frank Luther Mott, *American Journalism: A History of Newspapers in the United States* (Macmillan, 1947), 705; Randall Gould, *China in the Sun* (Doubleday, 1946), 179.

15. Edgar Snow to J. E. Snow, Jan. 2, 1931, ESC. *Kansas City Star*, Jan. 29, 1932.

16. Doenecke, *When the Wicked Rise*, 112–13; John Gunther, *Inside Asia* (Harper & Row, 1939), 116.

17. Interview with Helen F. Snow.

18. On Snow's bachelor life, Edgar Snow to Mildred Snow Mackey, March 31, 1932; to Dorothy Snow (Howard's wife), March 30, 1931, ESC.

19. For background on Helen F. Snow and marriage: Snow, *Journey*, 102–9; Edgar Snow, "Christmas Escapade in Japan," *Travel*, Jan. 1935, 34–47; Allison, *Ambassador*, 17–18; Helen Foster Snow, *My China Years* (Morrow, 1984), 19–81 *passim*, 292; interviews with Helen F. Snow; Edgar Snow to J. E. Snow, Jan. 2, 1941, ESC. Edgar Snow to Charles Hanson Towne, March 30, 1933, CHT.

20. For details on life in Peking see Graham Peck, *Through China's Wall* (Houghton Mifflin, 1940), 16–26; Michael Blankfort, *The Big Yankee* (Little, Brown, 1947), 167; O. L., "Conquering the Gobi," *Saturday Review of Literature*, Nov. 25, 1933; Sven Hedin, *The Silk Road* (Dutton, 1938); Helen Snow, "Teilhard de Chardin in Peking," undated, Madison, Conn., Helen F. Snow files; interviews with Helen F. Snow, Harry Price, and F. McCracken Fisher. Edgar Snow to Charles Hanson Towne, March 30, 1933, CHT. H. Snow, *My China Years*, 93, 107.

21. Snow, *Journey*, 123–26, 147–48; "Keeping Posted," *Saturday Evening Post*, Aug. 19, 1944, 4. Edgar Snow to Charles Hanson Towne, March 30 and Nov. 10, 1933, CHT. Edgar Snow to Horace Epes, Dec. 9, 1933; to Col. Frank Knox, May 2, 1935, ESC.

22. On reading habits, Edgar Snow to Howard Snow, March 2, 1932, and Feb. 16, 1933, ESC. On George Bernard Shaw, Edgar Snow to J. E. Snow, Feb. 16, 1933, ESC; and Snow, *Journey*, 107, 138.

23. This talk can be found in Edgar Snow, "The Meaning of Fascism," *Peiping Chronicle*, Jan. 8, 9, 10, 11, and 12, 1935. Snow, *Journey*, 137–38; interview with Helen F. Snow; Edgar Snow to Howard Snow, March 2, 1932, ESC.

24. On Snow's work with Chinese writers: Edgar Snow, *Living China* (John Day, 1937; reprint, Hyperion, 1973), 15–16; Edgar Snow, "Lu Hsun: Master of Pai-Hua," *Asia*, Jan. 1935, 40–43. Edgar Snow to Howard Snow, March 2, 1932; Feb 25, 1933; and Sept. 6, 1933, ESC. Interview with Helen F. Snow.

25. Henriette Herz to Edgar Snow, Nov. 13, 1936, Nym Wales Papers, Hoover Institution on War, Revolution, and Peace, Stanford University, Palo Alto, Calif., hereafter cited as NWP. Also Nym Wales (Helen F. Snow), *Notes on the Sian Incident* (mimeographed, n.d.), 169–71; interview with John S. Service.

26. Edgar Snow to Nelson T. Johnson, Feb. 6, 1937, Nelson T. Johnson Papers, Manuscript Division, Library of Congress, Washington, D.C., hereafter cited NJP. For a good discussion of Nationalists pushing writers to Left see Harriet C. Mills, "Lu Hsun and the Communist Party," *China Quarterly* 4 (Oct.-Dec. 1960):17.

27. Snow's early troubles with Red baiting in Snow, *Journey*, 23, 80–81. Snow's "radical" activities listed in undated summary of Shanghai Municipal Police reports, Edgar Snow file, Federal Bureau of Investigation, Washington, D.C., hereafter cited as FBI.

28. On Johnson: Snow, *Far Eastern Front*, 304; Russell D. Buhite, *Nelson T. Johnson and American Policy Toward China: 1925–1941* (Michigan State University Press, 1968), 1–16, 27.

29. Details of episode in memorandum of conversation by Nelson T. Johnson, July 5, 1933, NJP.

30. Interview with Helen F. Snow.

31. Edgar Snow, "The Ways of the Chinese Censor," *Current History*, July 1935, 381–86; Edgar Snow, "Weak China's Strongman," *Current History*, Jan. 1934, 402–8; Eastman, *Abortive Revolution*, 25–30; Hallett Abend, *My Life in China: 1926–1941* (Harcourt, Brace, 1943), 103–4. Additional background found in Lin Yutang, *A History of the Press and Public Opinion in China* (University of Chicago Press, 1936). Snow corresponded with Lin about censorship issues, Edgar Snow to Lin Yutang, March 29, 1936, ESC.

32. Edgar Snow to Howard Snow, July 20, 1935, ESC.

33. On personality, interview with John S. Service; Helen F. Snow to author, Dec. 23, 1973. On Yenching and Snow's relations with students: Philip West, *Yenching University and Sino-Western Relations, 1906–1952* (Harvard University Press, 1976), 91–92; Xiao Qian, "A Talk on Edgar Snow," delivered Feb. 1982, author's files; Liang Shichun, "Edgar Snow's Vision," *China Reconstructs*, May 1979, 23–24; and "Concerning Edgar Snow," note to author from Liang, Oct. 19, 1974; interviews with Helen F. Snow and Randolph Sailor, a politically interested member of the faculty.

34. Edgar Snow to Charles Hanson Towne, July 19, 1935, CHT. Edgar Snow, "Japan Digs In," *Saturday Evening Post*, Jan. 4, 1936, 58. For related articles see Edgar Snow, "Japan Builds a New Colony," *Saturday Evening Post*, Feb. 24, 1934, 12.

35. Details on Snow's involvement with December 9th student movement from: Snow, *Journey*, 139–46; Nym Wales (Helen F. Snow), *Notes on the Chinese Student Movement, 1935–1936* (mimeographed, 1959), *passim* but especially 172 and 194; John Israel and Donald W. Klein, *Rebels and Bureaucrats: China's December 9ers* (University of California Press, 1976), 31–50; Ch'en Han-p'o, "Amidst Student Movement," *Beijing Review* 25 (Feb. 15, 1972):23–25; interview with Huang Hua (Wang Ju-mei).

36. Interview with F. McCracken Fisher, his quote edited for syntax.

37. Jessie G. Lutz, "December 9, 1935: Student Nationalism and the Chinese Christian Colleges," *Journal of Asian Studies* 4 (Aug. 1967):637; H. Snow, *Student Notes*, 195; Charlotte Salisbury, *Long March Diary: China Epic* (Walker, 1986), 28; Helen F. Snow to J. B. Powell, Feb. 27, 1936, NWP; and editorial, perhaps by Powell, in *China Weekly Review*, Feb. 29, 1936. Also Powell's dispatch in *Chicago Tribune*, Dec. 17, 1935. Snow's press problems in Edgar Snow to Nelson T. Johnson, March 4, 1936, NJP.

38. Edgar Snow, "The Japanese Juggernaut Rolls On," *Saturday Evening Post*, May 9, 1936, 92.

39. The Communists' role in the December 9th Movement is a matter of dispute. As mentioned above, the Chinese Communist Party argues that it directed the movement. Among those on the other side is Snow, who believed in 1935 and later that the students led the movement and that they were anti-Japanese rather than pro-Communist. (See his "Comment: The December 9th Movement," *China Quarterly* 26 [April-June 1966]:171–72.) A good deal of American scholarship supports this view. (For good examples see John Israel, "The December 9th Movement: A Case Study in Chinese Communist Historiography," *China Quarterly* 23 [July-September 1965]:140–69; and Lutz, "December 9, 1935.") The comment from Wang Ju-mei, who later took the name of Huang Hua and became Foreign Minister in the People's Republic of China, comes from an interview with the author in Peking in 1985. Other comments supporting Snow's view: Lyman P. Van Slyke, *Enemies and Friends: The United Front in Chinese Communist History* (Stanford University Press, 1967), 66; Israel and Klein, *Rebels and Bureaucrats*, 33.

A related issue is the importance of Snow's involvement in the movement. His chief discussion of the subject is located in *Journey* where he wrote a chapter entitled "We Spark a Rebellion." When scholars began to use that chapter to describe Snow as a key figure in the initial stages of the movement, he played down his role. (Again see his "Comment: The December 9th Movement.") My own view, as described in the chapter, is that Snow did not guide the movement any more than the Communists did, but the students harnessed his active involvement. Additional useful comment on this found in John Israel, "Comment: The December 9th Movement," *China Quarterly* 27 (July-Sept. 1966):166–67.

Three: *Red Star over China*

1. Jean Strouse, "The Real Reasons," in William Zinsser, ed., *Extraordinary Lives: The Art and Craft of American Biography* (American Heritage, 1986), 181.

2. Cerf, "A Matter of Timing," 838.

3. On the Communist movement after 1927: Vincent Sheean, *Personal History* (Houghton Mifflin, 1969), 217; Jerome Ch'en, *Mao and the Chinese Revolution* (Oxford University Press, 1967), 125, 165–66; Dick Wilson, *The Long March, 1935: The Epic of Chinese Communism's Survival* (Avon, 1973), chapter 5; Harrison E. Salisbury, *The Long March: The Untold Story* (McGraw-Hill, 1987), 138.

4. On perceptions of the Chinese Communists: Edgar E. Strother, ed., "A Bolshevized China—The World's Greatest Peril," reprinted articles from *North China Daily News* and *China Press*, copy in Department of State Library; Kenneth E. Shewmaker, *Americans and Chinese Communists, 1927–1945: A Persuading Encounter* (Cornell University Press, 1971), 19; UP dispatch in *China Weekly Review*, March 8, 1930; Wilson, *Long March*, 45; Jonathan D. Spence, *The Gate of Heavenly Peace: The Chinese and Their Revolution* (Penguin, 1982), 269–70; Jerome Ch'en, *China and the West: Society and Culture 1815–1937* (Indiana University Press, 1979), 52; Agnes Smedley, *Battle Hymn of China* (Knopf, 1943), 73; Franz Michael, *The Taiping Rebellion*, vol. 1 (University of Washington Press, 1966), 69; Mary C. Wright, *The Last Stand of Chinese Conservatism* (Atheneum, 1966), 303. Also Philip Jaffe, "Odyssey of a Fellow Traveller," unpublished autobiography, 304, copy in Philip Jaffe Papers, Robert Woodruff Library for Advanced Studies, Emory University, Atlanta, Ga., hereafter cited PJP.

5. Snow, "The Strength of Communism in China—The Bolshevist Influence," 521. An accompanying article by Reginald E. Sweetland, a *Chicago Daily News* correspondent, came to much the same conclusion. Regarding Snow's early sources of information on the CCP: Edgar Snow, *The Other Side of the River: Red China Today* (Random House, 1962), 263; Smedley, *Battle Hymn*, 123–24; Otto Braun, *A Comintern Agent in China: 1932–1939* (Stanford University Press, 1982), 6; Dorothy Borg, *The United States and the Far Eastern Crisis of 1933–1938: From the Manchurian Incident Through the Initial Stage of the Undeclared Sino-Japanese War* (Harvard University Press, 1964), 595. Edgar Snow, *Red Star over China* (Random House, 1938), 163; unless otherwise noted, all citations from *Red Star* are found in 1938 edition. H. Snow, *My China Years*, 60, and Jay C. Huston, "Will Western Capitalism Be Willing to Save China from Chaos and Communism," Nov. 15, 1931, and "Sun Yat-sen, the Kuomintang, and the Chinese-Russian Political Economic Alliance," Aug. 1, 1931, Dept. of State Records, files 893.00b/857 and 893.00/11823, National Archives, Washington, D.C., hereafter cited as DOS. On Huston's first report the Consul-General wrote after his name approved "in general." He approved the second report "so far as read." Shewmaker, *Americans and Chinese Communists*, 41–42. Clubb did not recall discussing his report with Snow, but they did speak about Chinese communism when they knew each other in Peking (Edmund Clubb to author, April 27, 1982). Clubb's report was eventually published as *Communism in China: As Reported from Hankow in 1932* (Columbia University Press, 1968). Snow outlined his research activities in a proposal for a Guggenheim Fellowship, typewritten, n.d., ESC.

6. Snow's views on CCP in: Snow, "The Strength of Communism in China—The Bolshevist Influence," 523; Edgar Snow to Howard Snow, July 20, 1935, ESC.

7. On Snow's troubles reaching the Chinese Communists: Edgar Snow to Henriette Herz, Feb. 6, 1934, ESC; Cerf, "A Matter of Timing," 838; Wilson, *Long March*, 83.

8. On Long March and Communist situation upon arrival in the Northwest: Borg, *Far Eastern Crisis*, 202–7; Shewmaker, *Americans and Chinese Communists*, 32–33; Wilson, *Long March*, 219–39, 271–73; Salisbury, *Long March*, 296, 311–15; Van Slyke, *Enemies and Friends*, 61–62; Edgar Snow, "Mr. Hirota's Third Point," *Foreign Affairs* 14 (July 1936):603; Tuchman, *Stilwell*, 157–58; Snow, *Journey*, 152; Snow, *Red Star*, 16–24.

9. For Snow's efforts during this period to reach the Northwest see his Guggenheim proposal, cited above; Snow, *Journey*, 147; H. Snow, *Student Notes*, 36–41, 52, 127–41, 196–98; Ch'en, "Amidst Student Movement," 23; Ross Terrill, *The White-Boned Demon: A Biography of Madame Mao Zedong* (Morrow, 1984), 41–45. For a view that disputes Yu-Chiang relationship, see Roxane Witke, *Comrade Chiang Ch'ing* (Little, Brown, 1977), 495.

10. Leonid Polevoy, in letter to author, June 9, 1981, and in interviews. According to Leonid Polevoy, his father's acquaintances included Sun Yat-sen, Li Ta-chao (a founder of the Chinese Communist Party and professor at Peking National University), Lu Hsun and other writers, Chou En-lai, Liu Shao-ch'i, Mao Tse-tung (who worked as an assistant librarian at Peking National University), Mikhail Borodin, Adolph Joffe, and Galen. Leonid Polevoy further argues that his father was a Marxist, though not a member of the Communist Party, and had major differences with the Soviets whom he believed did not understand China. Polevoy does not loom as a major figure in literature about China but intriguing references appear in Chow Tse-tsung, *The May Fourth Movement: Intellectual Revolution in Modern China* (Stanford University Press, 1967), Dick Wilson, *Zhou En-lai: A Biography* (Viking, 1984), and Kai-yu Hsu, *Chou En-lai: China's Gray Eminence* (Doubleday, 1968). Chow (244) says that Gregori

Voitinsky, sent by the Comintern to China in 1920, met Polevoy "who started to sympathize with the Soviet government at the time, and through him Voitinsky came in touch with Li Ta-chao and some other intellectuals who had been active in the May Fourth Movement." Chow (249) also says "Palevoy [*sic*]" and Voitinsky's secretary helped establish a party branch in Wuhan. According to Hsu (21–22), Chou En-lai visited Polevoy, "a Russian teacher at Peking University who served at the same time [1917] as the cultural liaison for the Comintern." He agrees with Wilson (46): "This was [Chou's] first personal contact with international Communism."

11. On Snow's invitation to the Northwest: Edgar Snow, "Notes based on interview with Sun Li, student delegate to Sianfu from Tungpei University," typewritten, March 9, 1936, ESC. Snow, *Journey*, 152; Snow, *Red Star over China*, rev. and enl. ed. (Grove, 1968), 419, hereafter cited *Red Star* (1968); Israel and Klein, *Rebels and Bureaucrats*, 85; H. Snow, *Sian Incident*, 66; H. Snow, *Student Notes*, 37; Rewi Alley, "Some Recollections of Edgar Snow," typewritten, n.d., author's files; Shewmaker, *Americans and Chinese Communists*, 73. Shewmaker writes that Smedley was infuriated that Snow made it into Red China first. Interview with Helen F. Snow. Snow does not mention Polevoy in his writing. Neither Helen Snow nor Lois Snow are aware that Polevoy helped Snow. After the Japanese attacked Peking in 1937, they jailed Polevoy for seventeen months. He subsequently went to the United States where he joined the Harvard faculty to work on a Chinese language dictionary.

12. Background on circumstances contributing to Snow's invitation: Warren I. Cohen, "The Development of Chinese Communist Policy toward the United States, 1922–1933," *Orbis* 11 (Spring 1967):220. Cohen argues that before reaching Shensi, the CCP "was not in a position to make foreign policy." On secret notes to students, James M. Bertram, *Return to China* (Heinemann, 1957), 4. For a discussion of tension with Wang Ming see, Gregor Benton, "The 'Second Wang Ming Line' (1935–1938)," *China Quarterly* 61 (Jan.-March 1975):61–94; Wilson, *Long March*, 119–38 and 310–12. Huang Hua also notes that the trip would have been difficult for a woman, even of Smedley's mettle, and that Snow had proved himself in the student movement (interview with Huang Hua). Salisbury (*Long March*, 318) speculates Snow's invitation was facilitated by Comintern interest in the CCP establishing international connections.

13. Cerf, "A Matter of Timing," 839. Details on preparation for trip and layover in Sian in Snow, *Red Star*, 10, 23–24; H. Snow, *Sian Notes*, 5–6; H. Snow, *My China Years*, 182; Snow, *Red China Today*, 262–65; Edgar Snow, *Random Notes on Red China, 1936–1945* (East Asian Research Center, Harvard University, 1957), vii. Interviews with Harry Price, Helen F. Snow, F. McCracken Fisher, and Huang Hua. Helen Snow says she had the job of filing for her husband and later turned the chore over to Fisher.

14. Arrival in Paoan: Snow, *Red Star*, 58; Snow, *Random Notes*, viii; L. Snow, *Edgar Snow's China*, 112. In her account, Lois Snow changed tenses of verbs. I have changed them back to what the original was likely to have been.

15. Interviews with Mao: Snow, *Random Notes*, ix–x, 73–76; Snow, *Red Star* (1968), 432–34, 444, 487, 505; Snow, *Red Star*, 80, 133–35, 167, 191–92; Edgar Snow, "Interviews with Mao Tse-tung, Communist Leader," *China Weekly Review*, Nov. 21, 1936. On Chang's blunders, Salisbury, *Long March*, 315–23.

16. Snow, *Red Star* (1968), 430, 479, 484; Braun, *A Comintern Agent*, 24; Helen F. Snow to author, Jan. 14, 1982; Snow, *Random Notes*, 29, 32, 60, 62.

17. Snow, *Random Notes*, 83, 131; Snow, *Red Star*, 232, 291.

18. On impressions of CCP relations with ordinary Chinese: Snow, *Red Star*, 44, 73, 94, 105, 209, 215, 250–52; Edgar Snow, *Shanghai Evening Post & Mercury*, Feb. 3, 1937; Snow, *Random Notes*, 117; Edgar Snow to Helen Snow, Aug. 3,

1936, Helen F. Snow files. For another discussion of factory conditions, see Spence, *Gate of Heavenly Peace*, 220.

19. On impressions of Red Army: Snow, *Red Star*, 94–102, 262–64, 338–45.

20. Van Slyke, *Enemies and Friends*, 38–65; Benton, "The 'Second Wang Ming Line,' " 61–65.

21. Edgar Snow, *China Weekly Review*, Nov. 14 and 21, 1936; Snow, *Random Notes*, 56–59; Van Slyke, *Enemies and Friends*, 64; Benton, "The 'Second Wang Ming Line,' " 69–71.

22. Snow, *Red Star*, 255, 365; Snow, *Journey*, 179.

23. On Snow's impression of rural equalitarianism: Snow, *Red Star*, 100, 106, 211, 218, 225, 433–45; Snow, *Shanghai Evening Post & Mercury*, Feb. 4, 1937. On Mao: Maurice Meisner, *Mao's China and After: A History of the People's Republic*, rev. ed. (Free Press, 1986), 41–45; Snow, *Red Star*, 66, 69–70; Snow, *Red China Today*, 267; Snow, *Journey*, 180; H. Snow, *My China Years*, 156. For a study of these American images see John William Ward, *Andrew Jackson: Symbol of an Age* (Oxford University Press, 1955).

24. Dr. George Hatem, speech commemorating the tenth anniversary of the death of Edgar Snow, Feb. 15, 1982, Helen F. Snow files; Snow, *Red Star*, 95–96, 373.

25. On Snow's homecoming: "Edgar Snow's Seal and Bracelet," *China Reconstructs*, May 1975, 30; Snow, *Random Notes*, 113–14; Snow, *Red Star*, 390; Snow, *Journey*, 179–80.

26. H. Snow, *Sian Notes*, 51; Snow, *Journey*, 183–84; *New York Herald Tribune*, Oct. 28–29, 1936; *Washington Post*, Oct. 27–28, 1936; Nelson T. Johnson to Secretary of State, Oct. 28, 1936, 811.91293/222, DOS; Snow, *Red Star*, 8; interview with Mildred Snow Mackey.

27. Reception to Snow's reports: Snow, *Journey*, 184, 191; H. Snow, *Sian Notes*, 53, 58, 66, 158; Edgar Snow, *China Weekly Review*, Nov. 14 and 21, 1936; Edgar Snow, "Direct from the Chinese Red Area," *Asia*, Feb. 1937, 74–75; Snow, *Shanghai Evening Post & Mercury*, Feb. 3, 4, and 5, 1937; C. E. Gauss to Nelson T. Johnson, Feb. 9, 1937, 893.00/14044, DOS; John S. Service, "Edgar Snow: Some Personal Reminiscences," *China Quarterly* 50 (April–June 1972):211; interview with Randolph Sailor; Edgar Snow to Nelson T. Johnson, Feb. 6, 1937, NJP; Sheean, *Personal History*, 238.

28. On Sian Incident: Edgar Snow to Randall Gould, Nov. 24, 1936, in H. Snow, *Sian Notes*, 64–65, also see 67–68, 79, 92–94, 160; James M. Bertram, *First Act in China: The Story of the Sian Mutiny* (Viking, 1938), 28-39, 125–27; Snow, *Red Star*, 409–10; Borg, *Far Eastern Crisis*, 221–25; Smedley, *Battle Hymn*, 149–50; Snow *Random Notes*, xi, 1–11. Edgar Snow to Nelson T. Johnson, Nov. 13, 1936; Johnson to Snow, Nov. 14, 1936, NJP. Interview with F. McCracken Fisher. In his book, Bertram did not use Fisher's name, referring to him instead as "Don."

29. For details on Japanese aggression: Snow, *The Battle for Asia* (World Publishing Company, 1942; original ed., Random House, 1941), 16–21. Snow, *Journey*, 186–87; James M. Bertram, *Unconquered: A Journal of a Year's Adventures among the Fighting Peasants of North China* (John Day, 1939), 55–56; Tuchman, *Stilwell*, 168–69; *Kansas City Star*, Dec. 11, 1937; Spence, *Gate of Heavenly Peace*, 312; Edgar Snow, London *Daily Herald*, Dec. 18, 1937.

30. On American attitudes: Borg, *Far Eastern Crisis*, 283–317; Tuchman, *Stilwell*, 189; Isaacs, *Scratches*, 157–64; poll data in Arthur S. Link, *American Epoch: A History of the United States since the 1890's*, vol. 2, 3d ed. (Knopf, 1963), 476; Hadley Cantril and Mildred Strunk, eds., *Public Opinion: 1935–1946* (Princeton University Press, 1951), 1156; Irving Howe and Lewis Coser, *The American Communist Party* (Beacon Press, 1957), 235, 312, and 329–37; Richard H. Pells,

Radical Visions amd American Dreams: Culture and Social Thought in the Depression Years (Harper & Row, 1973), 300.

31. Interview with Helen F. Snow; Cerf, "A Matter of Timing," 839; Harrison Smith to Henriette Herz, Oct. 29, 1936, NWP; Snow, *Red Star*, vii.

32. Malcolm Cowley, "Red China," *New Republic*, Jan. 12, 1938, 287; B. C., *Evening Express*, Jan. 8, 1938; Bruce Catton, *Knoxville Sentinel*, March 13, 1938; David Lord, *Florida Times-Union*, Jan. 23, 1938; Dorothy Wents, *Daily Republican*, Feb. 10, 1938; *Wisconsin State Journal*, Feb. 27, 1938; R. L. Duffus, *New York Times*, Jan. 9, 1938; Snow was on the cover of *Saturday Review of Literature*, Jan. 1, 1938. The sample of reviews is based almost exclusively on files maintained by a now defunct clipping service, Reviews on File, and includes long reviews as well as notices running no more than a paragraph. Some of the reviews, such as Catton's, ran in more than one newspaper. Regarding sales: Henriette Herz to Edgar Snow, cablegram, Feb. 10, 1938, ESC; Cerf, "A Matter of Timing," 838; Service, "Edgar Snow Reminiscences," 212; Ch'en, *China and the West*, 55. Impact of book: Harold L. Ickes, *The Secret Diary of Harold L. Ickes*, vol. 2 (Simon & Schuster, 1954), 327–28; interview with Hubert Liang; Doris Reubens, *Bread and Rice* (Thurston Macauley Associates, 1947), 41; White, *In Search of History*, 49–55; Milton Caniff to author, June 26, 1978; Isaacs, *Scratches*, 155; Arthur Miller, "In China," *Atlantic Monthly*, March 1979, 91; interview with Alejandro Roces. Statements similar to Miller's and Roces' about the impact of *Red Star* came by the score in interviews for this biography.

33. Communist reaction: "Keeping Posted," *Saturday Evening Post*, June 4, 1938, 80; Snow, *Red Star*, 374, 378; Snow, *Random Notes*, 3, 20; V. J. Jerome and Li Chuan, "Edgar Snow's 'Red Star over China,' " *The Communist* 5 (May 1938): 447. Asiaticus's critique and Snow's response in " 'Asiaticus' Criticizes 'Red Star over China,' " "Edgar Snow Replies," and " 'Asiaticus' Holds His Ground," *Pacific Affairs* 11 (June 1938):237–52. *Pacific Affairs* did not publish a second letter from Snow: Edgar Snow to Owen Lattimore, June 18, 1938, ESC. Background in Shewmaker, *Americans and Chinese Communists*, 115–16. Shewmaker incorrectly says Wittfogel was the only Westerner who seemed to have met Heinz Shippe; Snow met Shippe in Shanghai: see Heinz Shippe to Edgar Snow, Feb. 27, 1938, ESC.

34. Birthplace quote from Isaacs, *Scratches*, 163.

35. Snow, *Red Star*, 211. For examples in *Red Star* where Snow describes Communists as Communists see 76, 139, 167, 211–12, 218, 369–74, 415–16, 437.

36. H. Snow, *My China Years*, 310; Helen F. Snow, "Old Files on Indusco" (unpublished, n.d.), 5, Helen F. Snow files; R. L. Duffus, *New York Times*, Jan. 9, 1938; A. M. F., *Milwaukee Journal*, Jan. 9, 1938; Roger S. Green, *Worcester Telegram*, Feb. 13, 1938. "Unduly hard" comment on Chiang found in G. L., *Christian Science Monitor*, Dec. 29, 1937; Gunther, *Inside Asia*, 21–22. For background on Greene: Warren I. Cohen, *The Chinese Connection: Roger S. Greene, Thomas W. Lamont, George E. Sokolsky and American-East Asian Relations* (Columbia University Press, 1978), 199.

37. John Lewis Gaddis, *The United States and the Origins of the Cold War, 1941–1947* (Columbia University Press, 1972), 32; Dallek, *American Foreign Policy*, 124.

38. Interview with Harry Price.

39. Snow, "Edgar Snow Replies," 248; Snow, *Red Star* (1968), 426–30, 436, 448–49, 465. Snow too quickly dismissed the Mao-Chang Kuo-t'ao conflict as not needing to be discussed: Snow, *Red Star*, 192. Interestingly, Mao told Snow in 1960 that the struggle with Chang was the darkest moment of his life. (Snow, *Red Star* [1968], 432.) For examples of how Mao and others may have misled Snow, see William F. Dorrill, "The Fukien Rebellion and the CCP: A Case of

Maoist Revisionism," *China Quarterly* 37 (Jan.—March 1969):31–53; John Rue, *Mao Tse-tung in Opposition, 1927–1935* (Stanford University Press, 1966), 35, 77–78, 173–74, 213, 232; Tetsuya Kataoka, *Resistance and Revolution in China: The Communists and the Second United Front* (University of California Press, 1974), 2.

40. Opinions on Snow's sound judgment and accuracy come from two interesting sources: Tang Tsou, a critic of American reporting about Chinese Communists, acknowledged Snow's "generally accurate account" (*America's Failure in China, 1941–1950* [University of Chicago Press, 1963], 231); and Soviet representative Otto Braun, whom Snow described as having little standing in Paoan, notes "Snow was first and foremost a journalist and a writer . . . one of the first to perceive the intra-Party conflict" (Braun, *A Comintern Agent*, 252–53). Material from this section found in: Snow, *Red Star*, 73, 174, 195, 384; Snow, *Red Star* (1968), 186; Snow, *Random Notes*, ix, 101–2. Edgar Snow to Nelson T. Johnson, Feb. 6, 1937, NJP. Wang Ju-mei, Snow's translator, had orders to report to Mao on Snow's notes, interview with Huang Hua.

41. New York *Sun*, June 25, 1938. For comments on Snow's intense inquisitiveness, see Braun, *A Comintern Agent*, 252; and Ma Hai-teh, "A True Representative of the American People," *Beijing Review*, Feb. 15, 1982, 20.

42. On historical value of *Red Star* see Fairbank, Foreword to *Random Notes*, v–vii; Wilson, *Zhou*, 307; Stuart Schram, *Mao Tse-tung* (Simon & Schuster, 1966), 15, 166. In a good comparative analysis of the work of other journalists, Shewmaker concludes that Snow "was the most articulate and staunch advocate of the thesis that the Chinese Communists were Marxist revolutionaries aspiring to the attainment of absolute political power." Kenneth E. Shewmaker, "The 'Agrarian Reformer' Myth," *China Quarterly* 34 (April-June 1968):76; also Shewmaker, *Americans and Chinese Communists*, 254–55; Snow, *Red Star*, 212.

43. Snow, *Red Star*, 449.

44. A. T. Steele to author, Dec. 14, 1980. For an analysis arguing that Snow was influential see Shewmaker, *Americans and Chinese Communists*, chapter 4.

45. Paul Beckley, *Kansas City Star*, undated, Mildred Snow Mackey files.

Four: *Scorched Earth*

1. Descriptions of Snow's anxiety, perhaps circulated by his publisher to increase the drama of the book, appeared in short press notices, e.g., the Columbus, Ga., *Inquirer-Sun*, Jan. 31, 1938, and the Boston *Herald*, Feb. 5, 1938. Also Snow, *Journey*, 191; and Edgar Snow to Robert Haas, Feb. 10, 1938, RHP.

2. A. J. Brace, *Kansas City Star*, April 27, 1938; Edgar Snow to editor, *Kansas City Star*, June 23, 1938, ESC; "The Epigrams of Lusin," in Lin Yutang, ed., *The Wisdom of China and India* (Modern Library, 1942), 1090.

3. Edgar Snow to Earl Browder, March 20, 1938, ESC.

4. For discussion of political impact of Snow's journalism: Snow, *Red Star*, 373, 389; Snow, *Journey*, 192; Schram, *Mao*, 193; Liang, "Edgar Snow's Vision," 23–24; C. P. Fitzgerald, *Mao Tse-tung and China* (Penguin, 1977), 36; Warren I. Cohen, "The Development of Chinese Communist Policy toward the United States, 1934–1945," *Orbis* 11 (Summer 1967):553; Snow, *Red Star* (1968), 487; Snow, *Battle for Asia*, 259; Fairbank, Foreword, *Random Notes*, v; Derk Bodde, *Peking Diary: 1948–1949, A Year of Revolution* (Fawcett, 1967), 190; Zhao Rongsheng, "Snow Led Us to Yanan," in Wang Xing, ed., *China Remembers Edgar Snow* (Beijing Review, 1982), 67–72. Edgar Snow to Nelson T. Johnson, Feb.

6, 1937, and to T. T. Li, Feb. 4, 1937, NJP. Interviews with Helen F. Snow and Israel Epstein.

5. Snow, *Journey*, 158, 206; Nym Wales (Helen F. Snow), *My Yenan Notebooks* (mimeographed, 1961), 166; interview with Helen F. Snow; Snow, *Random Notes*, ix, 56–59. For an example of Snow praising Chiang see *Red Star*, 173. Jaffe talks of seeing a draft chapter on Chiang that was not included in *Red Star*; interestingly this comment is found in Jaffe's handwritten notes for "Odyssey" and not in the typed version. Jaffe may have been referring to a chapter on Ch'en Keng. Helen Snow recalls that while she was in Yenan Ch'en sent word through her asking that E. Snow not use a story describing how he saved Chiang's life on the battle-field. "Ed was really furious about cutting this great story" (Helen F. Snow to author, April 8, 1982). Snow did briefly mention the Ch'en Keng episode in "China's Fighting Generalissimo," *Foreign Affairs* 16 (July 1938):618, and much later at length in *Random Notes*, 90–99.

6. Shewmaker, *Americans and Chinese Communists*, 142–43; Powell, *25 Years*, 124; Borg, *Far Eastern Crisis*, 229–30.

7. George Hatem to Edgar Snow, Dec. 3, 1936, ESC; Edgar Snow, *China Weekly Review*, Nov. 14, 1936.

8. Snow, *Random Notes*, 22.

9. Edgar Snow, *Red Star over China*, rev. ed. (Random House, 1938), 385 and 369–80, hereafter referred to as *Red Star* (1938, rev.); cf. *Red Star*, 384 and 369-80.

10. Snow to Browder, March 20, 1938; Snow, *Red Star* (1938, rev.), 374, 378–79.

For an argument that Snow made revisions to conceal the Communists' real intentions, see Freda Utley, "Red Star over Independence Square: The Strange Case of Edgar Snow and the *Saturday Evening Post*," *Plain Talk*, Sept. 1947, 12–13. Utley singled out two passages. The italicized sections were deleted from the revised edition.

> And finally, of course, the political ideology, tactical line, and theoretical leadership of the Chinese Communists have been under the close guidance, if not positive *detailed* direction, of the Communist International, *which during the past decade has become virtually a bureau of the Russian Communist Party. In final analysis this means that, for better or worse, the policies of the Chinese Communists, like Communists in every other country, have had to fall in line with, and usually subordinate themselves to, the broad strategic requirements of Soviet Russia, under the dictatorship of Stalin.* (Snow, *Red Star*, and *Red Star* [1938, rev.], 374)

> The three periods of Sino-Russian relationship mentioned above accurately reflect also the changes that have taken place in the character of the Comintern during recent years, and its stages of transition *from an organization of international incendiaries into an instrument of the national policy of the Soviet Union.* (Snow, *Red Star* and *Red Star* [1938, rev.], 375–76)

Contrary to Utley's opinion, the revisions promote accuracy, rather than hide the truth. The first passage, for instance, is more nearly accurate in describing the CCP as relatively autonomous. Moreover, Utley took the revisions out of context. Although these passages played down the Comintern as "an instrument of [Soviet] national policy," other passages do not. The section from which the second passage is lifted makes the point that Comintern policies were a function of internal disputes within the Soviet Union and that Stalin, the winner in those disputes, directed the Comintern along lines congenial to the Soviet Union's internal needs. With Comintern setbacks overseas in the

1920s, Snow wrote in the revised edition, "the Party grew weary of adventures afar, and was ready to turn to construction at home" (378).

Helen F. Snow (interview with author) recalls that her husband developed doubts about some of his original statements on Comintern involvement with the CCP—though she seems to suggest otherwise in *My China Years* (310). The entire episode, in fact, is complicated by contemporaries' often self-serving and contradictory recollections. Left-leaning Philip Jaffe wrote in his autobiography (*Odyssey*, 74) that the "revised American edition [of *Red Star*] was published with much of the worst features of anti-Soviet material substantially modified, under Snow's direction and in part with my assistance." Jaffe's statement, on which he did not elaborate, is not credible. By his own admission, he did not know Snow well. In addition, Snow's revisions did not radically change the book, as Jaffe implies. (Cf. Karl August Wittfogel's 1951 congressional testimony discussed in chapter 7.)

In the 1960s Jaffe undertook a comparative analysis of various editions of *Red Star*, which is located in PJP.

11. Background on this little-known episode in Snow's life comes from H. Snow, *Sian Notes*, 173–82; Helen F. Snow, "Remembering 'Democracy'—A Lightning Flash of a Magazine," *China and US*, Sept.–Oct. 1974, 4; H. Snow, *My China Years*, 220–27; Ida Pruitt, "Days in Old Peking, 1921–1928" (unpublished ms, n.d.), 405–6, 421, Ida Pruitt files. Interviews with John Leaning, Helen F. Snow, Harry Price, and Hubert Liang. John Leaning to author, May 1982. J. B. Powell to Helen Snow, April 13, 1937, NWP.

12. "Introductory," *democracy*, May 1, 1937, 1.

13. Letter published in *democracy*, June 8, 1937, 77; *democracy*, June 22, 1937, 117; Shanghai Municipal Police Records, May 14, 1937, FBI.

14. Snow, *Battle for Asia*, 3–6; *Journey*, 188; James Bertram to author, Feb. 13, 1974, and Sept. 2, 1980. For a good description of foreign activity generally, see Peck, *Through China's Wall*, 324.

15. On Helen Snow's trip to Yenan: Shewmaker, *Americans and Chinese Communists*, 76, 82–83; Helen Foster Snow, *Inside Red China* (Doubleday, 1939; reprint, Da Capo Press, 1977),3–25, 279–80; Jaffe, "Odyssey," 195–98; H. Snow, *Sian Notes*, 172; T. A. Bisson, *Yenan in 1937: Talks with Communist Leaders* (University of California Press, 1973), 15. Edgar Snow to Philip Jaffe, June 22, 1937, PJP. Snow to Owen Lattimore, Nov. 15, 1952, ESC.

16. H. Snow, *Yenan Notebooks*, 162–69. Helen Snow's recollection on difference in personalities in letter to author, Dec. 29, 1973. Interviews with John Leaning, Harry Price, Ida Pruitt, John S. Service, Israel Epstein, and others; also Owen Lattimore to author, Aug. 29, 1979.

17. Background on Snow's trip to rejoin his wife: Snow, *Journey*, 188–92; Snow, *Red China Today*, 74; Snow, *Battle for Asia*, 6–8, 22–29; Pruitt, "Old Peking," 422–23; Service, "Edgar Snow Reminiscences," 213; Bertram, *Unconquered*, 65–79; H. Snow, *Inside Red China*, 282, 299–301; H. Snow, *Yenan Notebooks*, 176–77; Wilson, *Zhou*, 147.

18. For description of Snow's activities during this period: Edgar Snow, London *Daily Herald*, Oct. 15 and 28, Nov. 6 and 10, 1937; Snow, *Battle for Asia*, 45–54; Snow, *Journey*, 195; Blankfort, *Big Yankee*, 186–87; Phillip Knightley, *The First Casualty* (Harcourt Brace Jovanovich, 1975), 270–71; Helen Snow to author, June 23, 1978; Powell, *25 Years*, 301.

19. On attitudes toward war: Snow, *Battle for Asia*, 40; Edgar Snow, London *Daily Herald*, Oct. 16, Dec. 20, and Dec. 28, 1937; Van Slyke, *Enemies and Friends*, 93–94; Edgar Snow, " 'Red' Greetings to Nippon," *New Republic*, May 11, 1938, 6; Edgar Snow, "The Sun Also Sets," *Saturday Evening Post*, June 4, 1938, 33; Tuchman, *Stilwell*, 186.

20. Shewmaker, *Americans and Chinese Communists,*, 103–4; Blankfort, *Big Yankee*, 185. Blankfort explains that "gung ho" is only part of the Chinese phrase for "work together," though it subsequently became an accepted idiom in English and Chinese.

21. Snow, *Red Star* (1938, rev.), 460–61.

22. Borg, *Far Eastern Crisis*, 231; Snow, "China's Fighting Generalissimo," 625.

23. Snow, *Battle for Asia*, 78–91, 96; Dzung Kyi-ung, "The Chinese Industrial Cooperation Movement" (Ph.D. diss., Princeton University, 1944), 3–6; Rewi Alley, "The Edgar Snow I Knew," *Eastern Horizon* 11 (1972):17; Snow, *Red Star* (1938, rev.), 481; Edgar Snow, London *Daily Herald*, Oct. 21, 1937; Helen F. Snow, "The Summing Up," n.d., typewritten, Madison, Conn., 2.

24. On the beginnings of the Chinese Industrial Cooperative movement, see Nym Wales (Helen Foster Snow), *Notes on the Beginnings of the Industrial Cooperatives in China* (mimeographed, 1961), 1–38; Helen F. Snow, *China Builds for Democracy* (Modern Age, 1941), 42–43; Snow, *Battle for Asia*, 97–99, 117–18, 230; Snow, *Journey*, 197–225; Edgar Snow, "China's Blitzbuilder, Rewi Alley," *Saturday Evening Post*, Feb. 8, 1941, 13; Rewi Alley to author, April 22, 1982; *Chinese Industrial Cooperatives* (Hongkong Shanghai Industrial Cooperative Promotion Committee, 1939), 53–54; W. H. Auden and Christopher Isherwood, *Journey to a War* (Faber & Faber, 1973), 240. For a disinterested study see Douglas Robertson Reynolds, "The Chinese Industrial Cooperative Movement and the Political Polarization of Wartime China, 1938–1945" (Ph.D. diss., Columbia University, 1975). Snow said the raw idea for Indusco orginated with his wife; Alley recalls that he drafted the first plan and brought it to the Snows, who helped him work it over (Alley to author, Oct. 24, 1974; Rewi Alley, "Edgar Snow and Indusco," *China Remembers*, 47–50). Snow wrote about Yen's education experiment in "Awakening the Masses in China," *New York Herald Tribune*, Dec. 17, 1933. The comment on Clark-Kerr's anti-Americanism from Lord Oliver Franks, interview.

25. Snow, *Battle for Asia*, 75–76, 117–18.

26. Edgar Snow to Nelson T. Johnson, July 8 and 17, 1938; Johnson to Snow, July 8 and 18, 1938, NJP.

27. Snow, *Random Notes*, 20–23; Edgar Snow, "China's Japanese Allies," *Asia*, June 1939, 341–43.

28. Interview with F. McCracken Fisher; H. Snow, *China Builds*, 59; Chalmers A. Johnson, *Peasant Nationalism and Communist Power: The Emergence of Revolutionary China, 1937–1945* (Stanford University Press, 1962), 37–38; L. Snow, *Edgar Snow's China*, 153.

29. Edgar Snow to Helen Snow, Aug. 12, 1938, ESC. Edgar Snow, "Han Ying's 'Lost' Red Army," *Asia*, April 1939, 203; and "China's New Fourth Army," *Asia*, May 1939, 257.

30. Snow, *Journey*, 207–8; H. Snow, *China Builds*, 59; Edgar Snow to Helen Snow, Aug. 28, 1938, ESC.

31. Interview with Polly Babcock Feustel; Helen Snow to author, May 1, 1982; Edgar Snow to J. E. Snow and Mildred Snow Mackey, Jan. 26, 1939, ESC; Edgar Snow, "Igorot Mutation," *Asia*, Sept. 1940, 474.

32. On Edgar Snow's views of the Philippines in *Asia* magazine: "Filipinos Change Their Minds," Sept. 1939, 494–96; "Japan's 'Peaceful' Invasion," Oct. 1939, 590–92; "Filipinos Want a Guarantee," Nov. 1939, 659–61. Edgar Snow, "They Love Us, They Love Us Not," *Saturday Evening Post*, April 29, 1939, 64–69. Interviews with Polly Babcock Feustel and Helen F. Snow. Also, Gunther, *Inside Asia*, 290.

33. Edgar Snow, "The Coming Conflict in the Orient," *Saturday Evening Post*, June 1936, 85–87; Snow, "The Sun Also Sets," 37; Snow "They Love Us, They Love Us Not," 64; Snow, "Filipinos Want a Guarantee," 661.

34. On Indusco activities in the Philippines: H. Snow, *Notes on Industrial Cooperatives*, 39–40, 44–46, 67; H. Snow, *China Builds*, 182–83; Snow, *Journey*, 207–10; Lynn Z. Bloom, ed., Introduction to Natalie Crouter, *Forbidden Diary: Record of Wartime Internment, 1941–1945* (Burt Franklin, 1980), xvi; Reynolds, "Cooperative Movement," 266; Edgar Snow to Henriette Herz, March 3, 1939, ESC; Helen Snow to author, April 8, 1982. On Alley's sense of time see Graham Peck's delightful *Two Kinds of Time*, rev. ed., abridged (Houghton Mifflin, 1967), 194.

35. Typewritten copy of Reuters dispatch, Feb. 8, 1939, Helen F. Snow files; Snow, *Journey*, 203; H. Snow, "Old 1939 Files on Indusco," 7; H. Snow, *Notes on Industrial Cooperatives*, 6–7; interview with Jonathan B. Bingham, who visited China in 1939.

36. Theodore H. White and Annalee Jacoby, *Thunder Out of China* (William Sloane, 1946), 5; A. T. Steele, *The American People and China* (McGraw-Hill, 1966), 25–26; Tillman Durdin to author, Oct. 5, 1981; Snow, *Battle for Asia*, 156–57; Ch'en, *Mao*, 215, 235; Van Slyke, *Enemies and Friends*, 105–7; Edgar Snow, "China's Precarious Unity," *New Republic*, June 8, 1940, 44.

37. This letter has no addressee or date, and had penciled notation "not sent" in margin, according to Reynolds, "Cooperative Movement," 133–34. Also, Reynolds, "Cooperative Movement," 144, 150–74, 306–7; Snow, *Battle for Asia*, 207–15.

38. Snow, *Battle for Asia*, 159–60, 199–238, 261–64; Snow, *Journey*, 230–33; H. Snow, *Notes on Industrial Cooperatives*, 29.

39. On Yenan: Snow, *Battle for Asia*, 266–78, 317–34; Snow, *Journey*, 231–34; H. Snow, *Notes on Industrial Cooperatives*, 56–65; Steele, *American People and China*, 26; George Hogg, *I See a New China* (Little, Brown, 1944), 19; Blankfort, *Big Yankee*, 247; Wilson, *Long March*, 280–81, 312–13; Snow, *Red Star* (1968), 505. Snow quote on Indusco products found in letter from Carlson to Robert Barnett, Jan. 11, 1940, Robert Barnett files.

40. On Mao-Snow relations: Snow, *Battle for Asia*, 283; Snow, *Random Notes*, 21, 69, 71–73; Snow, *Red Star* (1968), 460; Ch'en, *Mao*, 210; Edgar Snow to Helen Snow, June 4, 1939, Helen F. Snow files; Jaffe, *Odyssey*, 74–76; Edgar Snow, *China Weekly Review*, Jan. 13, and Jan. 20, 1940. For concern about the closing of the Burma Road see Snow, *Battle for Asia*, 403–4; also two newspaper articles by Snow, written mid-1940 (place of publication not known), entitled "Britain's Burma Road Decision—Was It Just an Oriental Munich?" ESC.

41. Snow, *Random Notes*, 24–25; Snow, *Battle for Asia*, 285–86.

42. Shewmaker, *Americans and Chinese Communists*, 125.

43. Snow, "China's Precarious Unity," 45; Edgar Snow, "Rip Tide in China," *Asia*, Oct. 1940, 511. For discussion of self-censorship see A. T. Steele, *American People and China*, 24: Kenneth E. Shewmaker, "The Mandate of Heaven vs. U.S. Newsmen in China, 1941–1945," *Journalism Quarterly* 46 (Summer 1969):274–86; and Shewmaker, *Americans and Chinese Communists*, 122–23. Shewmaker agrees that Snow is the first to break silence but dates this with 1941 book, *Battle for Asia*.

44. On CCP and change in China: Snow, *Battle for Asia*, 241–50, 276, 287–91, 295, 335; Edgar Snow, "The Dragon Licks His Wounds," *Saturday Evening Post*, April 13, 1940, 160. "Lovable" Communists remarks from Joy Homer, quoted in Shewmaker, *Americans and Chinese Communists*, 110–24, which describes overwhelming positive reports of the period.

45. On United States role in Asia: Snow, *Battle for Asia*, 399, 407, 416–22; Edgar Snow, "Things That Could Happen," *Asia*, Jan. 1941, 14; Edgar Snow, "Will Stalin Sell Out China?" *Foreign Affairs* 18 (April 1940):450–63. Edgar Snow to William Babcock, Nov. 18, 1939; to Charles Hanson Towne, Dec. 16, 1939, ESC.

46. The size of Indusco is from Reynolds, "Cooperative Movement," 179, 427–30. "New Industries," *Time*, April 22, 1940, 31–32, reported that Indusco had fifty thousand members and two thousand units, figures often cited by the movement's supporters. Robert W. Barnett, "China's Industrial Cooperatives on Trial," *Far Eastern Survey*, Feb. 28, 1940, 51–56; Peck, *Two Kinds of Time*, 170–97; Edgar Snow to Edward Carter, May 3 and May 10, 1940, Robert Barnett files. Also, Snow, *Journey*, 218; Snow, *Battle for Asia*, 174–75, 205.

47. Edgar Snow to Henriette Herz, July 13, 1940, ESC. Snow to Robert Haas, May 24, 1940, RHP.

48. Edgar Snow, *New York Herald Tribune*, Dec. 26, 1940, and Jan. 22, 1941. The *Herald Tribune* editorial, undated, is in ESC. For an example of initial sketchy reports on the incident see United Press dispatch in *New York Herald Tribune*, Jan. 18, 1941. For background, Snow, *Journey*, 235–38; White and Jacoby, *Thunder*, 75–77.

49. Edgar Snow, "Is It Civil War in China?" *Asia*, April 1941, 169.

50. Interview with Polly Babcock Feustel; Snow, *Journey*, 240; Edgar Snow to "Mr. Chen," Jan. 4, 1964, ESC.

Five: *People on Our Side*

1. Bennett Cerf, "Trade Winds," *Saturday Review of Literature*, Dec. 15, 1945, 12.

2. On Snow's homecoming: Edgar Snow to "Tony," July 11, 1968, ESC; Edgar Snow, "Showdown in the Pacific," *Saturday Evening Post*, May 31, 1941, 40; Lin Yutang, *San Francisco Chronicle*, Feb. 23, 1941; Tracy B. Strong and Helene Keyssar, *Right in Her Soul: The Life of Anna Louise Strong* (Random House, 1983), 204; Anna Louise Strong and Edgar Snow, "Judgment Seat," Anna Louise Strong Papers, Suzzallo Library, University of Washington, Seattle, Washington. Interview with Richard Nickson.

3. Reception of *Battle for Asia*: Freda Utley, *New York Times*, March 9, 1941; interview with Freda Utley; Freda Utley, *The China Story* (Henry Regnery, 1951), 103–8; Freda Utley, *China at War* (Faber & Faber, 1939), 73–74, 192; Freda Utley, "Will Russia Betray China?" *Asia*, April 1941, 170; Snow, *Battle for Asia*, 289–90; Snow, *Red Star* (1938, rev.), 489; Shewmaker, *Americans and Chinese Communists*, 252–53; R. B., New York *Sun*, Feb. 26, 1941; Philip A. Adler, *Detroit News*, June 29, 1941; Paul Jacoby, *Chicago Tribune*, Feb. 19, 1941. A representative sampling of other reviews includes, F. G. H., *Philadelphia Inquirer*, Feb. 14, 1941; Paul M. A. Linebarger, Durham, N.C., *Morning Herald*, March 9, 1941; Arthur Coleman, *Dallas Morning News*, Feb. 23, 1941; and (unusually critical) Andre H. Berding, Buffalo *News*, March 15, 1941. *Publishers' Weekly*, April 5, 1941, 1470. Henry Luce to Edgar Snow, Feb. 25, 1941, ESC.

4. Interviews with Claude Mackey and Helen F. Snow; *Saturday Review of Literature*, March 1, 1941; Eleanor Roosevelt, "My Day," *Washington Daily News*, Feb. 27, 1942; Hope Ridings Miller, "Capital Whirl," *Washington Post*, March 5 and 6, 1942.

5. Edgar Snow, "How America Can Take the Offensive," *Fortune*, June 1941, 69; Edgar Snow, "Books on the Asiatic Front," *Publishers' Weekly*, May 31, 1941, 2138–42; "Keeping Posted," *Saturday Evening Post*, May 31, 1941, 4. Henriette Herz to Belle Becker, Feb. 15, 1941, RHP. Edgar Snow to J. E. Snow, May 17, 1930, ESC. Interview with Lois W. Snow.

6. Edgar Snow, *People on Our Side* (Random House, 1944), 4; Dallek, *American Foreign Policy*, 129; Cantril and Strunk, *Public Opinion*, 970–71; Cohen, *America's Response*, 150–51.

7. On Snow and FDR: Edgar Snow, "Fragments from F. D. R.," *Monthly Review*, Jan. 1957, 316–21, and March 1957, 395–404; Snow, *Journey*, 253–58; Snow, *Random Notes*, 125–30. Edgar Snow to Steve Early, FDR's press secretary, Feb. 21, 1942, and Edgar Snow, Memorandum to the President, Feb. 24, 1942, Franklin D. Roosevelt Library, Hyde Park, N.Y., hereafter referred to as FDRL. It is not clear if Snow gave FDR the memorandum during their talk or, inspired by the conversation, drafted it just afterward. Edgar Snow to Mildred Snow Mackey, April 1, 1942, ESC. Helen Snow to author, Dec. 29, 1973.

8. Sources on FDR and his China foreign policy: John Dos Passos, *District of Columbia: The Grand Design* (Houghton Mifflin, 1952), 417; Arthur M. Schlesinger, Jr., *The Imperial Presidency* (Houghton Mifflin, 1973), 224; Tuchman, *Stilwell*, 174; James MacGregor Burns, *Roosevelt: The Soldier of Freedom* (Harcourt Brace Jovanovich, 1970), 549–51; Cohen, *America's Response*, 140; Michael Schaller, *The U.S. Crusade in China, 1938–1945* (Columbia University Press, 1979), 24–84; Dallek, *American Foreign Policy*, 143. Nelson T. Johnson to Stanley Hornbeck, April 24, 1941, Stanley Hornbeck Papers, Hoover Institution on War, Revolution, and Peace, Stanford University, Palo Alto, Calif., hereafter referred to as SHP. Snow, "Is It Civil War in China?" 170.

9. Burns, *Roosevelt: The Soldier*, 592–93; John Morton Blum, *V Was for Victory: Politics and American Culture during World War II* (Harcourt Brace Jovanovich, 1976), 279–92; *New York Times*, Feb. 25, 1942.

10. Presidential aide Lauchlin Currie forwarded Snow's two reports to FDR. Roosevelt's comments are in Franklin Roosevelt, Memorandum For Hon. Lauchlin Currie, Oct. 22, 1942, FDRL. A good indication of Snow's thinking at the time is found in two of Snow's *Saturday Evening Post* articles: "Must Britain Give Up India?" Sept. 12, 1942, 111, and "Must We Beat Japan First?" Oct. 24, 1942, 94; also Edgar Snow, in G.N. Acharya, ed., *They Speak for India* (S. K. Kombrabail, 1943), 1–13; and Edgar Snow, Introduction to M. Thein Pe, *What Happened in Burma* (Allahabad Law Journal Press, 1943), 9–19. M. Thein Pe is probably the Burmese whose views Snow passed to FDR. On being reminded of Roosevelt's reaction years later, Currie "was startled by F. D. R.'s rough treatment of the Report on China . . . a very uncharacteristic reaction." Lauchlin Currie to author, March 14, 1987.

11. Contrasting views on capitalism: Snow, *Battle for Asia*, 422; Snow, "How America Can Take the Offensive," 180; James MacGregor Burns, *Roosevelt: The Lion and the Fox* (Harcourt, Brace, and World, 1956), 328–36, 243; Paul K. Conkin, *FDR and the Origins of the Welfare State* (Crowell, 1967), 74; Frances Perkins, *The Roosevelt I Knew* (Viking, 1946), 330; New York *News*, Feb. 2, 1941. Edgar Snow to J. E. Snow and Mildred Snow Mackey, Jan. 26, 1939, ESC.

12. On Snow's general approach to issues: Interview with O. Edmund Clubb; other examples, and there are many based on interviews for this book, include W. Averell Harriman and British journalist Felix Greene, men otherwise rather dissimilar. As one concrete example, John Service was struck by Snow's open-mindedness when they met during the war in Chungking. Snow considered Ambassador Clarence Gauss too conservative and anti-Chinese but was receptive to Service's argument this was not so (Interview with John S. Service). On Snow's relations with the Left: Richard H. Pells, *Radical Visions & American Dreams: Culture and Social Thought in the Depression Years* (Harper & Row, 1973), 328; Snow, *Battle for Asia*, 289–90, 299; Snow, *Journey*, 247–48. Edgar Snow to Franklin Folsom, Executive Secretary of the Congress, June 6, 1941, ESC. Interviews with Richard Nickson and Pat Tobin.

13. Edgar Snow, "We Learn the Hard Way," *Saturday Evening Post*, Feb. 21, 1942, 54; Edmond Taylor, Edgar Snow, and Eliot Janeway, *Smash Hitler's*

International: The Strategy of a Political Offensive against the Axis (Greystone, 1941), 49–71; Steel, *Lippmann*, 393–94.

14. *Philadelphia Evening Bulletin*, June 4, 1941. Edgar Snow's *Saturday Evening Post* articles: "They Don't Want to Play Soldier," Oct. 25, 1941, 14; "What is Morale?" Nov. 15, 1941, 16; "Made-in-America Blitz," Feb. 7, 1942, 12. *Kansas City Star*, Feb. 21 and Feb. 22, 1942. Interviews with Polly Babcock Feustel and Helen F. Snow. Snow refers to Fields in letter to Charles Hanson Towne, Sept. 14, 1941, CHT.

15. On government job possibilities: Snow, *Journey*, 253–58; Snow, *People*, 5–6; Edgar Snow, "How to Blockade Japan," *Saturday Evening Post*, March 14, 1942, 57. Edgar Snow to Howard Snow, March 16, 1951, ESC. Snow to Early, Feb. 24, 1942, FDRL. Snow mentions "Donovan committee" in a letter to Bennett Cerf, Dec. 23, 1941, RHP; circumstances of his recruitment or stated reasons for not taking the Donovan job are unclear but Snow knew many of the journalists being recruited. Also see, Thomas F. Troy, *Donovan and the CIA: A History of the Establishment of the Central Intelligence Agency* (Aletheia, 1981), 85–86; A. M. Sperber, *Murrow: His Life and Times* (Freundlich, 1986), 210; Joseph C. Goulden, *The Curtis Caper* (Putnam, 1965), 48; Burns, *Roosevelt: Lion and Fox*, 337.

16. On *Saturday Evening Post*: Snow, *Journey*, 259; Goulden, *Curtis Caper*, 27–67; Paul Gallico, *Further Confessions of a Story Writer: Stories Old and New* (Doubleday, 1961), 434; Karen Vaughn, "Just Plain Ben," *Media History Digest* 2 (Summer 1982):35–39; Sommers obit in *Philadelphia Evening Bulletin*, July 14, 1963; Martin Sommers, "What Jehol Means to Main Street," *New Outlook*, Feb. 1933, 26–29; "Report," *Quill*, Nov. 1978, 20; Gunther, *Inside Asia*, 207. Interview with Robert Fuoss.

17. Snow, *Journey*, 258; Martin Sheridan, *Boston Traveller*, Dec. 7, 1941. Interviews with Howard Snow and Richard Nickson, who watched Peg and Ed Snow interact in Hollywood. Snow refers to irregular communications with Peg in letter to Henriette Herz, Aug. 11, 1944, ESC. Helen Snow discusses the marriage at length in "learn from Edgar Snow," undated, typewritten article, Helen F. Snow files.

18. On Asia visit: Snow, *People*, 8–57; Snow, "Must Britain Give Up India?" 109; Edgar Snow, "The Pathology of the Oppressed," *Saturday Evening Post*, March 25, 1944, 6; Edgar Snow, "What We Can Expect from China," *Saturday Evening Post*, Aug. 8, 1942, 67; Snow, Introduction, *What Happened in Burma*, 16; Snow, *Journey*, 273–76; Jawaharlal Nehru, "India Can Learn from China," *Asia and the Americas*, Jan. 1943, 25–26. The communications officer's impressions of Snow in Fred Stires to author, April 6, 1981.

19. Snow, *Journey*, 260–63; Snow, *People*, 7; Edgar Snow, "China's Flying Freighters," *Saturday Evening Post*, Aug. 1, 1942, 20–21; Snow, "Must Britain Give Up India?" 10. G. R. Herrman to Edgar Snow, May 8, 1971, ESC. Interview with Robert Barnett.

20. Press treatment: Snow, *People*, 156–57; Edgar Snow, "The Lights Go On Again in Russia," *Saturday Evening Post*, Sept. 16, 1944, 26.

21. Knightly, *Casualty*, chapter 11; Snow, *People*, 118, 159–60; Snow, *Journey*, 338; Maurice Hindus, "Report on Russia." *Reader's Digest*, Nov. 1942, 92; Harrison Salisbury, *Russia on the Way* (Macmillan, 1946), 102. Edgar Snow to Raymond J. Marcus, Jan. 21, 1951, Raymond J. Marcus files. Interview with John Melby. Churchill and Clark-Kerr comments found in Edgar Snow's untitled, typewritten notes on personalities he met in Soviet Union, ESC, hereafter referred to as "Personalities."

22. Snow's feeling toward Russians: Edgar Snow, "How Russia Upset Hitler," *Saturday Evening Post*, Jan. 30, 1943, 90; Alexander Werth, *Russia at War, 1941–1945* (Dutton, 1964), 890–93; Edgar Snow, "Here the Nazi Butchers Wasted

Nothing," *Saturday Evening Post*, Oct. 28, 1944, 18; Snow, *People*, 46, 93, 186; Snow, *Journey*, 290–95, 335–37. Elizabeth Vincent, wife of diplomat John Carter Vincent, recalls Snow telling of Maidanek, interview.

23. Snow's personality: interview with Harrison Salisbury; Harrison Salisbury, *A Journey for Our Times* (Harper & Row, 1983), chapter 21. David M. Nichol to author, March 4, 1987; John Hersey to author, Aug. 18, 1980.

24. Snow, *People*, 67–68.

25. On Snow's assessment of communism in the Soviet Union: Snow, *People*, 104–17, 158, 214–16; Snow, *Journey*, 277; James Bertram to author, Sept. 2, 1980; Alec Nove, *An Economic History of the U.S.S.R.* (Penguin, 1984), 187, 240–41, 258–59, 388, and chapter 11; Edgar Snow, "Guerrilla Tactics in Soviet Defense," *The American Review on the Soviet Union* 4 (Oct.–Nov. 1941):5; Edgar Snow, *The Pattern of Soviet Power* (Random House, 1945), 133, 212; Edgar Snow, "The Stalin Truman Faces," *Saturday Evening Post*, June 30, 1945, 64; Vitaly Rapport and Yuri Alexeev, *High Treason: Essays on the History of the Red Army, 1918–1938* (Duke University Press, 1985), 275–78; Snow, "Meet Mr. and Mrs. Russia at Home," *Saturday Evening Post*, Dec. 22, 1945, 65.

26. Salisbury, *Russia*, 119; interview with Harrison Salisbury; Nove, *Economic History*, 226–27, 240, 277–78; Snow, *People*, 105; Robert Conquest, *The Nation Killers: The Soviet Deportation of Nationalities* (Macmillan, 1970), 11, 49; Snow, *Soviet Power*, 144–48; Henry Cassidy, *Moscow Dateline, 1941–1943* (Houghton Mifflin, 1943), 358; Knightly, *Casualty*, 256; Walter Durranty, *New York Times* magazine, July 30, 1944; Melvin Small, "How We Learned to Love the Russians: American Media and the Soviet Union during World War II," *Historian* 36 (May 1974):464–65.

27. Much study remains to be done on wartime reporting of the Soviet Union. One area that deserves attention, for instance, is the impact of censorship on the quality of news coverage. Two studies mention Snow. Although useful in many respects, they portray Snow one-dimensionally, calling his reports, "ecstatic" and fatuously classifying him as a "fellow traveller": Small, "How We Learned to Love the Russians," 455–78; Paul Willen, "Who 'Collaborated' with Russia?" *Antioch Review* 14 (Sept. 1954):259–83. Regarding common misconceptions that Snow did not embrace, see Edmund Stevens, *Russia Is No Riddle* (Greenberg, 1945), 77; Snow, *People*, 251; Snow, *Soviet Power*, 188–89.

28. Snow, *People*, 252; Edgar Snow's *Saturday Evening Post* articles: "Will Russia Invade Germany?" Sept. 11, 1943, 16; "Eastern Europe Swings Left," Nov. 1, 1944, 9–10; "What Russia Wants to Do to Germany," Dec. 2, 1944, 88; "Will Russia Fight Japan?" Oct. 9, 1943, 92. Also Gaddis, *Cold War*, 78–79.

29. Edgar Snow, "How Russia Will Fight Japan," *Saturday Evening Post*, March 3, 1945, 92.

30. Edgar Snow in *Saturday Evening Post*: "What the Russians Think of Us," Sept. 25, 1943, 91; "How Fast Can Russia Rebuild?" Feb. 12, 1944, 20; "The Ukraine Pays the Bill," Jan. 27, 1945, 84.

31. Snow, *People*, 250–51; Snow, "Eastern Europe Swings Left," 70; Harriman conversation in Snow, "Personalities."

32. Edgar Snow, "Strictly Confidential" typewritten notes on conversation with Litvinov, October 6, 1944, FDRL; Snow, *People*, 244–55; Snow, *Soviet Power*, 211–12; Nove, *Economic History*, 286–90; Frederick C. Barghoorn, *Soviet Foreign Propaganda* (Princeton University Press, 1964), 96.

33. Snow, *Journey*, 312–17; Edgar Snow to Grace Tully and Franklin Roosevelt, Dec. 28, 1944, FDRL. For background on Litvinov see Salisbury, *Journey for Our Times*, 216–17. Litvinov's comment to Harriman from interview with John Melby.

34. Franklin Roosevelt to Edgar Snow, Jan. 2, 1945, FDRL; Snow, "Fragments from F. D. R," March, 395–404; Snow, *Journey*, 341–45; John H. Crider, *New York Times*, March 2, 1945. For an example of other communications, Edgar Snow to Franklin Roosevelt, Nov. 18, 1942, FDRL.

35. Gaddis Smith, *American Diplomacy during the Second World War, 1941–1945* (Wiley, 1965), 63, 70, 153; Gaddis, *Cold War*, 14–18; Robert James Maddox, *The New Left and the Origins of the Cold War* (Princeton University Press, 1973), chapter 2, which discusses this issue with reference to Snow's conversations with Roosevelt; William Taubman, *Stalin's American Policy: From Entente to Detente to Cold War* (Norton, 1982), 132–33; Vojtech Mastny, *Russia's Road to the Cold War: Diplomacy, Warfare, and the Politics of Communism, 1941–1945* (Columbia University Press, 1979), 223, 283; Snow, "Fragments from F. D. R.," March, 399.

36. Smith, *American Diplomacy*, 74; Gaddis, *Cold War*, chapter 2; Wendell L. Willkie, *One World* (Simon & Schuster, 1943), 87; Frank Luther Mott, *Golden Multitudes: The Story of Best Sellers in the United States* (Macmillan, 1947), 331; Cantril and Strunk, *Public Opinion*, 962.

37. On Snow's books: Blum, *V for Victory*, 36; Ernest Cady, *Columbus Dispatch*, July 15, 1945; John Weilburg, *Chicago Sun*, Sept. 24, 1944; Snow, "Fragments from F.D.R.," March, 395, 402; Bennett Cerf, "Trade Winds," *Saturday Review of Literature*, Feb. 17, 1945, 25; "Council Chooses Snow Book as New 'Imperative,'" *Publishers' Weekly*, Sept. 30, 1944, 1399–1400; "Keeping Posted," *Saturday Evening Post*, Feb. 3, 1945, 4; Harry Hansen, *New York World-Telegram*, July 11, 1945; Edgar Snow, "What Kind of Man Is a Russian General?" *Saturday Evening Post*, April 17, 1943, 20; *Book-of-the-Month-Club News*, Sept. 1944, 26; Snow, *Soviet Power*, v; Toronto *Globe and Mail*, Nov. 15, 1943; Ralph Peterson, Louisville *Courier-Journal*, Aug. 19, 1945. For examples of Snow blending larger issues and people in his stories see "Must Britain Give Up India?" 9, and "China's Flying Freighters," 20; "Keeping Posted," *Saturday Evening Post*, Oct. 24, 1942, 4. Bennett Cerf to Edgar Snow, March 28, 1945, RHP; Snow to Frances Merriam, Jan. 31, 1945, RHP. Snow to "Mr. Chen," Jan. 4, 1964, ESC.

38. Edgar Snow, "They're Getting Their Alibis Ready," *Saturday Evening Post*, July 28, 1945, 12; Snow, *Journey*, 350–56; Edgar Snow, "Behind Russian Lines in Austria," *Saturday Evening Post*, Aug. 11, 1945, 18.

39. "Keeping Posted," *Saturday Evening Post*, Sept. 1, 1945, 4.

40. Snow, "The Stalin Truman Faces," 20; Edgar Snow to Saxe Commins, July 21, 1945, RHP.

Six: In the Path of the Storm

1. Blankfort, *Big Yankee*, 340; J. B. Powell, "I Was a Prisoner of the Japanese," *Readers Digest*, Nov. 1942, 63–66; Powell, "Missouri Journalists," 45–55; Powell, *25 Years*, 338–42, 370–404; interview with John W. Powell; *Chicago Tribune*, Jan. 30, 1944; Rozanski, "American Journalists," 372; Snow, *People*, 6; Bertram, *Beneath the Shadow: A New Zealander in the Far East, 1939–46* (John Day, 1947).

2. Snow, *Journey*, 287; Snow, *People*, 46, 260; "Hibbs and the Satevepost Happy 10-Year Marriage," *Business Week*, March 15, 1952, 67.

3. John Gunther, *Inside U.S.A.* (Harper, 1946), 281, 288; Gaddis, *Cold War*, 46; Blum, *V for Victory*, 255; George Sessions Perry, "Kansas City," *Saturday Evening Post*, Aug. 25, 1945, 14, 39.

4. Edgar Snow, "Meet Mr. and Mrs. Russia at Home," *Saturday Evening Post*, Dec. 22, 1945, 15; Snow, *Journey*, 321.

5. Edgar Snow, "Russia Still Suspects Us," *Saturday Evening Post*, Nov. 17, 1945, 9–10; Snow, *Journey*, 360–61, 382; George F. Kennan, *Memoirs (1925–1950)* (Bantam, 1969), 267–71; interview with George Kennan. Snow offered an analysis of his thinking about the Soviet Union after the war in Edgar Snow to Raymond Marcus, Jan. 25, 1951, Raymond Marcus files.

6. House Committee on Foreign Affairs, *European Study Trip, August 12 to October 13, 1945*, 79th Cong., 1st sess., 1946, Committee Print, 11–19.

7. Edgar Snow, "Oil and the King of Arabia," in Overseas Press Club of America Editorial Committee, ed., *Deadline Delayed* (Dutton, 1947), 118–32; Snow, *Journey*, 373–82.

8. Background and quotes on Snow's travels in Thailand and Indo-China found in his *Saturday Evening Post* articles: "Secrets from Siam," Jan. 12, 1946, 12; and "No Four Freedoms for Indo-China," Feb. 2, 1946, 20. Snow mentioned his Kunming visit in passing, *Red China Today*, 602.

9. Edgar Snow to Saxe Commins, Nov. 10, 1945, ESC; Beckman to author, n.d. and May 21, 1981; Snow, *Journey*, 390–91; Luis Taruc recalled Snow's visit in interview with Bryant George, Jan. 23, 1985, conducted on behalf of author.

10. Edgar Snow, "The Philippines Cry for Help," *Saturday Evening Post*, March 16, 1946, 14–15.

11. Luis Taruc, *He Who Rides the Tiger: The Story of an Asian Guerrilla Leader* (Praeger, 1967), 25–33.

12. Edgar Snow, *Red Star over China* (Modern Library, 1944), ix, hereafter referred to as *Red Star* (1944).

13. Xiao, "A Talk on Edgar Snow."

14. Background on press relations with China from 1939 to 1945 in Shewmaker, *Americans and Chinese Communists*, chapters 8, 9, 10; Shewmaker, "Mandate of Heaven vs. U.S. Newsmen," 274–86; White and Jacoby, *Thunder*, 213. Material on developments in China and U.S. policy toward China is drawn from Spence, *Gate of Heavenly Peace*, 327–52; Tuchman, *Stilwell*, 455–509; Schaller, *Crusade*, 87–229.

15. Chou En-lai to Edgar Snow, May 18, 1942, ESC; Snow, *Red Star* (1938, rev.), 476; Tsou, *America's Failure*, 51; C. P. Fitzgerald, *Mao and China*, 58–64.

16. Edgar Snow, *Village in August* (Smith & Durrell, 1942), ix–xix; Edgar Snow to Evans Carlson, March 13, 1945, ESC. Background on Indusco: Reynolds, "Cooperative Movement," 179, 353–58, 430; Hogg, *I See a New China*, 196–200; Helen Snow to author, June 7, 1982; H. Snow, *Notes on Industrial Cooperatives*, 80–81; "New Industries," 32; Snow, *Journey*, 233, 237–38; Edgar Snow, "China's Guerrilla Industry," *Asia and the Americas*, May 1944, 211; Snow, *Random Notes*, 126.

17. R. W. Barnett, memorandum to C. B. Fahs and Charles Stelle, Aug. 8, 1942, Robert Barnett files. It is difficult to underestimate the degree of self-censorship. For another example see Evans F. Carlson's admission that he held back criticism, Carlson to Raymond Gram Swing, Nov. 1, 1944, Raymond Gram Swing Papers, Manuscript Division, Library of Congress, Washington, D.C. Snow helped journalist Doris Rubens meet Mme. Sun in Hongkong before the war. Afterward Rubens wrote *Bread and Rice* and sent Snow proofs. He asked her to delete "gossip," apparently derived from Mme. Sun, which dealt in part with China relief activities, Edgar Snow to Doris Rubens, Oct. 24, 1946, Doris Rubens Macauley files.

18. Dallek, *American Foreign Policy*, 123; Steele, *American People and China*, 22–28; Isaacs, *Scratches*, 175–76; Willkie, *One World*, 120–21.

19. Ambassador Johnson to Secretary of State, Feb. 23, 1941, and Davies note, file 893.00/14650, DOS. John Paton Davies, Jr., *Dragon by the Tail: American, British, Japanese, and Russian Encounters with China and One Another* (Norton, 1972), 163; Buhite, *Nelson Johnson*, 144; Senate Committee on the Judiciary,

Morgenthau Diary (China), vol. 1, 89th Cong., 1st sess., 1965, Committee Print, 460–61.

20. Shewmaker, *Americans and Chinese Communists*, chapter 10; Tuchman, *Stilwell*, chapter 18; Smith, *American Diplomacy*, 94; Nathaniel Peffer, *New York Times*, Oct. 28, 1945; Edgar Snow to Trudie Schafer, June 4, 1969, Trudie Schafer files.

21. Snow, *Red Star* (1944), epilogue; Edgar Snow, "Sixty Million Lost Allies," *Saturday Evening Post*, June 10, 1944, 11–13.

22. For the debate with Lin, see Lin, *History of the Press*, 163; Lin Yutang, *San Francisco Chronicle*, Feb. 23, 1941; Lin Yutang, *My Country and My People* (John Day, 1939), 352, 391–92; Lin Yutang, *The Vigil of a Nation* (John Day, 1944), 111, 125, 224–42; Edgar Snow, "China to Lin Yutang," *The Nation*, Feb. 17, 1945, 180–83; Lin Yutang, "China and Its Critics," *The Nation*, March 24, 1945, 324–27; Edgar Snow, "China to Lin Yutang—II ," *The Nation*, March 31, 1945, 359. For examples of Snow's finely balanced views on CCP goals and timing in achieving them, see Snow, *Red Star*, (1938, rev.), 436–39, and Snow, *Battle for Asia*, 290–95. For his views in 1944, see Snow, "Sixty Million Lost Allies," 44; Snow, *People*, 290–94; and "War and Change in China: A Talk by Edgar Snow," an unpublished, undated speech probably delivered in late 1943 or 1944, NWP. For examples of more careful analysis see Snow, *Red Star* (1944), 502, 514; Edgar Snow, "Must China Go Red?" *Saturday Evening Post*, May 12, 1945, 9–10; Snow, *Soviet Power*, 132–45; Snow, "Fragments from F.D.R.," March, 397. Salisbury (*Long March*, 326) notes that many of those living in Yenan thought the revolution would not succeed quickly.

23. Snow, *Soviet Power*, 141.

24. Snow, *Soviet Power*, 140; Tuchman, *Stilwell*, 486, 511; Snow, *Random Notes*, 127–28; Tsou, *America's Failure*, 176–236; Tang Tsou "The American Political Tradition and the American Image of Chinese Communism," *Political Science Quarterly*, 77 (Dec. 1962):570–600. Tsou's illuminating discussion of American perceptions of Chinese communism overdramatizes Snow's change of attitude in 1944. As discussed above, the change was a shift rather than an entirely new stance.

25. Max Eastman and J. B. Powell, "The Fate of the World Is at Stake in China," *Reader's Digest*, June 1945, 16; Powell, *25 Years*, 422; interviews with John W. Powell and Elizabeth Hart Woo; *Chicago Tribune*, Sept. 2, and Oct. 3, 1942; Aug. 6, 1946; March 1, 1947; Ross Y. Koen, with Richard C. Kagan, ed., *The China Lobby in American Politics* (Harper & Row, 1974), 51.

26. Herbert Feis, *The China Tangle: The American Effort in China from Pearl Harbor to the Marshall Mission* (Princeton University Press, 1953), 362–63; 406–12; Schaller, *Crusade*, 273.

27. Interview with Israel Epstein; Cohen, "Chinese Communist Policy toward the United States, 1934–1945," 562–63; Agnes Smedley, "Red China in the News," *New Republic*, March 12, 1945, 363–64; Snow, *Journey*, 266; Shewmaker, *Americans and Chinese Communists*, 162; Isaacs, *Scratches*, 163; Edgar Snow, notes from conversation with Mao Tse-tung, 1960, ESC.

28. Tuchman, *Stilwell*, 523–24; "Edgar Snow Barred by Chungking Government," *Publishers' Weekly*, Dec. 15, 1945, 2623; "The Unacceptables," *Time*, Dec. 17, 1945, 58; *Washington Post* and *New York Times*, Dec. 8, 1945. Copy of Snow's protest, as well as related correspondence to U.S. officials, in Harry S. Truman Library, Independence, Mo., hereafter referred to as HSTL. In HSTL see especially Ben Hibbs to Harry S. Truman, telegram, Dec. 16, 1945.

29. Edgar Snow to Ben Hibbs and Martin Sommers, Aug. 12, 1946, ESC.

30. For Japan material see three 1946 articles by Edgar Snow in *Saturday Evening Post*: "What the Jap is Thinking Now," May 11, 9–10; "Hon. Spoils Rot in Japan," June 15, 22–23; "Is Japan Drifting toward Socialism?" June

22, 20. Also Snow, *Journey*, 391–92; Bertram, *Beneath the Shadow*, 226–27, 241–42. A translation of Snow's interview with Japanese Communists Kyuichi Tokuda and Yoshio Shiga, from *Minshu Shimbun*, Dec. 15, 1945, in PJP.

31. Edgar Snow, "We Meet Russia in Korea," *Saturday Evening Post*, March 30, 1946, 18–19; Snow, *Journey*, 393–98; Snow, "Fragments from F.D.R.," Jan., 318; Smith, *American Diplomacy*, 93.

32. Walter LaFeber, *America, Russia, and the Cold War, 1945–1966* (Wiley, 1967), 21–65; Gaddis, *Cold War*, 282–315. Ben Hibbs to Stewart Alsop, Nov. 18, 1947, Joseph W. and Stewart Alsop Papers, Manuscript Division, Library of Congress, Washington, D.C., hereafter referred to as JSAP.

33. David Caute, *The Great Fear: The Anti-Communist Purge under Truman and Eisenhower* (Simon & Schuster, 1978), 25–29; Richard M. Freeland, *The Truman Doctrine and the Origins of McCarthyism: Foreign Policy, Domestic Politics, and International Security, 1946–1948* (New York University Press, 1985), 115–34.

34. Walter Millis, ed., *Forrestal Diaries* (Viking, 1951), 177–78; John Gunther, *The Riddle of MacArthur: Japan, Korea and the Far East* (Harper, 1951), 64–71; William J. Coughlin, *Conquered Press: The MacArthur Era in Japanese Journalism* (Pacific Books, 1952), chapter 9; Bertram, *Beneath the Shadow*, 268; Walter Simmons, *Chicago Tribune*, Aug. 6, 1946; Utley, "Red Star over Independence Square," 9. Edgar Snow to Bennett Cerf, April 12, 1946, RHP. Yoko Matsuoka to Snow, May 3, 1947; and Snow to George Seldes, Feb. 13, 1954, ESC.

35. Rosemary Misurelli, member of Yaddo staff, to author, May 21, 1981. Edgar Snow's *Saturday Evening Post* series appeared in 1947 as: "Why We Don't Understand Russia," Feb. 15, 18–19; "How It Looks to Ivan Ivanovich," Feb. 22, 23; "Stalin Must Have Peace," March 1, 25. Snow's articles appeared in *Stalin Must Have Peace* (Random House, 1947), from which the quotes in this section are taken: see pages 23–24, 37, 55, 58, 87, 125, 141–42, 174. Ben Hibbs, "An Open Letter: To Generalissimo Stalin and Other *Post* Readers," *Saturday Evening Post*, Feb. 15, 1947, 19; Martin Sommers's introduction adapted from his article, "Why Russia Got the Drop on Us," *Saturday Evening Post*, Feb. 8, 1947, 25. For an example of *Post* editorial feeling at the time see "The Atom Argument Isn't So Simple," *Saturday Evening Post*, April 27, 1946, 120. For examples showing how close the *Post*'s wartime view was to Snow's see editorial, "The Russians Were Expendable," June 19, 1943, 108; Demaree Bess, "Let's Quit Pretending," Dec. 18, 1943, 9–10. The *Post* presented Bess's article as "representing the views" of the magazine.

36. Sommers's introduction did not appear in later editions. Lois Snow does not recall why, interview.

37. Edgar Snow to Martin Sommers, March 29, 1947, ESC; Snow to Charles G. Ross, Jan. 21, 1947, HSTL.

38. A description of the episode and the public's reaction is found in Richard Strouse, "Friendly Surprise," *New Republic*, March 3, 1947, 42–43; letters to the editor, *Saturday Evening Post*, March 22, 1947, 4. Snow did not tell the *New Republic* that Hibbs wanted to make editorial changes. Snow "thought if I went into all the mechanics of the production it might come out in some distorted form." Edgar Snow to Ben Hibbs, March 17, 1947, ESC.

39. Snow, *Stalin Must Have Peace*, 33–34. Patrick Hurley to Ben Hibbs, Feb. 15 and June 11, 1947, Patrick J. Hurley Papers, University of Oklahoma Library, Norman, Okla. Hurley to Hibbs, Feb. 28, 1947; Hibbs to Hurley, March 4, 1947; Hibbs to Edgar Snow, March 11, 1947; Snow to Hibbs and Snow to Hurley, March 17, 1947; and Martin Sommers to Snow, April 24, 1947, ESC. *Chicago Tribune*, Feb. 23, 1947. For background on Hurley-Stalin meeting see Feis, *China Tangle*, 287–89.

40. Snow to Jerry Crouter, Dec. 1947, ESC; H. E. Salisbury, *New York Times*, April 27, 1947; H. A. W., *Trenton Times*, May 4, 1947; W. H. Chamberlin, *Chicago Tribune*, May 11, 1947.

41. Martin Sommers to Edgar Snow, April 14, 1947; Helen Mangold, president of Social Service Employees' Union, to Edgar Snow, March 5, 1947, RHP.

42. Utley, "Red Star over Independence Square," 9–20; Patrick J. Hurley, "The Satevepost's's Mr. Snow," *Plain Talk*, March 1947, 23–24. For a detailed discussion of Utley's critique of changes Snow made in *Red Star* see chapter 4, note 10.

43. Ben Hibbs to Edgar Snow, March 26, 1948, ESC.

44. Snow, *Journey*, 370; also reported in *Philadelphia Bulletin*, Nov. 23, 1947.

45. Edgar Snow to Ben Hibbs, July 12, 1947; Hibbs to Snow, July 15, 1947, ESC.

46. Martin Sommers to Edgar Snow, Oct. 6, 1947, RHP; interview with Lois W. Snow.

Seven: Ishmael in His Native Land

1. "The Strange Case of John P. Davies," *U.S. News & World Report*, Dec. 23, 1953, 26; John T. Flynn, *While You Slept: Our Tragedy in Asia and Who Made It* (Devin-Adair, 1951), 29, 45; Budenz, "The Menace of Red China," 23; Caute, *Great Fear*, 361, 368, 452. The latter book powerfully chronicles the horrors of the era.

2. Interviews with Lois W. Snow and Elizabeth Vincent; L. Snow, *Edgar Snow's China*, xi.

3. Interview with Lois W. Snow.

4. Edgar Snow articles in *Saturday Evening Post*: "The Rover Boys in Burma," May 19, 1948, 26–27; "The World's Queerest State," July 14, 1948, 24–25; "Has Britain Won Back India?" April 3, 1948, 30–31; "Can Gandhi's Heir Do His Job?" Aug. 29, 1948, 28.

5. Edgar Snow, "The Message of Gandhi," *Saturday Evening Post*, March 27, 1948, 24–25; Shirer, *Gandhi*, 227; Snow, *Journey*, 389–412; Vincent Sheean, *Lead, Kindly, Light* (Random House, 1949), 203–7. Interview with Margaret Parton.

6. Edgar Snow to Ben Hibbs, March 18 and 29, and April 5, 1948; Hibbs to Snow, March 26 and April 12, 1948, ESC.

7. Martin Sommers to Joseph Alsop, Dec. 27, 1946; to Stewart Alsop; Aug. 29, 1947; Ben Hibbs to Joseph McCarthy, Aug. 10, 1950; Joseph Alsop to Sommers, Sept. 9, 1951, JSAP. Joseph Alsop, "The Strange Case Of Louis Budenz," *Atlantic Monthly*, April 1952, 29–33; Joseph Alsop, "Will the CIO Shake the Communists Loose?" *Saturday Evening Post*, Feb. 22 and March 1, 1947, 15–16 and 26–27; and "Why We Lost China," *Saturday Evening Post*, Jan. 7, 1950, 47.

8. Edgar Snow in *Saturday Evening Post*: "Will Tito's Heretics Halt Russia?" Dec. 18, 1948, 22–23; and "Will China Become A Russian Satellite?" April 9, 1949, 30–31. Martin Sommers to Stewart Alsop, July 23, 1948; Sommers to Joseph and Stewart Alsop, Jan. 10, 1949, JSAP. Sommers to Edgar Snow, Feb. 7, 1949, ESC.

9. Edgar Snow's *Saturday Evening Post* articles: "The Venomous Doctor Vyshinsky," Oct. 21, 1950, 19–20; "Flagstaff, Arizona," Jan. 14, 1950, 34; "World Capital on Turtle Bay," June 17, 1950, 28; "Broadway Comes to Main Street," Oct. 28, 1950, 32–33; "Mexico City," May 12, 1951, 26; "Acapulco, Mexico," Aug. 4, 1951, 33. Edgar Snow to Martin Sommers, March 24 and April 5, 1950; to Maud Russell, executive director of Committee for a Democratic Far Eastern Policy, April 28, 1949; and to Messrs. Jinnet and MacFarlane,

Federal Bureau of Investigation, June 17, 1953, ESC. Edgar Snow to Raymond Marcus, Jan. 25, 1951, Raymond Marcus files. "Snow's Article Record with SEP," ESC. Strong and Keyssar, *Right in Her Soul*, 266, 271. A good summary of Snow's attitude toward the Soviet Union is found in *Journey*, 329–31, 362–69, 385–86.

10. Interviews with Harrison Salisbury and Charles Hogan; Gay Talese, *The Kingdom and the Power* (Laurel, 1981) 526–27.

11. White, *In Search of History*, 391–92; Stanley I. Kutler, *The American Inquisition: Justice and Injustice in the Cold War* (Hill & Wang, 1982), chapter 4; Snow affidavit to Mrs. R. B. Shipley, Director Passport Office, June 11, 1953, ESC. Edgar Snow in *Saturday Evening Post*: "He Could Wreck Marshall's Plan," Oct. 4, 1947, 26–27; "Why Michel Didn't Vote Communist," Dec. 27, 1947, 8; "Why France Can't Feed Herself," Jan. 10, 1948, 24; "Where Presidents Are Hired Men," Feb. 14, 1948, 12; "Here's How the Socialists Run a British Town," March 6, 1948, 28–29. Edgar Snow, "What We Could Do About Asia," *The Nation*, Jan. 28, 1950, 75–79.

12. Ben Hibbs to author, Oct. 22, 1974; Hibbs to Edgar Snow, June 16, 1953; Edgar Snow to Howard Snow, Feb. 2, 1951, ESC. Interviews with Lois W. Snow, Robert Fuoss, and Robert Sherrod, who reported for and later became editor of the *Saturday Evening Post*.

13. Edgar Snow, "Stalin's Sinister First Lieutenant," *Saturday Evening Post*, May 17, 1952, 29; and "Red China's Gentleman Hatchet Man," *Saturday Evening Post*, March 27, 1954, 24. Interview with Robert Sherrod, who recalled headline problems with the stories he filed from Asia.

14. Interviews with Lois W. Snow and Howard Snow; Edgar Snow to Mildred Snow Mackey, Feb. 17, Nov. 3, and Nov. 23, 1948, and undated 1949 letter, ESC.

15. Edgar Snow to J. E. Snow, July 7, 1952, ESC.

16. Portraits of Ed and Lois Snow and their time in Snedens Landing and Rockleigh are based on numerous interviews: Lois W. Snow, Mary Heathcote, Howard Snow, Dorothy Salisbury Davis, Harry Davis, Margaret Parton, Helen Zimbalist, Norman Rose, Madeleine Gekiere, Leonard Schwartz, Trudie Schafer, David Loth, Charles Hogan, and Elizabeth Vincent. Also, Owen Lattimore to author, Aug. 29, 1979; Randall Gould to author, Oct. 12, 1979; Lois Wheeler Snow, *A Death with Dignity: When the Chinese Came* (Random House, 1974), 17–36, 139.

17. Snow, *Journey*, 412.

18. Edgar Snow, "The Heir to Confucius' Name and Fame," *Asia*, Oct. 1930, 719. Edgar Snow to Howard Snow, Jan. 5, 1953, ESC. Interview with Claude Mackey.

19. Quoted congressional testimony found in R. C. Davis to Mr. Welch, "Re: Edgar Snow," Jan. 21, 1944, FBI. Also see Stuart Lillico testimony in House Committee on Un-American Activities, *Investigation of Un-American Propaganda Activities in the United States*, vol. 4, 75th Cong., 3d sess., 1939, Committee Print, 2510–11. Caute, *Great Fear*, 88–89.

20. J. Edgar Hoover to SAC, New York, Jan. 27, 1944; Davis to Welch, "Re: Edgar Snow," Jan. 21, 1944; J. C. Strickland to D. M. Ladd, May 25, 1945; D. M. Ladd to the director, Sept. 4, 1947; FBI report on "Edgar Parks Snow," June 4, 1951; SAC, New York, to Director, FBI, "interview with Edgar Parks Snow," June 29, 1953; "Report on Edgar Parks Snow," October 20, 1955. The above documents from Snow's FBI files, provided under the Freedom of Information Act (FOIA), cannot be considered complete. FOIA staff deleted names of informants and, in some instances, refused to release entire pages from their files. When asked about excluded information, a FOIA officer volunteered that the information was not "as interesting as shoot'em up bank

robberies." Although that is a matter of opinion, the general tenor of the reports suggests that omitted material would not substantially change the conclusions reached in this chapter. Other background: Leo P. Ribuffo, *The Old Christian Right: The Protestant Far Right from the Great Depression to the Cold War* (Temple University, 1983), 184; Richard Gid Powers, *Secrecy and Power: The Life of J. Edgar Hoover* (Free Press, 1987), 214–15.

21. Interview with Charles Seib, who covered Capitol Hill at the time for the International News Service.

22. Interview with John Leaning. Edgar Snow to Owen Lattimore, Nov. 15, and to Howard Snow, Dec. 22, 1952, ESC; Kutler, *The American Inquisition*, chapters 7 and 8; E. J. Kahn, Jr., *The China Hands: America's Foreign Service Officers and What Befell Them* (Viking, 1975), 267–73. For a favorable account of Kohlberg see Joseph Keeley, *The China Lobby Man: The Story of Alfred Kohlberg* (Arlington House, 1969).

23. Interview with Lois W. Snow; Steven MacKinnon to author, Nov. 20, 1981; Chalmers Johnson, *An Instance of Treason: Ozaki Hotsumi and the Sorge Spy Ring* (Stanford University Press, 1964), 60–66; Edgar Snow, "MacArthur's Fantasy," *The Nation*, Jan. 19, 1949, 202–3.

24. House Committee on Un-American Activities, *The Role of the Press in the Communist Conspiracy*, 82d Cong., 1st sess., 1952, Committee Print, 2192; Senate Committee on Foreign Relations, *State Department Employee Loyalty Investigation*, pt. 1, 81st Cong., 2d sess., 1950, S. Rept. 2108, 594–95; Senate Committee on the Judiciary, *Institute of Pacific Relations*, 82d Cong., 2d sess., 1952, S. Rept. 2050, 100, 115–16; Senate Subcommittee on Internal Security, *Institute of Pacific Relations*, pt. 2, 82d Cong., 1st sess., Committee Print, 680; Senate Subcommittee on Internal Security, *Interlocking Subversion in Government Departments: "Army Information and Education,"* pt. 20, 83d Cong., 2d sess., 1954, Committee Print, 1637; Senate Subcommittee on Internal Security, *21-Year Index: Combined Cumulative Index—1951–1971*, vol. 2, Aug. 1972, Committee Print, 1386; Edgar Snow, "Soviet Society in Northwest China," *Pacific Affairs* 10 (Sept. 1937):266–75; *Chicago Tribune*, June 3, 1950.

25. Davies's testimony on Snow contained in Senate Subcommittee on Internal Security, *Institute of Pacific Relations*, pt. 14, 82d Cong., 2d sess., 1952, Committee Print, 5461–68; Snow, *Journey*, 332–34; Kahn, *China Hands*, 244–46, 257–63; White, *In Search of History*, 384.

26. Senate Subcommittee on Internal Security, *Institute of Pacific Relations*, pt. 1, 82d Cong., 1st sess., 1951, Committee Print, 303. G. L. Ulmen argues that Wittfogel was correct and notes that Philip Jaffe, for whom Ulmen was a research assistant, thought Wittfogel influenced Snow's views on the Comintern. In his autobiography, however, Jaffe wrote that *Red Star's* "anti-Soviet bias undoubtedly reflected what Snow saw and heard in Yenan." G. L. Ulmen, *The Science of Society: Toward an Understanding of the Life and Work of Karl August Wittfogel* (Mouton Publishers, 1978), 202–3; interviews with Wittfogel and Ulmen; Jaffe, *Odyssey*, 74. For what it is worth, Snow quoted Wittfogel on another issue in *Red Star*, 78. Snow comments on sending draft *Red Star* material to Wittfogel in Edgar Snow, "China since the Bomb," unpublished typewritten manuscript, VIII–5.

27. Irene Corbally Kuhn, "Why You Buy Books That Sell Communism," *American Legion Magazine*, Jan. 1951, 58–60; Joseph P. Kamp, *America Betrayed* (Constitutional Educational League, 1950), 22–23; Flynn, *While You Slept*, 59–61, 73–74, 82, 88; Freda Utley, *The China Story* (Henry Regnery, 1951), 157. Interview with Freda Utley. For other comments on Snow see Louis Francis Budenz, *The Bolshevik Invasion of the West* (Bookmailer, 1966), 206; Anthony Kubek, *How the Far East Was Lost: American Policy and the Creation of Communist*

China, 1941–1949 (Henry Regnery, 1951), 365, 371–72; Joseph McCarthy, *McCarthyism: The Fight for America* (Devin-Adair, 1952), 63.

28. William Fulton, *Chicago Tribune*, Feb. 26, 1951; Willard Edwards, *Chicago Tribune*, Feb. 16, 1952; *New York Times*, Feb. 17, 1952; James B. Reston, *New York Times*, Dec. 9, 1953; Edgar Snow, letter to editor, and Reston reply, *New York Times*, Dec. 12, 1953; Edgar Snow to Howard Snow, Jan. 5, 1953, ESC. Reston comments more strongly on the problems of covering McCarthyism in his book, *The Artillery of the Press: Its Influence on American Foreign Policy* (Harper & Row, 1967), 16. Interview with Charles Seib; and not-for-attribution interview. For analysis of Luce's anti-Communist hostility, see John Hersey, "Henry Luce's China Dream," *New Republic*, May 2, 1983.

29. Interviews with F. McCracken Fisher and Harry Price; Allison, *Ambassador*, 115–16; Caute, *Great Fear*, 282. The State Department Office of Security apparently lost or destroyed the files on Snow; the files are not among State Department records in the National Archives. Michael Q. Lee, State Department Information and Privacy Staff, to author, Aug. 19, 1981.

30. Senate Subcommittee on Internal Security, *Institute of Pacific Relations*, pt. 6, 82d Cong., 2d sess., 1952, Committee Print, 1781–82.

31. Charles Alexander, *Holding the Line: The Eisenhower Era, 1952–1961* (Indiana University Press, 1975), 54; Samuel A. Stouffer, *Communism, Conformity and Civil Liberties* (Wiley, 1967), 30; LaFeber, *The Cold War*, 137–38; Walter Sullivan, *New York Times*, June 11 and June 22, 1953; Edgar Snow, letter to editor, *New York Times*, June 16, 1953; Edgar Snow to Dwight D. Eisenhower, June 30, 1953, to Karl Mundt, June 24, 1953, and to Mildred Snow Mackey, Aug. 8, 1953; Ben G. Crosby, State Dept. Director of Congressional and Public Information, to Edgar Snow, July 31, 1953, ESC.

32. L. Snow, *Death with Dignity*, 23–25; Edgar Snow to Arthur Hays Sulzberger, Oct. 4, 1958, ESC; interviews with Lois W. Snow, Charles Joelson, and Harry Davis. Joelson later became a congressman and judge.

33. T. M. O., *Kansas City Star*, Oct. 7, 1944; interviews with Claude Mackey and Robert Long.

34. "A Long Footnote," *One Man's Opinion*, Feb. 1956, 9; John Birch Society files, located in Belmont, Mass. Howard Snow to Edgar Snow, Dec. 29, 1952; Edgar Snow to Howard Snow, June 18, 1953, and Feb. 22, 1956; Edgar Snow to Mildred Snow Mackey, July 14, 1953, ESC. Caute, *Great Fear*, 349; interviews with Howard Snow and Helen Laney, librarian at NAM.

35. Mildred Snow Mackey to Edgar Snow, June 13, 1956; Edgar Snow to "Mickey," March 27, 1956, to Robert H. W. Welch, Jr., July 21, 1956, and to Darrell Berrigan, Oct. 2, 1954, ESC. FBI report on "Edgar Parks Snow," June 4, 1951, FBI. Louis F. Budenz, *The Techniques of Communism* (Henry Regnery, 1954), 228.

36. Carey McWilliams to author, Oct. 24, 1975; Edgar Snow to Howard Snow, July 29, 1954, and Nov. 19, 1955, ESC. Edgar Snow's three-part editorial in "Nationalism-Colonialism: The New Challenge," *The Nation*, Oct. 22, 1955, 333–34, Oct. 29, 1955, 353–55, Nov. 12, 1955, 409–11; Koen, *China Lobby*, 131; Carey McWilliams, *The Education of Carey McWilliams* (Simon & Schuster, 1979), 182–83; Caute, *Great Fear*, 454; Service, "Edgar Snow Reminiscences," 215. For example of letter to editor see Edgar Snow, *New York Times*, Feb. 26, 1955.

37. Edgar Snow to Howard Snow, Dec. 13, 1954, ESC.

38. Edgar Snow to Saxe Commins, May 1, 1951, RHP. Edgar Snow, "Slave Girl," *Saturday Evening Post*, Oct. 20, 1951, 42–43; L. Snow, *Death with Dignity*, 23. Snow's 1960 interview with Mao Tse-tung, ESC. Edgar Snow to Mildred Snow Mackey, March 22, 1954, ESC. Manuscript of "Where the Blue Sky Begins" located ESC.

39. Background on *Journey to the Beginning*: L. Snow, *Death with Dignity*, 23; Dorothy Commins, *What Is an Editor? Saxe Commins at Work* (University of Chicago Press, 1978), 175–76; interview with Mary Heathcote; Edgar Snow to Darrell Berrigan, Oct. 27, 1952; to Howard Snow, Feb. 2, 1951; and to Mildred Snow Mackey, Nov. 14 and 16, 1958, ESC. Reviews: Philip Foisie, *Washington Post*, Oct. 26, 1958; Annalee Jacoby, *Saturday Review*, Nov. 22, 1958; C. L. Sulzberger, *New York Times*, Oct. 25, 1958; A. T. Steele, *New York Herald Tribune*, Oct. 26, 1958; and, for an example of a wholly positive review, James Nelson Goodsell, *St. Louis Post-Dispatch*, Oct. 14, 1958. Lee Mortimer, *New York Mirror*, Dec. 13, 1958.

40. Snow, *Journey*, 413–23; Edgar Snow, "From 'Brinkmanship' to Negotiation," *United Asia*, April 1957, 99; Edgar Snow, "China: The Ghost at the Summit," *The Nation*, May 23, 1959, 467–71; Edgar Snow, "Red China at Geneva," *The Nation*, April 24, 1954, 350–52; Alexander, *Holding the Line*, 79–81, 284–85.

41. Interview with Charles White.

42. McWilliams, *Education of Carey McWilliams*, 147–48, 183; Snow, *Journey*, 240; Service, "Edgar Snow Reminiscences," 216.

43. This discussion of Snow's perception of America draws from: Edgar Snow to Howard Snow, Dec. 22, 1952; May 1, 16, and 17, and June 5, 1953; Aug. 15, and Dec. 13, 1954; June 1, 1955; Feb 10, 1959; Edgar Snow to Darrell Berrigan, Nov. 16, 1953; and Howard Snow to Edgar Snow, May 11, 1953, ESC. Edgar Snow in *The Nation*: "All for One: The Corporation Is All," Oct. 2, 1954, 292–96, and "Point IV for America," May 12, 1956, 394–97; Alexander, *Holding the Line*, chapter 4; John Brooks, *The Great Leap: The Past Twenty-five Years in America* (Harper Colophon, 1968), chapter 2. Walter Prescott Webb's views found in his *The Great Frontier* (University of Texas Press, 1964); Webb quote is on page 132.

44. Edgar Snow to Howard Snow, May 24, 1955, ESC; Edgar Snow, "He's Betting on the Atom Age," *Saturday Evening Post*, Sept. 1, 1956, 28; Snow, *Red China Today*, 720.

45. *Kansas City Star*, Aug. 7, 1949; Edgar Snow to Howard Snow, Jan. 4, 1954, ESC; Snow, *Journey*, 231.

46. Edgar Snow to Howard Snow, March 1 and April 1, 1957, and to Rewi Alley, April 24, 1956, ESC.

47. Interviews with Lois W. Snow, Karl Jaeger, Calvin Kytle, and R. Roger Majak. Also Karl Jaeger files, Bath, England.

Eight: The Long Perspective

1. Edgar Snow, "Main Street Moves to Amirabad," *Saturday Evening Post*, Sept. 2, 1944, 18; Steele, *American People and China*, 31–35; Caute, *Great Fear*, 90; Alexander, *Holding the Line*, 90–91; Cohen, *America's Response*, 215–26. Also see Warren I. Cohen, "Acheson, His Advisers, and China, 1949–1950," and John Lewis Gaddis, " 'Defensive Perimeter' Concept, 1947–1951," both in *Uncertain Years: Chinese-American Relations, 1947–1950*, ed. Dorothy Borg and Waldo Heinrichs (Columbia University Press, 1980).

2. Chiang Kai-shek, *China's Destiny* (Roy, 1947), 229; Edgar Snow, "Asia and the Future of Co-Existence," address to the Council on World Affairs, Cleveland, Ohio, March 28, 1955.

3. For background on CCP advances and setbacks, see Meisner, *Mao's China*, especially chapters 8, 12, and 14; Roderick MacFarquhar, *The Origins of*

the Cultural Revolution: The Great Leap Forward, 1958–1960 (Columbia University Press, 1983), especially conclusion; John K. Fairbank, *The Great Chinese Revolution: 1800–1985* (Harper & Row, 1986), chapters 15 and 16; Spence, *Gate of Heavenly Peace*, chapter 12; World Bank study, *China: Socialist Economic Development* (World Bank, 1983), vols. 1–3; Thomas G. Rawski, *Economic Growth and Employment in China* (Oxford University Press, 1979), 193–97; Anthony M. Tang and Bruce Stone, *Food Production in the People's Republic of China: Research Report* (International Food Policy Research Institute, May 1980), 13–16. Rewi Alley to Edgar Snow, Sept. 1, 1968, ESC.

4. William W. Alfeld, "Newsgathering and the Right to Travel Abroad," *Journalism Quarterly* 36 (Fall 1959):423–30; Alexander, *Holding the Line*, 86–87; Peter G. Filene, *Americans and the Soviet Experiment* (Harvard University Press, 1967), 59; Tom Engelhardt, "Long Day's Journey: American Observers in China, 1948–50," in *China and Ourselves: Explorations and Revisions by a New Generation* ed. Bruce Douglass and Ross Terrill (Beacon Press, 1970), 112–13; John McCook Roots, *Chou* (Doubleday, 1978), 120–29; "China: High Tide of Terror," *Time*, March 5, 1956, 27–33; Julian Schuman, *Assignment China* (Whittier, 1956), 185–92; Steele, *American People and China*, 164; John Strohm, *Milwaukee Journal*, Oct. 13, 1958.

5. Snow, *Red China Today*, 334, 371. Edgar Snow to editor, *Time*, April 2, 1956, 8. Edgar Snow–Rewi Alley correspondence, especially Alley to Snow, Sept. 28, 1955; April 24, 1956; Feb. 25, 1958; June 5 and 14, 1958, ESC. Also Edgar Snow to Han Yang-seng and Lao Sheh, March 1, 1957, and July 3, 1958; to Hilda Selwyn-Clark, June 14, 1958; to Israel Epstein, Jan. 29, 1959, ESC.

6. Snow, "Asia and the Future of Co-Existence"; Snow, "Red China's Gentleman Hatchet Man"; Edgar Snow, "Recognition of the People's Republic of China," *Annals of the American Academy of Political and Social Science* 324 (July 1959):75–88.

7. Interviews with Lois W. Snow and Karl Jaeger. Background on school located in ESC and Edgar Snow to Harry and Dorothy Salisbury Davis, Jan. 25, 1960, Davis's files. Edgar Snow to Donald Klopfer, May 18, 1960; Dan Mich to Snow, cable, June 15, 1960; Mich to Snow, Aug. 29, 1960, RHP. R. O. L'Allier to A. H. Belmont, June 11, 1960, FBI. Ben Hibbs to author, Dec. 8, 1974. Snow, *Red China Today*, 4–11, 77; "Snow Job," *Time*, July 25, 1960, 60.

8. Snow, *Red China Today*, 20.

9. Ibid., 314, 337–38, 544.

10. Ibid., 22, 206, 302, 393, 454. Not-for-attribution interview with Chinese official familiar with Snow's travels.

11. Snow's interview with Chou in "Red China's Leaders Talk Peace—On Their Terms," *Look*, Jan. 31, 1961, 86–87. Also Snow, *Red China Today*, 73–101.

12. Edgar Snow, Notes of Conversations with Mao Tse-tung, Oct. 22 and 27, 1960, ESC, hereafter referred to as "Mao Conversations." Also, Snow, *Red China Today*, 115, 120.

13. Utley, *China at War*, 74; interview with not-for-attribution Chinese source; Snow, *Red China Today*, 4, 43, 73–75, 105, 190, 267–68, 284, 455; Terrill, *White-Boned Demon*, 233; Snow, "Mao Conversations"; Strong and Keyssar, *Right in Her Soul*, 297–98.

14. Edgar Snow to Bennett Cerf, RHP. Edgar Snow to Chou En-lai, Aug. 18, 1960, ESC. Snow, *Red China Today*, 606–7.

15. Mme. Sun Yat-sen to Edgar Snow, Nov. 3, 1960, ESC. Interviews with Charles Hogan and Felix Greene. Snow, *Red China Today*, 31.

16. Snow, *Red China Today*, 207–8, 366, 531, 541–42, 579, 587, 602. For an example of Snow worrying about CCP impressions of his journalism see Edgar Snow to Rewi Alley, March 11, 1961, ESC.

17. On Snow's difficulties and frustrating reporting see *Red China Today,* 22, 27, 58, 65, 293, 379, 439–40, 464, 538, 541. Examples of his criticism of the Communists: 9, 181–83, 395, 711, 714. Also interview with Israel Epstein.

18. Snow, *Red China Today,* 4, 402–3.

19. On Snow's views of democracy and equity see *Red China Today,* 187, 240, 248–57, 289, 292–300, 562, 590. Also, Edgar Snow to John W. Powell, April 7, 1961, ESC. Interview with Lois W. Snow.

20. On Snow's use of comparisons, see *Red China Today,* 43, 106–7, 326, 341, 352, 358–63.

21. On cult of Mao, A. T. Steele, *New York Herald Tribune,* Feb. 4, 1949; interviews with Israel Epstein, R. Roger Majak, and not-for-attribution Chinese source. Also, Snow, *Red China Today,* 120–22, 145, 150–52. Snow said he did not voice concerns about the cult to Mao until 1965, but notes of his 1960 meeting show that he at least indirectly raised the issue then: Snow, *The Long Revolution,* 67.

22. Snow, *Red China Today,* 360, 641–42; for one subsequent version of the P'eng story, see MacFarquhar, *The Great Leap Forward,* chapter 10; also Clare Hollingworth, *Mao and the Men against Him* (Jonathan Cape, 1985), 350; Meisner, *Mao's China,* 460. The Harvard student was Edward Friedman, interview.

23. Snow, *Red China Today,* 148, 154. Salisbury, *Long March,* 327.

24. On famine see Snow, *Red China Today,* 51–54, 147, 172–76, 188, 280–81, 620–24. Rewi Alley to Edgar Snow, May 2, 1961; other examples, Alley to Snow, Feb. 5, Feb. 20, Aug. 26, and Oct. 5, 1961, ESC. FitzGerald, *Mao and China,* 119. For discussion of grain production figures see especially Thomas P. Bernstein, "Stalinism, Famine, and Chinese Peasants: Grain Procurements during the Great Leap Forward," *Theory and Society* 13 (May 1984):339–77; also, Tang and Stone, *Food Production,* 26, 88–89, which cites grain production figures exceeding 150 million metric tons; World Bank, *China: Socialist Economic Development,* vol. 2, 54. Joseph Alsop, "The Coming Explosion in Red China," *Saturday Evening Post,* Aug. 11–18, 1962, 79–83; *Time,* Dec. 1, 1961, 28–29.

25. Snow, *Red China Today,* 101, 642; Snow, *Random Notes,* 5.

26. Snow, *Red China Today,* 559–61, 741–42.

27. Ibid., 732.

28. Edgar Snow to Mildred Snow Mackey, Feb. 5, 1961, ESC. Snow, *Red China Today,* 716–17.

29. Interviews with Lois W. Snow; Service, "Edgar Snow Reminiscences," 216. Snow repeated this incident to many other friends.

30. In *Look,* Jan. 31, 1961: Editor's note, "A Report from Red China," 85; Snow, "Red China's Leaders Talk Peace—On Their Terms," 86–87; A. Doak Barnett, "What Chou En-lai's Words Mean to Us," 105. Snow, *Red China Today,* 86; Edgar Snow to Harry and Dorothy Salisbury Davis, Jan. 2, 1961, Davis's files; *Kansas City Star,* Jan. 16, 19, and 21, 1961. Senate Committee on Foreign Relations, *Nomination of Chester Bowles: Under Secretary of State-Designate,* 87th Cong., 1st sess., 1961; Chester Bowles, "The 'China Problem' Reconsidered," *Foreign Affairs* 38 (April 1960):476–86; Chester Bowles, *Promises to Keep: My Years in Public Life, 1941–1969* (Harper & Row, 1971), 391–403. Edgar Snow to Dan Mich, June 19, 1961, and to Donald Klopfer, June 23, 1961, RHP. Interview with Doak Barnett.

31. Interviews with Mary Heathcote and Harrison Salisbury. Edgar Snow to Kung P'eng, Feb. 14, 1961, and to Israel Epstein, May 22, 1962, ESC. Edgar Snow to Donald Klopfer, April 15, 1960; June 7, July 30, and Aug. 6, 1961, RHP. Edgar Snow to Harry and Dorothy Salisbury Davis, Dec. 2, 1961, Davis's files. Snow, *Red China Today,* 480; Felix Greene, *Awakened China: The Country Americans Don't Know* (Doubleday, 1961).

32. Book reviews: William M. McGovern, *Chicago Tribune*, Dec. 23, 1962; Mark Mancall, *New York Herald Tribune*, Dec. 2, 1962; John K. Hutches, *New York Herald Tribune*, Dec. 3, 1962; R. C. Lewis, *Book-of-the-Month Club News*, Jan. 1963, 14; *Time*, Dec. 14, 1962, 94; *New Yorker*, Dec. 29, 1962, 77; Harold C. Hinton, *Commonweal*, Jan. 11, 1963; George O. Totten, *Annals of the American Academy of Political and Social Science* 349 (Sept. 1963):212–13; Michael Lindsay, *New York Times*, Dec. 9, 1962. Snow–Lindsay exchange in *New York Times*, April 7, 1963. Also, Edgar Snow to Bennett Cerf, Dec. 2, 1962; Bennett Cerf to Edgar Snow, Dec 7, 1962, RHP. Edgar Snow to Mildred Snow Mackey, Dec. 16, 1962, ESC. Interviews with Mary Heathcote, John S. Service, and Michael Lindsay. Lindsay's 1940s perspective on China in Shewmaker, *Americans and Chinese Communists*, 131–34, 245–46. Steele, *American People and China*, 172. Snow, *Red China Today*, 36, 594.

33. Edgar Snow to Editor, *New York Herald Tribune*, Jan. 2, 1963, RHP. Edgar Snow to Editor, *Kansas City Times*, March 8, 1962, ESC. Edgar Snow, *The Long Revolution* (Random House, 1972), 7; *Publishers' Weekly*, Feb. 4, 1963, 128.

34. Snow, *Red China Today*, 718; Edgar Snow, Introduction, dated Dec. 10, 1963, to *China, Russia, U.S.A.: Changing Relations in a Changing World* (Marzani & Munsell, n.d.), x.

35. Steele, *American People and China*, chapter 6, plus appendix by Martin Patchen, "The American Public's View of U.S. Policy toward China."

36. M. A. Jones to Mr. DeLoach, Dec. 4 and Dec. 12, 1961; Director, FBI, to New York SAC, April 7, 1966, FBI. Kagan, Introduction to *China Lobby*, ix; Steele, *American People and China*, 121–22; Allan H. Ryskind, "Red Refugees Refute Old China Hand," *Human Events*, Jan. 5, 1963, 17; *Fresno Bee*, Jan. 12, 1962; Francis Xavier Gannon, *Biographical Dictionary of the Left* (American Opinion, 1968), 544–45; Sunwoo Nam, "The Taming of the Korean Press," *Columbia Journalism Review*, March/April 1978, 43–45.

37. James C. Thomson, Jr., "On Making of U.S. China Policy, 1961–9: A Study in Bureaucratic Politics," *China Quarterly* 50 (April-June, 1972):220–43; LaFeber, *The Cold War*, 217–18, 228–29; Cohen, *America's Response*, 216, 230–37; David Halberstam, *The Best and the Brightest* (Fawcett Crest, 1973), 375–423; Roger Hilsman, *To Move a Nation: The Politics of Foreign Policy in the Administration of John F. Kennedy* (Delta, 1967), 275–357; Harris Wofford, *Of Kennedys and Kings: Making Sense of the Sixties* (Farrar, Straus, Giroux, 1980), 29–30; Terrill, "John Carter Vincent and the American 'Loss' of China," in *China and Ourselves*, 127; Snow, "Personalities." Harrison Salisbury to Edgar Snow, April 14, 1966, ESC. Edgar Snow to Charles O. Porter and Ernest T. Nash, June 10, 1963, copy in Grenville Clark Papers, Baker Library, Dartmouth College, Hanover, N. H., hereafter referred to as GCP. Interviews with W. Averell Harriman and Robert Barnett, in whose files is a copy of Harriman's "Memorandum of Conversation with Snow," July 16, 1961.

38. Rockefeller report quoted in "Report from Red China," 85. Interview with Lawrence O. Houstoun.

39. Snow, *Red China Today*, 736, 760.

40. Ed Sullivan to Edgar Snow, Dec. 27, 1962, RHP.

41. Joseph Alsop, *New York Herald Tribune*, European Edition, June 26–27, 1965; Alsop, "The Coming Explosion in Red China," 80; John Hohenberg, *Between Two Worlds: Policy, Press, and Public Opinion in Asian-American Relations* (Praeger, 1967), 418–19. Edgar Snow to Martin Sommers, Oct. 11, 1963, ESC. Interviews with Trudie Schafer and Stanley Karnow.

42. Edgar Snow to Donald Klopfer, April 18, 1963; Aug. 31 and Oct. 7, 1964, RHP. Edgar Snow to Mildred Snow Mackey, Dec. 16, 1962, ESC. *Boston Herald Traveller*, June 1, 1963. Interview with Helen F. Snow.

43. Interview with Lois W. Snow. L. Snow, *Death with Dignity*, 43–44. Edgar Snow to Howard Snow, Dec. 8, 1962, and July 7, 1965; to Cecil Thomas, March 12, 1965, ESC. Edgar Snow to Grenville Clark, Aug. 21, 1964, GCP. All quotes from Snow correspondence with Clark appear in Kenneth E. Shewmaker, "The Grenville Clark—Edgar Snow Correspondence," *Pacific Historical Review* 45 (Nov. 1976): 597–601.

Nine: With Honor

1. Edgar Snow to Hernando Abaya, Dec. 17, 1969, ESC; Strong and Keyssar, *Right in Her Soul*, 304, 311.

2. K. S. Karol, *China: The Other Communism* (Hill and Wang, 1967), 2–10; George Hatem, "A True Representative of the American People," *China Remembers*, 35; Irving Dillard, "Grenville Clark: Public Citizen," *American Scholar* 7 (Winter 1963-64):1–8. Edgar Snow to Mao Tse-tung, May 10, 1963; to Ernest T. Nash (co-founder of Committee to Review China Policy), April 7, 1963; and to George Hatem, May 4, 1963, as well as other correspondence in GCP. Edgar Snow to Rewi Alley, Nov. 12, 1966, and to Abe Fortas, Sept. 5, 1964; George Pratt to Mary Dimond, n.d., plus other Pratt-Snow correspondence in ESC, especially Pratt to Snow, Jan. 20, 1963; Snow to Pratt, Feb. 5, 1963; Pratt to Michael Straus, July 10, 1964.

3. Edgar Snow to Kung P'eng, Sept. 21, 1963, ESC. Interview with Lois W. Snow. Steele, *American People and China*, 156.

4. Edgar Snow, *New York Times*, Feb. 3, 1964 (a more complete version ran in the *Washington Post*, Feb. 3, 1964); A. M. Halpern, ed., *Policies toward China: Views from Six Continents* (McGraw-Hill, 1965), 496–97. Edgar Snow to John Hillelson, Jan. 28, 1964, ESC.

5. Edgar Snow to Grenville Clark, April 10 and Sept. 28, 1964, GCP. Edgar Snow to Kung P'eng, Sept. 5, 1964; to "Mr. Chen," Jan. 4, 1964, ESC.

6. Edgar Snow to "Mary," Nov. 1, 1964, ESC. The book, never published, was entitled *China since the Bomb*; the manuscript is in ESC.

7. Snow, *The Long Revolution*, 67–70 191–237; Edgar Snow, "Interview with Mao," *New Republic*, Feb. 27, 1965, 17–23; *Washington Post*, Feb. 14, 1965. Related stories based on Snow's reports in *Stern* and *Le Nouveau Candide* can be found in *New York Times*, Feb. 12, 1965, and Bernard D. Nossiter, *Washington Post*, Feb. 20 and 26, 1965. Allen S. Whiting, Memorandum of Conversation, April 2, 1965, FBI; editorial "Let's Open the Door to China," *Saturday Evening Post*, July 25–Aug. 1, 1964, 84.

8. Israel Epstein, "Snow Speaks through Letters," *China Remembers*, 26. President Johnson's remarks in *New York Times*, April 8, 1965; Steel, *Lippmann*, 557–64. Edgar Snow to Harrison Salisbury, Jan. 30, Feb. 8, April 12, 1965; and Salisbury to Snow, Feb. 3 and March 19, 1965; Snow to George Pratt, Feb. 20, 1965; Snow to Kung P'eng, Feb. 28, 1965, ESC. Snow to Grenville Clark, March 15, 1965; March 4, 1966, GCP.

9. Edgar Snow to Mildred Snow Mackey, April 13, 1965, ESC. Snow to Grenville Clark, n.d., and Sept. 18, 1965, GCP. Interview with Mary Heathcote.

10. On Cultural Revolution see Fairbank, *Chinese Revolution*, 320; Spence, *Gate of Heavenly Peace*, 395–99; Meisner, *Mao's China*, 310, 338; Margaret Coffey, Jonathan Frerich, and Robert Bishop, "China Watchers and the Cultural Revolution," *Journalism Quarterly* 54 (Spring 1977):77–83; Anthony Grey, *Hostage in Peking* (Doubleday, 1971), 361; Michael Lindsay, "China Revisited," unpublished ms., Michael Lindsay files, 18. Rewi Alley to Edgar Snow, Jan. 24 and

Oct. 22, 1967; Sept. 1 and 23, 1968; Snow to Alley, Jan. 15, 1967; to Chou En-lai, July 10, 1967; to Israel Epstein, March 1, 1968; to Anthony Grey, March 1, 1970; draft letter to Kung P'eng, n.d., ESC. Snow to Trudie Schafer, July 20, 1968, Trudie Schafer files. Snow to Grenville Clark, Sept. 29, 1966, GCP. Interview with Israel Epstein.

11. Snow, *Red Star* (1968), 456, 471, 482, 508, 515; Edgar Snow, "China in 1966—and1986?" draft introduction for European editions of *Red China Today,* 8, ESC (dated Oct. 26, 1966); Edgar Snow, "The Man Alongside Mao," *New Republic,* Dec. 18, 1966, 15–18; Edgar Snow, "Why China Went Red," in Emil Schulthess, *China: A Story in Photographs* (Viking, 1966). Among other bits and pieces Snow wrote see Edgar Snow, Introduction to Joshua S. Horn, *Away with All Pests* (Hamlyn Publishing, 1969). Interviews with Trudie Schafer and Mary Heathcote. Edgar Snow to Howard Snow, July 15, 1968; to John Fairbank, July 12, 1968; to Mildred Snow Mackey, Nov. 3, 1968, and Jan. 8, 1969; to Israel Epstein, July 19, 1966; to Frank Taylor, July 14, 1969, ESC. For discussion of Mme. Mao and Mme. Liu, see Terrill, *White-Boned Demon,* 273–83.

12. Edgar Snow to Howard Snow, June 1, 1965, and May 22, 1969; to Mildred Snow Mackey, March 10, and May 17, 1970, ESC. Edgar Snow to Grenville Clark, Aug. 21, 1964, GCP. "Red China Gets Ready to Fire Its A-Bomb," *Business Week,* Aug. 1, 1964, 34.

13. On Vietnam see Edgar Snow to National Conference on the United States and China, April 26, 1965, a complete copy of which is located SHP; *Washington Post,* April 30, 1965; Snow, *Red China Today,* 726; Edgar Snow, "Barkinson's Law on Bombing," *Columbia University Forum Anthology* (Atheneum, 1968), 309–14 (originally appeared in the *Forum* in Spring 1967); Henry Steele Commager's favorable comment on Barkinson article, and one unfavorable remark, found in "Letters," *The Columbia University Forum* (Summer 1967):2; Lois Wheeler Snow, *New York Herald Tribune,* Feb. 16, 1966, March 9–10, 1968; Doris Kearns, *Lyndon Johnson and the American Dream* (Harper & Row, 1976), 252; Halberstam, *Best and Brightest,* 504–11, 630, 742. Edgar Snow in the *New Republic*: "Is Peace Still Possible?" May 22, 1965, 20; "Deeper into the Trap," Dec. 25, 1965, 15–18; "China and Vietnam," July 30, 1966, 12–14. Edgar Snow to Grenville Clark, Sept. 9, 1965; March 4, April 14, and June 10, 1966, GCP. Edgar Snow to George Pratt, April 4, 1965; Snow letter, undated, no addressee, ESC. Interviews with Richard Moose and William Fulbright. Fulbright quote from speech delivered shortly before Tonkin Gulf resolution, March 25, 1964, *Congressional Record,* 88th Cong., 2d sess., 6227–45.

14. Merry Selk, "The Five Principles—A New Approach," in *China after the Cultural Revolution* (Vintage, 1970), 213–16; Meisner, *Mao's China,* 397–412; Edgar Snow, "Mao and the New Mandate," *New Republic,* May 10, 1969, 17–21.

15. Everett Feay, *Fresno Bee,* July 21, 1968; Edward Radenzel, *San Francisco Chronicle,* Sept. 29, 1968; Welles Hangen, *Saturday Review,* July 27, 1968, 28; *New York Times,* Feb. 9, 1969; William Borders, *New York Times,* March 24, 1967; *Kansas City Times,* April 14, 1968; Epstein, "Snow Speaks through Letters," 27; Douglas and Terrill, Introduction, *China and Ourselves,* xxi.

16. Lois Wheeler Snow, "All You Need to Know for a Trip to China," *Saturday Review,* Oct. 23, 1971, 36–39; *Washington Post,* Aug. 15, 1970. Consul General cable to Sec. State, Aug. 14, 1970, FBI. Edgar Snow to Mao Tse-tung, July 30, 1969; to Howard Snow and Mildred Snow Mackey, Oct. 22, 1969; to Howard Snow, July 16, 1970, ESC. Edgar Snow, "Note regarding my state of health," July 1, 1970, ESC. Details of this trip taken from Snow's diary entries, July 31, Aug. 3, 5, and 11, 1970, ESC, hereafter referred to as "Diary." An Australian woman, married to an American and working for a San Francisco

newspaper, visited China in 1965; she did not tell the Chinese of her American connections; see Lisa Hobbs, *I Saw Red China* (McGraw-Hill, 1966).

17. For background on Sino-American diplomacy and Snow's role see Snow, "Diary," Aug. 16, 18, and 20–21, Oct. 1, 1970; Snow, *The Long Revolution*, 3–12 167–76; Henry Kissinger, *White House Years* (Little, Brown, 1979), chapter 18; Marvin Kalb and Bernard Kalb, *Kissinger* (Dell, 1975), chapters 9 and 10; Service, "Edgar Snow Reminiscences," 217. Nixon said he learned of Mao's invitation "within a few days after he made it to Snow," Richard Nixon, *The Memoirs of Richard Nixon* (Grossett & Dunlop, 1978), 547. For a brief report that may throw light on Chou's shifting views on the possibilities for Sino-American rapproachement, see William Safire, *New York Times*, Jan. 16, 1978.

18. On Snow's travels in China and his analysis of the Cultural Revolution, Snow, *The Long Revolution*, 75, 95, 117–29, 139–44; Snow, "Diary," *passim*; typed interview at Cereal Store No. 19, Sept. 26, 1970, ESC; L. Snow, *Death with Dignity*, 89; Rewi Alley, speech at 1982 commemoration of Snow's death, typewritten, author's files. Also interviews with Lois W. Snow and Huang Hua. For examples of the varying degrees of positive feelings mustered by others about the Cultural Revolution see William Hinton, *Turning Point in China: An Essay on the Cultural Revolution* (Monthly Review Press, 1972); Neale Hunter, *Shanghai Journal: An Eyewitness Account of the Cultural Revolution* (Praeger 1969); Jack Chen, *Inside the Cultural Revolution* (Macmillan, 1975).

19. Snow, "Diary," *passim*; L. Snow, *Death with Dignity*, 26–29; *Hongkong Standard*, Dec. 23, 1970, and Feb. 10, 1971; *South China Morning Post*, Dec. 23, 1970. Edgar Snow to Huang Hua, Jan. 11 and 30, 1971; to Lois Snow, Feb. 17, 1971, ESC. Lois Wheeler Snow's book appeared as *China on Stage: An American Actress in the People's Republic* (Random House, 1972).

20. Interview with Lois W. Snow. L. Snow, *Death with Dignity*, 32–34; Edgar Snow's articles in *New Republic*, 1971: "The Open Door," March 27; "Aftermath of the Cultural Revolution," April 10; "Population Care and Control," May 1; "The Army and the Party," May 22; "China's 70,000 Communes," June 26. Edgar Snow, "A Conversation with Mao," *Life*, April 30, 1971, 46–48; Kissinger, *White House Years*, 720; Nixon's TV announcement in *U.S. Policy toward China: July 15, 1971–January 15, 1979* (Department of State, 1979), 5; *Washington Post*, April 27, 1971. Edgar Snow to Howard Snow, July 31, 1971; to George McGovern, March 8, 1971; to Mao Tse-tung, May 16, 1971; to Eric Linder, Dec. 13, 1971, ESC.

21. Edgar Snow, "China Will Talk from a Position of Strength," *Life*, July 30, 1971, 22–24; Edgar Snow, "Why Nixon Is Relatively Good," *Time*, Aug. 2, 1971, 13; *Chicago Tribune*, July 17, 1971. Edgar Snow to Rewi Alley, April 20, June 18, and July 31, 1971; Ralph Graves to Snow, Oct. 20, 1971; Snow to Graves, Nov. 14, 1971; Jean Pohoryles to Snow, Oct. 7, 1971, ESC.

22. L. Snow, *Death with Dignity*, *passim*; Edgar Snow to Howard and Dorothy Snow, Oct. 20, 1971, ESC.

23. The exchange in the letters to the editor section of the *International Herald Tribune*: Lois and Edgar Snow, June 10, 1971; Joseph Alsop, June 21, 1971; Edgar Snow, June 26, 1971. Joseph Alsop, "Has China Changed?" *Foreign Policy* 10 (Spring 1973):73–76. On Alsop's changed attitude, *New York Times*, Feb. 4, 1973, and interview with Harrison Salisbury.

24. Kissinger, *White House Years*, 698, 701–2, 715, 1051; James Thomson, Jr., "Watching the China-Watchers," *Foreign Policy* 4 (Fall 1971):138–47; Tad Szulc, *The Illusion of Peace: Foreign Policy in the Nixon Years* (Viking, 1978), 664; Meisner, *Mao's China*, 408; Dallek, *American Foreign Policy*, 258–71; Lloyd C. Gardner, Introduction, *The Great Nixon Turnaround* (Franklin Watts, 1973), 1–44; Nixon, *Memoirs*, 559; Richard Nixon, "Asia after Vietnam," *Foreign Affairs* 46 (October 1967):111–25; Richard Nixon, "The New China Policy," *Department*

of State Bulletin, March 13, 1972; Nixon speech to Congress in *New York Times*, Feb. 29, 1972; Cohen, *America's Response*, 241–47; Edgar Snow, "East Asia after the Vietnam War Is Over," *New Republic*, July 6, 1968, 21–24. Shanghai Communiqué is printed in *U.S. Policy toward China: July 15, 1971–January 15, 1979*, 8. Edgar Snow to Howard Snow, May 18, 1970, ESC. Discussion of American interest in peace found in William Schneider, "Conservatism, Not Interventionism: Trends in Foreign Policy Opinion," in *Eagle Defiant: United States Foreign Policy in the 1980s*, ed. Kenneth A. Oye, Robert J. Lieber, and Donald Rothchild (Little, Brown, 1983), 42. For an example of how closely the Chinese could be attuned to nuances of gestures such as Mao standing with Snow on T'ien An Men Square see Nien Cheng, *Life and Death in Shanghai* (Grove, 1986), 306.

25. Edgar Snow, Preface, *China and Ourselves*, vii-xi; Robert Pearman, *Kansas City Star*, April 11, 1968; Nils Gunnar Nilsson, *Politiken*, Nov. 28, 1971. Edgar Snow to Owen Lattimore, May 19, 1970; to Mildred Snow Mackey, June 29, 1971, ESC. Interviews with Lois W. Snow and Trudie Schafer. News release on WCBS interview, Aug. 2, 1971, located author's files. Richard Nixon to Edgar Snow, Jan. 31, 1972, printed in *New York Times*, Feb. 20, 1972.

26. Edgar Snow to John Service, Nov. 25 and Dec. 6, 1971, John S. Service files. Soong Ch'ing-ling to Edgar Snow, Nov. 11, 1971, ESC. Interview with Lois W. Snow. John Burns, *Washington Post*, July 29, 1971.

27. Snow, *The Long Revolution*, 66, 188; L. Snow, *Death with Dignity*, 72. (Snow's final written words also located in his *Life* article, "China Will Speak from a Position of Strength.")

28. Details of Snow's last days in L. Snow, *Death with Dignity*, *passim*; interview with Lois W. Snow.

Ten: Righting the Wrongs?

1. L. Snow, *Death with Dignity*, 77, 132–37. Obituaries: *Kansas City Star*, Feb. 16, 1972; Alden Whitman, *New York Times*, Feb. 16, 1972; "The Man Who Knew Mao," *Newsweek*, Feb. 18, 1972, 46; Aldo Beckman, *Chicago Tribune*, Oct. 29, 1972; "Mao's Columbus," *Time*, Feb. 23, 1972, 45–46. *Cross and the Flag*, Dec. 1971, 30. Over the next years criticism of Snow surfaced from time to time in other places, for example, Frederick W. Williams, Letters to the Editor, *Editor & Publisher*, Nov. 2, 1985, 9. Williams protested that the magazine had described Snow, as well as Agnes Smedley and Anna Louise Strong, as journalists.

2. Interviews with Jerald ter Horst, Charles Bailey, and Philip Foisie—the latter *Washington Post* managing editor for foreign news who thought China coverage a scandal. It was Foisie who had proclaimed years earlier that Snow had lost his reporter's legs. J. F. ter Horst, "Peking," Robert L. Keatley, "Shanghai," and Charles W. Bailey, "A Hell of a Story," in *The President's Trip to China*, (Bantam, 1972), 17–18, 130, 139–44. Jerald F. ter Horst in "and how it was covered," *Quill*, April 1972, 10. John Chancellor, "Who Produced the China Show?" and Stanley Karnow, "Playing Second Fiddle to the Tube," both in *Foreign Policy* 7 (Summer 1972): 88–103.

3. Lois Wheeler Snow, "The Burial of Edgar Snow," *New Republic*, Jan. 26, 1974, 9–11; Sian Snow's comments quoted in Lois Snow to Mildred Snow Mackey, April 31, 1973, ESC.

4. For examples of Snow being cited in contemporary news reports: Ross B. Munro, *Washington Post*, Dec. 2, 1975; Edgar Snow, "Between God and Ma-

gog: An American Memoir," *Time*, Sept. 20, 1976, 18–19 (draft Mao obit in ESC); "The Talk of the Town," *New Yorker*, Nov. 29, 1976, 29–30; Chalmers Roberts, *Washington Post*, Jan. 14, 1979. On the enduring fame of *Red Star*: interview with Caio Kock-Weser, of World Bank, and June Plecan, former Peace Corps volunteer. Angela Davis, *Angela Davis: An Autobiography* (Random House, 1974), 51; Dong Leshan, "Edgar Snow and 'Red Star over China,'" *China Remembers*, 63. Example of Lu Hsun picture from author's own experience.

5. AP dispatch in *Kansas City Star*, Feb. 21, 1982.

6. James Truslow Adams, *The Adams Family* (Little, Brown, 1930), 24.

7. Interview with Roy Fisher.

8. Snow's first sale to the *Saturday Evening Post* was for $750. In the mid-1980s, fifty years later, the *New York Times* Sunday magazine paid $750 to $1500 for short articles and $1500 to $2500 for long pieces. *Writer's Market* (Writer's Digest Books, 1985), 497.

9. John F. Burns, "A Reporter's Odyssey In Unseen China," *New York Times Magazine*, Feb. 8, 1987, 29–31; James P. Sterba, *Wall Street Journal*, July 24, 1986.

10. Snow, *Journey*, 283.

11. Edgar Snow to "Mr. Chen," Jan. 4, 1964, ESC; Snow, *Journey*, 84.

12. Xiao Qian, "Snow and 'Living China,'" *China Remembers*, 56. Xiao's story in *Living China* was "The Conversion."

13. For a study of disaffected American intellectuals being deceived by Communist regimes, see Paul Hollander, *Political Pilgrims: Travels of Western Intellectuals to the Soviet Union, China, and Cuba* (Harper Colophon, 1981), especially chapter 8, "The Techniques of Hospitality: A Summary." Significantly Hollander gives scant attention to Snow, and then in several cases as a positive example. In one case where Hollander is negative about Snow, he misses the point. Hollander notes that Snow traveled in Chou En-lai's special train, implying that this colored Snow's reporting of China. Hollander fails to mention that Snow also described how average rail travelers had difficulty finding adequate food. Hollander, *Pilgrims*, 307, 365; Snow, *Red China Today*, 43–44, 73–74. Also relevant in the question of Snow's idealism is the comment of Simon Leys, a witty, acerbic, and elitist critic of the Chinese Communists. Leys has grouped Snow with Han Suyin and John King Fairbank. He finds fault with each, Snow's sin being that he was "naive." Yet Leys notes that "they are each uncommon personalities in their fields with superior information at their disposal. In the West, Maoism has no more convincing advocates, because (unlike the other members of that flock) they know whereof they speak—even if they do not say all they know." Simon Leys, *Chinese Shadows* (Viking, 1974), 213–14. Owen Lattimore discussed Chinese Communist views of Snow in Introduction to *China Shakes the World*, xi.

14. For a modern statement of Snow's views on the Soviet Union, see Robert Reich, *Tales of a New America* (Times Books, 1987), 65, 98–99. Bishops' statement quoted in Robert Shaplen, "Reporter at Large," *New Yorker*, Sept. 28, 1987, 70.

15. Henry Bamford Parkes, *The American Experience: An Interpretation of the History and the Civilization of the American People* (Knopf, 1947), 128. A similar statement along the same lines is found in David M. Potter, *People of Plenty: Economic Abundance and the American Character* (University of Chicago Press, 1954), *passim* but especially 136–37.

16. Snow's prediction came in typewritten draft, dated Aug. 1, 1966, of his preface to the Italian edition of *Red China Today*, ESC. The preface included other extravagant predictions (e.g., that Chinese GNP might equal the Soviet Union's in 1986), as well as some that were on the mark (e.g., dramatic increases

in industrial and agricultural output). Also see Snow, *The Long Revolution*, 22, 61, 66, 148–50.

17. Emily Hahn to author, Feb. 21, 1984.

18. *Kansas City Star*, Sept. 19, 1979.

19. John Maxwell Hamilton, *Boston Globe*, Jan. 7, 1986; Lou Cannon, *Washington Post*, April 22, 1984; George E. Condon, Jr., *San Diego Union*, May 3, 1984; "The Words of Chairman Deng," *World Press Review*, March 1987, 14; *China Daily*, March 11, 1985. U.S. response to Chinese reforms in the 1980s parallel the enthusiastic applause Americans gave to Lenin's reformist New Economy Policy in the early 1920s, see Filene, *Americans and the Soviet Experiment*, 71–75.

Index

About the Author

John Maxwell Hamilton has worked as a journalist in the United States and abroad in Africa, the Middle East, Asia, and Latin America. He served in the U.S. Agency for International Development during the Carter administration and, subsequently, on the staffs of the House Foreign Affairs Committee and the World Bank. His first book, *Main Street America and the Third World,* looked at the ways events in developing countries shape Americans' lives. He lives with his wife and son in Alexandria, Virginia.

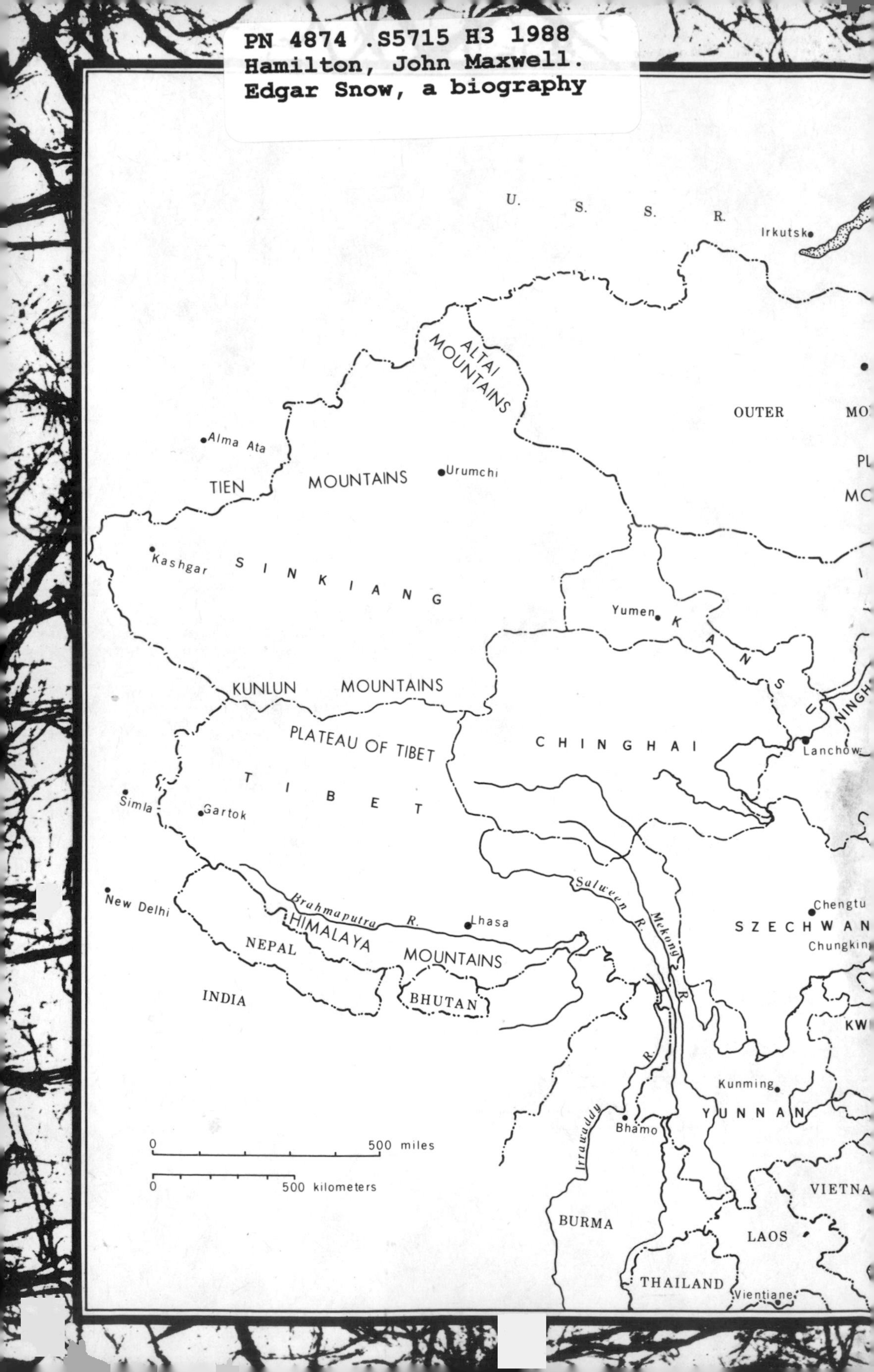
U. S. S. R.
Irkutsk
ALTAI MOUNTAINS
OUTER
Alma Ata
TIEN
MOUNTAINS
Urumchi
Kashgar
S I N K I A N G
Yumen
K A N S U
NINGH
KUNLUN MOUNTAINS
PLATEAU OF TIBET
C H I N G H A I
Lanchow
T I B E T
Simla
Gartok
Salween R.
Mekong R.
New Delhi
Brahmaputra R.
Lhasa
HIMALAYA MOUNTAINS
Chengtu
S Z E C H W A N
Chungking
NEPAL
INDIA
BHUTAN
Kunming
Y U N N A N
Irrawaddy R.
Bhamo
0
500 miles
0
500 kilometers
VIETNA
BURMA
LAOS
THAILAND
Vientiane